OF GARRISONS AND
GOALSCORERS

OF GARRISONS AND GOALSCORERS

HUGO SAYE

authorHOUSE®

AuthorHouse™
1663 Liberty Drive
Bloomington, IN 47403
www.authorhouse.com
Phone: 1-800-839-8640

Published by AuthorHouse   07/16/2012

ISBN: 978-1-4685-8618-3 (sc)
ISBN: 978-1-4685-8619-0 (e)

Acknowledgements

The existence of this book has been reliant on the kindness of so many people that it becomes difficult to know where to start. Of course, every single person at Harbour View Football Club has my enormous gratitude, and the club itself will always be in my heart. To all the players who accepted me and talked openly to me, to all the staff and management who welcomed me and assisted in any way they could and to the incredibly dedicated chairman Carvel Stewart, I say a huge thank you.

Outside the club I must thank Ian Burnett, Lasana Liburd, Dr Amanda Sives, Andrew Jennings, Jeremy Wilson and Nicole Caldi for the help they offered in various forms. Also those involved in the Jamaican national team who spoke freely to me and allowed me into their world.

My time in Jamaica was not just what you read in this book but nine months of real life and all the food-shopping, electricity bills and empty evenings that come with it. With that in mind I have to thank the people that helped me settle and enjoy my time over there: Leah and Tim; Emmelie and Lindy; Annika, Laura, Nick, multiple Andrews and all the others. And lest I forget, the Irishmen of Digicel who had me along for Tuesday night kickabouts and beers.

The list is nearly done, but I have saved the most crucial for last. There are two final thank yous to people who really did make the whole thing happen, and for that I dedicate this book to them. Firstly to my family, and in particular my brother Adam. They know the countless ways in which they have helped and supported me and so for me to explain here would be needless. All I can say is thank you.

And finally, to Clyde Jureidini, whose tireless efforts to help me both professionally and personally went a million miles above and beyond what most others would deem necessary. My gratitude is endless.

Finally to all those who have helped and supported me since my return from Jamaica, thank you. To anyone I have forgotten, I apologise sincerely about my memory and I thank you equally.

Who's Who

For ease of identification, all players will generally be referred to by their surnames, or by their 'shirt names' if this creates a clash, e.g. John-Ross Edwards becomes John-Ross. Non-players, unless made clear otherwise, will be referred to by their first name or nickname.

HARBOUR VIEW F.C.

PLAYERS
5. **Nicholas 'Josh' Beckett**—Midfield
6. **Lamar 'Panucci' Hodges**—Defence/Midfield
7. **Kemar 'Baggio' Lawrence**—Midfield
8. **Richard 'Short Man' Edwards**—Midfield, Club captain
9. **Kavin 'Tittyman' Bryan**—Striker
10. **John-Ross Edwards**—Midfield
11. **Andre 'Bullet' Fagan**—Striker
11. **Fabian 'Koji' Taylor**—Striker
12. **Kamar 'Petra' Petrekin**—Striker
13. **Oneil Fisher**—Midfield
13. **Elton 'Juice' Thompson**—Striker
14. **Kimorlee 'Bibi' Brissett**—Left back
15. **Lamar 'Wonka' Nelson**—Midfield/Forward
16. **Andre 'Zidane' Steele**—Midfield
17. **Rafeik 'Far Right' Thomas**—Striker
18. **Romario 'RomRom' Campbell**—Midfield
19. **Ranique 'B.G.' Muir**—Striker
21. **Daveion 'Vavi' Woodhouse**—Defence/Midfield
22. **Fabian 'Fame' Campbell**—Midfield
23. **Jahmali 'Chooksy' Spence**—Striker
25. **Robert 'Joe' Williams**—Centre back
26. **Dicoy 'Ding' Williams**—Centre back
27. **Christopher 'Jammel' Harvey**—Right back

29. **Lennox 'Calico' Creary**—Striker
31. **Marcelino 'Bassa' Blackburn**—Midfield
32. **Michard 'Button' Barrett**—Goalkeeper
34. **Devon 'Bats' Haughton**—Goalkeeper
36. **Kemeel 'Zidane' Wolfe**—Midfield
45. **Jaron 'JJ' Richards**—Right back
47. **Montrose 'Grinch' Phinn**—Centre back
51. **Jermaine 'Maestro' Hue**—Midfield

NON-PLAYERS

Carvel 'Daddy' Stewart—Club Chairman and Vice President of the Premier League Clubs Association.

Clyde 'Jerry' Jureidini—General Manager of the club. Also works with the PLCA and commentates on national TV and radio.

Donovan 'DV' Hayles—Head Coach, guiding them to the title the previous season. A former national team goalkeeper.

Vin Blaine—Club Manager.

Andrew 'Bowa' Hines—Physical trainer and head coach of Under 21s side. Former Harbour View and national player.

Jermaine 'Twinny' Malcolm—Kit manager

Ann-Marie Massie, Barry, Brucky, Corey, Deighton, Ebba, Gene, Ludlow Bernard, Mally, Teet—Club management, help and support.

OTHER

The Rt. Hon. Edward Seaga—Former JLP leader, MP for West Kingston and Prime Minister of Jamaica, Chairman of the PLCA and president of Tivoli Gardens Football Club.

Captain Horace Burrell—President of the Jamaica Football Federation.

Austin 'Jack' Warner—Vice President of FIFA, President of CFU, CONCACAF, and highly influential in the Trinidad & Tobago Football Federation. Also Minister for Works & Transport in the Trinidad Government.

Theodore 'Tappa' Whitmore—Coach of the Jamaican national team.

ORGANISATIONS

JLP—Jamaica Labour Party, current Government, right of centre
PNP—People's National Party, current Opposition, left of centre
JFF—Jamaica Football Federation
PLCA—Premier League Clubs Association, self-governing body of clubs running the Premier League.
CFU—Caribbean Football Union
CONCACAF—Confederation of North, Central American and Caribbean Association Football

FOREWORD

The Beautiful Game

'I've really gone off football recently. It's just a game played by arseholes.'

The long-awaited and much-hyped South African World Cup has reached its uninspiring and underwhelming closing stages. As I stand in a pub somewhere in the south west of England the above words have just been spoken to me by a friend, one who has been a keen supporter of 'the beautiful game' his entire life but now finds himself disillusioned by the way it has evolved. He is not one of those cynical, pretentious types who gains an obtuse pleasure from pouring scorn on sport, quite the opposite in fact. Nor is he, at 26, a bemused old timer feeling left out by progress' ceaseless march and longing for the good old days. It is just that for him football has become so grasping and vacuous that it barely even warrants watching anymore.

What is sad is that in this modern era he is far from alone in thinking that way. There are millions of devotees out there who are nagged by the same doubts, who now look at the sport that has become core to their very identities as little more than a playground of callous mercenaries and shameless delinquents. Moral-free players have become hopelessly detached from the real world due largely to the absurd wages paid them by clubs which themselves have gone from being the hearts of their communities to worldwide corporations lifting their skirts to the global markets in desperation for that extra pound, euro or dollar. And it is all governed over by corrupt men whose snouts have been in the trough for so long that they neither know nor care what is right or wrong so long as it comes with a healthy cheque attached.

But isn't this the people's game? Where have all the people gone? Too many of us now feel like an afterthought as the vacuum-packed instant-thrill of the English Premier League ignores us and flirts with the lucrative audiences overseas instead, but we are still there. Of course we are, we can't help ourselves. As fans it is our weakness and the game's strength that we are imbued with an irrational love for our teams so strong that we continue to happily hand over extortionate amounts of cash despite knowing full well that we are being ripped off and that the romance is entirely one way. Gradually though, the spell is wearing off and people are walking away, their once-bottomless reserves of affection finally exhausted. And yet we're all sure that there once was a time when things were better, that our relationship had meaning and substance, and that football did love us back.

I was of that number. The dedication of my two older brothers had ensured that I was indelibly Arsenal before I even really knew how football worked, and still my love for my club continues uninhibited. And yet the wider game as a whole was starting to become a bit distasteful. I wanted, therefore, to leave the multi millionaires and the histrionics behind. I wanted to find football at a level that more reflects its natural self.

Contrary to media representation, league football is not something exclusive to Brazil, Argentina and Western Europe; 208 nations sit under FIFA's umbrella and each and every one of them plays out its own leagues, crowns its national champions, forms its national teams, hails its stars and bemoans its villains. And all while the wider world focuses its adoration on those select few 'arseholes'. Who are the people that play the game in these countries, I wondered? Who are the people that watch it, run it and have become legends in it? What are their stories? How do their lives unfold?

Jamaica is one such country. It is a place we all like to think we know and it enjoys a much higher global profile than its size and wealth might suggest. Rum, Rasta and reggae have seen to that along with global icons like Bob Marley and Usain Bolt. It's a place of white sand beaches where everyone has dreadlocks and smokes ganja, while its capital, Kingston, is a shanty town of chilling gangland killers where almost certain death awaits the visitor. These are the facts that we all know about Jamaica. In terms of sport they play cricket and they sprint remarkably, but football takes a less glorious role. The island briefly flashed into the consciousness of a world that gleefully embraced it at the '98 World Cup in France, but before and since that peak it has sat in the shadows while everyone else watched the big parties going on elsewhere. As far as we are all concerned Jamaican football existed only for a few quick weeks back in June 1998.

But football is actually the country's most popular sport, by a long way. The national team, meanwhile, played its first game in 1925 and the country has had a full national league running since the 1970s, and both institutions are still going strong today. And there is more to the country than dreads, spliffs and guns.

It was these thoughts that took me to Kingston where I would spend a whole season with the reigning champions of the national Premier League, Harbour View F.C., as they went about trying to defend their title. While there I would come to know the people who make the game happen and understand, partly at least, what life on the global footballing margins involves for those distanced from the media frenzies and the super-money.

But this was not all I went there to discover. I wanted to learn about one of the most fascinatingly complex societies on the planet, and the important role that sport plays in a place where endless street wars have taken the murder rate to levels akin to the Afghan front line. It is a country where the gangland and the sports field are closely connected by politicians who use both to garner unwavering support. I would meet the people who created such a situation.

Without realising it at the time, I would also find myself in a prime position to watch the downfall of one the game's most infamous tyrants, encountering him a number of times through what would be his final year in sport. And, in a sense, the way that everything reflected back on England showed me that there is still some merit left in our own game back home.

What I am hoping this book does, therefore, is illustrate the way of life in the *real* global game. But more than that, I am hoping to show that football does still have some good in it, that it does still matter. It is not all oligarchs and sex scandals, brash Champions League finals and multi-million pound salaries. To show that these things are simply the very in-your-face tip of football's iceberg and the reality of the game for the overwhelming majority of those involved in it is something entirely different. And it should be remembered that the story of this one little country is not an isolated case study, but the story of the masses. When you look beyond the big leagues, many of the tales of struggle, strife and survival coming out of Jamaica could be replicated in at least three quarters of those 208 nations within FIFA. This is what football really is. This, to me, is football's true face, and it is so much more than the vacuous, grasping circus so many of us now take it for.

CHAPTER ONE

Into The New World

From the air Jamaica is a crumpled verdant mass, as though someone has screwed up a green sheet of paper and tossed it onto a shining blue sea where it is slowly unfurling itself again. As you descend through thin wisps of cloud scattered houses become visible along tracks which offer occasional punctuation to the endless jungle stretched across the mountainous landscape. A ribbon of bright turquoise wraps itself tightly around the island's perimeter, fading to a deep, dark blue ocean. Gradually more and more roads come into view and the buildings start to grow more and more dense until you are looking, for the first time, on the great urban sprawl of Kingston. By now you can see the spit on which the airport sits in the harbour, and if you trace it to the point where it meets the mainland then draw your gaze slightly northwards, past the bulk of the houses to where the Blue Mountains rise up from the careworn suburbia, it is just about possible to make out, right at their foot, the most significant structure in Jamaican club football: Harbour View Stadium. The Compound, as it is more commonly known, is the home of Harbour View Football Club, reigning Jamaica Premier League champions and the people with whom I would be spending the next eight months in order to experience life on the 'other side' of the beautiful game.

'And what brings you to Jamaica, sir?' the man behind the desk asks as he thumbs through my passport. He had previously adopted an air of pleasant curiosity as I explained that I am there to research a book on Jamaican football. This had dissipated, though, when I made the mistake of revealing my attachment to Harbour View. His face dropped and the mood instantly blackened, and I am now apparently much less welcome. Clearly not a fan, the man demands why them? Why Harbour View? There are plenty of clubs in the country, so what made me choose them? Weary from the ten hour flight and totally unprepared, I stumble my way through some sort of answer about wanting to see the operations of the current champions but it has little impact, the casual nature of our early rapport has gone for good and the simple formality of stamping my passport is becoming an interrogation.

Suddenly I find myself on the defensive, fending off questions about my life at home, my work, my finances. Punch drunk, I stagger from answer to answer until he lands his summation, and his biggest body blow yet:

'So you've just turned up in a country you've never been to before with no actual job, no visa, no return flight date and no letter from the club confirming what you're doing. What did you expect to happen?' When he puts it like that I have to admit he does have a point, and a pretty good one at that. As I will not actually be earning I had therefore just intended to get by on a standard holiday visa, perhaps arrogantly hoping that a UK passport might buy me some leeway in a country where Queen Elizabeth II is still Head of State, but clearly life isn't going to be that simple.

He continues to ask me questions and explain to me exactly how and in what myriad ways I am in the wrong, while disdainfully flicking through my documents in that way border control officers do when they want you to know that your fate is entirely at their discretion. He soon establishes that I didn't actually work for anybody in particular back home either and have no fixed, regular income—the weight of the realisation that I tick all the boxes of an undesirable keeps growing until suddenly he simply stamps a page and hands the passport back to me. 'Take care then,' he adds courteously. It had taken only a matter of minutes in the country for me to experience the deep partisanship of the Jamaican people that would become so central to the coming months. Next time, I resolve, I will keep my club loyalties private.

Sitting in the back of an airport taxi, the screamed pleas from its engine to be moved up a gear being stubbornly ignored, with a vista of towering cement works on either side, I am hit by a reality that suddenly feels overwhelmingly daunting. At 24 years old, and completely alone, I have thrown myself into an entirely alien yet infamously dangerous country where I will not see friends, family or even a single person I know for the next eight and a half months. I'm sweaty, I'm tired, I've just been bollocked by Immigration and I'm four and a half thousand miles from home: what the hell am I doing here? My eyes had been bigger than my stomach, I think to myself, there's no way I can do this.

Such a feeling is not a pleasant one, yet it is this that hangs over me as I arrive at The Durham, the guest house where I will be staying for my first few days in Kingston. Having been shown to my room, a small box of grey walls and metal bars over the outside door and windows, I sit on the bed and suddenly it all gets the better of me. I long for the home I left just a matter of hours ago. I miss my friends and family in a way that feels both pathetic and completely illogical given the insignificant amount of time that has elapsed since I last saw them and I curse myself for ever even coming up with this absurd project.

Yet my malaise is soon broken by the most potent of all Jamaican national characteristics: their sociability. I had left my room and been drawn into a conversation about the pros and cons of the Monarchy with the people who run the guest house and a few of their friends. They proceed to ply me with rum while telling me, having given the Queen their blessing, that the biggest problem with Jamaican footballers, and sportsmen in general, is indiscipline. They don't like to train I am told, and they lack the intelligence and education to be able apply themselves adequately to their craft. The West Indian cricket team is given as an example of the latter. They lack the mental flexibility to move from Twenty20 to the five day Test format (one of them does suggest it is irrelevant because they're hopeless at all forms of the game these days anyway) and this lack of thought is due to the failings of the education system. Not because schools should be expressly teaching pupils that it is in fact OK to play a forward defensive occasionally when you have to make a cricket match last for five days, but that a good education equips the mind with the ability to reason, to understand and to adapt on the sports pitch as well as in life.

I wonder how much of what they are saying about athletes I will find to be true over the coming season, and how much is just stereotyping. But I am enjoying myself, and the thought of spending eight months on this tropical island no longer seems quite such a hardship. The drained rum glasses pile up and conspire with the jetlag to make the broad accents and patois, the country's own unique take on the Queen's English, harder and harder to follow. After simply watching the conversation pass me by through a fog of alcohol and sleep deprivation for about an hour I make my excuses and go to bed, feeling much more content with my lot than I had done at the beginning of the evening.

I had arranged to have my first meeting with the Harbour View team a couple of days later, and this is to be in the form of a training session. At about half past three, when the temperature is slightly less aggressive than earlier in the day, Clyde Jureidini, the club's General Manager, arrives in his BMW to drive me there. Ordinarily the squad trains at the stadium but with the ground staff busy trying to get an unusually dry pitch into a playable condition for the opening game this coming weekend, pre-season has so far involved training at schools, universities or any other pitch the club can get hold of. Today's training session will be at Belleview, a mental hospital and therefore, some cynics might suggest, an appropriate home for the madness of football. As we turn into the facility Clyde looks towards the yellow and blue painted hospital buildings. 'They've got our colours,' he remarks, the tone of his voice suggesting he feels it a positive omen to have an institution for the criminally insane decorated in such a way.

The pitch itself is more like a patchy meadow than the sprinkled, manicured acres of England's top training grounds. With every step and every pass of the ball a cloud of dust puffs up and disperses in the strong cross wind coming in from the sea a few blocks away. A metal chain-link fence surrounds the perimeter, separating the dry field from the maze of ramshackle houses beyond. It transpires that the first team had actually trained in the morning and we have instead turned up to witness the high school players being put through their paces, a rag tag bunch of kids wearing an assortment of kits from English teams, American teams and even other Jamaican teams. Despite this there is still more than enough talent on display to impress the casual observer, of which a few who have stopped to gaze curiously on.

As we arrive a friendly bet is developing over whether anyone can hit a stray ball that sits about 30 yards from the group. Smugness grows among the naysayers after a few failures before one of the lads, almost unnoticed, casually places a ball on the ground and curls a perfect pass with the inside of his right foot which makes satisfying contact with the target. Suddenly the group erupt in shrieks of celebration while the victor sprints away, arms outstretched either side, chased by screaming team-mates. After it ends as these things inevitably do, with the celebrating boy pulled to the ground and jumped on by a heap of his pursuers, there is suddenly the last noise I had ever expected to hear in Jamaica.

'Oo! Oo! Oo!'

Unbelievably, someone in the core of this group of black boys is making monkey noises. To a European (any right-minded one at least) this is one of the most disgusting sounds in football, the sort of noise that upon hearing your stomach sinks in depression at the fact that people moronic enough to make it still exist. It is what racist fans around the continent—though thankfully the practice scarcely exists in England anymore—have long since done whenever a black player touches the ball, the implication of course being that evolution has somehow left the honed black athlete floundering behind those oh-so-advanced white men grunting over their beer-bellies in the stands. So what on earth is it doing here? Astonishingly the boys picking themselves up from the floor all join in, even lowering their knees, hanging their arms down to their sides and jumping around like apes. I look over to Clyde who watches on with the smile of an amused father.

'It's just a joke amongst themselves, not like when they jeer the players in Europe,' he says, clearly noticing my surprise. Suddenly I view the whole scenario in a very different light. I hope that these young players, all just teenagers, are not even aware of the connotations of their humour. Perhaps naively, but then perhaps not, I hope that their existences have so far been untouched by this horrible European disease.

I talk to Clyde as we watch the boys going through various exercises, knocking the ball around between cones and occasionally garnishing their drills with effortless flicks and tricks. It soon becomes clear that running a football club in Jamaica, even the champions of the Premier League, is primarily an endless struggle to remain afloat. While it is obviously nice to have the best players playing in their team, the real benefit of this talent is to export it to where the big money comes from, Europe and America. It has become harder, he says, since the national team fell out the top 70 in the world rankings because Britain will no longer give work permits to players coming directly from Jamaica. Now they have to spend enough years in the EU to become nationalised Europeans before they can reach our Promised Land, and by then of course that player's old Jamaican club no longer has any claim to his transfer fees. The Scandinavian leagues are regular customers, I am told, but the money that can be gleaned from them is relatively small pickings.

The boys are now playing out an attacking drill whereby they advance in threes and put the ball past a defenceless goalkeeper. There is some impressive play: dummies to drag the keeper out position, perfectly executed long shots and a high standard of finishing, which is admittedly much easier in the absence of an opposition defence. At one point though, a boy in a Robin van Persie-named Arsenal shirt attempts to score by flicking the ball round his legs and simply misses it. 'Look at that! He tries all the tricks but he's just got to finish.' Clyde mutters despairingly.

It was often said in the Eighties and early Nineties that John Barnes' skill and ability on the ball, his love of dribbling and trickery, was a result of his Jamaican upbringing. Following van Persie's blunder I ask if that was an accurate judgement of the way these islanders play the game.

'Oh yes, we like things seasoned. It has to be spicy. They like to do things they can tell their friends about again and again, like: "Did you see when I did that?"'

This national love of flamboyance, in football and life, is a theme he returns to a few times over the course of the afternoon. 'Every little event in Jamaica is a movie, everything's a drama,' he tells me in the car later. 'We don't like things to be normal. Normal's boring.'

Training continued but we leave early. Clyde is also the coach of Harbour View's masters team and they are playing a training match against a side from the third division at Heroes Park. Unlike Upton Park, Selhurst Park or indeed the national stadium here, Independence Park, Heroes Park literally is a park. It is, as you might expect from the name, an area dedicated to Jamaica's National Heroes, but it also happens to include a football pitch or two. A race track in a past incarnation, it is right in the centre of the city and ringed by a broad road housing various large ministerial buildings, adding to the air of municipal significance around the place.

We drive in and pull up at the corner of a pitch even more dry and tired than the one we had left quarter of an hour before to the sight of seven or eight half-changed players tugging socks over their feet and engaging in a fierce debate. On closer inspection it seems that the main unrest is actually coming from just one gentleman, the unfortunate effects of middle age on his once-honed physique being remorselessly betrayed by a tight fitting Chelsea shirt, who is ranting to everyone and no one about the problems plaguing their midfield. The others simply humour him or just laugh. Evidently this is not the first time they have seen this show.

Things continue in this vein for a while with little progress seeming to be made on any front with regards to some football actually being played. I ask Clyde when the game is supposed to start. 'Ahh well, we'll see. Whenever everyone gets here from work.' Eventually enough players have arrived to start while Clyde, himself a former player for Harbour View and the national youth teams, walks up the touchline to watch on from his managerial berth.

With the match underway, complete with regular cries to a referee who I'm not even sure exists, one man who has remained in our car park/changing room corner begins to tell me his story. He is the spitting image, albeit slightly rounded by the years, of Ivory Coast international Kolo Toure and had once played for Kingston-based Premier League side Arnett Gardens. He had been, in his own modest words, 'instrumental' in getting them into the top tier, where they have remained ever since, and had played either with or against all the great and good of Jamaican football. There were two men from the Jamaica Football Federation who had approached him to play for his country, he tells me, but before the chance had materialised they were involved in an accident—'in Mexico or something like that'—and were both killed. I would later learn a lot more about these two important men, both still very fondly remembered today, with one even having the Kingston and St. Andrew regional cup named in his honour. 'My hopes faded,' he says, still sounding deeply mournful, although seemingly only about his own hard luck rather than the loss of life and clearly still unhealed by the intervening decades. He never did get to play for the Reggae Boyz.

Football's boulevard of broken dreams is a long and crowded one. For every success story there are ten, a hundred, a thousand stories of disappointment. My mind drifts to those boys I had been watching earlier in the afternoon. Most of them, as is the case with every academy in the world, will never make it to the top. Will they too spend their autumn years hanging around the park, lamenting their tragic histories to complete strangers? Perhaps they will have moved on to some alternative form of greatness? Or will they, having missed out on the escape route of football, even manage to survive Kingston's notorious streets long enough to reach that age? It is a sad fact of sport that not everyone can be the best, and if you're not the best you simply have to be turfed out into the world of mere mortals.

The evening light fades quickly, as it does in the tropics, yet the players play on undeterred. Harbour View had gone a goal behind some minutes ago and the play is drifting back and forth between the two midfields. Kolo Toure is by now engaged in an animated conversation with some passing dog walkers in undecipherable patois, the occasional use of the word 'Rottweiler' being about all I can pick up, while a group of school children carrying musical instruments walk past, banging their drums and cutting freely across the corner of the pitch on their way to wherever they are going. The only other spectator from our corner, a nine year old boy bouncing with excitement about his birthday the following morning, has taken the spare ball and gone to practice his keepy-ups behind the goal his dad is reluctantly keeping in.

It is not long before the advancing night reaches the stage where seeing the far goal is impossible and as such it became fairly pointless even trying to keep track of the score. Clyde saunters back from his coaching position after admitting defeat in his attempt at piecing together a coherent football match from the various shouts and sporadically visible movements escaping from the darkness in front of us. Finally a whistle rings out to put an end to proceedings. 'That's a good sound,' he chuckles and it is hard to disagree. One resourceful onlooker does though, and optimistically turns on the headlights of his Volkswagen van in a fairly pitiful attempt at preventing the game's termination, but the beam merely limps a few meters forward before collapsing, exhausted, onto the touchline having achieved little more than raising a cheap laugh for everyone else present. Without thousands of pounds worth of floodlights it is impossible to fight nature's will and so the time has come to climb back into the cars and go home.

Leaving our match the radio news announces, as if timing it deliberately to most emphasise the disparity between the countries, that England's top clubs are spending the night fretting anxiously ahead of tomorrow's draw for the UEFA Champions League group stage. I wonder what Clyde would give to be burdened by such troubles. At the moment Harbour View are desperately seeking sponsorship money just so they can afford to even turn up to the Caribbean's Champions Cup.

As we drive through the highrise buildings of the city centre the radio station KLAS Sports FM (equivalent of the UK's TalkSport) has an interview with Glendon 'Admiral' Bailey, manager of last year's runners up and vanquished champions Tivoli Gardens. He talks of their preparations for the coming season and, strangely in this world of anti-'tapping-up' laws, names a list of players they are to trying sign. 'Our biggest problem is that we're not scoring enough goals', he offers in summation. Clyde emits a high-pitched laugh.

'They had three of the four top goalscorers in the league last season. They have **too many** strikers and they get carried away with it.' I ask if the players who had been mentioned were all strikers too. 'Yes, and strikers from lesser teams who haven't been performing as strikers.' His scoffing seems to contain a little pleasure and I sense he isn't too disappointed to see his rivals committing what he clearly feels is such an obvious error on the eve of the new season.

CHAPTER TWO

Where The Money Is

At 11 o'clock the following morning, the season is officially opened in the form of a launch event for the league competition. For the big ceremony I force my far-from-acclimatised body into a collared shirt and some suit trousers and get a lift with Clyde to the headquarters of the Jamaica Football Federation. Up the stairs we file and into a function room where the set up is basically that of a press conference. Rows of chairs face a small stage which holds a long table and a podium covered with various microphones, all in front of a backdrop heavily branded in the logo of Digicel, the mobile phone network which sponsors the league. The front and rear sections of seating are separated by a bank of television cameras and microphones, and a large table has been set up to the side which strains under the weight of all the kit and computers which are needed to support the media circus that follows football's every move.

As we wait for the event to begin, Clyde takes me around introducing me to executives, officials and various high flyers in the sporting press. 'You made the right choice with Harbour View,' one grimly informs me while Clyde is looking the other way. 'That's where the money is.' And, despite what I had discovered on my first day with the club, he is actually right. In a league where most players are scarcely paid for their efforts, if at all, Harbour View is one of only two or three fully professional teams, with first team players typically earning somewhere between £12,500 and £16,000 per year. By no means a poor salary here, but this is the very top of the Jamaican pile; John Terry earns that in a few hours.

I have a lingering handshake with Harbour View's grinning chairman Carvel Stewart, the wild nature of his hair and beard pleasantly out of keeping with the stereotypical ideas of such a successful businessman, who welcomes me warmly before being dragged away to press more flesh. Continuing our networking, we then speak to a producer from CVM, the television station which broadcasts the Premier League and with it this morning's event. After out introductions the producer turns to his presenter and, as though it had been the plan all along, tells him, 'This will almost definitely start late so at 11 o'clock we'll go to you for a quick chat with Clyde and Hugo here before we go to a break.'

Excuse me? Have I misheard? You want to interview me? Yes, it turns out they do. Before I've even had a chance to let this sink in we are positioned this way and that under a bright spotlight—and have repeated checks on exactly how my surname is pronounced—before the director begins the countdown from behind his bulky computer screen.

'20 seconds'. I have only been live on TV across a nation once before and that had somehow involved drunkenly dancing on a catwalk with lingerie-clad models before a large crowd on a Filipino beach. In its way this seems equally bizarre.

'Ten seconds.' The butterflies flap in my stomach. The director holds up three fingers, two, one and points the presenter into his introductory spiel. He then asks Clyde some questions about the coming season before turning to me. I had only turned up to watch some speeches and now here I am with a spongy yellow microphone hovering in front of my face being interviewed live on national television. I am asked something about what I know of Jamaican football and bumble out a couple of answers to his questions before being mercifully relieved of duty by an advertisement break. At this point I think back and realise I have absolutely no idea what I have just said to the Jamaican people, only really aware that I am left with the vague sensation of looking foolish. But at least it's done, I think with relief, and with what would turn out to be a premature sigh of relief at having fulfilled my unexpected media commitments, I sit down for the show

Not a moment too soon the event finally starts. After a brief introduction from the Master of Ceremonies, who seems oddly prepossessed with the exploits of his stage fellows in both sport and war, Captain Horace Burrell, President of the JFF, takes to the podium.

He slowly plods his way through a good five minutes of welcoming and thanking various people present, his main praise being reserved for the scantily dressed troupe of 'beautiful young ladies' representing Digicel. So taken is he by these girls that he meanders off into a slightly odd reminiscence about Edward Seaga—former Prime Minister, an important man in football and the next speaker on the stage—telling him that the success of a man comes from the company of females. 'So now,' he concludes, 'I surround myself, following your suggestion Sir, with a lot of ladies,' he pauses for dramatic effect, 'In my business of course!' Cue hearty chuckles from the audience. All good, blokey fun, but of fairly questionable professionalism. And with the joking now over, he gets down to the serious stuff.

'I cannot over-emphasise the importance of football to Jamaica's development, in every respect of the word. Mr Seaga once said: "If football is frequently played in the volatile areas, chances are that crime and violence would be reduced or would be non-existent." And it is true. It is because of football that Arnett Gardens and Tivoli Gardens now interact in the way that they do today. It was football that created that atmosphere and therefore all of us need to recognise the importance of football in uniting our people. In a country like ours, where crime and violence certainly is like a cancer, we must concentrate on the remedies which could rid our society of this serious cancer.'

This issue is the bottom line of why I had chosen to come to Jamaica, warring communities settling their differences over a game of football, but surely it couldn't really be that simple? It is a nice theory but to me it just seems a little too neat and convenient. I am curious to find out just how far the idea of football as the great social force can actually be applied to reality. And if football really had produced such a radical change, you have to wonder why? What is it about the game that made this happen? Over the coming season it is my primary aim to go some way towards finding out.

Burrell then continues about various plans to encourage the expansion of the Jamaican game, from FIFA courses for club management to refereeing improvements, before moving on to the country's facilities and a Mr David Mais of the Government-sponsored Sports Development Foundation, who is overseeing a project to enhance grounds and sporting infrastructure nationwide. Burrell chooses this very public platform to tell Mr Mais, in no uncertain terms, that he is doing his job very poorly indeed. 'I have a recommendation,' he declares, sounding much like that man in the pub who firmly believes that he has the answer to all the world's problems. 'And my recommendation is that we should identify at least four venues across the country.' His grand scheme, to fire their resources richly into just a few facilities rather than spread them thinner across more places around the island, apes that of Trinidad who will be holding their second ever World Cup (the under 17 women's World Cup, to be precise) in just a matter of weeks. This recognition is what he wants for his own Federation.

'The entire world will descend upon Trinidad & Tobago and it is because they have approximately four venues similar to the ones I have just outlined.' It is also because Trinidad is the home of Jack Warner, a FIFA Vice President, head of CONCACAF and the CFU as well as FIFA President Sepp Blatter's dearest and most loyal ally, but dutifully we all ignore that rather large elephant in the room. You can see the argument he is putting together and it does have some logic behind it. But without Warner's near-limitless influence over FIFA behind them, is it really worth Jamaica shooting for the two weeks of glory that come from hosting these tournaments instead of spreading their resources more evenly to provide for the game on a wider and deeper level?

'Going around and trying to build 20 facilities benefits no one,' he goes on, clearly forgetting the 16 extra places benefiting greatly that would be simply ignored under his four-venue scheme, 'because it would not work.' He doesn't trouble himself with an explanation as to why it would not, just a simple statement that it is so. He is in effect telling poor Mr Mais, who was by now looking decidedly uncomfortable in the audience: 'You're wrong because you're wrong.'

'I hope that my suggestion, Mr Mais, has not fallen on deaf ears. I sincerely hope that Sir,' he rounds off, with a faintly threatening air. He finishes (the MC later jokes that they tried to call time on him about halfway through) by mentioning plans to ensure all coaches are properly qualified in order to improve standards. And that is my introduction to the man overseeing Jamaican football. It is clear he is passionate about achieving his goals and has some well developed ideas to do so, but there is something about him that makes me feel uneasy, and as the season goes by I will find out that such a feeling is indeed well-founded.

Next up is the Most Honourable Edward Seaga, President of the Premier League Clubs Association, managing director of Tivoli Gardens FC and former Prime Minister. He gives a speech that could have been taken directly from the CEO of any big European club, all 'brands' and 'products', but does make a few interesting points about Jamaican development. And as he reaches the end he drops a bombshell that hits home the one huge gulf between football's two worlds.

'This season, I will admit to you, we seriously considered cutting the league in half because some of the clubs could not do a full season. There was a lot of scrounging around to find money. The Sports Development Foundation came to our assistance in the late stages with a donation, a contribution, of five million dollars to help out. We never had from the beginning the amount of funds that we needed, so we are playing catch-up and there is only so long you can be playing catch up for. At some point you actually have to catch up.'

This is how little money there is in football here, that the league was nearly cut in half because the clubs don't have the funds just to travel to a full set of fixtures. Five million Jamaican dollars, the amount that rescued them, is about £38,000. Collectively the twelve clubs of the Premier League were desperately scratching around for under forty grand just so that they could complete a full season. The same amount of funding in England's Premier League would pay Yaya Toure's wages at Manchester City for around 26 hours.

A short speech from the CEO of Digicel Jamaica and some presentations to the 'MVPs' of each team the previous season follow. Typically organised, they plum forget to announce that Tivoli's Navion Boyd—remember the name—was the overall league MVP until being asked by a reporter in the ensuing Q & A session. The few Harbour View players present are awarded with a Nokia phone for their triumph in May and then it is all over.

I am once again whisked round the room on a tour of introductions. Carvel Stewart approaches me again with another broad smile and shakes my hand once more while asking if I have acclimatised yet, and no sooner have I answered than he is being hauled away again for more questions elsewhere. 'I never get a moment off,' he mumbles as he leaves. Immediately a man from KLAS approaches me to fill the vacancy, introducing himself as Roger, then takes my name and phone number before saying, 'OK, I'll call you later. I'd like you to appear on the show tonight.'

Clearly Roger had not seen my awkward, shuffling appearance on CVM earlier. It would just be over the phone he offers by way of reassurance but nonetheless I remain unconvinced that it would be of comfort enough to coax out of me a media-worthy performance. But it is settled nonetheless, and off we go to the buffet. There various players, wearing their team strips and now freed of the constraints of formal proceedings, sit in groups laughing and joking and admiring their new toys. Every time I look around Carvel is standing in front of a different camera and I think fleetingly of his earlier lament before unsympathetically tucking in to some chicken. I now have press concerns of my own.

Back in my room at the guest house that afternoon, I receive a call from KLAS where I am informed that I will be on at 4:15 and asked, as with CVM earlier, how my surname is pronounced. 'See?' the man suggests. 'No, Saye, like to *say* something'. He tries again, 'Sayee?' I am running out of ideas about quite how I can make it any clearer. 'No Saye. Saye'. 'Sigh?' He suggests one last time. I give up, there is no way to win this game. 'Umm yeah, yeah that'll do.' The next hour and a half are then taken up by twitchy preparations: would it be best to talk outside or in? Should I turn off the fan? It will blow down the phone. But won't I get too hot?

The phone rings. Fidgeting time is over. They check it is me and put me on hold, playing what is currently going out on air down the phone line to me. I listen to the conversation about US$700 being stolen from an office that has something to do with West Indies cricket and realise that this is a proper, grown up serious radio station and next up, live, is me.

A few last adverts on hold are sharply interrupted by a producer. 'Excuse me Hugo, how do we pronounce your surname?' Good grief. Then, post-commercial break, I am brought into the action to talk about everything from what I hope to achieve to what I have already learnt, to what I have done in the past. Once underway, my first ever radio interview is surprisingly comfortable. With growing confidence I am soon rambling on in the manner of a seasoned pro, even referencing Captain Burrell's speech from that morning. And ten minutes later, with sweat pouring off me (the fan should be off, I had decided) it is all over.

I sensed a thread of naivety weaving through much of what I had said but on the whole it had been surprisingly painless. They even replayed clips of it on the news afterwards so it cannot have been too bad. In Jamaica as in England, football's great media monster rumbles on and that Thursday I served my role in its upkeep, being swallowed up and devoured by it and usefully filling a few transient minutes of its insatiable airtime hunger.

There is a point in late summer when the football fan's world starts turning again. Starved of the game since the previous May, or early July in a tournament year like this one, they spend the summer months in a kind of suspended half-existence, simply going through the motions of life until the alternative reality of the football league wakes from its slumber and gives all those empty, dragging weekends meaning again.

No matter where you are in the world, football's annual renaissance always brings the same thoughts. Will our new striker score goals? How will we cope with selling our best midfielder? Will our new manager implement some revolutionary new system to sweep away all before us? Oh sod it, just give me football again!

Looking up from outside the Compound and seeing people climb the steps up the stand, hanging around the television tower and milling around the street itself there is the familiar frisson of excitement that ritually precedes any game. Today of course has that added sense of anticipation; we can finally release ourselves back into the real world: the new season is here at last.

There are warm smiles all round. People greet the familiar faces they have not seen since May, all full of the optimism that comes with August's clean slate so ready to be filled with innumerable possibilities, while the tension that every champion must bear of having all to lose is also tangible.

The Compound is a sturdy concrete structure, painted in a yellow that has been robbed of its sharpness by years of twelve-month sunshine yet still retains a welcoming charm. It sits snugly surrounded by the lower reaches of the rainforest-draped Blue Mountains, which give the occupants of the houses dotted over the tree covered slopes beyond the far Roxy Williams stand a free view of the football within. I had seen a picture or two online but they never quite capture it right. The difference between a photograph of a stadium and seeing it 'in the flesh' is the same as the difference between a television picture viewed in widescreen and then in regular format. All stadia appear low, broad and echoingly vast when looked on remotely then suddenly seem to reach much higher, closing in to become tight and compact when you are actually there. Even the modest Compound, whose advertisement adorned bleachers hold a maximum of 7,000 people, elicits this sorcery and it becomes a very enjoyable place to watch football.

Driven there again by Clyde, we enter the section of the Linval McKenzie Stand that is free from the burden of the general public and stroll up a short flight of steps. At this point you find yourself at the back of the stand, behind the players' 'tunnel'—essentially the area where the two dressing rooms face each other and are bridged by the concrete media platform above—in which people mingle before heading up more steps to their seats. It had rained all afternoon and the floodlights are on early, adding their limelight glamour to the already charged atmosphere. We are occupying the opening day's evening kick off slot, although we have been brought forward half an hour so as to fit neatly into CVM's planned Sunday evening TV schedule, and the sky is already fading into a grey twilight.

I am guided to the 'press box', a long-ish metal desk across the tunnel bridge, where I am placed between a reporter from the *Jamaica Observer* by the name of Howard Walker and Hitz 92 FM's live radio commentary duo. The defence of Harbour View's title is to begin against the quaintly-named Humble Lions F.C., a traditionally Rastafarian club from the centre of the island and the only side they had failed to beat in three attempts during last season's competition.

With kick off approaching Clyde picks up a microphone and now becomes the stadium announcer ('Everyone at the club, we all have to take on multiple roles,' he had told me earlier in the week—clearly he was not lying), reading the names of those who had made the two starting line-ups over the PA system. Below us the owners of said names form into two neat columns ready to take to the pitch, more eager than anyone to put the summer to bed. At last it is time to get back to doing what they do best and play some football. With the teams lists read, FIFA's rousingly grand yet gratingly smug anthem blasts out and the teams file onto the pitch, led by a group of children carrying the yellow fair play banners so familiar to anyone who has watched a World Cup match. We stand while the national anthem rounds off the formalities and then we are, at last, underway.

Harbour View fly at the rusty Lions. Richard Edwards, the recent incumbent of the captains' armband following the January departure of Lovel Palmer to America, sends forward an early ball from his own half. The Lions' defender suddenly finds himself under it with his limbs entangled and he slips, allowing John-Ross Edwards a clear run at an isolated goalkeeper, the season's first victim helplessly awaiting his fatal blow . . . it goes over the bar, a momentary reprieve.

The next attack is almost immediate. A tricky run by national striker Kavin Bryan is followed by a low cross that is gratefully hoofed away. He follows it up with a straight run into the area only for a lunging last-man tackle to knock the ball against his shins and out for a goal kick. The first five minutes are all Harbour View. Edwards, also a Jamaican international, sits deep and directs all the play and the inevitable goal will come at any moment.

But then Humble Lions win a corner. They are shaking themselves from their summer-long stupor and begin making a few chances of their own. Suddenly we're the ones having to defend. A dangerous cross. A shot from distance. They are just starting to creep ahead on points when they are awarded a harmless looking freekick by the far touchline and in their own half. A long ball is floated into the crowded box where it is headed back across the scrum. Criminally, our defenders allow it to bounce seven yards out and it finds Lions striker Roberto Fletcher waiting. With a great swing of his right boot he attacks it, but mercifully sends the ball high, wide and over the relieved supporters in the West Stand. 'He hit that out of the ground ladies and gentlemen!' screeches the radio commentator next to me, both unable and entirely unwilling to conceal his amusement at the sorry state of poor Fletcher's ropey finishing.

A few chances come and go at either end with nothing more than wasteful shooting sparing the blushes of both defences. Fletcher's already forgettable day then gets worse when he is booked for a shameless hack near to his own corner flag. The resultant freekick pops and loops off various heads before the goal opens up for the briefest of moments only for yet another scuffed shot to flop lamely wide.

Approaching half time Harbour View are taking control of possession again but look unable to do anything with it. The fourth official raises his board, its red LEDs searing against the now-dark sky, to announce two minutes of stoppage time. Thoughts drift to chances missed as the final few seconds are dutifully played out in a procession when suddenly the white clad figure of Kirk Duckworth dashes up to Harbour View's Rafeik Thomas and inexplicably swipes his legs from behind. Down crashes Thomas while the gesticulating Lion, having already been booked, adopts the familiar role of innocent bystander. But it is, as it always is, wasted effort. The ref, like everyone else in the Compound, buys none of his performance and out shoots his yellow card, followed swiftly by the red. Duckworth holds his head in a show of bewilderment, the necessary final act in the dismissed footballer's play of injustice, before plodding glumly to the showers.

He is given just a few seconds to compose himself before the half time whistle sends his team mates in after him. Nil—nil, and drab fears of an anticlimactic start are beginning to surface. But not to worry: Digicel, clearly concerned about the potential side-effects of fifteen minutes to think for ourselves, have taken it upon themselves to 'entertain' us during the break. An over-excited man asks the crowd a cringe-worthy assortment of questions about Digicel products, promotions and slogans, rewarding right answers with a few dollars phone credit and an array of branded tat. Next is Puma who is introduced as an 'international dancehall star' and yet is swiftly reduced to the status of normal, embarrassed bloke when he runs on to sing with a faulty microphone and has to slink off to find an alternative while his backing music plays on unaccompanied. To his credit he subsequently performs with sufficient authority to largely rebuild the illusion by the time he is replaced by no less than 50 Digicel dancers who come on to perform a routine to a song about the company's latest campaign which tells us to 'jus Buss'. Sadly though they are cut short because an inconsiderate group of lads want to use their grassy stage to play the second half of some sort of football match.

Having lost a defender, Humble Lions make a change at half time in a bid to remain solid enough to repel the Harbour View threat. The unlucky man whose afternoon was cut short, 'the sacrificial lamb' as the radio man jabbers into his mic, was the unfortunate Roberto Fletcher. It is the final humiliation on a day he would no doubt rather forget. Somehow you don't suspect that this had been what his excited imagination had conjured up when he woke that morning, full of anticipation for the big opening game ahead.

The second half begins at a high tempo, full of fast running and clever tricks, but failing to produce any chances more significant than a few hopeful shots from distance. Harbour View are fortunate that the teams are not levelled when Kimorlee Brissett ploughs two-footed into the legs of the opposing midfielder right in front of us, the hearty crack of studs on shin pads and the ensuing shriek audible from up on the media desk. There follows a flowing move across the pitch which results in the ball being chested down into the path of Marcelino Blackburn inside the Lions' box, only for him to send yet another chance high and wide.

Midway through the half the Lions' keeper Shawn Sawyers picks up a slight injury, and while he is being treated Clyde takes the opportunity to introduce me to the local people. 'Welcome to British sports writer Hugo Saye who will be with Harbour View for the entire season,' he announces over the PA to a completely indifferent audience. Walker's ears do prick up though and at this point he decides he wants to do an article about me for the *Observer*, so takes my email address and ordered his photographer into an impromptu photo shoot of me gazing, *Cotton Traders*-esque, across the pitch. I am relieved to see Sawyers get back to his feet and the game resume. He, however, will probably wish at full time that he'd just gone off instead.

Harbour View are building the pressure and making more chances. Sawyers scrambles one off his goal line having been caught out of position; Brissett makes a fortuitous run into the area and puts his shot wide. But there is still danger lurking at the other end. Lions win a corner and swing it into the area where it is thrown around like a hot potato before their striker shoots powerfully at the exposed goal from no more than four yards out and yet somehow contrives to send it wide again. 'Unbelievable!' exclaims the delighted radio man next to me. I almost sense that any display of competent finishing from either side would severely dampen his enjoyment of the day.

With full time approaching the play starts to get more desperate, the defending more scrappy. Our imposing centre back Dicoy Williams dribbles the ball forcefully forward in the way that only a fed-up defender on a mission can, but the resultant chance is headed over.

Then we are awarded a free kick no more than two yards in from the near touchline and about 40 yards from goal. John-Ross stands to take it as a jumble of players tussle in the area. His cross bypasses them all and floats high towards the far post. It is one of those balls that seems to spend forever in the air and about half way through its journey a realisation hits. I start to raise myself up from my seat in anticipation. Hang on, that's going in! Sawyers too is struck by this, having come way off his line to claim the expected cross, and desperately tries to get back to base in time, but for him it isn't to be. The ball's smooth arc drops perfectly into the far top corner. It is, in its execution and its enigma, *that* Ronaldinho moment in Japan at the 2002 World Cup, only from further out. For a second or two there is just a stunned silence. John-Ross, seemingly as surprised as anyone and wearing the look of a man who isn't quite sure exactly what has just happened but knows he enjoyed it, turns to his nearest team mate and simply stares at him open mouthed in the blank moment before anyone reacts. Within seconds he is being jumped on by all and sundry as the team yells through the fence at the crowd in fierce celebration. Sawyers, meanwhile, stands with hands on hips and chin on chest, a figure of despondency.

For a while now it has seemed that any goal someone managed to scrape would be the only one and so it turns out. The final few minutes see little action bar a wasted one-on-one that could have made it two-nil, but otherwise the biggest highlight is a small laugh spreading through the press area when a Humble Lions flag blocks the Hitz commentator's view of the corner of the pitch, causing him to strain and bounce on the spot. The final whistle comes, and is greeted by local children running excitedly across the pitch to their heroes only to be berated over the PA by Clyde.

As everyone gets up to leave, satisfied with the opening result, one of the youngsters in our section, looking no more than ten years old, comes up to me and demands to know which football team I play for. I explain to him that I am simply here to write about football, not play it, but he is immediately joined by a young girl, emboldened by her friend's vanguard action, who runs up to me, grinning widely. 'Do you play for Brazil?' she asks excitedly. I can only laugh and point out that I am in fact English. 'So you play for England then!' announces the first boy, clearly glad to have solved the riddle. I reiterate to them that I am just a journalist and do not actually play for anyone and suddenly they look at me as if I have just cancelled Christmas. I have to admit, compared with the idea of playing for Brazil I even slightly disappointed myself with my reality check.

'So what are you doing watching the DPL then?' the boy mumbles painfully through his crushing feeling of anti-climax, as though it is all he can do not to turn and walk away from me there and then. I explain that I am here to watch Harbour View for the season and all of a sudden the gloom lifts. Indeed, with this news the girl whoops with such glee down the ear of the still on-air Hitz commentator that she is immediately chastised and shooed away. As she trots off, huge grin still plastered across her face, she lets me know that she definitely likes me again. It is pleasing to see the young fans of Jamaica showing such an attachment to a local team. Here, as in much of the world, the European leagues reign supreme over the affections of the nation's football fans but the domestic sides desperately need the loyalties of the paying public in order for any progress to be made. These children are a hopeful omen for the future.

It had been a good, if unspectacular, opening. Carvel, wearing his replica Harbour View shirt and finally getting to enjoy his longed-for moment off, comes and shakes my hand again. 'Your baptism!' he declares and we discuss the game for a minute or so, concluding that three points in the bag is the main thing after the first game. Driving away from the ground Clyde explains that the free kick was something they had worked on since their former coach, who unlike me had been a real Brazilian, had noticed that Jamaican keepers always come out too far at set pieces. 'I would think it was a fluke too if I hadn't heard the conversation myself and seen it work time and time again,' he insists. 'But it was definitely deliberate.' I'm not so convinced but what the hell, a goal's still a goal and a winning start's still a winning start.

Looking across the pitch from the press desk at the Compound. Behind the Roxy Williams stand on the far side can be seen houses which overlook the pitch from the mountain.

Sunday 29th August

Benfica	1	3	Tivoli Gardens
Boys' Town	4	2	St. George's
HVFC	**1**	**0**	**Humble Lions**
Reno	0	1	Portmore United
Sporting Central	0	2	Waterhouse
Village United	2	2	Arnett Gardens

National Premier League

	P	GD	Pts
1. Boys' Town	1	2	3
2. Tivoli Gardens	1	2	3
3. Waterhouse	1	2	3
4. Portmore United	1	1	3
5. HVFC	**1**	**1**	**3**
6. Village United	1	0	1
7. Arnett Gardens	1	0	1
8. Reno	1	-1	0
9. Humble Lions	1	-1	0
10. St. George's	1	-2	0
11. Benfica	1	-2	0
12. Sporting Central	1	-2	0

CHAPTER THREE

The Great Developmental Conundrum

The international break is a much-maligned entity. 'Why?' people often demand of FIFA, 'Why do you insist on these absurd interruptions?' No one seems to want them. They bring only frustration for fans who have waited all summer to see the their team swing back into league action only for it to be paused after a solitary game so the national team can jet off to some distant corner of football's atlas and play 90 entirely pointless-feeling minutes of football. The clubs are equally unenthusiastic about them. Even if their players are not injured during these games, the fixture pile-up that has been created later in the season to accommodate them will no doubt send a number of victims hobbling into the treatment room. Directly or indirectly, these early season FIFA jollies will inevitably result in the wage-paying clubs seeing critical players missing critical matches.

For their part, the Reggae Boyz will be entertaining Costa Rica at Independence Park in the aggressively advertised first preparatory step along the JFF's 'Road to Rio' and the 2014 World Cup in Brazil. And this is where these friendlies play their trump card. At the League launch event Edward Seaga had spoken of the importance of the clubs pursuing a thorough youth programme. 'The next World Cup is four years away,' he explained. 'It is the under 17s and under 21s that are going to take pride of place in these next few years to bring the players up that have the talent for Captain [Burrell] to put on the field the best squad of Jamaican players for the next World Cup.'

Jamaica are going through what is known commonly in football as a period of transition. Things are changing and the old is being swept out and replaced with the new. The stars based in the English Premier League, the two Ricardos Gardner and Fuller, are not being considered as options for Brazil 2014 and so the squad is filled with younger players who will spend the next four years developing into a team worthy of a place in those shiny glass bowls at the World Cup draw. And the Caribbean Cup is just a couple of months away, on which qualification to the CONCACAF Gold Cup this summer also hinges, so the pointless jaunts of the international break actually become rare moments of preparation for national coach Theodore 'Tappa' Whitmore as he seeks to provide the next generation with match experience.

Not that the break means life is quiet for the next two weeks. The *Observer* article on me hit the shops with, much to my own personal amusement, my half-page spread dominating the column inches ahead of a story about some wannabe called Usain Something-or-other on the opposite side. Of much more relevance to everybody else in the country though is Captain Burrell's speech at the league launch and the fracas it had begun that the media have now decided to pick up on and run with. The fallout had rumbled on in the papers and the radio phone-ins and the following week the two 'warring parties', the Captain and David Mais, are invited to air their views on TVJ's *Eye on Sports*.

Development is really the core issue in Jamaican football, and the argument centres on what is the best way to go about achieving it. It seems I have found myself entering into their world at a turning point in the game's history and the course of action eventually decided upon might determine the future of Jamaican football for decades. To spread their resources and provide for the local communities or to fire their cash into a few grandiose schemes for the world to admire?

The show opens with Burrell wearing the self congratulatory expression of someone who knows he is right and will get his own way. Mais appears less familiar with the camera lens, carrying the resigned aura of impending defeat in the face of mob-pleasing grand-standing. At the beginning it is relatively childish before Mais takes control. We're there to provide for everyone, he says, clubs make requests to us and we need to be able to develop them all. He gives the example of Humble Lions, at the Effortville Community Centre in Clarendon, who recently applied for money to install floodlights. This was a necessity but would be impossible to provide if they follow the Captain's scheme. There just isn't sufficient funding being put into sport, from either the government or the private sector, to be able to do everything. He then further pops Burrell's bubble by pointing out that it's all well and good building these 10,000 seat arenas, but how many grounds in the country ever even get close to actually bringing in that number of people? None, so what's the point in the long term?

Burrell fights back, floating higher and higher into the clouds with every passing minute, by telling us that he's thinking globally. 'I am not thinking about the local situation,' he pompously announces, despite the fact that thinking about the local situation is exactly what his job is all about. Returning to the subject of Jack Warner's Trinidad and their pending world tournament, he states that there would be millions of US dollars flowing into the country from it that are entirely unattainable for Jamaica in its present state.

It's a comfortable theory but the truth is, as agreed upon by global economists and almost all past research into the subject, that hosting such tournaments does not actually increase tourism, full-time employment or a nation's economic growth one bit. Indeed, Simon Kuper and Stefan Szymanski report in their book *Why England Lose* that three of the world's top sporting economists flew to South Africa prior to the 2010 World Cup, at the behest of the nation's finance minister, and said that the *best* the country could hope for was that the tournament would *not reduce* economic growth.

Kuper & Szymanski go on to discuss a study that Holger Preuss from the University of Mainz and his team of economists conducted into the 2006 World Cup in Germany. Over half of the 'visitors' watching World Cup games, they discovered, were actually locals. Locals, of course, who are just spending money at the football that they would otherwise have spent elsewhere in the German economy. Then there are the real visitors who happen to be in the country anyway so just pop along to a game out of curiosity, and those who had intended to visit the country at some point in their lives but now arranged their trip to coincide with the tournament. All of these people add little or nothing because their money would, at some point, have gone into the country's economy regardless of the football.

Only a fifth of attendees had actually come to the country specifically to watch the World Cup and these people generated spending of 2.8 billion—a large sum indeed but far less than the German state had spent on hosting the competition. And that was for the proper, real World Cup—you can say with some confidence that there won't be legions of beer-drinking, meal-eating, hotel-booking Brits descending on Trinidad to watch the under 17 girls' quest for glory.

Burrell is well away though, salivating lustily after his pie in the sky while casting envious glances across at the neighbours, desperately trying to keep up with the Warners. Mais counters, attempting to bring him back down to earth. 'We get out there and listen to what people say,' he tells the Captain. 'The reality is we have to deal with club level, school level, community level.' But the JFF President is having none of it. The SDF must ask the government for more money! The great talent of Jamaica deserves to be able to enjoy bigger facilities! He has become a politician tossing dreams out to the starry-eyed masses like crusty loaves to a starving mob.

We are trying to encourage corporate Jamaica to buy into our sporting product in order to raise more funds, offers a wearying Mais. But Horace's runaway train has long since left the realms of reason and is not coming back any time soon: 'We must go out and seek loans to do this!' The JFF is on financial death-row, with $100m (around £770,000) of unpaid debts outstanding to various creditors who are rapidly losing patience. Two days from now they will sell a site formerly earmarked for an academy to the Government for $36m, money that all has to go straight into making repayments, and here is the tub-thumping President demanding that they take out vast loans to fulfil some far-fetched pipe dream.

He becomes so detached from reality that he even begins to undermine his own arguments. Dane Richards, 'our own Dane Richards,' he emphasises, is currently playing so well in the MLS because he gets to train and play on good surfaces every day. This allows him to really hone his skills in a way that is impossible on the rough, patchy surfaces of Jamaica, he declares triumphantly.

So how would this problem be solved by just upgrading four select pitches? Surely this requires improving facilities throughout the league, exactly in the way that Mais and the SDF are trying to do?

It is becoming farcical. Fortunately the host brings it to an inconclusive end, but not before giving Burrell a chance to stoke the fires ahead of this weekend's international friendly.

'Costa Rica did not want to come here', he blasts. 'Because they believe our standard of football is not good enough to give them a match. They believed they would just run over the Reggae Boyz!'

No doubt he over-elaborated slightly on his tale but that all adds to the pantomime and the message is clear: let's have everyone fired up and ready show the world not to underestimate feisty little Jamaica. It was a somewhat incendiary remark, and as such probably quite inappropriate from a man of his position, but actually I found charm in that. No lofty FA chief would ever say that before an England match and for it I warm slightly to him for the first time. The man genuinely cares, there can be no doubting that. By Sunday night we will have the definitive answer as to whether or not the Costa Ricans had been right. Jamaica's great developmental conundrum, however, looks set to run and run.

Independence Park was designed and built to host the 1968 Commonwealth Games, and these days it is home to just about every single significant sporting event in Jamaica. It can accommodate 33,000 people at full capacity but as a football ground it ticks all the unfortunate boxes of the perfect atmosphere-killer: uncovered stands which allow any noise to dissipate skywards; a running track around the pitch and even a velodrome around that, making the fans and players two entirely distinct populations, removed and utterly detached from one another.

But you can take even a staid, humourless bowl like this and give it character and life simply by putting a load of Jamaicans in it. Based on the running track a DJ and an MC scream at the crowd through an ear-splittingly loud PA system. The crowd themselves, almost all wearing some form of yellow, are slowly filling the grandstand as well as bleachers on the opposite touchline. 'Whagwan bleachers!' the MC screeches, a greeting literally meaning 'what's going on' that encapsulates the clipped way in which patois works. 'Big up yourselves grandstand!' Scores of yellow inflatable clappers are waved and hit while a lone vuvuzela has somewhere infiltrated the grandstand, its owner still clinging achingly on to the spirit of the South African World Cup last summer.

With twenty minutes until kick off the Costa Rican players, still in shorts and flip flops, amble onto the grass for a casual pitch inspection and conclusions are being drawn in the stand that perhaps this game might not start exactly on its scheduled time of six o'clock. Sure enough, within minutes the MC's microphone is commandeered by a business-like JFF official who informs us that, due to matters beyond the JFF's control, kick off has now been moved to seven o'clock. As the news is broken the vuvuzela blurts out a regretful parp of surprise, as though in possession of a tail that someone has just trodden on, while the rest of us merely acknowledge the inevitable and wonder how we are going to fill the next hour and a quarter. 'This is due to matters outside the control of the JFF,' the official repeats, making doubly sure that no blame would be attributed to the Federation.

Clyde, the man of a thousand jobs, is tonight working as a co-commentator for one of the radio stations covering the game, but before being pressed into duty he takes me on a brief tour of the stadium. He is one of those people that seems to know everyone and with his sway we soon find ourselves walking down the tunnel, with the gap framing the yellow-sprinkled bleachers ahead of us looming larger with every step, and out to the entrance of the pitch. Here we loiter in the mouth of the tunnel as the players pass us to go and warm up. Navion Boyd of Tivoli Gardens, he who had been made league MVP for last season, has not been selected and lingers by the wall across from us in his training kit looking dolefully on as those who have been chosen go about their loosening drills. His gaze is only broken when one young female staffer stops inches in front of him facing out towards the pitch, and his eyes immediately drop down to become firmly fixed on the shapely curves closely wrapped in her tight jeans. He is, after all, only human.

By this point Clyde's deadline to be on air is fast approaching so he and myself head back to our seats as the DJ keeps booming out songs and the excitable MC intermittently tells various people—media, sponsors, administrators etc.—to 'big up' themselves. He is determined for the mood not to flag. 'Music and football, what a perfect combination!' he shouts, as though trying to convince us all that the one hour delay is, in fact, a delightfully unexpected bonus. It is a testament to the Jamaican nature that many people seem to believe him, dancing in their seats and thoroughly enjoying every minute of it. As an Englishman, with all the boring, rhythmless reluctancy that goes with it, I can't help but feel glad to hear FIFA's ubiquitous anthem striking up to announce the arrival, at last, of the players onto the pitch.

As the players move out, the JFF official has again managed to prise the microphone away from the MC in order to read out the teams. The Costa Rican squad is a bizarre mix of archetypal names both Latin (no. 16—Jose Miguel Cubero) and Anglican (no. 3—Roy Smith), but features no weighty personnel that suggests there is too much to fear. The names of the Reggae Boyz are read out along with their parent clubs as part of an ongoing campaign to emphasise that club ties are no boundary to national unity—every league ground features a billboard depicting a group of young people, each in a different team's strip, laughing together beside the slogan 'Rivals for 90 minutes, friends for life.' The starting XI features three from Harbour View.

Kick off. I find myself drawn into Burrell's rhetoric and desperately willing the Reggae Boyz to avenge the Costa Ricans' arrogance. 'We can't lose this.' I'm thinking. *We?* I've only been here two weeks, it's like spending a fortnight on the Costa Brava and using it to claim some sort of share in Spain's World Cup win. But never mind, there's no time for semantics now—we have a game to win.

And that game is taking on a familiar pattern, with Jamaica having the majority of possession but giving away the best chances to the other side. Somewhere a few rows behind and to my right the Central American commentator is living up to his tuneful stereotype, all rolling Rs and lingering As, as the play lolls from end to end. The visitors are good, their passing sharper, more purposeful and more inventive, but the Boyz work hard and are not without skill of their own. In the first half chances come both ways, the best of which sees Bryan Ruiz balloon a shot way over from 5 yards after the home defence is sliced wide open. But despite all this the excitement levels aren't quite there.

Jamaican crowds are strange to someone used to the noisy grounds of England, with the fans being largely reactive rather than proactive. They won't sing about their team or their players in a bid to inspire their side to greater things, instead they simply react noisily to a chance or a foul then return to their watchful silence. In fairness though, the nature of this stadium makes any kind of crowd participation difficult, as do the vast swathes of empty seats on this occasion, but it still gives the spectacle a strangely hollow feel.

One small boy in front of me tires of banging his clappers together and decides it would be far more fun to use them to hit the man two rows ahead round the back of the head. His father, busy talking on the phone, frantically tries to stop him and simply finds himself being made the target instead. Other people turn and strain to see the source of the elaborate Hispanic commentary with amused looks on their faces, as though pleased to discover that Latin Americans really do narrate matches in such a way and everything they've been told on the subject isn't just an urban myth. The game itself, way out on that distant patch of grass, is being reduced to the status of just another sideshow in the carnival.

Costa Rica, for their slight technical superiority, have become confined to little more than the occasional breakaway attack as the determined Jamaicans pass and probe around their half, searching for that moment of incision. Chances come but Patrick Pemberton, a man who sounds like he should be playing the tuba in a Yorkshire brass band rather than goalkeeping for the Costa Rican national team, is managing to keep them all out and it all amounts to nothing. As the half time whistle sounds there is still no goal.

Thankfully this half-time there are no men from Digicel yelling patronising questions to those in the stands. Instead we are treated to a succession of dancehall stars performing their latest singles and even a brief cameo from the internationally-known local hero Beenie Man. By the time it climaxes with Mr G's brilliantly titled current hit **Swaggarific,** the entire crowd is on its feet dancing and seem almost disappointed when the players, who by now are back in formation on the pitch and ready to go, put an end to the concert in order to play the second half.

And rightly so, because it offers little to raise the pulse in the way the music had done. Like so many international friendlies it descends into a revolving door of substitutions which jar all rhythm and momentum out of the play. Costa Rica played in Panama just 48 hours ago and show signs of fatigue, barely troubling the home defence throughout the entire half. The Reggae Boyz continue in much the same vein as before, controlling possession but doing relatively little with it. Then comes the breakthrough everyone has been waiting for, and for all the short passing that has been attempted it comes via good old fashioned route one.

A long ball is pumped up the field and Ryan Johnson out-muscles the Costa Rican defender, leaving him sprawled across the floor, then smashes the ball left-footed past Pemberton inside the near post. A delighted crowd leap to their feet as Johnson and his team-mates run to the corner flag where they line up to perform celebratory samba moves. And that's it. The game peters out amongst an array of substitutions long before the referee calls time. But the Reggae Boyz have successfully negotiated their first tentative step towards Brazil, and feisty little Jamaica has shown yet another part of a doubting world that it is not to be taken lightly.

Costa Rica players examine the pitch
before kick off at the national stadium.

CHAPTER FOUR

The Plight Of The Eagles

'It is our conviction that coaching is incomplete without nurturing the spiritual development of the player. When a player realises that the pursuit of earthly glory never satisfies; yet the Glory of God is not only fulfilling but ever-increasing, the God given potential in that player will begin to emerge.'

The Charlotte Eagles are an American soccer team. More than that though, they are a heavily Christian institution who see it as their primary objective, even ahead of winning football matches, to spread the Word of God via the playing of football. For a team to be geared entirely towards something other than winning seems to jar heavily with all modern concepts of competitive, professional sport, but to them it is a small part of a bigger picture. They are run as a charitable organisation and rely on large donations from various benefactors in order to survive. This is not something any team can do—Manchester United could not suddenly register themselves as a charity and find themselves receiving all the tax benefits that came with it—but the Eagles are not your average football club. They travel the world, hosting seminars and instilling in trainers the skills to become what they call, 'complete coaches'.

There are, they say, traditionally considered to be four dimensions of coaching: tactical, technical, physical and psychological. The Eagles believe there is a fifth element, something they feel every coach needs to pass on to his players in order to be 'complete': the spiritual. And it is this that brings them to Jamaica, and to Harbour View. Their coaches, in line with an organisation called Global Sports Ministries, are to lead a two day seminar at the Compound about football and, more importantly, about God, flying in to turn the coaches of Jamaica into 'complete coaches' within the space of two working days.

They have chosen a good breeding ground for their ideas. The Guinness Book of Records lists Jamaica as the most church-filled nation on earth, with more per square mile than any other country. The latest census reports that around 65% of Jamaicans are Christian, a lower proportion than claim to follow the doctrine in England and Wales, but faith here is much more active and explicit that it is in modern Britain. A large number of people attend regular services and will often point out to you 'their church', while houses will commonly have a cross or other symbol on display. The public school system also promotes the church in a way ours has long since ceased to do. Compared to Britain, the people of Jamaica are much more receptive to religious faith and open to the ideas and ways it preaches.

Before any of this is to take place though comes the business of a friendly between the two teams. It is difficult to place internationally the level at which Harbour View play. During my radio interview a couple of weeks ago I had been told by the hosts that I would probably find the standard equivalent to that of League Two in England, but much of what I have seen since suggests that had been a harsh assessment. What makes it difficult though are the vast differences between the two styles of play. There is more skill on show in Jamaica certainly, and the ball spends more time on the ground than in England's lower structure, but who's to say that necessarily makes them 'better' in terms of winning games? It is like putting Bach next to the Beatles and asking which was 'better', they are two entirely different animals and so drawing any pan-Atlantic comparisons is very difficult.

Which is what makes the contest between Harbour View and the Charlotte Eagles such a fascinating one. I had once done the obligatory stop of any Englishman visiting Los Angeles and gone to see the Galaxy playing in the MLS, two leagues above the Eagles' USL 2. Beckham aside, who really was a man among boys, I had seen nothing there that suggested a standard way above Jamaica's and with the American style being much more similar to the English this game would provide a useful reference point for Harbour View's place in the world. Especially as the Eagles gave Bolton Wanderers a run for their money just a couple of months ago, only going down to late goals in a 3-1 defeat.

The start is fairly even. After five minutes Marcelino Blackburn crosses for Christopher Harvey to head Harbour View one up only to concede just six minutes later from a Desmion Tachie header, this time from a corner. No one side really takes control and thus it continues for a while, with the Eagles even looking better at times, switching play intelligently and making the more inventive passes. Then Harbour View win a free kick in the far channel outside the area and never look back. The cross is powerfully fired in, by Blackburn again, and Kemeel Wolfe rises to put it past the keeper with another header.

When the game's fourth goal comes soon after, it too is from the head. 'We struggle to defend crosses and set-pieces,' one of the Eagles players admitted to me at the seminar a couple of days later and really I could do very little but agree with him on the evidence I had seen. This time Blackburn makes the glory touch, steering Kemar Petrekin's cross from the right wing past the keeper.

The second half is a typical friendly; slow and over-comfortable, the play twisted by an endless stream of rotating substitutions. As time plods on Harbour View win themselves a penalty which is duly converted by Jahmali Spence to make it 4-1. In fairness, there are mitigating factors for the visitors: they had only arrived in Jamaica last night and then spent the whole day at a local orphanage. They also seem to be struggling with the pitch, the grass patchy, dry and a good few inches too long. But as the scoreline rises those excuses held less and less water and by the time Fabian Campbell sweeps a low shot into the bottom corner from outside the area they have run dry entirely. 5-1. Comprehensive, emphatic and by no means a fluke. 'We were shocked, we weren't prepared for that standard of play,' Eagles substitute Steven Jackson later confessed to me over a lunch of the favourite local dish, curry goat. Further evidence that this is an island that produces some fine footballers, and when you consider that a number of top players were missing, including our internationals who had gone to Fort Lauderdale in Florida for a friendly with Peru, it isn't a bad night's work at all.

But it is not until the seminar two days later that I really come to understand exactly what it is that the Eagles came here to do. 'We use soccer as a platform to teach about Jesus Christ,' Paul Banta of an organisation calling itself Global Soccer Ministries explains to the group of coaches that has assembled from all over the island. 'It's not about us, it's about Him.' In short, they coach coaches to teach their players not just about football but about the 'Glory of God'. I watch on from the stands, not feeling particularly comfortable with the concept being laid out in front of me. A person's religious choices are a very personal thing, is it really the role of a football coach to impose himself on that?

My unease grows further as Banta makes way for Eagles head coach Mark Steffans to address the group. They stand in a line facing him, attentive to a man. 'Wherever you go—Africa, Jamaica, England—you bring out a soccer ball and kids will come,' he tells them. 'But you can be sure they won't set foot in a church.' Something about this idea carries an unnerving element of subterfuge. If you decide to go to church it is because you have chosen to embrace religion, it is not sprung on you from behind a veil of sport. Aren't they just using football as a pretence to lure impressionable children into a position from which they could exercise an ulterior motive of preaching Christianity? Christian, Muslim, Jew, atheist; religious beliefs should be discovered, explored and arrived at by a person at their own discretion, they certainly should not, I felt, be pressed upon a child by someone who has been entrusted by that child's parent with the responsibility of coaching them sport.

The bulk of the seminar swims by in a haze of drills and training games that the coaches could pick up on and take back to their teams, exactly as you might expect from any other course. But there are occasions when we break off from football to touch base with Christ, with prayers and lectures punctuating the course.

The second day begins with the Eagles taking about 100 or more local children, all involved in Harbour View's First Kickers programme, for a well-enjoyed session before continuing in much the same way as the first. By now I am curious to see more of the Eagles on a personal level outside their organisational concept and so I spend the early afternoon session lounging around on one of the TV tower's upper platforms with a few of the players, and I ask about their experiences from similar tours in the past. Speaking to Chad Smith, he tells me about the Eagles' tour to Medellín, Colombia and the case of the Bellavista Prison. This had been the most dangerous penal institution in the world during the 1980s and 90s as the drug war from the streets—Medellín being the city of Pablo Escobar—shifted to within the walls of the prison, and for a long time there was an average of two murders a day amongst the inmates. But then a pastor went up onto a hill that overlooked Bellavista and prayed for the prison. A chapel was set up along with a 'Church Behind Bars' programme and various other Christian initiatives. Over time the murderous inmates turned to God, the remarkable result being that today Bellavista is the least violent prison in Latin America.

There are online documentaries you can watch that corroborate this transformation and it is a truly remarkable turnaround for the most violent place on the planet. It is here that you start to see just how valuable the work of the Christian ministries can be. Of course there is a difference of opinion as to exactly what brought about the change, they would likely say God has touched the inmates and now works through them to change their ways, others would say it is a psychological change brought about by those at rock bottom being opened up to a new set of positive virtues that they had simply never encountered before, with Christ acting as a kind of spiritual placebo. But whether it is God or psychology, not one of those individuals would have changed without the church's influence and it is this that brings us back to Jamaica. Whatever your feelings about the Eagles' methods, no one can deny that it is better to have the children on the streets of Downtown Kingston reaching for a Bible than an AK-47.

Over the course of the two days my views towards the preaching of the Eagles have certainly softened. They are not about numbers and mass conversion, acting on some sort of recruitment drive to pack the churches with young footballers like child soldiers in God's barracks. They are trying to bring the positive virtues that Christianity preaches—love, acceptance, fair play—to young people who might otherwise simply grow up into a moral vacuum and find guidance in gang culture and violence. If leading them into a decent life requires converting them to follow Jesus then so be it.

Indeed, despite my misgivings, I am fully convinced that the work of the Eagles contains much to admire. They go to the world's most deprived areas and seek to help those in need, funded entirely by charitable donations. And they are, let's not forget, a professional team competing in the third tier of US football, but they do so with a Corinthian spirit that seems sadly out of place in the modern game. I had been impressed after the match to see the players stay around on the pitch performing tricks and ball skills with groups of local children, something they continued to do throughout both of the coaching days. Arriving as they have the week after it was revealed that a certain England striker cheated on his wife throughout her pregnancy with local prostitutes—just the latest in a long series of depressing acts committed by our players—this generous spirited team, one of the most genuinely nice groups of people you could ever hope to meet, are a wonderfully refreshing change. And if part of that stems from their beliefs then that is a tremendous advert for the virtues of Christianity. However, as much as I appear to be contradicting myself, my concerns do still linger and before the seminar is over I feel I should try and address them.

With the coaches going through the last exercises of the course I sit in the stand on the far side of the stadium and voice my feelings to Steve Shak, assistant coach of the team. 'It's my conviction, and the conviction of our players, that this is basically what we are established to do,' he responds to me. 'To influence the lives of people not just for the here and now but for eternity. What we do is create an environment where kids can come to a place where they really want to be where they can learn about Jesus, where they can learn about what we feel is the most important thing. Now if your heart doesn't agree with that belief system there's obviously going to be a tension there.'

'But we have a cross on our logo. If you look on our website, if you just come to one of our training sessions we pray, somebody shares some Bible and we finish with prayer every single training session. Part of our mission statement, the mission statement of the team, is to communicate the message of Jesus Christ through the environment of soccer. We are not hiding anything.'

Evidently someone has beaten me to the punch in suggesting to him that there may be something slightly deceptive about their methods, and he goes on to talk about how they bring footballers to the club. 'We're a professional team but we're very upfront in the recruiting process, we do not go to the best player and go, "How can we trick them into playing for the Eagles then get him with the Bible?" There's another step for us. I can pick the best player, that's not a problem, but now what are the chances that this guy is going to really believe in the mission of the Eagles and fit in with our programme?'

I put it to him that, rather than adult staff recruitment, the real issue is them going out into the world and pressing their message upon children under the disguise of football. 'You could view it as a disguise, we view it as a bridge.' He then refers back to the session that morning. 'Put it this way, most of the kids that came in here walked away and didn't respond. We're not trapping people in the stadium and saying: "You can't leave until you become a Christian." This is about love. This is why we came, because we love the people of Jamaica. It's not like I'm here preaching Satan, preaching evil, telling people that murdering, killing and cheating is the best way to raise your social status. We're preaching Jesus because Jesus is the one they call the Prince of Peace. I don't care if one person comes to Jesus or not, I'm here to express love to these people. I'm here to share my soccer knowledge that I have, but you can't be around me and not hear about Jesus because I understand my conviction and my belief. And the way I see it, and the truth that I've discovered, is that He is the only way.'

You may not like the way they go about it, or you may find the saccharine nature of Shak's religious dialogue a bit much, but the Eagles exist primarily to bring positive changes to parts of the world that desperately need them—from Africa to their own backyard of inner-city Charlotte—regardless of whether the end product is one more child following God or not, and for that I now really only see them as a good thing.

Once it is all over everyone mills about outside the changing rooms, saying their goodbyes and wishing each other luck with future projects, and I find myself suddenly feeling a stronger sense of happiness as I wander round than I have at any point since arriving in Jamaica. Many there would probably tell me I am experiencing the joy of being touched by God, I would simply call it a good mood. I have just spent the last two days with a fantastic group of people, American and Jamaican, who were all here to enjoy themselves and their football, and whatever your religious beliefs may be you can't go far wrong with that.

CHAPTER FIVE

Life On The Road

There has never been a title won in football without a bit of luck. No matter how good a team is, without having what they call 'the rub of the green' somewhere along the line—a favourable refereeing decision, a fortuitous bounce, a lucky deflection—that team is likely to end up empty handed. Harbour View had, arguably, enjoyed having it in their favour with the winner against Humble Lions, and on our first away trip of the season lady luck would come along and interfere with the result once again.

The League is finally back, and I am to get the team bus to the north coast parish of Portland where St. George's Sports Club is based in the small town of Buff Bay. Not having been to an away game yet, the process is new and unfamiliar but I am instructed to take an early morning taxi to the Compound. It drops me off in the car park outside the main building with plenty of time to spare and I am directed to a long common room upstairs where a few of the players are lounging on plastic garden chairs in front of a live Spanish league match. More and more of them fill the room as John-Ross Edwards gets up from the front, walks to the set-top cable box and changes the channel to a live English Premier League offering just in time to see Asamoah Gyan score on his Sunderland début against Wigan Athletic, and receive a chorus of loud cheers from around the room for doing so.

It is not, it seems, that too many loyalties are attached to the Mackems, just that Gyan himself appears a popular figure. Perhaps, having shot from obscurity to the big leagues on the back of an impressive World Cup with Ghana, these players can relate to his past and he represents The Dream that they all share. Or perhaps they all just appreciate a good player. Either way his goal, and all subsequent replays of it, are accompanied by delighted sound effects from the boys of Harbour View.

Shortly after the goal, the Harbour View manager, Donovan 'DV' Hayles, enters the front of the room to address his side before they make the journey through the mountainous centre of the island to the north coast. He is not a tall man but he retains the athletic physique of his youth when he played as a goalkeeper for both Harbour View and the national team. He was always known as eccentric even for a keeper, and I'm told it was not unusual to see him tearing up the field with the ball at his feet during a game. He possesses a vividly expressive face which is at almost all times adorned by a baseball cap, and a thin sliver of a moustache sits on his upper lip.

Standing before his players, he warns them about the effects of the heavy rain for which the Portland area is known. The tricks and dribbling will not work in the wet mud, he tells them, and they must be prepared to win another way. 'We are talented enough,' he presses. 'To play the long ball and adjust our game successfully.' As he says these words I imagine the English players of the League Two sides to which Harbour View had been compared worrying about having to play a long ball game because conditions did not favour their usual style of short passing and flair dribbling.

He then produces a marker pen and positions the starting line up on a white-board, indicating exactly what he expects of each individual as he does so. Expecting a lot of long shots from George's, the coach impresses upon his defence the need to be alert to the threat of the keeper getting behind the ball and spilling it in the wet conditions, before encouraging a similar tactic at the other end from his midfielders and strikers. 'Don't end up crying over spilt milk,' he warns. 'We have to catch the spilt milk and make them cry over it so we can walk away with our three points. *Our* three points.' He finishes by running through a couple of set pieces on the board and sends the team away to change and prepare for the bus.

The vehicle itself is little more than a mini bus onto which we all squeeze in like school children ahead of a class trip. 'Don't sit next to him on the bus,' DV had jokingly warned me during the team meeting, pointing to Kemeel Wolfe. 'Everything he eats comes up again.' As I take the last empty seat I look to my left and there, across a small isle down the centre, is Wolfe. I feel duly relieved to see him produce a flowery pillow and curl himself up against the window, slightly open to offer both fresh air and an exit strategy for the sandwich he had consumed twenty minutes earlier. With everyone on board, including a young boy somehow involved with the club—'Let him on, he's the future,' Lemar Hodges had shouted. 'He's the next Dicoy Williams'—we pull away from the car park and a CD is passed forward to the driver. Dancehall is the high tempo, twenty first century progression of reggae music that is pretty much ubiquitous in Kingston and soon it is pounding down from four speakers planted onto the ceiling of the bus. In the seat next to me Romario Campbell has been muttering quietly into his phone and immediately he protests about the sudden blast of music which is then turned down temporarily by his sympathetic team mates.

We move down through Harbour View, straight roads taking us past the single story, detached houses, each with small yards fronted by elaborately decorated walls. The windows and doors, as with all homes in this city, are covered with grilles of iron, painted white in an attempt to make them seem more decorative and remove the unwelcome connotations of what they are really there for. The shopping centre—a supermarket with a few fast food joints outside—lies at the bottom of the community and then you arrive at a large roundabout. The first exit takes you further east to the rest of Harbour View and beyond, straight ahead is the spit taking you out to the airport. We pass both turnings and go right onto the boulevard that passes the cement works and joins Harbour View to the main bulk of Kingston.

So this is it. Here I am in a rarefied and privileged position for any journalist in the world, sitting on the team bus of the national Premier League champions as they travel to an away clash against one of the league's other big names, and with a number of international players in our midst to boot. What will the experience be like, I wonder. What am I going to learn about life at the pinnacle of Caribbean football? Just a hundred or so metres down the boulevard, the bus is pulling over to the side of the road. We have been going no more than a minute or two, what possible problem could have arisen already? There is a few seconds of confusion before someone at the front excitedly yells, 'We got no Far Right!' The players quickly scan the bus to confirm the story before breaking out into screams of laughter. It is true, the Champions have driven off from the Compound for their first away game of the new season without their starting striker, Rafeik 'Far Right' Thomas. The player who, just a few days before, I had overheard being told by a coach that he could be the country's leading striker had fallen asleep back at the stadium and missed the bus, and his team mates are absolutely loving it. Behind me the imposing Nicholas Beckett, somehow folded into the back row of seats, gets out his mobile to inform the manger, who has gone by car, that we will be delayed, and he can barely contain his joy when he gets to the juicy reason as to why. We sit on the dusty layby, cars flying by and shaking the bus as they go, while various phone calls are made to arrange Thomas' transport. When it is ensured that he has been dragged out of bed and plonked on another mini bus carrying food and kit—'Fuzzy bus' as it is known within the club after its principle driver, Cornel 'Fuzzy' Austin—we pull out and back into the flow of traffic headed for urban Kingston, this time with a full complement of players.

We pass up through town and out on the route carrying us north. The bus climbs roads that get slowly steeper and more winding, the houses growing increasingly scattered and the towering greenery of the rainforest now becoming the dominant feature of the landscape. A few of the players seem somehow to be sleeping through the chest-thumping bass blasting from the ceiling. Beside me Wolfe has produced a bright pink blanket and curled up beneath it, determinedly ignoring the laughter of everyone else on board.

The road through Jamaica's heart is a narrow one cut into the side of the mountains. At all times one side is flanked by a rocky face or grassy bank, topped by looming trees and always covered with large-leaved ferns and grasses that reach down towards the travellers below. The other flank supports palms, bamboos and shrubs that do little to shield you from the vast and immediate drops down into deep gulleys. Not that you are bothered by that when driving through a landscape this stunning. As it opens up slightly you look out onto the rising and falling of dozens of individual peaks, each carpeted by the thick jungle, and plunging slopes running down to a charging river lying at various times twenty, fifty, a hundred feet below.

'We're coming for your faggots!' In this surrounding it is easy to be drawn away from Jamaica's many problems but this is the country, and Kingston the city, that gave the world so-called 'Murder Music', something that was now being demonstrated by the deejay (the confusing dancehall term for a singer) announcing that he was going out with his Tec-9 to shoot homosexuals, or 'batty bwoys' as they are known. The strength and depth of the anti-gay sentiments here, stemming from both a macho-man culture and Bible-based laws criminalising the practice, once led to an American journalist calling it the most homophobic place on earth. This is a strange and contrasting country, one that can enchant and appal in equal measure.

We reach the low coastal regions again and pass into the parish of Portland. It is an area with a chequered history and tales of boom, bust and movie stars echo down the years, due in no small part to its own unique micro-climate. Receiving far more rainfall than the rest of the island it has an even richer natural appeal, covered in thick foliage and famous for its rivers and stunning natural waterfalls. These are perfect growing conditions and in the latter part of the nineteenth century a banana boom exploded here that brought swathes of pickers, planters and farmers to the area in a 'green gold' rush. It wasn't to last though and by the 1930s these good times were largely over, but Portland's most colourful decades still lay ahead.

The real Champagne days were also induced, albeit less directly, by the natural wonders. 'Never had I seen a land so beautiful. Everywhere there is a blanket of green so thick that the earth never shows through,' wrote Hollywood star Errol Flynn after moving to the parish's capital of Port Antonio in the 1940s. Endearing himself to the natives by downing white overproof rum in the local bars, his rakish lifestyle soon became legendary. He is said to have won an island just off the northern coast in a bet and he reportedly set a crocodile loose on the streets of Montego Bay. Playwright Noël Coward was another resident in the area and the regular parties at his Blue Harbour home were attended by the likes of Alec Guinness, Sir Laurence Olivier, Katherine Hepburn and, of course, Flynn himself. The pair were also cohorts of James Bond creator Ian Fleming who lived further west at Oracabessa and used Jamaica in much of his work.

Today the region is quieter and exists very much as the forgotten cousin to the more celebrated destinations of Montego Bay, Negril and Ocho Rios, but this does not detract from its appeal which is very much the same now as it always was. And Portland does still occasionally flirt with Hollywood; recently Tom Cruise and Cameron Diaz found themselves here to shoot parts of their movie *Knight and*

Day. But football does not require stardust to exist, and this green and lush land provides our first away destination in our own quest, the endless pursuit of Premier League points and sporting heroism.

Up to this point my contact with the players has been patchy at best. As we pull over into a car park next to one of the remaining banana fields I hope this might change, and everyone climbs out of the cramped transport to stretch their legs and indulge in a lunch of rice and peas with chicken. Once everyone has taken theirs one of the kit men, a man known as Brucky, thrusts a polystyrene box of warm food into my hands and I walk over to sit on the grass with a small group of players to eat. And this is where you realise that socialising is not as easy as you might hope. Like most teams this is a group of young men who all get on very well, laughing and joking, generally at each other's expense, and keeping the mood high ahead of the game. But in Jamaica, officially an English speaking country, hearing a conversation is like hearing people speak in a language you learnt at GCSE but have not spoken since. You can catch the gist of the occasional sentence but most of it passes you by in a blur of indecipherable sounds and noises.

Patois was developed in the 17th century by the African slaves brought to the island who picked up on the language of their masters and nativised it. Over the centuries it has evolved into a dialect all of its own and to an outsider, even a native English speaker, it might as well be Russian. Because of this I sit there silently, just watching the conversations happening around me and no doubt giving off the impression of a terrified child too scared to say a word to these new people when in reality I just have no idea whatsoever what's going on. I felt like they see me as a bit odd and so find myself feeling a bit odd as a result. Apparently Daveion Woodhouse senses my awkwardness and he walks to the kit van, returning with a drink which he hands to me with a friendly smile. Perhaps they have accepted the idea of having a foreign writer around, but they strike me as still a bit unsure about exactly who I am.

We are still around twenty minutes from Buff Bay. The bus had left Kingston four and half hours before the game in order to get through the twisting mountain roads before eating—'It's a bumpy journey, it can upset the players' stomachs,' I had been warned the day before—and of course the club's budget does not stretch to staying in a hotel overnight, while flying is not even an option. The teams of the national Premier League are faced with logistical concerns that would not even occur to Jose Mourinho or Sir Alex Ferguson.

We pile back into the bus, with Thomas now transferred to ours and perched on the fold-out aisle seat between me and Wolfe, and drive along the coastal road, fringed with palm trees that droop down towards the frothy waves a few feet below.

This highway takes us through Buff Bay and then straight past the turning into the small ground. 'Woah, woah driver! It's there,' shout some of the senior players who have clearly been here more often than the driver as the St. George's Sports Club sign flashes past the window. We reverse and turn up the bumpy lane where we sit beeping outside the padlocked metal gate to the car park. With over two hours still to go until kick off the locals had clearly not expected us this early. The one or two of them who are already inside do not seem to like being distracted from their working (or idly sitting around) to let these city boys into their car park but eventually they get up and do so, however begrudgingly.

Lynch Park is a small ground with a number of concrete bleachers dotted around the outside of the pitch painted in the red and white of St. George's Sports Club and capable of holding, at a push, around 2,000 people. Its focal point is a large concrete clubhouse with its grand, pillar-fronted and slightly colonial-looking balcony, and one of Jamaica's many lush mountains looming up behind. The whole field is hemmed in by a breeze block wall, also painted red and white, from behind which you can hear the rise and fall of the Caribbean Sea on the other side of the road. Like most Jamaican stadia, what it lacks architecturally it makes up for scenically.

From the gravel car park we pass through a gate into the fenced off area surrounding the clubhouse. Adorning the metal link fence are two signs, the first of which would be seen in any sporting arena in the world while the second is uniquely Jamaican. 'PLAYERS AND OFFICIALS ONLY' reads the top sign, with the one below it adding importantly: 'NO GANJA TO BE SMOKED IN THIS AREA'. With two hours to kill the players inspect the pitch while chewing on sugar cane, the local way to raise energy levels before the match, before retiring to the changing room. I sit with a few of the coaches and The Next Dicoy Williams in the away dugout and listen to live radio commentary of the Tivoli—Sporting match which is being picked up by a strategically placed mobile phone. Behind us a slightly deranged-looking local man dances and sings on the other side of the fence, clearly feeling thoroughly excited about the match ahead. While he does so, Navion Boyd, back to league action with a point to prove to national coach Theodore Whitmore, scores what turns out to be the only goal of the game, making a win for us this evening essential in order to keep up the early season pace with our biggest rivals for the title.

In drips and drabs the players emerge in training kit to warm up and run through a series of passing drills as coach Andrew 'Bowa' Hines looks on, pouncing on the basic errors which are discouragingly frequent. George's had finished fifth last season and, despite a poor result the week before, would be no easy meat. Carvel Stewart had arrived by car shortly after us and was now flitting around with his business face on, referring frequently to an assortment of papers in his hand and talking at length to DV by the far goal mouth. With one last running exercise completed the players drift back to the changing room and I make my way through the clubhouse and up to the balcony to watch, via a brief exchanging of pleasantries with the determined Carvel.

Upon entering, I find that the balcony is not a neutral press space. With no seats or desks, and filled entirely with George's supporters, I lean myself against the railings next to a man named Scotty. Like most people in these 'VIP' areas at Jamaican football clubs, Scotty is a local man who had played for the team during his younger days. 'I'm expecting to beat your lot tonight,' he informs me after I explain who I am and what I'm doing in Jamaica. 'We didn't do well last week but we're back on our home ground now,' as though that is all it takes to guarantee a result. He goes on to express the hope that I might, in fact, be an undercover scout and that I will return to England with a list of names to pass on to the Premier League, as if I might secretly have Arsene Wenger on speed-dial so I could just whip out my phone as soon as I land at Gatwick to let him know what I found. Despite me telling him that I am in no such position, he proceeds to point out a few of the red-shirted players, who had re-emerged onto the pitch in the meantime accompanied yet again by FIFA's inescapable anthem, including national captain Jermaine Taylor—a former Harbour View player—and his brother Ricardo.

'And this one's impressive too,' he says pointing to the young Dever Orgill. 'Just got out of school but he's going to be big.' Graciously he acknowledges that the reigning champions down the other end have one or two decent players themselves, but this admission does nothing to diminish his confidence. 'Did you see how Barcelona went down the other day?' he grins, referring to Spain's top team losing at home to newly-promoted Hercules a couple of days before. 'Being champions means nothing.'

Unaware of the verbal lashing they have just received, Harbour View make all the early running. The Current Dicoy Williams picks up on a loose ball and fires it over from twenty five yards before Marcelino Blackburn, carrying on where he had left off against the Eagles, crosses only for Kemar Petrekin to shoot wide under intense pressure from the defender. But then that is it. Our domination of the first few minutes slips and George's make some chances of their own. The best passing move of the game allows them to swing in a cross towards dangerously lurking strikers but it is slightly over-hit and goes out for a goal kick. Yet it is a sure warning sign that they are not going to make it easy.

As time passes the first half starts to drift. Our standard of play becomes sloppy, and is looser and more haphazard than anything I have seen since arriving in the country. The referee is seemingly buying everything the players sell him and the free kick tally grows. As at any ground in the world, the fans around me bemoan his every move, declaring with unwavering certainty that he is favouring the opposition every time he blows his whistle. The evidence, as a red-shirted defender smashes his studs into the knee of Romario Campbell while the ref turns a blind eye, does not necessarily support their claims but football fans only ever see what is convenient, and this lot would never have let a trifling incident like that prevent them from venting their anger.

The momentum is now with the home team and another attack leads to another corner. With the players wandering into position for the set piece a rogue ball is thrown into the six yard box by one of the young ball boys. Suddenly down below us a man bursts through the gate by the half-way line and runs towards it. It is the very same man who had been manically dancing behind our dugout during the warm up. The crowd are immediately up on their feet and roaring him on as he slaloms through the bemused players and slots the extra ball into the bottom corner of the net before running off with his arms outstretched in celebration. A few officials finally decide something should be done about him and half heartedly jog onto the field, but they are never going to catch the enthusiastic runner and he shoots out through the gate on the far side of the pitch. No police detainment and life-time ban for him though. As far as the authorities are concerned it is out of sight, out of mind and once he has sat down again in the far stand, next to the 25 or so Harbour View fans who have made the journey, the irritated stewards return to their stations. The corner is comfortably cleared.

But the pressure is still on and after Dicoy horribly miscontrols a pass at the back, Michard Barrett finds himself with Leon Irving sprinting towards his goal and no defenders around to protect him. The shot slides wide but it is yet another warning. Yet another loose ball then loops up into the channel beyond the far side of the Harbour View box and brings a moment of magic as Orgill leaps spectacularly with his legs above his head and fires a bicycle kick towards goal. In the end it is a relatively comfortable save for Barrett, but was a stunning attempt nonetheless. 'Now *that* was good,' says a smug Scotty, turning towards me and looking very pleased with himself indeed.

At the other end Campbell fires a rare shot just over from about 25 yards but it is Harbour View who are clinging on for half time. 'BALL THEM GEORGE'S!' yell the men around me, sensing their superiority and the need to make the most of it. Then, just as the half time break looms, the game is turned on its head. As George's break Orgill once again picks up the ball on the right flank and cuts inside, tussling with Kimorlee Brissett who tugs his shirt back for a clear foul, but as the whistle is blown Orgill flings his right arm out and his elbow connects firmly with Brissett's cheekbone. Immediately the ref produces a red card and the entire stadium erupts in fury. The rules are simple enough though, and a raised arm to the face has to be dealt with in that way. Seconds later at half time Scotty is incredulous when I tell him as much, insisting that it had not been at the face and simply responding with an exasperated sigh when I point to the icepack planted firmly against Brissett's cheek as he walks to the changing room. But there is nothing he could do about it and for the second league game out of two we have a goalless first half but with Harbour View going into the second with a one man advantage.

We start it by dominating possession but every time our forwards are given the ball they are dribbling down blind alleys, always being closed out and cut off by the home defence. And George's are making their own chances too, with Jermaine Taylor firing a shot just over the bar from just inside the half-way line. Then we finally give ourselves a tangible advantage. Richard Edwards picks up on a loose ball and sends it through the home defence to the on-running Kemar Petrekin who slashes it past the keeper and into the far corner. Despite my best efforts a muted celebration escapes me right in the middle of the silenced George's hardcore, the release of pressure that comes from a vital goal getting the better of me. The real surprise though was the fact that I had been feeling that pressure in the first place. I have only been here three weeks and already Harbour View Football Club is drawing me in.

And now we're playing again. Straight from the kick-off we win the ball back and force a mix up in their defence which tees up Campbell for a shot that flies just wide. We are piling on the pressure and for a while it looks like the only remaining matter to be settled in the game is how many we would score. 'Make a change coach, we need to change,' bellow uneasy voices around me to the dugout down in front of us.

But before the coach has time to act they get the lucky break they need. An optimistic shot is deflected wide of the Harbour View goal and out for a corner. It is swung in harmlessly but is scrappily addressed by our defence who leave Girvan Brown free to head the bouncing ball past Barrett and into the net. With that the momentum swings entirely and all the attacking movements are now flooding into the Harbour View end. They win a free kick that is hit low into a knot of players and Jermaine Taylor finds himself, through fortune rather than design, with the ball at his feet inside the box and with only the keeper in his way. Fortunately he finishes like the centre-back he is and smashes it over, but it is now George's who looked like they had an extra player on the field.

We are becoming sloppy again, passes going wayward, poor touches and miscontrolled balls appearing in all areas of the pitch. The really ominous thing is what appears to be a lack of commitment:

fifty-fifty balls being lost every time, no one really sprinting, 'busting a gut' as they say back home, to get onto the end of a pass or a through ball.

But it is said that the mark of true champions is to be able to produce a win even when you are playing badly. In those moments there is someone that will take control, something about the team that will force a win through sheer strength of will. Or they might just get lucky. The George's defender will be haunted for some time by the horribly under-hit back pass he tried to play to his keeper, but Romario Campbell seized the opportunity it afforded him and suddenly he is sprinting towards goal with the ball at his feet. The defence desperately scramble back but Campbell pulls it across the box to substitute Kemeel Wolfe. He lingers on it, a defender now blocking his way. Shoot you idiot! He jinks this way and that but his chance has gone. Instead he lays it back across to Campbell, who looks for all the world like he is in an offside position, but the linesman does not flag and he tucks the chance away. George's are furious. All around me people stretch over the balcony rail to get those few extra inches closer and scream their anger that bit harder at the referee while the furious players surround the offending linesman. Campbell and the Harbour View players, meanwhile, sprint to the bench to celebrate with DV and the subs. The goal stands, and it is no less than Campbell deserves having been one of the few bright points in the side's otherwise dull performance. The remaining minutes see the occasional scare but the goal had all but killed off the game and the full time whistle seems no more than a formality when it comes.

I make my way pitch-side and speak to Carvel who had watched from the dugout and is far more concerned with the standard of the performance than the points won. 'It was disappointing,' he tells me glumly. I walk over to the dugout where Blackburn sits next to the captain, national midfielder Richard Edwards, who is holding an ice-pack on his knee. He explains that he had slipped and jarred it a few minutes from time, the sort of injury that could be fine in a day or two but could equally be something much more serious. He gets up and hobbles back to the changing room, supporting himself on Blackburn's shoulder, leaving me to help the equipment manager Jermaine 'Twinny' Malcolm carry the emptied water barrels and medical kit back to the bus. And everyone I speak to insists that Campbell had definitely *not* been offside.

As everyone is preparing to leave DV approaches me. He hands me some tapes, explaining that they are the footage of the game and that I am to pass them on to Clyde to give to the TV station for their highlights package—Jamaica in a nutshell—and then he offers to buy me a beer. 'The players aren't allowed to drink,' he informs me as we walk towards the concessions stand, 'but we are.' He looks very pleased with the Heineken that is already gripped tightly in his hand. He explains that the performance was being attributed to tired legs after the long, cramped bus journey, which makes the fact that a night in a hotel is unaffordable seem all the more desperate.

With a Red Stripe in my hand I am directed into the car of Neville 'Mally' Malcolm—one of the senior club men and DV's former boss at the Airport Authorities of Jamaica many years before—along with DV and Sydney McFarlane of the under 21s for the journey home. But no sooner have we pulled out of the ground than DV yells for us to pull over into a roadside jerk centre. Portland is the home of jerk and it is decided that the Englishman has to sample some pork.

The centre is little more than a concrete shack divided into two parts, one side being the grill area for preparing the meat and the other a tiny bar. As we approach, a large woman drunkenly staggers out to announce, 'Anyone who can pick me up gets to take me home.' She then continues on her way into the night, the effects of the drink rendering her oblivious to the mocking laughs that linger behind her.

With ten minutes until the food is ready, we settle around a table outside. A local in the bar spots us through a glassless window and, noticing the Harbour View training kit the others are all wearing, begins remonstrating with us for so clearly having the referee on our side. Immediately DV leaps to his team's defence, arguing that every team gets decisions going for and against them during the season, and that the man wouldn't even remember the 'offside' goal if George's had taken the chances they should have done and won the game. Jamaicans argue with a passion we are not accustomed to in England, voices are quickly raised and take on a violent tone and it always seems like the first punch is just one wrong comment away. But this is just 'their way' and they could be the best of friends a couple of minutes later. Shouting does not necessarily mean aggression like it does at home.

The argument develops and becomes one of those bizarre situations where I have to remind myself I am not with a group of fans but the management of the national Premier League champions. I try to imagine Carlo Ancelotti, decked out in Chelsea attire, sitting outside a café at the side of a road near to Goodison Park with a bottle of Heineken in his hand and engaging in a loud slanging match with the locals after a tight win away at Everton. Jamaican football, though, has not yet found the need to distance itself from the common man in the way that our own cash-rich Premier League has. And while privileged Jamaicans may read this from an Englishman and react by once again calling into question their professionalism as a nation (as is the vogue among the educated classes), I find it endearing and hope they can instead find the charm in the scene. Football has become too precious at the top, here it is as it is supposed to be.

Back in the car, as it winds its way back up and through the mountains, I chew on the spicy meat that is sitting foil-wrapped in my lap and feel a sense of relief at our fortunate win. It would have been a long way to come in order to lose, which we arguably should have done. There were definite concerns about the way we played and about the state of our captain's left knee, but we will be entertaining Arnett Gardens in three days time with six points from six in the bag, and that's as much as you can really ask for.

Sunday 12ᵗʰ September

Arnett Gardens	0 3	Reno
Humble Lions	0 1	Boys' Town
Portmore United	3 0	Village United
St. George's	**1 2**	**HVFC**
Tivoli Gardens	1 0	Sporting Central
Waterhouse	4 1	Benfica

National Premier League

	P	GD	Pts.
1. Waterhouse	2	5	6
2. Portmore United	2	4	6
3. Boys' Town	2	3	6
4. Tivoli Gardens	2	3	6
5. HVFC	**2**	**2**	**6**
6. Reno	2	2	3
7. Arnett Gardens	2	-3	1
8. Village United	2	-3	1
9. Humble Lions	2	-2	0
10. St. George's	2	-3	0
11. Sporting Central	2	-3	0
12. Benfica	2	-5	0

CHAPTER SIX

The Prosperous Cheat

There is something satisfying about the mathematics of a league table. It is definitive and unequivocal, the best rise to the top while the worst fall to the bottom and everything is exactly where it should be. Like pouring thick treacle over a rough surface, it moves and sorts itself out before the whole lot settles neatly into its place leaving the end result smooth and tidy. That is the theory at least. Which is what makes looking at a table after two games so frustrating. You want it to tell its story and reveal its secrets about the teams it contains but at this stage the reality is far more random, it offers tantalising hints but gives no real answers like the mature table does. In compensation, this dearth is often made up for early in the season by the thrill of someone kicking off with an unexpected dip or peak whereby almost every year one of the big teams finds itself in the bottom half after a couple of games while some carefree newcomer, fresh from promotion the previous May, goes flying into the top four or five. The team at the top could have had a freak start, two easy fixtures or some lucky goals. The team unexpectedly at the bottom, meanwhile, could have been slow beginners after the summer, had some injuries or unfortunate refereeing decisions. Whatever the reason for this turn, the fact that we know it is not a true reflection of status and that it is inevitably just a flash in the pan makes for something to pique our interest in the absence of the table's more considered revelations that come later in the season.

The Jamaica Premier League, though, does not even have that injection of excitement in its favour. After two games, five of the twelve teams have six points and they are exactly the teams you would expect them to be, while Premier League first-timers Benfica sit pointless on the bottom and have already clocked up a five goal deficit to boot. In short, it is about as immaterial a league table as you could ever hope to see. But matchday three brings the first set of midweek league fixtures and with them, for better or worse, the metronomic order of the first two games will crash spectacularly.

The previous Saturday, Paul Banta of Global Soccer Ministries had conferred a sacred status upon the Compound. In the fevered atmospheres of South American and European football this is nothing new, and the psuedo-religious clichés are hurled so hard and with such frequency at the big stadia, or sporting cathedrals as they are often referred to, that those grounds are already their own special brand of 'sacred'. But that is not what Banta had in mind. 'Let's make this a Holy place,' he had declared after one discussion about accepting Christ's ways. 'A place where we can give ourselves to Jesus.' Jesus hadn't liked this, or at least someone hadn't. In fact, something about his consecration had so displeased whatever deity happened to be listening that tonight, the night of the season's first Wednesday game, a Biblical plague of flying insects has been cast onto the Compound.

From the street outside warning signs are visible as groups of them swarm in the glare of the floodlights and once inside they are everywhere, covering the walls, the seats, the floor and filling the air. The press platform is worst of all, its lights drawing them in and mesmerising them so that they envelop the desks, the ground and any unfortunate people who also happen to be in the vicinity. Swigging from a bottle of Pepsi I have to ensure the lid is securely screwed back on within milliseconds every time in order to prevent them overrunning that too. Fighting back, Clyde sets out pots of water to draw them in and stamps his feet across the living carpet developing on the concrete floor, but as a battle against sheer weight of numbers it is entirely futile. In the end all we can do is switch off the lights and hope for the best, leaving the media highflyers of Jamaica to work by the borrowed glow of the floodlights alone.

In the midst of the frenzy I am introduced to the happy, bouncing Martin Davis, a 13 year old from the youth set-up who had recently spent a couple of weeks in Spain with Valencia as part of an exchange programme organised by the two clubs. He tells me excitedly about his time over there and the couple of first team players he had managed to meet, and how he cannot wait to go back. Due to play for the Jamaica under 17s, Martin had so impressed on his trial that Valencia have offered him a full-time place in their academy and at the end of the month he is to head over there, alone, to set himself up for a new life in eastern Spain.

As his family will remain in Kingston and he does not speak any Spanish, I ask if he is nervous at all. 'Not really, I'm just excited,' he replies with a wide grin that tells me he really means it. His voice has not even broken yet and he is full of a child's innocent delight, yet I'm troubled by the nagging cynicism that comes with a few extra years and cannot help but worry for him. Clearly he is exceptionally talented but professional football can be the cruellest of paths to follow and should it not work out he will feel a million miles from home. And even if it is a success life will still be difficult for him. I think of the occasional pangs of homesickness I have experienced myself since moving to Kingston, but Martin is just a child and does even not speak a word of the local language—how much worse might it be for him? Having said all that though, it really is an unbelievable opportunity for a Jamaican boy and one that I sincerely hope might work out well. I wish him the best of luck and he laughs with an encouraging humility when I tell him I will be looking out for him in the Champions League ten years from now. Always lurking closely behind that dream, though, are countless very real dangers for a young boy undertaking his journey to football's summit. If there really is a God looking down on us in the Harbour View Stadium, I hope he keeps a close eye on Martin's future.

Mercifully the insect storm has subsided slightly by the time the players stride out onto the pitch. Once again we are in the late kick off slot and results earlier in the day have been kind to us. Tivoli lost, as did Waterhouse while Portmore gave Benfica their first ever Premier League points after going down 2-1 at Drax Hall. And here we are playing Arnett Gardens, the team that has just lost 3-0 at home to League newcomers Reno. The next 90 minutes are just a formality in moving three points clear of almost all our biggest rivals.

Only they aren't. Arnett are comfortably the weakest team I have seen since I arrived in Jamaica and it seems like only a matter of time until we score the first of many. But we never do and after about half an hour Kevin 'Pele' Wilson scores for them having been left unmarked at a freekick. In reply we produce nothing that can get us back into it. The full time whistle puts an end to the most frustrating of nights as we let a big opportunity in the league slip. Suddenly the fact that we have bumped along to slightly fortuitous wins in our first two games looks ominous. When will our season get going? With Sunday bringing us a trip to Portmore United we cannot afford to wait too much longer.

According to official sources, Harbour View Football Club was established in 1974. Official sources here though are not always entirely accurate, or at least don't always tell the full story. Jamaicans are not wonderful record keepers and have retained the 'campfire culture' of their African roots, preferring to pass their histories on verbally rather than writing them down, and as such the stories of the past are often to be found in conversation rather than a library.

The people at the club today are the people who have been at the club since the beginning. Clyde, DV, Carvel and others all built Harbour View themselves and today they are the richest resource for finding out where it came from. Of course this doesn't make things easy as discrepancies arise between different versions, but the majority still remains constant.

The community was built by a private company called the West Indies Home Contractors and its initial foundation of 1,800 homes was completed in 1961. It was designed as a place for the middle classes to move out of the city and into the suburbs for a quieter life, and this family-orientated focus resulted in scores of children coming into the community. The one thing children do, of course, is play, and this was essential in the birth of the football club. With no dedicated areas built for recreation, any patches of open space were descended upon for football, cricket and any other games that could be formulated, and among these makeshift playgrounds was a site at the bottom of the mountains known as the Compound that had been left empty when the contractors and engineers moved out. 'More and more of the boys gravitated to that area,' Clyde recalls. 'There were a lot of old tractors and machinery and long cables going underground and the earth was just messy. But bit by bit little areas were cleared and more and more of the boys moved into the area.'

According to DV the first community football club was founded in response to the activities of the church. The St. Benedict's Catholic Church took up a central role within the area at that time, providing both schooling and youth organisations. It was the CYO that first formed a football team and that was followed closely by the Altar Boys group for the younger children in the church, with the two teams playing against each other in informal practice matches and against other teams from other areas in competitions on weekends. But this did not include everybody. Harbour View is split by a river and in those days the residents on either side were drawn into conflicts, with those on the eastern side being of a more rebellious nature.

'Over that side you see more bad eggs,' DV says. 'The river, for no reason at all, created a division. Not just physically but mentally and socially and somehow the people over that side thought, because we were closer to town, that we believed we were higher class than they . . . . And so there developed a lot of tension in the community.' It was the non-churchgoers over on that side who felt left out at the football being played by the Catholic boys and decided to form their own team, calling it the Eastern Thunderbolts. 'I would think that the baby stage, that little dot in the mother, would have been the church and then after two or three months in the womb it became the Eastern Thunderbolts because it broke away and became the wider community,' DV says about the early days.

The Thunderbolts had talent. Lindy Delaphena was the first Jamaican to play in the English top division and, on returning to the island as his career drew to a close, he picked out the team as one of the best in the area, but they lacked structure and their experiment barely even lasted a year. 'They saw themselves as outlaws,' says DV. 'And they basically just wanted to smoke ganja, do them ting and then play football.' Actually being organised was never part of the fun.

In 1966 the bottling company Desnoes & Geddes formed the Minor League competition for under 17 teams in the Kingston and St. Andrew Corporate Area and this was the cue for Harbour View to try again. It was the first side from the community to take part in formal competition and included in the group were Carvel's brother Owen as well as Neville 'Bertis' Bell, the current coach at St. George's. DV's older brother took on the captaincy and as a result his family got increasingly drawn into the club, with his mother even cooking meals for the players before games. As the young boys got increasingly organised their results got better and in their third season in the Minor League they reached the final only to lose on penalties. As a few years passed that team became too old and the next generation came up to the take their places, and under Clyde's captaincy they won the Minor League in 1972, beating Elliston Flats in the final. Not only was this the club's first ever trophy but it proved to be the incentive they needed to keep on developing. By 1974, the year the official history states as the starting point, the club was already very much up and running, and the whole of Jamaican football was turbulently shaking through some enormous changes.

The TV in the common room jumps and flickers. On it, commentators run through the pre-game build up for the Clarendon derby between Humble Lions and Sporting Central Academy, and seven or eight players sit around on the white plastic garden chairs watching it. I had climbed out of a taxi and joined them just in time to see highlights from the midweek games. 'Champions Harbour View lost one-nil at home to Arnett Gardens,' announces the enthusiastic presenter over footage of their goal and a number of our missed chances, sparking angry comments from around the room at the way fate had turned on them on Wednesday night. It is a relief when they move on to today's live game instead.

DV comes in and sits at the front, joining in the players' banter as they all eat chicken and rice from plates in their laps. 'Come on the Lions, four in a row!' Shouts Blackburn, sitting with a bag of ice on his left ankle, in reference to the home side's three defeats from three so far this season. The commentators do their best to up the drama of a fairly lacklustre game, discussing one Sporting player who had moved from the Lions and equating it to Luis Figo's transfer from Barcelona to Real Madrid. The plodding nature of the football and the thousand or so passive looking souls watching on from the bleachers hint that the real nature of this rivalry might be somewhat less intense. DV then calls the players away to a different room for the team talk and, as they pick up their chairs and carry them next door, the television offers an example of one of Jamaica football's biggest problems and a stark forewarning of what would trouble us in Portmore later that evening: poor refereeing.

The exiting players pause to watch, chairs hanging from their hands, as a Sporting player runs past the last defender and has his shirt pulled back. Unperturbed, the striker drives on, opens his body up and slides the ball past the keeper into the bottom corner of the net. And this is the point at which the ref chooses to blow his whistle and award Sporting a penalty, even though the foul had occurred outside the area and the striker had gone on to score anyway. No referee in the world, not even a helpful parent in charge of a primary school under 9s match, should be making decisions like that and this is the sort of thing the Jamaican league must deal with on a regular basis. Fortunately in this instance the penalty is scored anyway, but matches and leagues can turn on that sort of decision.

Having been given their instructions by the manager, the players come back to the common room to check the score and gather their things before the journey. Nickolas Beckett idles up to me as I rise from my chair in front of the TV, slaps my hand in greeting and puts on his best, and most carefully enunciated, British accent, ''Ello Yugo, are you orlroit?' It is pure Dick van Dyke but I compliment his attempt and he smiles and walks away. I head downstairs and out to our transport, this time joining fitness coach Andrew 'Bowa' Hines in his Mitsubishi for the short journey into the neighbouring parish of St. Catherine to Portmore.

The geography has developed in a way that means there is no countryside between Portmore and Kingston, the growth of the shipping port having brought them together into one large conurbation. The main road along the wharf side gives a virtually direct route there from Harbour View and as we travel it, constantly passing and being passed by the player-crammed minibus, Bowa points out the various sights it has to offer. Kingston Prison, Downtown, the port and, moving into St. Catherine, a stretch known as Back Road which couples as the area's red light district are all revealed to me.

It is not, one must say, one of Jamaica's more scenic drives, but at the end of it Portmore United's Freddie Neeta Park is not without its charms. The pitch is hemmed in on two sides by red and white painted bleachers, with another side taken up by the two story concrete clubhouse and the other end simply fenced off from the world beyond. The area itself is slightly elevated, meaning that from my seat next to the TV cameras on the roof of the clubhouse the lights of Portmore and Kingston can be seen stretching away into the darkness below the eastern goal and its accompanying stand. The corner between there and the stand along the far side is overlooked by a church, yellow-painted walls and blue roof giving it a typically Caribbean appearance, which backs on to a hill that rises up before sloping down into the bay. The whole thing is surrounded, as most things are around here, by palm trees which reach over the tall metal fences and sway gently in the breeze.

The game itself is largely characterised by sloppy mistakes, bad refereeing and shameless cheating. Portmore striker Steven Morrissey spends the entire match throwing himself to the floor at the slightest opportunity. Down and down he goes, over and over again. It starts early when he runs across the top of the box and flings himself through the air on passing a defender, twisting to scream towards the ref before he even hits the ground, and it continues for the entire match. Portmore attack, Morrissey dives and squeals; a thoroughly repetitive vision. Which makes it all the more galling when he is central in the scoring of their first goal. He shoots from the edge of the area and it is parried by Barrett, but instead of pushing it wide he can only deflect it straight back out and right onto the feet of Errol Stevens who tucks away the easiest of finishes.

This happens just before half time, and equally close on the other side of the break comes their next. Just seconds into the second half Kimorlee Brissett is fouled in his left back position. Taking the free kick quickly he passes it to Richard Edwards on the edge of his own box and, clearly unready to be receiving the ball, the captain dallies and tries to move it on but is caught in possession by the alert Morrissey. It is he who picks our captain's pocket, runs the few yards into the area and side-foots it into the bottom corner within a minute of the restart. It could not have gone any worse.

Before the end he makes himself Edwards' nemesis again. As he once more spins to the ground screeching after a challenge which inflicted minimal contact, the skipper picks up the ball and throws it back down in exasperation which, unlike the constant diving, the ref considers to be a completely unacceptable way for a player to conduct himself. Over runs the official and produces his yellow card, which happens to be Edwards' second, and then the red. The deplorable Stevie Morrissey has finally done as he desired and succeeded in getting our captain sent off. Had the ref done his job correctly Morrissey would have been booked himself right at the beginning and none of this would have happened.

The full time whistle puts an end to an unsuccessful Harbour View onslaught that had taken up the entire second half, but produced only one of the goals we needed. To their credit, the players had not collapsed after going two-nil down, they had fought and continued to do so right up until the very end, led on by their captain until his injury time dismissal. But that does not hide the fact that they had been unable to score the second goal and have now suffered two consecutive defeats. The defending champions have six points from their first four games and, alarmingly, have only scored four goals, two of which we were arguably pretty lucky to have. Back in England, Chelsea's fight to retain their title has yielded five wins from five, with 21 goals scored and conceded just one, and that it the sort of form you want to begin a season with. Our stuttering fallibility is not only damaging for ourselves but offers our rivals a huge mental boost as well.

But this is not England. The English Premier League, we like to constantly tell everyone, is 'the most exciting league in the world'. Yet at the beginning of each season there are only ever two or three teams seriously considered to be contenders to win the league. In Jamaica it is generally thought to be between five teams from a league of twelve. Put another way, at the beginning of the season nearly half the teams in the competition are genuine, realistic contenders for the title. Almost every week there is at least one big clash, the sort of scenario that could make Sky Sports executives positively wet themselves with excitement at the thought of all those Grand Slam Sundays they could blare out from our screens. But this also means that a title winning team's statistics will be much less impressive than we are used to in England. Last season Harbour View lost seven times and scored just 44 goals from their 38 games. Tivoli Gardens in second amassed just 66 points, meaning it took a minimum of 67 to become champions, a lower total than has ever been required to win the English league in its 38 game format.

So all is not lost. Due to the way results have gone we are still only three points from the top, making us one of eight teams that could potentially be leading the way after the next round of games, and we've actually got two points more than we did at this stage last year. It's been a long way from the start we would have wanted but due to the genuinely exciting and unpredictable nature of the Jamaican Premier League, we are at least still alive.

Wednesday 15th September　　Sunday 19th September

Benfica	2 1	Portmore United		Arnett Gardens	1 0	Boys' Town
Boys' Town	1 0	Tivoli Gardens		Humble Lions	1 1	Sporting Central
HVFC	**0 1**	**Arnett Gardens**		**Portmore United**	**2 1**	**HVFC**
Reno	2 0	Humble Lions		St. George's	0 1	Benfica
Sporting Central	4 1	St. George's		Tivoli Gardens	4 0	Village United
Village United	2 0	Waterhouse		Waterhouse	1 0	Reno

National Premier League

	P	GD	Pts.
1. Tivoli Gardens	4	6	9
2. Portmore United	4	4	9
3. Waterhouse	4	4	9
4. Boys' Town	4	3	9
5. Arnett Gardens	4	-1	7
6. Reno	4	3	6
7. HVFC	**4**	**0**	**6**
8. Benfica	4	-3	6
9. Sporting Central	4	0	4
10. Village United	4	-4	4
11. Humble Lions	4	-4	1
12. St. George's	4	-7	0

CHAPTER SEVEN

They Just Love Boys' Town

The Rastafarians of Kingston are up in arms. All week the national news has been dominated by the court trial of Jamaican reggae and dancehall artiste Buju Banton in Tampa, Florida and they are determined that he should be freed. He had been caught by a professional US Federal informer taking part in a cocaine deal and this, along with possession of a firearm, could potentially see him serving a life sentence in an American jail.

Buju is a man who stirs mixed feelings in his home country. He largely pioneered the 'Murder Music' scene and as such made himself thoroughly unpopular amongst the, admittedly rare, liberal and, even more rare, homosexual sectors of society. But his conversion to Rastafari had changed his outlook on life and his more recent music tended to be more positive in content, speaking out against gun violence and even promoting safe sex, as demonstrated by what is probably the most perfectly-titled song of all time: *Willy, Don't Be Silly*.

What is most important about Buju to the average Jamaican though is that he is a star internationally. Chances are you have never heard of him but he has made a name for himself in the dancehall scene around the world and is reportedly worth US$4 million, and that does not happen by just being big in Jamaica. This means that he is something that projects the name of this proud but small nation onto a much bigger screen and keeps the world aware of its continued existence, and this is exactly why the general population desperately want to believe that he was set up and is entirely innocent.

They do have some hope on their side. A special agent from the Drug Enforcement Agency told the court that he had investigated Buju for a whole year and been unable to find any hard evidence to pin on him. But there are voice tapes and photographs that started to chip away at the public's faith in his innocence, and even film footage of him tasting the drug. The trial had run throughout the week, making front-page headlines with every day, and had been so tight that the jurors were unable to call it, causing their deliberations to spill over into a second morning.

It is on that second day, the Friday, that I walk along the busy Hope Road, one of Kingston's major thoroughfares, back to my flat from the supermarket and find myself being beckoned over by a small group of Rastas. This is not uncommon, it happens pretty much every time I pass that particular corner and one of the group will inevitably give me a hard-knocks story before asking for 'a likkle money'—the frequency with which it happens is one of the more irritating by-products of being a white face in Kingston—but this time they have another purpose. 'Free Buju!' one of them, whose name I had been told before but without comprehension, pleads as he comes over to meet me. Another one I am familiar with, called Steve, follows him and he is furious: 'If im a go jail deh's gon be nuff blood spilled in Jamaica,' he spits while stabbing his finger into my chest, his face tightened with such rage that it is as though I am the very man who had 'set-up' and arrested Buju. The pretence that all Rastas are absolutely committed to pacifism was broken decades ago.

With that off his chest, Steve walks away to cool off before returning no more than thirty seconds later with a smiling 'Whagwan' and a genial fist bump. Meanwhile the other, much calmer, Rasta has been telling me why the trial is so important to their people in particular. To them Buju is a successor to Bob Marley in being an ambassador for their beliefs. Marley had opened the eyes of the world to the existence of this relatively new religion and spread its message but, as the man put it, 'Bob's now sleeping' and what he had been to the previous generation, Buju is to this.

Our nation and 'our' religion will always be in the public eye. The world will never simply forget about Britain or the Anglican Church because both are far too prominent, too central on the international scene. But Jamaica and Rastafari do not have that luxury—they need to constantly reaffirm their position in order to remain in the global consciousness, and while they generally do a remarkable job given their size and resources, the wheels need to keep rolling. At the

Premier League launch event Edward Seaga had spoken of countries building their 'brands'. 'In Jamaica we cannot complain,' he had said. 'We have been branded since Independence as a country with world class music. Jamaica has been branded in recent years as a country with world class athletes. But brands do not stay in place, they are put in place and they soon lose their impact if they are not continuously refurbished. And they do. And the brands that we have in music can be lost, so too the brands we have in athletics can be lost. There are signs in both. But we can refurbish them, and we can have new brands.'

But they need people like Buju in order to do so, to keep refreshing our awareness of Jamaica's place in the worldwide community and this is why the whole nation has spent the last week trying to swallow their doubts and pray for a result of not-guilty—because he cannot fulfil that role if he is locked up behind the bars of the Florida State Prison. I tell the two Rastas that I hope he will be freed and wish them luck as I walk away. As it turns out, unanimity evades those 12 Florida men and women for yet another day. The island, after all that tension, will have to wait until next week for their verdict.

On Sunday morning I receive a phone call from a man known throughout most of Kingston simply as 'Boys Town Man'. He lives in Harbour View and so attends most of their home games but he is actually a part of the west Kingston club from which he gets his nickname and, as they are playing against Reno early in the afternoon, he offers to take me there before driving me over to the Compound in time for Harbour View's evening kick off with Waterhouse.

The club is based in Trenchtown, a region right in the heart of Kingston's rough western districts and the place from where the term 'Yardie' originates in reference to the central courtyards around which the government housing projects were built. Boys' Town is sandwiched between two of the city's most notorious 'garrison' communities, the fanatically People's National Party (PNP) supporting Arnett Gardens to the north and the equally fanatically Jamaica Labour Party (JLP) supporting Tivoli Gardens to the south. The small community itself has a history of JLP support but lacks the infamy of the warring neighbours and the literal middle ground between those two areas is not a nice place to be—we are not talking English politics where there might be some slightly raised voices over a policy disagreement between a Tory and a Labourite in the pub. I will get to the details of how and why at a later time, but hardline Jamaican politics developed as a street-war strewn with guns, bullets and murder in which everyone became a soldier, and Arnett and Tivoli are about as hardline as they come.

Touring the area with a man who knows it well, and is well known within it, strikes me as a good way to broaden my horizons so I take him up on his offer and he comes by to pick me up from my flat. As we drive over to the Collie Smith Drive Sporting Complex he tells me more about himself, explaining that he is a teacher by profession (earning him the moniker of 'Teach' in the Boys' Town community) but also does a lot of social outreach work and is therefore a popular and well-respected figure in these impoverished and volatile regions, so much so that he tells me he rarely even bothers to lock his car when he leaves it parked.

On the streets outside clusters of people stand around on the pavements in front of small shanty houses or run down shops and Teach regularly pulls over to speak to them. Others stare across suspiciously at the white face peering out of the open passenger window as we drive past. Unlike middle class Harbour View, the buildings here are ramshackle affairs often constructed from sheets of corrugated metal that have rusted on exposure to the elements. Similarly, the clothing on display is more ragged and dirty, with the men often not even bothering to dress their top halves. It is not somewhere I would comfortably walk alone, at least not during my early months in Kingston.

Teach proudly boasts about his club and when we arrive at the ground he eagerly shows me around, pointing out various indicators of the site's history as an all-round sports complex. Painted across the inside wall of one building is a large banner listing the 'immortals of West Indies cricket' who have played there, Sir Garry Sobers, Everton Weekes (erroneously spelt as 'Weeks' on the wall) and George Headley among them. He explains that whenever Australia and England tour the West Indies they always come here: 'They just love Boys' Town!' he declares joyfully. I am not entirely sure how much truth is in that statement but I like the idea, and I have no intention of phoning the MCC to find out if he had actually been using a little Jamaican artistic licence in his story.

The ground itself bears the least resemblance to a football stadium of any I have seen. Other than a small steel-framed stand occupying about one quarter of one side and a couple of small buildings, it is more like park football than Premier League football, with the spectators standing along the touchlines, huddled under umbrellas behind metal fences. The club is, I am told, saving its money to develop the place, and they are currently fabricating their own blocks on site as part of the process, but for now they are some way behind most of their rivals.

The game kicks off at three and the day has seen such heavy rainfall that there are large puddles all over the pitch through which the ball cannot pass and simply stops dead in a wave of muddy water. Every time it hits these lakes the only way to move it along is to get the foot right underneath it and just keep scooping it forward a few feet until it is back on dry land. They really are farcical conditions for a football match but the question of it being postponed is never even raised. We were never in for a classic, and as such the 0-0 scoreline seems like it had always been inevitable when the end arrives.

With the final whistle been and gone, Teach gives out sweets to some of the local children, on the condition that they promise to go to school tomorrow, and hands bags of corn flour out to the players to take back to their families, his small but noticeably appreciated way of helping the stars of this cash-poor Premier League that is still a long way from being fully professional. We drive away with little time to spare before the Harbour View kick off but Teach has designs on showing me more of the local area and we have barely moved before we turn into a small side street, pulling up outside a house which, he explains, is where Bob Marley had lived as a child and now exists as a humble Rasta-run museum in the shadow of its much larger counterpart in one of the more affluent parts of town. After a brief snoop around, including sneaking a photo of Bob's old bus, something which is apparently strictly forbidden on a proper tour, we get back in the car and travel to Arnett's Anthony Spaulding Sports Complex. The ground lies just a few hundred yards from Boys' Town at the other end of the Collie Smith Central Road, and here they are hosting Sporting Central. Our whistle-stop tour of west Kingston concludes after a few minutes watching and, already late for Harbour View, we leave with the score still 0-0 to make the short drive from Arnett through Tivoli to Port

Royal Street. This carries us past the eastern fringe of the port area and onto the home straight of the Sir Florizel Glasspole Boulevard.

By the time I have found my spot on the media desk half an hour of our match has disappeared and we are already 1-0 down thanks to a deflected own goal. 'We cannot lose on Sunday,' DV had passionately impressed upon his players after Friday's training session. 'When you are down it is very easy to sit there and ask: "What can I do about it?" We are down now, we have lost two in a row, but we are not going to sit and ask ourselves that—we are going to get up. We are going to stand up and do whatever it takes to win on Sunday. If we have to pick up the field to win, we pick up the field. If we have to move those mountains to win, we move those mountains. If we have to empty that ocean to win, we empty that ocean. In short, we must do even the impossible to make the possible happen.'

Well boys, let's see it.

Our play is bright, the midfield working it around well, but we still look too toothless in the final third of the pitch. DV had told the press after the defeat at Portmore that, 'we need to make some adjustments for our next game.' Out has gone the 4-4-2 of the early season and we now have five midfielders behind Andre Fagan as a lone striker. Romario Campbell is out of the quintet, as is Richard Edwards who is suspended after his red card the week before, with Nicholas Beckett and Kemeel Wolfe replacing them and senior player Jermaine Hue, freshly back from an elongated summer in New York where his wife lives, taking the final spot.

But this new look side is suffering from the same malaise and they are finding chances hard to come by, until a few minutes before half time when Hue swings the ball into the area and, from the midst of a tight knot of defenders, Fagan leaps to head it in. Scores level and a full half to get that much-needed win.

But try as we might, the second half can't gives us what we need. We don't play badly and it's certainly not for lack of effort, but it just doesn't happen for us. The result is a third straight game without a win when, once again, we had been doing all the attacking but we just could not get those vital goals when it mattered. The players had pushed on those mountains as hard as they could, but had been short of the cutting edge they needed to make them move.

Sunday 26th September

Arnett Gardens	0 2	Sporting Central
Benfica	0 2	Village United
Boys' Town	0 0	Reno
HVFC	**1 1**	**Waterhouse**
Humble Lions	P P	Tivoli Gardens
St. George's	1 1	Portmore United

National Premier League

	P	GD	Pts.
1. Portmore United	5	4	10
2. Waterhouse	5	4	10
3. Boys' Town	5	3	10
4. Tivoli Gardens	4	6	9
5. Reno	5	3	7
6. Sporting Central	5	2	7
7. HVFC	**5**	**0**	**7**
8. Benfica	5	-3	7
9. Arnett Gardens	5	-3	7
10. Village United	5	-5	5
11. Humble Lions	4	-4	1
12. St. George's	5	-7	1

CHAPTER EIGHT

'A Necessary Evil'

While last week's front pages had been full of tension over Buju's fate, those on the back of the papers were excitedly anticipating the arrival of Jack Warner and, most importantly, the FIFA president himself, Sepp Blatter. They arrived on Sunday for a groundbreaking ceremony at the JFF's new academy at the University of the West Indies' Mona Campus on the eastern fringe of Kingston, and had been stirring plenty of excitement. They had already performed the groundbreaking for one such centre in 2003 in Portmore—the plot that was recently sold off to ease the debts—but tumultuous inner politics at the JFF saw that attempt fail and they have now decided to have another crack at it, this time at Mona.

Having spent Sunday night sipping champagne on the lawns of Jamaica House, Monday morning is when they are called into their much-publicised duty. On arrival at UWI the traffic snakes from the bottom of the 'Bowl', up the hill, right through the campus and all the way back onto the outside road. Despite this, the large marquee which has been set up to house the event on the muddy site is largely empty when I arrive. Inside are two wide columns of seats either side of a central aisle which all face a stage at the far end of the tent, while a number of boards have been dotted around the circumference detailing exactly what the final academy will provide and how it will look.

A few national team players, dressed in Jamaica polo shirts and black trousers, loiter near one that depicts plans for a 9,500 capacity mini-stadium around the blue athletics track that had been opened the year before, and among these I see our own Dicoy Williams. I amble over and say a quick hello, trying to strike up a conversation about the plans in front of us. He, however, is much more interested in playing with his Blackberry, and simply gives an awkward, monosyllabic response before returning to the safety of his phone. He's not one of the players with whom I have really familiarised myself yet and he is clearly far more comfortable with his friends than some foreign journalist he doesn't even know, so I look quietly at the plans before diligently moving away to look at the other boards and wait for the main event.

Long after the 9:30 deadline by which we were supposed to be seated the tent is still only just starting to fill. JFF officials, sponsors and dignitaries all mill around, keenly taking full advantage of an unmissable opportunity to network and schmooze as the press men mingle between them all, hoping to pick up on some sort of exclusive. The photographers, distinguishable from the rest by their scruffy shorts and t-shirts, bob and weave through the crowd, their cameras seeming to separate them from the real world, taking pictures of anything that takes their fancy as they pass the dead time before the Big Game move into view.

At about quarter past ten we are finally told to take our seats for the arrival of the guests of honour. The photographers suddenly swing into action, descending on the entrance in pack formation to await the appearance of their real prize while the opening strains of the FIFA anthem, of which I now know every note, boom from the speakers set up by the stage. And then there they are. Preceded by a swarm of paparazzi, the main attractions enter. Professor Gordon Shirley of UWI; Minister of Culture, Youth & Sport Olivia Grange; Captain Burrell and of course, those resplendent men of football royalty, Warner and Blatter.

So just who are Austin 'Jack' Warner and Joseph 'Sepp' Blatter? Officially, Warner is a Vice President at FIFA and the President of the Caribbean Football Union, CONCACAF and highly placed in the Trinidad & Tobago Football Federation, all while holding down a position as Minister of Works and Transport in the Trinidad government. Blatter, meanwhile, is a trained lawyer who has worked at FIFA since 1975 and, having attached himself to all the right people, became its President in 1998. I could explain all the reasons why I, and just about everyone else in Britain, dislikes the fact that he runs the world's favourite sport but that is not the point of this book so instead I will just make casual mention of Andrew Jennings' essential work *Foul! The Secret World of FIFA: Bribes, Vote Rigging & Ticket Scandals* and move on to Warner, whose story will shed some light on Blatter anyway.

Warner is, in short, a fairly unpleasant man who is about as corrupt as they come, and the 2006 World Cup offers two fine examples as to how. This tournament was the first time that Trinidad & Tobago had ever made it to the World Cup and, eager to line his pockets, Warner took a large number of the tickets allocated to his Federation and sold them himself through his family's own travel agent Simpaul Travel, earning the Warner clan a tidy US$1 million. Blatter and FIFA, keen to be seen to be doing the right thing, fined them a sum equal to their profiteering in punishment, but as yet they have only seen around a quarter of that paid. The world saw Blatter hand out his swift retribution and so now he does not really seem too bothered about whether or not it is actually fulfilled and simply sends a gentle reminder in the post every once in a while. What's a million dollars between friends anyway?

Staying with the topic of that World Cup, Warner's TTFF came to a deal with their history-making players to split all proceeds from the tournament 50:50. The problems came when the TTFF declared that they brought in TT$18.2 million which, after costs have been deducted, gave the 23 players TT$141,102 to share between them. The squad, which included names familiar to any follower of the English Premier League like Dwight Yorke, Shaka Hislop and Kenwyn Jones as well as significantly less well-off local players, did not accept this as sufficient and, after a lengthy and dirty battle, accounts from the Government released under the Freedom of Information Act revealed that the TTFF had actually banked TT$173,690,113.50, nearly ten times what they declared, of which the London-based Sport Dispute Resolution Panel ordered that half be paid to the players. Currently Warner's organisation, which technically still trades under the name of TTFA, is trying to persuade Parliament to officially change their name to TTFF as, according to Hislop, 'a ploy . . . to get out of paying debts they owe to creditors and players.'

Add to this the facts that Warner once tried to get the Scottish FA to make out the cheque for Trinidad's share of the gate receipts from a friendly to him personally rather than the TTFF, has been caught on film making racist statements and, in being an MP, violates Article 5 of

FIFA's Code of Ethics which states that all officials must be 'politically neutral', and it becomes increasingly hard to see how he still has his job. Researching this book I contacted Jennings who summed the whole situation up in saying that the fact he does, 'tells you all you need to know about Blatter' as well. Warner needs Blatter's power and Blatter needs Warner's federations' votes and neither one is prepared, yet, to let a little thing like upholding the moral values FIFA supposedly represents put the brakes on their gravy train. No one knows yet that seven or eight months from now the relationship will crumble as the world looks on, half in joy, half in disgust. For now they are still both allies and pals.

So how does Jamaica's Captain Burrell fit into the picture? He is currently in his second stint as JFF President, having won the post back in an unopposed election in 2007 after then-incumbent Crenston Boxhill had decided not to stand. In this role he has become one of Warner's, and therefore Blatter's, most loyal disciples who has been known to come to his friends' aid in less-than-ethical ways in the past and has slotted himself neatly into their boys' club. More importantly though, he is said to be positioning himself to take Warner's seat at the top of CONCACAF should Blatter, as is rumoured in some areas of the press, finally tire of the Trinidad man's perennially embarrassing behaviour and move to get rid of him.

These are not popular people in English football, least of all Warner who appears to have some sort of personal vendetta against us, but elsewhere that is not quite so. Exactly how you see these men seems to depend very much on where you are standing and, as their work has brought much-needed money and help to the region as well as additional World Cup spots, they are given a much warmer reception in the Caribbean than they could ever hope for on a trip to London. Both go about their business with methods that we in England, our huge money pots affording us the luxury of being able to largely adhere to the moral structure, deem to be abhorrent but locally they are generally considered the best men for their jobs because they get results for the organisations they represent, organisations which are happy to turn a blind eye to their ways and take the funds that they so desperately need. One important figure in Jamaica described Warner to me as 'a necessary evil'.

And so it is that these three heroes or crooks or whatever you want to call them, come to stride down the centre aisle of the marquee in the Mona Bowl to genuinely rapturous and adoring applause. Marching together they all look the best of friends, displaying no signs whatsoever that they may be holding daggers above one another's backs, and they settle comfortably behind their table on the stage facing their enamoured audience.

Our host steps up to the podium to introduce us to the guests, starting with Grange before moving on to someone whose, 'reputation precedes him.' Oh? Who could that be? The speaker continues: 'This man needs no introduction and so his will be the shortest of all.' Blatter's eyes raise and he is just arranging his features into a smile of feigned embarrassment when the host unravels his little mystery. 'When you hear the word "Captain" these days you just assume it will be followed by Horace Burrell.' Blatter's face falls back into neutral, as though trying to prove to anyone who saw that he had never presumed even for a second that such a warm introduction had been for him. His own name is read out last in a much more formal and awed way than the Captain's had been, and as it is done he looks slightly disappointed that it does not fit in with the friendly tone he seems to want for this gathering of the 'FIFA family'.

Each of the guests make a short speech and in the main they are exactly what you would expect to hear at such an event, platitudes about the worth of such an academy before lovingly heaping personal praise on one another, like a group of dogs standing in a circle admiringly sniffing each other's backsides. Burrell even ventures as far as to say that Blatter will be remembered by future generations as 'a real genius in football development.' To me that is the most amusing joke anyone has told all day but, as I choke back a laugh and consider the one or two other ways in which people might look back on his reign, heads all around me nod in sage agreement. Sepp is among friends here.

In introducing Warner to the podium, the host sums up exactly why the work of this mob is popular here by telling a David and Goliath story of how Warner once described the English FA as an 'irritant' and then got them to come out to Trinidad for a friendly, painting the picture of a man who has the organisation that gave football to the world desperately scrambling to meet his every whim.

In truth, after one barb too many the FA had finally decided enough was enough and offered to send some of its stars for a friendly in Trinidad on the condition that Warner stop making his frequent and absurd statements about them and apologise, so he snivelled that 'the time has come' for England to host another World Cup and the FA duly sent its team to Port of Spain.

So far I have cast Warner very much in the role of the pantomime villain but life is never that black and white. The real world is not made up of people who are simply 'good' and 'bad' and as such he does not arrive at the microphone and cackle the deranged laugh of a power-mad maniac before launching into a militant rant. In fact he speaks warmly and enjoyably. 'I will be quick,' he begins, 'because you have not come here to hear me, you have all come to hear the man after me.' Even a little modesty thrown in to the mix too. He goes on to poke fun at Burrell and the JFF, saying that 'only in Jamaica' could they break ground for an academy then take seven years before anything actually comes of it. He comes out with one or two points that do not sit too well but on the whole he makes an endearing speech which frequently has the audience, myself reluctantly included, laughing out loud. In fact, had I arrived at the ceremony entirely unfamiliar with who he is I would almost certainly have left thinking what a good bloke he seems, but all the pleasantries and jokes in the world cannot disguise his reality, so instead I take his speech for what it is, and with a huge pinch of salt, and forget about it.

Finally Blatter himself takes to the podium, and as he does so the heavens open. His welcoming applause is punctured by the abrupt sight and sounds of the Reggae Boyz in the rows in front of me diving for new seats to avoid the rain suddenly pouring down onto them through a number of small holes in the roof. He notes this development and hopes aloud, to appreciative mirth from the audience, that it is not an omen of any kind. But he need not worry when he is safely ensconced in the Caribbean. He might be Swiss but it is regions like this in which he is at his safest, with as few European faces in the crowd as possible. They love him here, here he is always more than welcome.

'This technical centre is meant primarily for young people, and it is hoped it will open many doors for them,' he says, echoing the easy sentiments of everyone else, before alluding to its social importance.

'The game can play a role in social and cultural development of countries. For example, the promotion of women's football can help bring about recognition for them in some parts of the world.' And Sepp is full of good ideas for the promotion of women's football. 'They could, for example, have tighter shorts,' he famously told the media after pondering the issue back in 2004. What a progressive thinker!

'As a school of life, football has an educational role to play,' he goes on today, 'and this academy can provide a legacy for Jamaica because here football can play its part in education and culture. Football is more than just kicking a ball, it is based on discipline and respect.'

And he is right, football can teach the next generation of Jamaicans important lessons and values for life, and hopefully the academy will provide another important stepping stone in the process of giving the country the means to develop its sporting talent in the way it needs. Because the game really is more than just kicking a ball, and this academy, or more precisely these social connections it pertains to, is precisely why I am in Jamaica in the first place.

With Blatter's speech over, the guests of honour put up their umbrellas and venture out into the tumultuous weather, followed by the more foolhardy members of the media, for the ceremonial acts of unveiling a plaque and breaking the ground before Sepp and Jack jet off to Anguilla for another similar function. Instead of going to watch I take the same option as the players, dignitaries and saner press men and go into the buffet tent next door to take my place in the lunch queue, watching on as a couple of young women—dolled up to the nines in an effort to bag themselves a footballer—meander up and down the line, draping themselves all over anyone in a yellow polo shirt.

Slowly the event packs up. After lunch people dash through the rain and back into the main tent where they mingle or gaze out towards the car park in the vain hope of getting to their vehicles without being drenched. One of the potential WAGs from the buffet queue saunters by, hanging off the arm of a young player who looks both bemused and delighted, and evidently disapproves of the older gentleman her friend is posing for photos with, ordering their retreat by drawling, 'O . . . M . . . G LaShawna, let's go,' in a trendy Jamerican accent.

I stand under the leaky garden gazebo that has been acting as a foyer and try desperately to get through to the overloaded taxi company on the phone as campus security ferries people around through the mud. The weather has now eased off slightly, to the extent where the dull outline of the hills which formed the sides of the tight 'Bowl' is just about discernible again through the opaque sheet of rain, and in this lull Blatter and Warner's lift arrives. A nice blue and white helicopter, on FIFA expenses of course, sets itself gently down by the building in which they have been sheltering from the weather, because it simply would not do to have men of their stature making the 20 minute journey to the airport by car.

I have no such convenience and, being one of the last to leave while the workers clear away the morning's festivities around me, I finally settle into the front seat of a typically shabby taxi, whose windscreen wipers are losing a hard-fought battle with the elements, and plunge into flood-water a good few inches deep on roads which had been completely dry just an hour or two earlier. As the traffic slowly pushes through the torrent, the sky grows thickly grey and the maelstrom displays no signs of letting up. The omen cast by Sepp takes a hold.

The guests of honour chat before going to break the ground. L—R: Olivia Grange, Sepp Blatter, Capt. Horace Burrell and Jack Warner

CHAPTER NINE

The Curious Case Of Jermaine Hue

What began the moment Blatter stood before his adoring audience does not cease for days afterwards. For the week or so since then, Tropical Storm Nicole has been brushing past the island, dumping down rains that cause widespread flooding and result in utter carnage. Thirteen people are reported dead and a further eight missing, including two killed in Harbour View. Paling in comparison to that, but still not entirely insignificant, is the news that the complete nationwide activity of the Premier League has also been swallowed up by the deluge, not to be seen again until the rains finally subside.

How the time drags. People are barely able to leave their homes during the storm and the country grinds to a halt. Security forces are mobilised to protect the public and prevent looting; schools are closed until further notice; buses and planes cease operations. 'The storm forces us once again to look at the thorny issue of the country's fragile infrastructure,' laments *The Observer* as roads and bridges collapse, leaving entire communities stranded, and forty per cent of the population is cut off without power. All anyone can do is twiddle their thumbs until Nicole decides to move on.

By the time that does eventually happen two fixtures have disappeared and next up come fellow title aspirants Boys' Town at the Compound. And after two weeks without football, barring a dreary international friendly, it is a nice feeling to be watching the now-familiar names and faces warming up on the pitch of our comfortable little stadium. Sitting at my press desk again, I feel I am back where I belong.

Boys' Town have already beaten Tivoli this season and they are being spoken of as dark horses for the league. With kick off approaching, Teach, dressed in his red Boys' Town polo shirt, approaches to say hello before disappearing again to his seat. During our tour the other week he had been very pleased with the fact that he had been part of the team that beat Harbour View 4-2 in the Masters league last season. A repeat today, he says, would send him home very happy indeed.

On the eve of the new season DV had told the papers that he expected it to take four or five games for his team to reach peak match fitness. Well five games have now gone and they haven't been particularly convincing. The excuses are now exhausted and it is about time Harbour View stand up and produce the sort of results that defending champions should.

The game begins at a frantic pace and barely lets up for 90 minutes. It has hardly even begun when Jahmali Spence, given his first start of the season, finds himself free on the edge of the six yard box only to smash it right across the goal and wide of the far post. More chances come and go, but for all the hectic pace and long shots the game is trapped between the two defences with neither side really managing to get beyond the opposing back line.

This soon changes. Some good passing by Harbour View after quarter of an hour picks out Andre Fagan on the edge of the box where he has his legs swiped from under him, an obvious free kick. Jermaine Hue and Christopher Harvey stand over the ball eyeing up the goal beyond a large, red Boys' Town wall, one of them shaping to blast it and the other to place it. To keep the keeper guessing until the last second both players approach the ball simultaneously. As Harvey pulls out only a step or so away, it is Hue that continues, stroking the outside of the ball with the inside of his left foot, lifting it round and over the wall and curling it perfectly into the top corner of the net. It is the most beautiful goal I have seen scored all season and, as if not wanting to besmirch the moment with gaudy celebration, Hue simply stands with his arms aloft while everyone else goes berserk around him.

And thus things stand when we reach half time, one-nil up thanks to the man known throughout football simply as 'Maestro'. It's a name he has earned over a career that is now in its autumn years, and these days Hue's status is that of a veteran who has been arguably the most gifted creator of his generation. Behind him are a collection of international caps that is solid enough but fails to truly reflect his abilities, particularly considering they have yielded more than one goal every three games, a very distinguished ratio for an international midfielder. There's a good chance you have even seen him play. You may recall that shortly before the 2006 World Cup England played Jamaica at Old Trafford, a game most famous for turning Peter Crouch into a cult hero as he danced his 'robot' for an enraptured crowd for the first time with a hat trick of goals. The focus of the visitors' midfield that day was a slightly dispirited Hue, a less enjoyable memory for him than for us.

But his impact on the national team has been limited, and many at Harbour View will tell you that is because of a conspiracy at the JFF that dates back over ten years. After impressing at the 1998 World Cup, a young star called Ricardo Gardner was transferred from Harbour View to Bolton Wanderers for the astronomical sum, by local standards, of one million pounds. Captain Burrell's eyes lit up and he decided that, because the national team had provided the platform for him to be noticed, the JFF should be given half of this money. This was, frankly, absurd, as Gardner was Harbour View's own asset and therefore the money from his sale goes to them. They did dole out $180,000 to each of the thirteen parish associations around the island, which was irregular and charitable enough, but did not acquiesce to the JFF's greedy wishes. Burrell has never forgiven this, and Harbour View claim to have been victims of a vendetta ever since.

Hue's misfortune, as the next 'marquee' player to come out of the youth system after Gardner, has seen him become the victim of this pettiness and as such he has rarely been given a look in for the national team. The bulk of his thirty caps to date came in the few years that Crenston Boxhill took Burrell's mantle and since the Captain resumed his position at the top a series of elaborate excuses have seen Hue's progress stall again. When presented with the opportunity, I asked national coach 'Tappa' Whitmore—a genuine man who I sincerely believe not to be 'in' on any kind of conspiracy—about Hue and he replied by saying: 'Jermaine Hue can help us. But sometimes you have to wonder if he **wants** to play for the national team because he has been through a particular period with a lot of coaches who have shunned him. So probably Jermaine Hue has given up on the national programme.' It is a terribly sad situation. And more than that, it simply isn't true. Hue himself would later tell me:

'Once you play up to a standard you should be playing for the national team. But if that doesn't work you don't stop there; you continue, and hopefully the media or the people of the country will see the good work and feel that you should be representing your country. But my mindset is that every game I go out there and perform to my best and if they want to call, they'll call me. I'm always ready to represent my country.' The media and the people do see his good work though, but still it doesn't appear to be enough. It seems conjecture and misinformation, whether deliberately fed or not, is costing Hue the chance to do what he wants the most.

So what exactly are the Reggae Boyz missing out on? Just two minutes into the second half Harbour View counter after Boys' Town have over-committed to an attack and Hue brings the ball forward with Fagan, Spence and John-Ross breaking ahead of him. He holds it, weighing up the options as the defence scrambles back. Just as it looks like he has dawdled too long and the chance has disappeared he sends the ball curling across the top of the penalty area to where Spence is running across to towards it. The pass is fractionally behind him but his run is merely a decoy that has dragged the last defender out of position, leaving the ball sitting up perfectly in front of John-Ross with nobody between himself and the keeper. From just outside the area he drills a first time shot straight into the bottom corner.

About twenty minutes later Hue scores another, smashed into the top corner from eight yards after Spence had teed him up. The onslaught continues, co-ordinated at all times by the Maestro. A penalty had made it three—one but when Hue whips in a free kick for Rafeik Thomas to head in we are three ahead once more. With the win now secured, DV takes the opportunity to rest the star man. The crowd stand to applaud him off loudly as he grins widely and acknowledges all four sides of the ground. He has scored two and set up the other two, and that it is only his second appearance of the season, with the first being a full two and a half weeks ago, makes it all the more impressive. If the conspiracy theories are true, Burrell is only shooting himself in the foot.

The match is rounded off when Blackburn picks up on a rebound and tucks it away. His performances all season have showed an enormous passion for this team and his celebrations, despite being for a largely inconsequential goal, are the wildest of the lot. More importantly for the wider community, a struggling Harbour View have faced one of their title rivals, who have been in daunting early season form, and smashed them 5-1. It is the sort of scoreline we have threatened a couple of times but tonight we managed to actually make goals from all our possession and with Tivoli, who lost at Waterhouse earlier in the evening, coming up on Sunday it is a huge boost to finally get our season up and running.

With the final whistle blown I disappoint yet more local children by explaining to them that, despite being from England, I do not personally know either Wayne Rooney or Steven Gerrard, unlikely as that may seem. Picking up the now abandoned plastic garden chairs from behind the press desk, I go downstairs and by the outside bar I chat to a lady named Simone whom I met at Portmore. There she had proclaimed herself to be Harbour View's single biggest fan and now she boldly guarantees me that we will 'run over' Tivoli at the weekend. DV comes out of the home changing room with a Pepsi in one hand and a box of Chester's Chicken in the other and produces a grin that is large even by his standards. Unable to shake him by his food-filled hands, we simply bump fists as he tells me that he too is full of confidence ahead of the massive game coming up. In fact we all seem to be, perhaps not quite as much as Simone, but it has been one of those nights that fills people with such feelings. The first, we can only hope, of many to come.

Wednesday 13th October

Benfica	1 1	Arnett Gardens
HVFC	**5 1**	**Boys' Town**
Reno	1 1	Village United
Sporting Central	0 1	Portmore United
St. George's	1 0	Humble Lions
Waterhouse	1 0	Tivoli Gardens

National Premier League

	P	GD	Pts.
1. Portmore United	6	5	13
2. Waterhouse	6	5	13
3. HVFC	**6**	**4**	**10**
4. Boys' Town	6	1	10
5. Tivoli Gardens	5	5	9
6. Reno	6	3	8
7. Benfica	6	-3	8
8. Arnett Gardens	6	-3	8
9. Sporting Central	6	1	7
10. Village United	6	-5	6
11. St. George's	6	-6	4
12. Humble Lions	5	-5	1

CHAPTER TEN

Sunday Afternoon
In The Gardens

If left to the imagination the name Tivoli Gardens brings to mind an idyll of rustic beauty. You might picture an Eden of foliage and waterfalls, or perhaps hanging baskets adorning whitewashed houses with the sun baking terracotta roof tiles, from where you gaze out across Tuscan olive groves in rolling hills.

It is not like that.

The drive to their ground takes you down the long straight roads of West Kingston's grid system. Crumbling pavements fall into broken roads which are flanked by telegraph wires drooping low between their poles in front of an endless progression of shabby, dilapidated concrete and brick buildings. Occasionally it opens up to reveal whole blocks of rubble that have become litter-strewn dumping grounds. Stray dogs slink through the mess in search of something to eat, fearfully looking over their shoulders as they go, while others simply lie dead in the street, victims of starvation, disease or traffic that have just been left in the spot where they exhaled their last desperate breath. Locals stand around on the pavements or in doorways while children run and play amongst the debris.

You may be familiar with the name but cannot place exactly where or when you might have heard it. In fact, even if it does not ring a bell, there is a very good chance that you have still seen or read of Tivoli. In May, just a few months before I arrived in Kingston, this community was at the centre of the world as the police and the army waded in and waged war against its inhabitants in an effort to hunt down local 'don' Christopher 'Dudus' Coke, and all the while the media services of the entire planet watched their every move.

As the British tabloids were screaming hysterically about a 'drug riot' in West Kingston, a state of emergency was put into effect to quell an unrest which took the lives of 73 civilians (although many people claim the real figure is more than double that) as well as three security officers, and resulted in the seizure of 47 guns, 84 explosive devices and 10,673 rounds of ammunition from within the community. All in the name of capturing the near-mythical Coke.

After the violent and mysterious death of his father, and while still at the relatively young age of just 22, Dudus inherited his position as leader of the 'Shower Posse'. This was no petty street gang or mob of bored hoodlums, the Shower Posse was one of the biggest and most violent criminal organisations in American history, a Jamaican gang operating from coast to coast in the US that was allegedly responsible for bringing 1,000 tons of cocaine into the country and committing 1,400 murders during their peak years of the 1980s. And the place in which the Posse had its roots—roots that ran so deep as to be irretrievably embedded into the social, economic and political fabric—was Tivoli Gardens.

This is an impoverished community in which vast numbers feel abandoned and let down by a succession of governments who have failed to create sufficient employment and fix the destructive social ruptures that have broken the peace on the streets, something in which it is by no means unique. But a man like Dudus can provide some of the things for which the people are so desperately yearning: resources, solidarity, security. Over the years, Coke and his predecessors have used their wealth for everything from school equipment to home repairs and his influence to keep residents safe from the attacks of other gangs in a way that official state security cannot. He has often been compared to Robin Hood, someone who can provide for the poor when the authorities have failed them and he has earned a cult-like or even religious following, with many of his supporters taking to the streets sporting signs that proclaimed, 'Jesus died for us; we will die for Dudus'.

But it is not just in Tivoli where dons revel in this kind of respect and it is not just the public who have come to rely on them and their influence over local communities. At the other end of the spectrum lie the parties and politicians whose manoeuvrings have become so intertwined with those of the dons that many believe one could not exist without the other, certainly not in their present state. And to answer the question of how such a situation has arisen is to explore the fundamentals of just what 'garrison communities' are and, more importantly, where they came from.

Every city on the planet must go through an adolescence, a phase in its development during which large-scale industrialisation and urbanisation tear it away from the nascent comforts of youth and plunge it into a period of uncontrollable change, filling it suddenly with vast new work opportunities and an even more vast mass of people looking to take advantage of them. For capital cities this effect is generally exaggerated and will almost invariably result in the rise of unprecedented social troubles as huge swathes of the population descend upon a town struggling to keep up and find themselves without the employment and opportunities they had dreamed big city life would provide. How well each city can cope with these problems depends largely on the resources it has at its disposal and the actions of those who control them. It was in the late 1950s and early 60s that Kingston first found itself facing its own industrial and social revolution but unlike many of the globe's more fortunate capitals it did not have anything even approaching a sufficient financial grounding to be able to support it. Over the course of the 60s unemployment in Jamaica rose from 12.7% to 31%. The capital was a city of around 600,000 people and of those it is estimated that there were over 100,000 potential workers unemployed; people capable and willing to work but left to spend their days on the streets instead because the jobs were simply not available on the necessary scale. While this was happening the overwhelming majority of the nation's wealth was being concentrated in the hands of a select few: it is estimated that 89.8% of Jamaica's corporate income was being shared between just 13.6% of its companies, many of which were controlled by foreign investors from Cuba, China or the US.

Unrest and violence in such a situation is not uncommon as people vent their pent-up anger about their situation towards the men in power who they feel have caused it. However, there was more to it in Kingston. Social academic Terry Lacey states that, 'most violence in Jamaica was neither outside nor against the established political order but sprang directly from it.' With the economy so dependent on foreign capital and international corporations, money earned off the back of the country's resources was simply being syphoned out into purses overseas and the public sector was proportionately a million miles behind the private. The Government therefore took the decision to focus virtually all of its investment in this area and leave the faster growing sections of the economy almost entirely to private enterprise, and with this came a previously unheard of opportunity for them to sweeten the population and create strongholds of overwhelming loyalty to their party. They were hugely influential in deciding where to direct construction and housing projects and could therefore concentrate goods, jobs and homes into areas for their own supporters.

And this is where the dons came into it. Having developed loyal communities the politicians needed men on the ground to maintain that authority, while the gangsters needed extra resources and protection from the law. So the politicians armed the public, turning the ordinary man on the street into a political soldier under the command of the top ranking gang leaders. Entry into the communities became controlled by these men and supporters of the rival party were hounded out and forced to set up squatter camps on the outskirts until the area was almost exclusively populated by supporters of the party in power. The 1997 Kerr Report into political tribalism asserts that, 'the creation, development and maintenance of garrisons are neither accidents of history or geography but part of a process deliberately fostered for political ends.'

Having been elevated into a position of great power within their locales and been given the weaponry to back that power up by the very people who were supposed to be bringing law and order to the country, the dons soon began turning their new-found resources onto other 'projects'. Their main use to the men in Parliament was during election years—ensuring that everyone in their area voted in the correct way—but that left them at something of a loose end for four out of every five years: what to do with all their guns and authority during the lean times? They had the means and the opportunity to do so much more, and they did so emphatically. Drugs, of course, became the main industry along with numerous other activities that were beyond the realms of legitimacy, and the best part of it was who was going to stop them? The politicians who gave them their guns in the first place? If the MPs tried to take down the dons, the dons would simply take the MPs down with them.

So safely insulated from the threat of reprisal, the criminal community was allowed to flourish and with the jobless masses unable to find employment they needed very little encouragement to gravitate towards the men driving the nice cars, flashing the big cash and offering their own form of 'work' as an alternative to the straight and narrow. Coupled with this was a chronic breakdown in traditional family roles as paternal absenteeism became (and remains still) all too common, leaving children to be brought up by mothers who frequently could not cope with the strain. Feeling abandoned at home and often failing to fill that hole with teams or social groupings at school, there were therefore scores of young men who could only really find a sense of belonging by turning to the welcoming 'family' of the don.

With these factors stoking the fires, gang life grew rapidly over the decades as communities became increasingly internalised and distanced from one another, especially those of opposing political standing, and the murder and crime figures climbed dramatically until they were wildly out of control. According to United Nations statistics from 2003, the good citizens of Jamaica killed each other at a rate that outstripped any other nation on earth bar South Africa and Colombia. With an average of 32.4 murders per 100,000 inhabitants its homicide rate that year was 23 times higher than that of the UK, and police statistics and World Bank population estimates indicate that by 2009 it had accelerated to a terrifying 62.2 per 100,000, compared to just 1.3 in England & Wales. In the worst areas of town that figure gets up around the 250 mark, and that is the sort of tally only normally seen in a warzone. It is because of this that Kingston has earned a reputation as the murder capital of the globe and now exists in the wider world's consciousness as a no-go city of lawlessness and death.

Of course it would be naïve to suggest that all gang activity is based solely around politics (or indeed that all murders are based around gang activity). In fact these days it is a relatively minor motive for the nation's violence and, as with everywhere else in the world, there are drug and turf wars, as well as revenge killings, to such an extent that gangs regularly fight unquestioningly with other gangs of the same party loyalty. However, it would be equally naïve to believe that in the twenty first century guns are never fired in the name of the JLP or PNP. The phenomenon of the garrison still exists strongly and all are highly volatile areas.

What is striking from a football point of view is that of the five Kingston & St. Andrew clubs currently playing in the Premier League, four are based in communities whose voting patterns earn them the 'garrison' label, with Harbour View being the only one to go about its business in relative neutrality. And the mother of them all, where 94% of voters sided with the JLP during the last parish council elections in 2007, is Tivoli Gardens.

The JLP was the ruling party from 1962 (when the country was granted Independence from British Governance) to 1972 under the official leadership of its founder Sir Alexander Bustamente and it was during this period that Tivoli was developed in an area previously occupied by a shanty dwelling known as Back-O-Wall. There were negative signs from the start; in the 1962 elections Back-O-Wall was the only place on the island to report any form of political violence with homes burned to the ground and a stabbing outside one polling station. Clearly, it seemed, with redevelopment the area would also need some control to be stamped upon it.

The man charged with doing this, and creating a community fit for the future, was the MP for West Kingston, none other than a young Edward Seaga. During the Dudus uprising Seaga appeared on TVJ's *Impact* programme where he spoke in utopian ideals about the early years of Tivoli Gardens, describing it as a 'model' society of social, cultural and educational progression which only went wrong when the PNP regained power in the 1970s. His aim had been to, 'create a community in which there were social services from the pre-natal stage—family planning et cetera—all the way through to infant school, primary school, secondary school,' he told the host. 'And then in a huge community centre—the biggest on the island—all the programmes you could want of a cultural nature: dance, music, fashion shows, drama, everything. And that was Tivoli Gardens . . . I created it. And having created it, it lasted for three or four years because for that period of time the JLP was still in office.'

For Tivoli's deterioration he did not blame his 'model' or the people of the community but the external political forces putting pressure on it from the outside, saying it was 'attacked' by these entities and knocked from the path it was originally intended to tread. But whatever the root cause of its downfall it is inescapable that the place today is a very distant one from the perfect world it was created to be and it now lives a paranoid existence, alongside its much smaller neighbour Denham Town, as a modest splash of JLP green surrounded on the map by large expanses of PNP orange. And it was from this environment that the Shower Posse sprang and where Christopher 'Dudus' Coke became a folk hero before he was claimed by the law.

The process of Coke's arrest was far from straightforward. In fact it became the single largest scandal of Prime Minister Bruce Golding's government so far—one which came within a rejected resignation of costing him his job—and its after effects continued to rumble on throughout my time in Jamaica. According to the US Drug Enforcement Administration Coke is one of the most dangerous drug traffickers on the planet and in 2009 Washington began extradition proceedings to bring him to trial on narcotics and arms offences, but Golding flatly refused to acquiesce to their requests on the grounds that the wire-tap evidence they presented was obtained illegally. And this is where it starts to get murky. American television network ABC tagged Golding as 'a known criminal associate' of Coke while British newspaper *The Independent* said the gang was 'on [the] payroll of the Jamaican Prime Minister', allegations which Golding dismissed as 'malicious' and 'clearly part of a conspiracy to undermine the duly elected Government of Jamaica.' It seems to most that the JLP Government was refusing the extradition request simply to protect 'their man', and they stepped up their efforts with some outside help.

In March 2010 an Opposition MP raised the issue in Parliament of an alleged agreement worth US$400,000 between the Jamaican Government and US law firm Manatt, Phelps & Phillips to lobby the US Government over the treaty dispute that had arisen from the Coke extradition. Golding vehemently denied the existence of it, saying: 'Let me make it quite clear. The Government of Jamaica has not engaged any legal firm, any consultant, any entity whatsoever, in relation to any extradition matter'. The trouble was that the contract was there for all to see and someone had paid the firm a lot of money, so if was not him who was it? In May he admitted to Parliament that he had indeed sanctioned the agreement but on behalf of the JLP rather than the Government, a story which still did not tie up with that of Manatt,

Phelps & Phillips. Less than a week later he addressed his country on live television to apologise for his role in the affair and to say that he would finally sign the extradition request for Dudus.

This was the signal for the residents of Tivoli Gardens to erect barricades across all entrances to the community as state security prepared to come and take Coke by force. A couple of days later two Police Stations were burnt to the ground and Golding called the state of emergency across Kingston and St. Andrew that would eventually see the US get their man—itself an act that many felt was a clumsy case of overkill, albeit one that got the right result in the end. In the months since the uprising the country's murder rate dropped by 40% but it still remains to be seen whether that is a temporary lull or a genuine turning point. The *Observer* this month lamented that the Government's post-Tivoli crime strategies were not being implemented thoroughly enough and urged Parliament: 'Let's not win the crime battle but lose the war'.

The dust had far from settled since the Dudus affair and in amongst it all there was one of the country's top football clubs pressing to regain the Premier League title it had lost the year before. And this is not a club that has been distanced from its surroundings by wealth, glamour and imported players; it is a club where much of the squad lives locally, as Harbour View's Rafeik Thomas and Fabian Campbell also do. These Premier League footballers obeyed the restrictions of the imposed curfew, endured mass killings in their streets, avoided the bullets while praying their families managed the same—two Tivoli players were even detained by the Police before being released without charge. The League was squarely wrapped up in the mess. Everywhere that football exists it has its links to politics; in West Kingston those links are as real as anywhere in the world.

Tonight we were there. This is the one, the night the Premier League's big two face each other down. This is Real Madrid—Barcelona, Internazionale—AC Milan . . . Tivoli Gardens—Harbour View. At the Compound before we go Richard Edwards speaks to me about how important it is that the team maintains its 'winning ways' after the big result against Boys' Town. Admittedly this is by no means the game anyone would have chosen to keep that fragile new momentum going, but a definite confidence runs through everyone in the common room and after Wednesday's results, why not?

Under a gun-metal grey sky the Harbour View convoy pulls through the gates to the Edward Seaga Sports Complex and bumps its way slowly up a drive that runs alongside an old disused railway, on which the rusting bulks of long-abandoned trains still rot, and round into a tightly enclosed car park. The main building is a tall, broad, looming structure of red brick that threatens like a large Victorian factory as the rain begins to fall. We carry the kit bags and warm-up equipment down the unlit central corridor to the away changing room, opposite which is a large metal fence that encloses the club's gym equipment like animals in a cage. Players from both teams pass and greet one another with friendly handshakes and hugs. A small group of local children hang around on the steps at the main entrance watching on, one or two of whom stare questioningly at the novel white man in the Harbour View shirt that walks back out past them, sneering some indecipherable comment as I go.

From the clubhouse you pass through a low chain link fence and out onto the pitch. Facing outwards the ground is walled in on all three sides with only the far touchline and the one that is now behind you holding some metal bleachers. Behind the goal to the left a couple of blocks of flats rise up from beyond the wall where residents perch on the edge of the roof or hang from windows in the stair well to get a free vantage point to watch the games inside. Looking east beyond the far touchline you would normally see in the middle distance the mountains that wrap themselves around Kingston, today though the rain was such that they had been swallowed by a deep grey void.

The stands fill up as the players go through their warm ups and Twinny hits crosses into the box for the two keepers to catch. After twenty minutes or so they go to change before coming back out for the biggest match of the season so far, a game which I will be watching, for the first time, from on the touchline.

We start well, winning an early free kick which Christopher Harvey fires wide before they respond with a quick break that releases Navion Boyd, but after cutting in he fails to get his boot around and his shot slices across the face of the goal and past the far post. One chance each, blow for blow.

Minutes later Jamahli Spence is set free, chasing a through ball into the Tivoli box where he collides hard with the keeper who, having bravely put his head in the way of the burly striker, does not get up again. He's down for so long as the medics assess him that Bowa leaps up and yells to the lingering players to jog around so as not to seize up. After a good seven or eight minutes of treatment on the pitch the keeper is stretchered off and replaced, being carried away looking reassuringly healthy and even managing to sit up on the gurney.

Play resumes with Tivoli picking up momentum, commanding the play and starting to take control. As a corner swings into the Harbour View box it needs only minimal contact to turn it in but Blackburn leaps defiantly and just manages to touch it away from a striker's head. As another attack unfolds Daveion Woodhouse, in at left back for the suspended Kimorlee Brissett, commits the cardinal error of following the ball and leaves Boyd glaringly open in the box. Fortunately the cross comes in behind his run and Woodhouse is let off the hook, but Tivoli's international forward is causing him non-stop problems and looking the best player on the pitch.

Then comes the moment that has been threatening since the early minutes. A long, cross-field ball lands neatly at Boyd's feet as he comes tearing into our box from the right. He effortlessly dodges Woodhouse, jinking in onto his left foot and striking it from six yards towards the far post. Michard Barrett makes his move but the ball strikes the lunging Dicoy Williams on the thigh and cannons off to the other side of our suddenly helpless keeper. One—nil Tivoli.

Seaga is, as always, watching on from the home bench as Boyd continues to taunt the Harbour View defence, running onto a through ball and squaring it to the lurking Keammar Daley who allows us to stay in the game with a tame shot straight at Barrett. But with the game progressing we start to make our own marks on it as we go in search of the equaliser. Hue plays in Harvey whose low cross is just cleared by the defender before Andre Fagan can turn it in. As they push for a second we go about trying to exploit the open gaps and a good passing move on the counter attack results in the ball teeing up for Edwards to volley goalwards from 30 yards. The keeper scrambles across his line but can't reach and is relieved to see it drop just wide of the post. 'Good try Eddie. Come again, come again,' come the appreciative shouts from the bench.

Before half time we have further shots from Spence and Blackburn that are desperately turned away, and as when the whistle comes it is us who are firmly in control.

The second half begins as frenetically as the first had finished. It is end to end. As a cross comes flying into our box it strikes Woodhouse on what looks suspiciously like an arm but the loud shouts for handball are ignored and the home players scream furiously at the linesman on the far side. I had been told a few weeks before that in places like Tivoli the officials can allow the intimidating crowds and the area's reputation get the better of them and it can therefore be very difficult for visitors to get results. Today though the refereeing has if anything been going in our favour, and this was another example of that.

With about twenty minutes to go it is Harbour View doing all the attacking while Tivoli just desperately try to maintain their lead of one fortuitous goal. Wolfe shoots tamely; Thomas has one that nearly squirms under the keeper; Wolfe has another one saved; Harvey puts it just over the bar from a corner.

Going into injury time our desperation grows while the home crowd become more and restless. Aggression is rearing up and the venom directed at the referee and his assistants turns an already edgy atmosphere decidedly menacing. It is sensed by the small group of heavily armed security men behind our dugout whose previously relaxed postures become upright and alert in response, their assault rifles clasped tightly in their hands. But back out on the pitch we have run out of ideas. After Harvey's effort we produce no more opportunities and the siege on the Tivoli goal is brought to a close by the ref's sharp whistle.

Yet another loss. Sure, Tivoli away is undoubtedly the toughest fixture of the season and we had been by no means outplayed, losing only to one deflected goal and then keeping them under constant pressure for large parts of the remainder of the game. But all the same, the defeats are now piling up and the gap between us and them is ever growing.

'Referee you suck pussy,' comes a furious cry from the stand as the players and officials leave the field, a shout that has a threatening edge to it that goes beyond the usual football ground banter. Throughout the latter stages of the game our surroundings have become charged and hostile and it is easy to see how some officials may be cowed by places like this, but tonight's had not. In fact, if he had been lenient to either side you would have to say it was Harbour View, but generally he managed to deliver one of the better and more balanced performances I have seen in the country, much to his credit. You might wonder why someone deserves to be singled out for praise just for doing their job adequately, but while doing so you should probably bear in mind that an adequate day's work for you most likely does not involve riling up 1,500 impassioned residents of Kingston's most notorious garrison. And you can bet your bottom dollar that there will be no special measures in place to ensure his safe passage home after the game.

From a Harbour View standing it is not too disheartening, as defeats go, and as such there is no need to let it damage our confidence as we prepare for a long away journey to Reno a few days from now. Every team anticipates that they will lose points over the course of a season—no one expects to win every last game—and this is one of those occasions where you can swallow the pill. The loss has not by any means derailed our title bid, but we certainly cannot afford another slip up in Westmoreland.

Sunday 17th October

Boys' Town	1 0	Waterhouse
Humble Lions	1 0	Benfica
Portmore United	0 0	Arnett Gardens
Reno	2 1	St. George's
Tivoli Gardens	**1 0**	**HVFC**
Village United	0 3	Sporting Central

National Premier League

	P	GD	Pts.
1. Portmore United	7	5	14
2. Waterhouse	7	3	13
3. Boys' Town	7	0	13
4. Tivoli Gardens	6	6	12
5. Reno	7	4	11
6. Sporting Central	7	4	10
7. HVFC	**7**	**3**	**10**
8. Arnett Gardens	7	-3	9
9.Benfica	7	-4	8
10. Village United	7	-8	6
11. Humble Lions	6	-4	4
12. St. George's	7	-7	4

CHAPTER ELEVEN

Smash And Grab

It is for a previously empty Wednesday evening that the first of the games consumed by Nicole is rescheduled. For us this means a long trip west to Savanna-la-Mar, home to fifth-placed Reno. In more prosperous times this would have been an occasion on which the club would put the players up in a hotel the night before, allowing them to arrive at the game relatively fresh. Unfortunately these are not prosperous times and that is a luxury that is simply not feasible, so when I phone for travel plans I am told we will be leaving the Compound at eight o'clock on the Wednesday morning to make the four hour journey in plenty of time for a four o'clock kick off.

But the night before that is the least of our pre-game worries. With around twenty hours until kick off, I venture online and discover that the US National Hurricane Centre website is painting an ugly picture which shows an area of low pressure over the north west Caribbean Sea that envelops the whole western half of the island and has, according to the reports, a 70% chance of becoming a cyclone over the next 48 hours. No one can say for sure whether it will or not. The effect of this is that instead of resting up in a comfortable local hotel the night before a big league game, Harbour View's players are 100 miles away wondering if the match will even be going ahead.

In a country where roads can be engulfed in minutes, the authorities do not have to just take into consideration whether or not the game itself can be played but whether the away teams will actually be able to get home afterwards, and as such the final decision on whether to play or not is invariably left unmade until the last possible minute. At about twenty past seven in the morning I am assured by phone that we have the all clear, so I climb into a taxi and head over to Harbour View.

Despite getting there about ten minutes before our scheduled leaving time, I am among the first to arrive. The bus will actually be leaving at nine, I had been told when I was already halfway there, and in a typically Caribbean display of timekeeping it would be an hour later than even that by the time we do eventually move out. In the meantime I place a chair by the window and begin to read while players start to drift up the stairs in ones and twos, shuffling towards the kitchen from where the homely smell of frying meat emanates enticingly.

The common room soon starts to fill and I pick up my seat to join the small group that has formed in front the TV, taking in a high-octane, low-plotline movie that seems to contain just about every 80s action star Hollywood could throw at it, as well as a couple of the newer generation for good measure. When it ends with Sylvester Stallone bidding The Girl goodbye and leaving her on the dock of some exotic, and now thoroughly blown-up, land before climbing into a plane with Jason Statham it tips the already unimpressed audience over the edge. 'Oh hell no,' Bowa cries. 'After all that he just leaves her?' He looks around for confirmation of his disappointment and the others seem to share his sense of anti-climax, drifting off to eat or play dominoes leaving just myself and John-Ross Edwards to take in a re-run of a Bayern Munich Champions League game from last night.

Eventually all food has been eaten and all instructions given, so we troop downstairs and out of the door to the dusty car park where the bus waits under the intense morning sun. Once again I squeeze in next to Romario Campbell near the back as Blackburn drops into the single seat by the window opposite holding a large cuddly toy dog so careworn that one of its big floppy ears has fallen off somewhere down the years. John-Ross stocks up on supplies for the journey from the small concessions stand by the wall as players shove coins out of the windows and shout their orders to him. DV emerges, putting his bags in the back of Bowa's car before looking over to his players' transport. Immediately he storms over to berate those who have removed their black and white match-day travelling kit, something he had specifically told them all to wear at the beginning of the season to get them into a professional mindset on the day of a game. Blackburn is a particular target for his fury, having completely forgotten to bring his shirt and turning up instead in a black Pringle-style jumper which he has since removed anyway. DV makes it very clear exactly how he feels about it.

Squeezing every last drop of value from the hiring of the bus, Simone and a few of her friends jump aboard to fill the last of the space and occupy the temporary seats which fold out into the central aisle. We then head out with music blaring and bass thumping, this time making our way through Downtown and the industrial port area, full of warehouses and factories, past the Red Stripe brewery and Wray & Nephew's rum bottling plant and towards St. Catherine. As we approach Portmore the traffic becomes increasingly thick until we are firmly stuck in a dense mass of honking horns and churning exhaust fumes. Using his uniquely Caribbean sense of craft, the driver pulls out onto the rough hard shoulder and accelerates, bypassing a vast stretch of stationary vehicles before cutting back into the queue with our position considerably advanced.

No sooner have we started slowly moving forward again than another minibus comes up from behind having followed our path along the outside. Someone recognises the faces inside it and soon both our bus and theirs are abuzz with excitement. Windows are opened and players leap up to lean out and shout greetings and jokes to the passengers opposite, who in turn fire back the banter gleefully. Journeying out of town beside us, it turns out, is the Boys' Town team bus on its way to Falmouth where they will be playing Village this afternoon. With the 5-1 result still fresh in the mind, the Harbour View players seem to resist the temptation to rub it in and instead exchange friendly chat across the motorway at thirty miles per hour. Blackburn, a resident of the Trenchtown area, yells to the driver to maintain a steady speed as he fishes a couple of bills from his pocket and passes them over to an outstretched hand that is bridging the gap, taking the serendipitous opportunity to conveniently pay off some past debt. With a few more handshakes and a couple more laughs the buses separate and concentrations turn again to our own business.

After turning off the clogged thoroughfare and being freed up by the unlocked traffic we blast down bumpy pot-hole filled roads, Harbour View's prize assets being tossed around in the rickety seatbelt-less bus like beads in a maraca. This provides endless ammunition for Nicholas

Beckett and Daveion Woodhouse to yell jokes to each other at the driver's expense from opposite ends of the coach. He is, apparently, 'driving like Ivor' and although I am not too sure exactly who Ivor is it seems clear he's not a man that impresses many driving instructors. As we bounce around a song comes on the CD about the singer having sex 'doggy style', which Blackburn excitedly stands up and demonstrates on his cuddly toy while the others all laugh around him. Wherever you are in the world, lads will always be lads.

The driver's pace does not let up as we get onto the highway, accelerating past vehicle after vehicle until finally our poor battered bus can take no more. A loud crack explodes from under the wheel arch below John-Ross' seat and a black flash of debris shoots towards the car we are currently streaking past to our left, causing its driver to duck momentarily behind his steering wheel in defence. The shard falls short and he pops back up, looking relieved to still be in one piece, and hastily speeds away as we swing in behind and pull over to the hard shoulder. The amused players take the opportunity to stretch their legs and file out to gaze on the shredded rear-left tyre before meandering down the hard shoulder to sit along the metal barrier. A few loiter around watching the sweating driver, now stripped down to a string vest to avoid getting grease on his Harbour View top, as he sets about removing the damaged wheel. 'Well, if you're going to drive like Ivor . . .'Woodhouse mutters disapprovingly, to no one in particular.

A Highway Patrol man stops to assist, only to confess that red-tape prevents him from actually doing anything other than laying out a few cones along the side of the road. After doing that he proceeds to just stand around among the group of onlooking players, many of whom have grown tired of the novelty and are now complaining that these circumstances are 'fucking bullshit'. The wheel-nuts have been proving tighter than anticipated and with 'Ivor' unable to make them budge Beckett and Spence, two of the larger-built members of the squad, are called in to the fray as weights to jump on the end of the long pole that is being used to loosen them.

But progress is slow. After sitting around for at least twenty minutes Blackburn comes sprinting back over from his spot on the crash barrier having spied Bowa's pale blue Mitsubishi approaching in the distance. 'DV coming! DV coming!' he shrieks through a mischievous grin.

Having already been shouted at once that morning for travelling in the wrong kit and keen to avoid receiving the manager's fury again, he dashes to the bus and throws his naked torso behind it just as the car passes. Unsurprisingly though, the sight of the Premier League Champions' entire squad sitting on the hard shoulder of a busy motorway is deemed reason enough for the coaches to pull over and investigate the situation. Within seconds a concerned looking DV is marching towards our stricken vehicle—and his shirtless winger—only too aware that the already-thin sliver of time his players have to stretch and warm up at Reno is draining away by the second.

It seems there are more pressing matters than the various states of dress on display and, not wanting to waste any more time than is necessary, lunch is taken there to save us having to take another long break further up the road. Once again polystyrene containers of chicken with rice and peas are handed around to everyone present and with that the Highway Patrol man, who has achieved nothing whatsoever up to this point, springs into action to insist that everyone puts all their rubbish in a bag and no litter is left by the road. Clearly Britain is not alone in suffering from the curse of the over-officious, yet entirely useless, civil servant.

While this was happening the brains and the brawn were finally winning their battle with the wheel nuts. Bowa, standing by the side of the bus, looks into the open window next to him and his eye is caught by the pink fluffy dog lying on one of the abandoned seats. He reaches in and grabs it, waving it around and demanding to know who owns it with the disappointed tone of a let-down father as the players laugh wickedly. He shakes his head despairingly at the suddenly sheepish looking Blackburn who is grassed up by his unsympathetic team mates.

With the wheel finally removed the spare is produced, squeezed and rejected as unusably flat. A brief discussion ensues, followed by some unsuccessful attempts to flag down passing lorries for an air pump, and it is eventually decided that we would put our faith in the remaining, inner left-rear wheel and continue on one down until we reach somewhere that could pump up the spare. After about fifteen minutes of uncharacteristically careful driving we arrive at a small roadside shack with bike tyres, tractor tyres and everything else in between piled up outside and the driver makes his final repairs. Carvel stops by to make sure that his team will actually be turning up to this afternoon's game and before too long we are back on our way again through the narrow, winding, jungle roads of central Jamaica.

Clarendon, Manchester, Saint Elizabeth. The southern parishes come and go as the hours drift by. As we cross into the western extreme of Westmoreland, home of Savanna-la-Mar, we are once again flanked by the coastal fringes of the island, and with this 'Ivor', who previously seemed to have taken on board the lessons of the shredded tyre, suddenly decides we are in the maddest of dashes to reach our destination and stamps down on the throttle again. When behind the wheel, Jamaicans often take on the philosophy that it is perfectly okay to overtake on blind corners, shoot red lights and basically drive how you want, where you want so long as you are beeping your horn as you do so. To them this simple act seems to absolve you of all responsibility and if someone crashes into you by carelessly coming the other way then, well, you did warn them you were coming. So with the horn almost constantly pushed down, we shoot past every car that happens to get in our way, showing no regard for what is in the road ahead and being thrown regularly from our seats as the bus crashes through the deep and numerous potholes that litter the country's roads.

Our speed gathers continuously, as though the brakes have long-since ceased to work and the accelerator is now the only thing the driver has left to play with. 'That's enough, driver!' Jermaine Hue shouts a couple of times from the back seat but to no avail. Outside the windows are picture postcard Caribbean scenes of colourfully painted wooden boats bobbing gently on a turquoise sea just off white sandy beaches, but they are gone in a flash as we are chucked around the roads by a driver who seems to have gone completely mental. We only slow up when a man driving what looks like a hybrid between a golf buggy and a milk float takes to entertaining himself by doing all he can to hold us up. The large grin spread across his face as we eventually overtake hints at the fun he has gleaned from his game, and we shoot forward again to arrive, on a wing and a prayer, in Savanna-la-Mar about twenty minutes later.

With kick off now less than an hour away, the players take the chance of some slower, town driving to change into their kit so as not to waste any more time once we arrive at Reno's Frome Complex home. It is a wet, grey day and the rains of 'Low Pressure Area 1' are coming down hard on the small, soaked town. Beneath sombre skies, Sav's rain covered streets are adorned by a number of pretty colonial buildings which give the small town an old-world charm that has been almost entirely driven out of concrete Kingston.

Exiting out the other side again, Ivor takes one last opportunity to toss us from our seats by hurtling into one final pothole. 'Bumbaclaat,' murmurs Beckett behind me as he is thrown skywards for the umpteenth time. Unlike the Americanised swearing earlier in the day, this fairly disgusting utterance is about the weightiest word in the Jamaican lexicon. It is one of a small cluster of similar curses all based around the excretion of menstrual blood and faeces and the cloths used to 'stem the tides'. Needless to say, it is a phrase that adorns most sentences uttered inside the country's football grounds, as well as the buses of the teams playing on them.

At twenty past three, having left Harbour View at around ten, we finally cross through the goat-filled field that doubles as Frome's public car park and into the ground itself. Passing through the gate the players cycle through the tracks on the CD for something up-tempo and with windows open and bass shaking the bus we boom past the onlooking spectators hanging around the clubhouse and on to another field where we park and trot out to another unlit concrete away changing room. Both toilets are broken so the players relieve themselves round the back before returning to the soggy field in which the bus has been parked, a cricket pitch during the drier months, to go through their warm up drills.

Without going back to the changing room, DV runs through his last minute instructions for the game and at about five to four the team climb through a gap in the low metal fence separating the two fields and line up on the sodden pitch for the national anthem. The Frome Complex is a nice, open ground in a scenic position. The clubhouse stretches out along one end while the backdrop to the opposite goal is a clump of trees which sit in front of three or four rows of rising hills which grow increasingly faint through the atmospheric haze. Some painted bleachers lie alongside one touchline, on which was currently a mass of coloured umbrellas, and the other one is open to the cricket field where the players had warmed up.

I place myself on the veranda of the clubhouse, the only sheltered area of the ground, in amongst locals who, whether trendy teenagers or grizzled old men, are all liberally enjoying their ganja and I stand to watch the game from within their twisting cloud of smoke. The pitch is completely drenched, certainly in no condition for a football match, but after travelling all this way, and shelling out all the expenses that go into such a trip, there is simply no chance of the game being called off now.

Large areas of the pitch are so inundated that they have become grand puddles and shots and crosses are regularly accompanied by flying lumps of mud. When on the floor, the ball hardly moves through the water and when sent high it returns to earth and just dies completely, giving defenders and attackers alike huge problems in judging its path and bounce. One long range Reno shot is followed by a deep ball which Montrose Phinn tries to head behind only for it to stop dead upon bouncing and remain in play, leading to a desperate scramble to get the ball out for the relative safety of a throw.

Our attacks are few and far between. John-Ross plays in Spence but the chance disappears as he slips at the critical moment. It is a similar story when Hue feeds him. Turning to shoot, he loses his footing and finds himself flat out in the mud again. As we start to find our way into the game debates rage around me as to the merits of various members of the home side. 'Number 14 nuh produce a bumbaclaat,' derides one man as the player in question sends a wasteful cross high and wide.

Shots are coming in from distance, often skidding off the mud and making life very difficult for the keepers. As our defenders and their attackers battle over first rights on the rebound from yet another such effort I think of DV's speech before travelling to St. George's about making sure we are not left crying over spilt milk, but generally the keepers seem to be handling the conditions well. Their number 14 has a chance to respond to his critic but squanders it, heading wide from a good position.

Another couple of decent Reno chances go begging before they finally launched the critical attack. Just inside our half a midfielder turns on the ball, slipping in process and wrapping his flailing fist around Richard Edwards' head as he falls. Our captain drops to the floor and they push forward right into the central gap that has been created in his absence, and from there the ball is played through to striker Christopher Harris who has been left criminally unattended inside our box. He fires the ball through the mud and into the bottom of Michard Barrett's net.

We respond well, making some dangerous moves deep into their half in search of the equaliser. Blackburn breaks into the box only to waste his pass, but the locals around me sense the danger and complain loudly that the defence had allowed him far too much space. Their worries are proved well-founded no more than sixty seconds later when John-Ross puts in a deep cross that the keeper tries to claim but misses. The ball finds its way back to Blackburn, again with far too much room, on the far side of six yard box from where he squeezes the ball inside the post from the tightest of angles.

It is amazing how the confidence of a goal can change a football match in a way that defies all reason and suddenly we are somehow pulling off the sort of passing moves that were getting bogged down just a few minutes ago, with Edwards, Hue and Blackburn combining neatly to set up Andre Fagan for a header that he puts just wide. We are still giving them hope though and after the referee awards the softest of fouls against Edwards a cross is fired in which their striker tries to win by launching himself shoulder-first into the out-rushing Barrett and knocking him to the floor. The elderly locals demand a penalty for Barrett's callous interruption of their player's attempt to score and share their displeasure at being denied one in no uncertain terms. 'Ras claat! Di referee a bloodclaat!' yells one, angrily. 'Bumbaclaat,' thoughtfully surmises another in sage agreement.

The maligned official blows for half time. As opposed to retiring to the distant changing room the players amble to the side of the pitch where they rest on the ground or, for a lucky few, on the cool boxes as DV gives his team talk. In the conditions he urges his players to fire in shots that would bounce just in front of the keepers. 'It is not about pretty football,' he tells them as fresh shirts are handed round—a luxury that few clubs besides the relatively wealthy Harbour View can provide—'it is a dogfight.'

Offering some final encouragement and pressing upon the team that Reno 'are just hanging on', he sends them back out for the second half. Reno had indeed just been hanging on, but they would not be for long. Within a minute of the restart we win a soft free kick, centrally positioned and around 25 yards from goal. 'Some teams get all the decisions,' complain the men around me, with some degree of justification, as Hue and Harvey line up the shot. The right back then moves away into the area, leaving it to his senior team mate who takes a few strides towards the ball and hits it low, never more than a foot or so from the ground. The keeper dives before it clips the wall, a connection which sends it to his other side and skidding through the mud into the bottom corner. From one down, Harbour View have snatched the lead.

Any match that can be described as a 'dogfight' is never going to be Jermaine Hue's ideal game but he has now produced the key moment, and the key goal. Confidence grows again and soon the players are coming up with some champagne moments, some of which work while others fail comically as they begin competing as much with the elements as the opposition. Fagan attempts a Cruijff turn in the Reno box only to trip over the ball as it becomes lodged in the mud halfway through the spin. More impressively, John-Ross brings the ball into their half where he nutmegs a midfielder before laying it off to Hue who takes one touch then dinks it lightly over the head of a defender into the path of Spence. He greets the ball with a first time flick off the back of his heel to the on-running John-Ross who has sprinted forward to collect it again, only to be hacked down as he does so. It was a beautiful move that deserved more than it gets, a free kick that is hit straight into the wall.

As if to prove how tough the pitch is to play on, a Reno cross flies dangerously in where it is met by the striker with a powerful header down towards the bottom corner of our goal. The people on the steps of the clubhouse are already starting to celebrate the equaliser when the ball hits the mud and just stops still a yard or two from the line. It did look like it was probably going wide anyway, but when some wet mud can become the decisive factor in determining who gets the points from a Premier League match you know something is awry.

Over in the cricket field car park Simone has left her dry viewpoint on the team bus and is now furiously berating the driver of the stand-by ambulance over some unrecognisable disagreement as Harbour View desperately dig in to repel the home team's constant attacks. Crosses flash unmet through our box and shots rain in on our goal. On the occasions when we manage to get the ball to players in a safe area they show no ambition other than to simply keep it there and waste some of those stretching, dragging seconds. The one flickering occasion where we do show some intent is squandered when Hue surprises everyone so much by actually attacking that nobody goes with him and his one man foray into the Reno half simply peters out.

But then it comes. Under feeble lights which cough their meagre glow into the darkening evening the referee blows the final whistle. We had held on and, rain-soaked and mud-caked, we had earned a difficult victory. 'We had to fight to win it,' DV says to me as the drenched players troop back to the dark changing room, and we really had, often literally in what had been a very physical game.

I get back onto the bus where Simone, her friends and the unused subs are already waiting and have been joined by a drunk, shirtless local with the remains of a bottle of rum in his hand. I had met him at the drinks stall before the game and then seen him again afterwards, by which time he had become significantly the worse for wear, and now here he is on our bus joyously declaring me to be his good friend and claiming he is an old class mate of Jermaine Hue's. Whether this is true or not, Hue does manage to coax him off before going to change after Simone's demands to go had fallen on deafly intoxicated ears.

In ones and twos the bus slowly refills with players. Beckett returns in need of something to dry his wet hair with, sees Blackburn's dog unguarded and pounces to use it as a convenient towel before returning it innocently to its place. Hue had left his clothes on board after getting changed in his seat on the way and he returns in just his underpants to get himself dressed again. Once everyone is back in their seats tin foil parcels of bread and chicken are handed round and the bus pulls off to make its way back out onto the now dark roads of Savanna-la-Mar.

By the time we are working our way through the fringes of Westmoreland the adrenaline has worn off and many of the players have settled down to relax in the darkness. To my left Blackburn, one of the bolder, brasher members of the squad, who half an hour ago had been shouting ecstatically down the phone to his girlfriend about his goal, is now curled up asleep, tightly hugging his toy dog to his chest.

It had been a long day and we were still a good four hours from seeing the twinkling lights of home on the horizon. When we finally draw over the brow of the final hill and down into the big, bright city the bus begins to stop here and there, dropping players off in the shadowy streets near their homes. They pick up their kit bags and hop out onto the pavements as we tour West Kingston. Waterhouse, Spanish Town Road, Trenchtown—not all Premier League footballers share a faux-Georgian mansion in the countryside with their pop star girlfriend. When I ask to be dropped uptown on Hope Road there are one or two looks that suggest the foreigner will never really understand their world.

Despite the hours we could have no complaints about the day. We had pulled a smash and grab job on what would become Tropical Storm Andrew, nipping into his threatening reach, snatching our three points and making the charge home before his fury could strand us on the west coast. As it turned out the rains never really came to Jamaica anyway, at least not to anything like the same extent as they had with Nicole, and the country's slow, expensive and uncomfortably introspective recovery from the damage of a few weeks previously was allowed to continue largely unheeded.

Harbour View's own recovery appears to be picking up as well. Since the break we have carved out two wins from three, both very impressive in their own different ways, and have only dropped points in the tightest of away defeats at the home of our strongest title rivals. We are still some way from perfect but it is starting to look like there just might yet be a happy ending to this crazy, up and down season.

Wednesday 20th October

Portmore United	0 0	Humble Lions
Reno	**1 2**	**HVFC**
Sporting Central	1 0	Benfica
Tivoli Gardens	3 0	St. George's
Village United	1 2	Boys' Town
Waterhouse	2 0	Arnett Gardens

National Premier League

	P	GD	Pts.
1. Waterhouse	8	6	16
2. Boys' Town	8	1	16
3. Tivoli Gardens	7	9	15
4. Portmore United	8	5	15
5. Sporting Central	8	5	13
6. HVFC	**8**	**4**	**13**
7. Reno	8	3	11
8. Arnett Gardens	8	-5	9
9. Benfica	8	-5	8
10. Village United	8	-9	6
11. Humble Lions	7	-4	5
12. St. George's	8	-10	4

Harbour View players recover during half time at Reno.
Visible from left to right are Blackburn, John-Ross (10),
Barrett (32), Phinn, Hue (51, seated) and Fagan (11).
Under the mac in the centre is Carvel Stewart.

CHAPTER TWELVE

The Democratic Process

Arnett Gardens versus Tivoli Gardens is the most notorious rivalry in Jamaican football. The reasons why that is so go way beyond the pitch though. Jungle versus Garden, as the areas are also known, is quite simply the most notorious rivalry in Jamaican society full stop.

For decades there were violent and deadly hostilities between the two communities and even now there often remains a palpable tension between residents. But the sparring has significantly cooled in recent years and this, many people argue, is due in no small part to football. Captain Burrell said as much at the League launch in August. 'It is because of football that Arnett Gardens and Tivoli Gardens now interact in the way that they do,' he trumpeted in no uncertain terms. This, he had implied, is the true value of the game in a country such as Jamaica.

And yet it is a claim that feels slightly counterintuitive. Football, as a manifestation of regional rivalries, often seems only to pour petrol on the fires of these conflicts, providing a battle ground on which the ordinary folk on either side can meet and then whipping them up into their partisan frenzies. See when Liverpool and Manchester United clash, or witness the reception teams from Italy's cultured north receive when visiting Napoli and the south. But the game is not without its documented occasions as a boundary-breaker and peacemaker either, one of the most spectacular examples being the spontaneous games played by British and German troops between their lines at Ypres on Christmas Day in 1914. And of course every World Cup is garnished with video clips of smiling multi-cultural faces, generally belonging to children, to make sure we all know exactly how important the tournament is in bringing different people together.

Football is one of the most potent social forces on the planet but clearly its implications are not one dimensional and defined in absolutes. It is not necessarily the great unifier FIFA would have us believe any more than it is necessarily divisive and inflammatory. In different contexts and at different times it has different effects.

So what is it in Kingston? Are the cheerleaders correct about the awesome power of the little round ball or is there more to the reduced tensions than they let on? I want to find out, and the first step is to look at the roots of the division and what caused it in the first place.

Having considered the fertile conditions of West Kingston that birthed the Tivoli 'model' in the 1960s it may come as no surprise that the boom years for neighbouring Trenchtown, in which Arnett Gardens lies within the St. Andrew South constituency, came in the following decade when the PNP won the tempestuous 1972 election and served two terms in office under Michael Manley. While Manley oversaw the great positive changes for PNP supporters, the real local hero was Housing Minister and MP for the constituency Anthony 'Tony' Spaulding; it was he who instigated the construction of 1,100 low-cost homes in Trenchtown and consequently transformed the area.

In much the same way as Tivoli was constructed with leanings towards JLP supporters, so Trenchtown's flourishing welfare was only open to those who backed the PNP. Speaking to the *Gleaner* in 2006, a priest who worked at the Ministry of Housing during Spaulding's time in office described him as, 'violently partisan . . . one hundred per cent of the homes went to PNP people. JLP people knew better than to come to the Ministry and apply.' In 1972 Spaulding had won the seat of St. Andrew South by just 102 votes; by 1976 he took it by over 13,000 and then by over 15,000 in 1980. On the other side of the Spanish Town Road, Seaga won the West Kingston seat in 1962 with 52% of the vote for the JLP; in 1980 he won the same seat with 94%. In no more than a few years the two had overseen the development of communities that gave their respective parties the safest seats in Jamaican politics.

It was during the PNP's time in office in the 70s that things got increasingly turbulent. As Prime Minister, Michael Manley declared that Jamaica's political future lay in 'Democratic Socialism' and swung the country heavily to the left. This development saw Manley align himself with Cuba and the Soviet Union from whom money and guns reportedly flowed and onto the streets of the burgeoning PNP communities, those like Arnett Gardens. It was the height of the Cold War and the US was, of course, particularly jumpy throughout the period and sought to fight back against the socialist spread by putting its own muscle behind Jamaica's political right, forming strong links between the CIA and the JLP, of which Seaga had by now assumed leadership.

It was also during that decade that the Shower Posse began to bloom under the guidance of Dudus' father, Lester Lloyd Coke, widely known as 'Jim Brown'. With Tivoli being a waterfront community the gang had access to shipping routes overseas and they used them to establish international drug running networks, aided, it is said, by the CIA as part of their efforts to fund the criminals that would destabilise the PNP Government. Philip Agee, a former CIA agent, said of that time: 'The CIA was using the JLP as its instrument in the campaign against the Michael Manley government. I'd say most of the violence was coming from the JLP, and behind them was the CIA in terms of getting weapons in and getting money in.' It is even suspected by many that an assassination attempt on Bob Marley in 1976 in which the singer was shot and wounded—stray bullet holes can still be seen in the wall of his former home in Kingston—was carried out by the Shower Posse and backed by the Americans, coming as it did just two days before he staged a free concert organised by the government to try to quell the political violence: the Rastafari in general were considered PNP supporters and Tony Spaulding was particularly active in ensuring the concert went ahead, suggesting the message was more pro-PNP than pro-peace. As the relationship between the two right wing partners became more explicit, opponents began to spell Seaga's name CIAga, a memory at which he laughed nostalgically when he later spoke to me about that time. 'The socialist PNP, they were definitely associated with Cuba and the Soviet Union, very definitely,' he told me, and showed no hint of secrecy when I asked about the relationship he formed with the US: 'You know, you fight back. And that was the way of fighting back . . . It was all part of the politics.'

While Seaga cemented his ties with America, Manley made a state visit to Cuba where he indulged his admiration for the revolutionary ways of Castro. His security on the trip did not come from any official government force but from Winston 'Burry Boy' Blake, the don who was one of Spaulding's associates in Arnett Gardens and the recipient of a string of lucrative government contracts, becoming the PNP's toughest enforcer in Kingston and St Andrew as he did so. He was frequently seen in public with Manley and led the war on the streets against the JLP. Along with George 'Feathermop' Spence, Burry Boy led an assault on the JLP headquarters in 1974 that resulted in an elderly guard being stabbed, and the duo were regularly involved in urban warfare against the Shower Posse and other JLP gangs. When he was shot dead in 1975, Burry Boy's funeral procession, led by Manley, became a stunt in the ongoing conflict when it needlessly turned off the Spanish Town Road and into Tivoli. Having been on the receiving end of the don's gunfire countless times, the residents saw the inflammatory move as a cheap 'dis' against them and soon bullets were flying from all directions while the mourners ran for cover.

With the JLP and PNP, and therefore Tivoli and Arnett, firmly at war, economic issues placed further strain on the 1980 election and made it one of the bloodiest in history; it is reported that 844 people were killed in the space of just two weeks. Speaking at her book launch, Manley's wife reflected: 'The night of the 1980 elections we didn't know if we would live or die. When I talk to JLP people now they will tell you they felt the same way.' But this marked the point at which Jamaica ran out of patience with Manley's thrust into socialism and voted Seaga and the JLP back into power. There followed the peak years for Coke's Shower Posse. The American government instructed Seaga, in return for their help in destabilising the Manley administration, to crack down on the marijuana trade that was so rife in Jamaica, an operation whose success was its biggest failure as it left a void in the criminal community that was instead filled by cocaine. Jamaica became a major international transhipment point for the drug, which flowed freely from Colombia—some say in planes leased by the CIA in an effort to fund the JLP's anti-left stance—through Kingston and on to the rest of the world.

Lester Coke's sprawling activities and vast network meant he was one of the first dons to free himself from any real need for the politicians and his criminal empire became self reliant. But this did not mean he neglected his roots: he used his money to pay for schoolbooks, for home repairs and for anything else the people of Tivoli needed, while his influence continued to keep the area safe from the outside. And he was still playing the warrior-king, personally leading an attack against the Rema community in 1986 that left seven people dead.

But as the Cold War approached its conclusion, so the 'glory years' of the gangs began to wane. With no more use for the right-wing criminals, the US turned to investigating them instead and began to bring them to task for the crimes they had committed on American soil. In 1988, 34 members of the Shower Posse, including Coke, were indicted by a grand federal jury and a month later 53 gang members were arrested in New Jersey. Coke himself remained free for another few years until being captured in the early 1990s when Jamaican state forces, by now under the instruction of Manley and the PNP again, brought him in and prepared him for extradition to the US. And this was what the dons feared the most: at home witnesses could be intimidated, officials could be bribed, people could be blackmailed—Coke himself had been charged by the police for 14 murders without conviction—but in America there was no way to cheat the law. One Shower Posse gunman agreed to testify against the gangleaders in return for immunity—during which he implicated himself in nine murders—and he described himself as a 'political enforcer' for Seaga's JLP before adding that, 'the United States made me what I am.' Coke himself never made trial. His network spread far and wide even beyond politics, having forged links from commerce to banking, from media to the clergy; there was a huge amount of information about a lot of people that would have come out in the wash during his court case. In 1992, while still awaiting extradition, he died violently in a fire localised solely to his Kingston prison cell. 'If you believe Jim Brown [Coke] just burned to death, by accident, in his jail cell you'll believe in the tooth fairy,' his lawyer said afterwards. 'The only thing I can tell you for sure—and I saw the body—is that Jim Brown is dead.'

Seaga led Coke's funeral procession, labelling him a 'protector of the poor', and the Shower Posse fell into the hands of Dudus. The new don was well educated and thoughtful, shunning the spotlight in a way that contrasts with some of the other, more showy, big men. But he continued his father's traditions and used his wealth to help Tivoli Gardens and its residents in any way he could, while also maintaining enough of a presence to keep the streets safe. In fact, in the recent years leading up to his arrest, Tivoli has enjoyed one of the lowest crime rates in Kingston.

Quite how much influence the dons maintained politically is questionable though. It is reported that Prime Minister Bruce Golding only got his safe JLP seat in the West Kingston constituency because Dudus agreed to it at Seaga's behest, having previously refused other candidates. But at the lengthy enquiry into the Manatt incident, Golding pointedly countered that by saying it was 'absolutely' true that anybody could stand for the JLP in West Kingston without needing to be sanctioned by Coke. 'There is a myth out there associated with Coke that is completely contradictory to the relationship that exists within the constituency,' he added. Who really knows for sure. What is certain is that Dudus' construction company continued to receive millions of dollars worth of government contracts right up until his arrest. On the other side of the fence, when Arnett don William 'Willie Haggart' Moore was killed in a triple murder in 2001, current St. Andrew South MP Dr. Omar Davies of the PNP attended the funeral and noted that he was, 'a good friend who always supported me.' Dr. Davies is also the president of Arnett Gardens Football Club.

Even though political violence is not what is used to be, the evidence clearly points to very distinct divides still existing in the modern age: in the most recent Parish Council Elections 94% of voters in Tivoli Gardens sided with the JLP and 85% in Trench Town with the PNP. If you drive out of the city along the Spanish Town Road there is a very obvious point at which the graffiti on the north side of the road suddenly changes from pro-JLP to pro-PNP as you pass from Denham Town (a relatively small appendage on Tivoli's northern border, 89% JLP) into Trenchtown. And as for the football clubs, not only are they run by politicians themselves but all it takes to see exactly how important the MPs are to the clubs is a look at the names of their stadiums: the Edward Seaga Complex in Tivoli, and the Anthony Spaulding Complex in Arnett. Named for the men who birthed garrison politics.

The Premier League has now reached matchday nine and today the two clubs will be meeting with Tivoli looking to go top. The game is to held at the Tony Spaulding Complex in 'Jungle' and that alone is testimony to the huge leaps forward taken by the people of both areas: in the past all games between the two sides had to be played at a neutral venue because they simply couldn't enter one another's communities safely. So how much credit for this can we give to football? As my first step in answering that question I put the idea to Dr Amanda Sives of the University of Liverpool, author of ***Elections, Violence and the Democratic Process in Jamaica 1944-2007,*** and her response is not too encouraging:

'To argue that football is the reason for the peace between Tivoli Gardens and Arnett Gardens seems a little disingenuous to me,' she replies. 'It is generally known that the reason for the peace in the area has been the role of the dons in using "informal methods" of crime control and in negotiating with, or being able to dominate, other dons to keep the peace. This is not to argue that football is not important in keeping some young men out of gangs and indeed it may foster positive relations on one level between the communities, but it is not the panacea that you seem to be suggesting.' Yet she is quick to advise caution with her words by mentioning that sport as a specific lies outside her main area of research, as it seems to do with most academics who have looked into the current 'peace'. Clearly there is more work to be done on this question. 'I would go back to your football contact and ask him to provide evidence of how football keeps the peace,' she concludes, and so that's exactly what I will do. That, though, will have to wait for another time.

I stand by the barrier outside my apartment building talking to the security guard about the upcoming game while waiting for my lift from Clyde. Benfica, the minnows playing in the Premier League for the first time in their history, are coming to three-time Caribbean champions Harbour View. 'You never know with these little teams though,' the guard warns, himself a Harbour View fan. 'They could come here and play really well and if the big team has a bad match they could be surprised.' It can undoubtedly happen, think of Hull City at the Emirates and Blackpool at Anfield in recent years as proof that the big boys can be caught off guard in front of their own fans by some lively newcomer. We will certainly have to be cautious of complacency tonight but a careful and solid performance should be enough to send them back to the north coast empty handed.

Unfortunately a careful and solid performance is a million miles away from what we actually produce.

The good news on arriving at the Compound is that national striker Kavin Bryan is back in the squad, having returned from a loan spell in Vietnam a few weeks before with a minor knee injury that has now healed sufficiently for him to take a place on the bench. The bad news is that the rest of the team simply fail to turn up at all. Benfica are decent if unspectacular but we give the most miserable performance of the season so far and fail to really do anything of note whatsoever. To make things worse Jermaine Hue jumps to contest a header with one of their midfielders after about twenty minutes and lands on the opposing player's leg, causing his ankle to twist down over it and his body to collapse under its own weight. He crumples into a heap and Marcelino Blackburn immediately hoofs the ball out of play to allow him attention. With no hope of him standing again the stretcher is required to carry him off, sobbing as he goes, and take him into the changing room from where he is sent on to hospital. 'I was feeling a lot of pain,' he tells me later, the desperate sight he made as he passed beneath the press desk on the stretcher suggesting that is something of an understatement.

So with Romario Campbell on to replace him, and Daveion Woodhouse coming on at half time for Kimorlee Brissett who also picked up an injury, the team continue to piss into the wind and achieve absolutely nothing. At one point a fan shows his displeasure by throwing a fist sized rock into the middle of a crowded penalty area before a corner, fortunately missing everyone in there but making a definite statement nonetheless.

And with less than five minutes to go comes the killer blow. A Benfica midfielder picks up the ball and about 25 yards from goal he leaps dramatically over John-Ross Edwards' foot and tumbles to the ground right in front of the referee who is clumsily drawn into his act. But you can sit and moan about an unfair free kick all you want, once it has been given you have to take responsibility for dealing with it and if you fail to do that properly then you only have yourself to blame for the end result. And we do fail to deal with it, only managing to clear it as far as another Benfica player who puts a cross in to Carlington Smith, the striker managing to find some space for himself and smashing it in from no more than three yards out.

The final minutes tick by accompanied by the oddly rare sound of unified singing as the jubilant away support chant, "'Fica, 'Fica, 'Fica" on a constant, ecstatic loop. We push desperately with even Dicoy Williams joining the front line to become our sixth forward, but it is, as everything has been this evening, entirely futile and the ref soon puts us out of our misery.

The Tivoli game finished with them beating their old rivals 1-0, which makes our result even worse. In the past few weeks we have smashed Boys' Town at home and scrapped to win in the downpour at Reno—two wins that sum up exactly what every pundit will tell you is the material of champions—but if you cannot do it consistently and you lose stupid games at home to lesser teams in between these wins then they add up to nothing more than mid-table mediocrity. No excuses, no mitigations; performances like that are simply unacceptable for a team looking to win the league.

Sunday 24th October

Arnett Gardens	0 1	Tivoli Gardens
Boys' Town	1 1	Portmore United
HVFC	**0 1**	**Benfica**
Sporting Central	0 1	Reno
Village United	0 1	Humble Lion
Waterhouse	3 1	St. George's

National Premier League

	P	GD	Pts.
1. Waterhouse	9	8	19
2. Tivoli Gardens	8	10	18
3. Boys' Town	9	1	17
4. Portmore United	9	5	16
5. Reno	9	4	14
6. Sporting Central	9	4	13
7 HVFC	**9**	**3**	**13**
8. Benfica	9	-4	11
9. Arnett Gardens	9	-6	9
10. Humble Lions	8	-3	8
11. Village United	9	-10	6
12. St. George's	9	-12	4

CHAPTER THIRTEEN

'They Are Just Like Us'

Last minute goals are football's Hollywood. They are the drama that can give meaning to an hour and a half of nothingness, with their impact lingering on in the league tables. In short, they are the cheap thrill with the deep meaning.

In looking to bounce back from defeat yet again, Harbour View next travel to Clarendon where Sporting Central wait for them. Standing in the car park watching kit, balls, players and staff being packed into the small buses and cars, I speak to the injured Hue about his ankle. He explains that an x-ray on Sunday night had showed that nothing is broken and it is just a sprain, something which he expects to keep him out for no more than a few weeks. His agony the other night hinted that it could have been worse and he is vital to the manoeuvrings of the young team, making this very welcome news indeed.

When everyone is settled it transpires that I am to travel to May Pen in Hue's car, driven by Bobby Cross, a committed long time follower of the club and a Master's player. While sitting in the vehicle waiting to leave, Shawnette Pike, a manager at the club, leans through the window to jokingly pat Hue on the head and ask how his ankle feels. 'Don't walk on it too much without those crutches darling,' she coos when he says it is improving. 'We don't want you crying again do we?'

Awaiting us at the other end of the journey is another example of one of Jamaica's biggest and most inescapable problems. Namely that Sporting's ground at Brancourt, like so many around the league, is a field. In the far corner is a small hut with two changing rooms in it and behind one goal is a set of bleachers, but apart from that it is a field. Having seen similar set-ups at Reno and at Boys' Town, the mind starts to wander back to the debate that raged at the beginning of the season over the future of Jamaican facilities and how best to spread the resources that will go into improving them. A couple of weeks ago David Mais of the SDF dismissed any notion of a conflict between himself and the JFF, claiming 'there's no issue between myself and Captain Burrell. We just have different views on how certain things are done.' And yet the concerns still linger and Jamaica's facilities are still inadequate for a country that likes to place itself in the 'world class' sporting bracket.

It was with this, and other issues, in mind that before travelling to May Pen I had visited the head of both the SDF and Independence Park Limited—the company that runs the national stadium—Major Desmon Brown in his office at the stadium to talk about the problems Jamaica has, touching as well on his thoughts on the future and the importance of sport to the country as a whole.

The SDF is a government owned company that was created in the mid 90s to dish out state funding to all sports nationwide. When the government realised sport was in desperate need of help it placed a tax on the lottery and this is where the Foundation gets its funds, doling them out it as it sees fit. It is telling that despite giving money to over 40 different sports, football receives over a third of all donations, a sum still woefully insufficient, with cricket the second most backed game with just 9%. And as well as not having enough cash, another striking obstacle for the Foundation's operations is that, given the nature of politics in Jamaica, does a government-run agency really serve with the best interests of the whole public at heart?

'It's not exempt from politics,' Brown muses at this suggestion, 'but I wouldn't say it's politicised because sports crosses political barriers, sports is sports. So there may be slants, but I think on the whole sports benefits from the activity of the SDF. To the point where some of the directors who are currently on the board are the same directors from the previous government. About half of the board.'

What little money the SDF has must go a long way. The 40-plus national associations must use their money to ensure efficient administration as well as overseeing the development of their sports. On top of giving to the associations, the Foundation has a separate branch that oversees infrastructure work, building hardcourts and pitches where needed and then working to maintain them. Finally there is the Athlete's Welfare division which offers support for current or former sportsmen who are suffering from injuries or financial troubles. So with just a little money having to be spread so widely, it is little wonder such intense debate arises over how and where it should be spent. I put the Mais-Burrell question to Major Brown, and am surprised to see him side against his chairman.

'Both sides have their pros and cons. In my personal view I support Captain Burrell on this one. I believe that we should focus on a number of regional centres and develop those. But there is a proviso: if you create these regional centres you have to put in management. The reason why the community ones are failing is because of poor management, and a lot of management depends on who is running it and if that person moves or he migrates the whole system falls down. So if you're going to have regional centres you also have to consider putting in professional management to operate them. If we do that, I will support it. But if we're going to do regional centres without that it's going to be a waste of money.'

Having previously listened to Burrell and indeed others have their say on the matter, I then hear Brown give his own slant on the scheme, questioning Burrell's choices of Drax Hall and Clarendon as locations. 'My view is that it would depend on the population density and not just where one wants to put it, because one of the issues is that we need a certain population to support these facilities. So my view would be to choose the location where we have the density and then look at locations there. And I'm not too sure if those two would qualify. Definitely Montego Bay is one, Portmore area is another without a doubt and then you're looking at other areas. But what is important is the population density to support it. You might find a good place somewhere but if to transport people there and to get people there is not convenient, people are not going to go. What is important in locating the stadiums is we need to stop looking at what exists now and look as if we are starting from scratch. Where is the population density that can support this facility, and go there and put it.'

'If you want people to come to a stadium they have to feel safe,' he continued. 'If you want people to come you have to provide an environment, a *family* environment. When you go to the average football field there are people in the corner smoking ganja, who is going to bring their family to that? And the people who are smoking ganja cannot support a football team, and the quicker they realise that they need to go after the family—the mother and father, all of them will buy a jersey, they will buy something and they will spend some money buying hot dogs—those are the people who are going to support your team. Not the ganja smokers! And that is why we have the problem we have.'

'You can't build a stadium now only for sporting events, you cannot. Because it is not sustainable. In England, if you look at the new stadiums they build there, they are built for multi purpose. During the week you have places that can turn into rooms you can rent to companies to have seminars. People have weddings at stadiums in England now. In other words, you have to design a stadium now where sporting activity is one thing. In this company that I have here, entertainment is my biggest income. Church activities are my second biggest, followed by sports. Sports not the main, it's a sporting complex but the majority of my income doesn't come from sport. So if I were part of a design team, sport would only be a part. I would design it so people could have their weddings and events, companies could have seminars there. It would be designed so you could have properly managed entertainment events. Anybody who builds a stadium solely for sport isn't going to make money, not in today's world. And it's a world I live in now.'

It is becoming clear why poorer countries may take so long to make these things happen. When the budget isn't there to allow for any mistakes or second chances and with so many things to consider it becomes almost impossible to form concrete plans out of all the different opinions. It is not an easy task facing the SDF and its planners.

Moving away from facilities, I was keen to get Major Brown's opinion on how and why sport is so important to the country, given the position he holds as the counterpoint between the government and the sporting fraternity. 'It's a socialiser,' is his succinct response. 'It is one of these things that when you have a football match you have people from all different societies playing; it's a social equaliser, I believe, and everybody starts at the same place. I think also, one of the reasons the government and SDF commit so much money, is it allows people to vent off. When you come from work, or you don't have work, and sit down and you don't have anything to do, that just creates all kinds of evil thoughts. And there is something for them to do in sports, it gives them a way to vent their energy. I think it's an important tool in fighting crime. I wish we had the money, for instance, in some of our inner cities to put in some courts with lights, and pay for the lights so people could be on the court playing at night. Because I really believe that sport should be a serious tool in crime reduction.'

'You find that people congregate and have nothing to do. You know the saying: "The Devil finds work for idle hands"—that's part of it. They can't afford to go to places and spend money, they can't go to the movies—they don't have the money to go—so they sit on the street corners and get themselves in trouble. Put them on the field, get them out there! I wish we had more money to spend on that kind of activity.'

I can't help but wonder if similar sentiments could be applied to England. Demographics at football grounds are changing with bloated ticket prices meaning that crowds now are filled with supporters who are on average much older and wealthier than in the past. If teenagers are being isolated from their local clubs, coupled with a reduction in playing fields in recent years as land is sold off for development, are the young men and women of the UK finding themselves increasingly pushed away from football and into other, less welcome, activities? It is an idle musing, but perhaps it holds some water.

What sport gives to a society is often abstract and intangible, and those who do not participate or follow it may often fail to see why it has such importance placed upon it. I ask Major Brown how he might respond to those who question why the Jamaican government is spending its scant resources on something that is, essentially, a hobby. 'Actually that's part of the problem in Jamaica,' he notes with sense of frustration.

'People also see sports as a contribution and are not seeing the benefit. For instance, look at when Bolt won the gold and the relay, look at the coverage that Jamaica got. You think Jamaica could pay for that? We couldn't pay for that kind of PR, so the country benefits.' It is a return to Mr Seaga's Jamaican brand, being continuously refurbished by sporting excellence. 'You have to understand the social implication of sports and what sport can do for our society. The problem is people won't put a dollar figure to the exposure, they won't put a dollar figure to the social implications and what it does so they might say there is no positive return, but there is a lot of positive return. And part of our job is to get people to understand.'

'A study was done and what it shows is that 2% of our GDP is in the sporting industry—people who play the sports, those who make the uniforms, those who sell to the people in sports—so it is an industry by itself. So that is part of our issue here—to convince people that when they make contributions to sports it's not a hole in the ground they're throwing money in, there is a positive return. And the money that is spent now will not be spent later building prisons or on drug rehabilitation or crime prevention programmes—spend the money now, don't let them go down that road.'

With these thoughts in mind I put to him Captain Burrell's words at the league launch and ask how much stock he puts in the 'Tivoli-Arnett effect' of football on Jamaican society. 'I really do believe that is true. I think sport has a serious value in terms of bringing people together. It happens in Iran, Israel—you've got Arabs on the Israel team.' Unlike Dr. Sives he is clearly convinced by the theory, so I push further to find out exactly why he feels this effect occurs.

'It's just a matter of different people realising that we're the same. It happens in some countries: I've travelled the world, I tell you that all Englishmen are wicked. So I see an Englishman and I want to kill him, but when I sit before an Englishman or we play on a team, I realise that you are not any more wicked than we are. So it's a matter of perceptions that have been placed in peoples' heads, until you actually meet him and then you say, "He's not as bad as I thought he was." So it creates an environment for people to recognise that, "They're just like us."'

The only thing really warning me off the idea is that it seems just a little too clichéd, but that doesn't necessarily mean it isn't true. There are evidently other factors involved in the 'peace' between Jamaica's warring communities, but locally the people in the know seem in little doubt that football plays a major role. Before the season is over I'll discuss the idea with someone who perhaps knows best of all, and he will be yet another major advocate of football's reformative power.

By the time we arrive, having had to stop to deal with another breakdown in the convoy, the players are already well into their warm up. The Sporting team is just emerging from their changing room in the far off corner of the field and the solitary stand is gradually starting to fill. 'Blackburn you a pussy!' screams one man in the crowd. 'You gonna take that Bassa?' laughs Bowa, looking up from some one-on-one stretches he is doing with John-Ross, 'That man just called you a vagina!' But Blackburn does the only thing he can do and laughs the insult off while continuing to skip around the cones laid out on the floor. Following some more lengthy drills and stretches they return to the dug out to put on their match shirts and say the traditional pre-game prayer.

The game is a tale of frustration and angst. In the technical area DV cuts an agonised figure, and as decision after decision seems to go against his side he becomes increasingly resigned to not getting what he deserves. When Blackburn is the victim of a wild hack that goes unpunished, the player remonstrates angrily with the ref only to be told off by his now-forlorn manager. 'Bassa just play man,' he hollers to his midfielder. 'Expect that, expect it. It's not gonna change.'

In the break the players gather round the bench, flopping down to the floor and sucking on bottles of Lucozade. By this time DV is on a final warning for his behaviour and offers guidance to his team while the suspicious fourth official circles, carefully watching for any potential misdemeanour. Failing to find one with the management he rounds on me and demands that I leave the bench area. 'You're not on my match card,' he whines officiously when I ask for an explanation. Looking down the line to the home bench I see a clutch of young children sitting there who I am confident are not on the match card either, but not wanting to draw further scrutiny to the Harbour View dugout I do as I am told and dutifully stand up and move the metre or so that is required for me to be in an acceptable spot.

The second half, like the first, sees chances missed and opportunities wasted for 45 minutes. It all comes down to injury time. With the League slipping away Harbour View are unable to drop any more points, we need to score. Then Fagan goes down on the corner of the box when he really could have stayed up and Bryan runs through on goal only to be bundled over by the last defender, our cries for a penalty are rightly waved away by a ref who saw that the ball had been won. With 91 minutes gone Bryan picks up the ball again and is brought down 25 yards from goal. In all honesty it looked a soft decision but we're not complaining and the home side's protests are roundly ignored as Hue and Harvey stand over the set piece. Both take a step or two towards the ball before Hue pulls away, Harvey carrying on and hitting the ball low and straight. It should have gone harmlessly into the wall but as the kick is struck the barrier breaks apart and offers a way through. More than this, a perfect storm of bad defending collides when the ball pings off the leg of a defender who should have blocked it and completely changes trajectory. The keeper has already moved and immediately tries to switch direction but his momentum is too strong, all he can do is turn his head and follow the ball as it trundles past him into the bottom of the net.

The whole bench leap to their feet and the players chase each other round the field in jubilation. With just seconds left on the clock we have taken all the points from despondent Sporting. 'Match done,' Bowa boasts cockily, turning to the stands behind the goal in which we had just scored, 'match done.' A raw sense of injustice always makes a victory that much more pleasing and the primal emotions of the Harbour View contingent finally explode in aggressive, passionate joy. There is still a minute of play to go but as far as anyone is concerned Bowa is right, it is match done.

Afterwards a relieved and significantly calmed DV diplomatically tells the press that it had been 'a very hard game', while the rest of us retire to the car park with the kit bags and cool boxes. As we stand around arranging transport home Clyde and Kavin Bryan distance themselves and are immersed in quiet conversation. It is not public knowledge yet, but winning that free kick would turn out to be Bryan's last act in a Harbour View shirt, for this season at least, and as everyone else tucks in to some food the two of them are discussing the latest on what would be a longer term move to Vietnam. But that's life here. We get back one of our most talented players for a couple of weeks then have to ship him off in return for a bit of cash in order to stay afloat. Jamaican clubs are on the bottom rung of the ladder, always having to bring through young players from nowhere and then push them up to the next level so they can get the funds to develop the next one. Without the means to become the buyer rather than the seller the Jamaican clubs are simply treading water and don't have the scope to break into the powerful forward march that they want to.

But for the moment Bryan's move is not known and all the thoughts in the Harbour View camp are positive ones. We have managed to hit back after our shocking performance against Benfica and even when things were going against us we had kept going and claimed a big win, a big win that keeps us in touch with the leading pack at the top of the table.

Wednesday 27ᵗʰ October

Arnett Gardens	1	1	Humble Lions
Benfica	2	1	Boys' Town
Portmore United	0	1	Waterhouse
Sporting Central	**0**	**1**	**HVFC**
St. George's	0	1	Village United
Tivoli Gardens	2	1	Reno

National Premier League

	P	GD	Pts.
1. Waterhouse	10	9	22
2. Tivoli Gardens	9	11	21
3. Boys' Town	10	0	17
4. HVFC	**10**	**4**	**16**
5. Portmore United	10	4	16
6. Reno	10	3	14
7. Benfica	10	-3	14
8. Sporting Central	10	3	13
9. Arnett Gardens	10	-6	10
10. Humble Lions	9	-3	9
11. Village United	10	-9	9
12. St. George's	10	-13	4

CHAPTER FOURTEEN

He's A Very Naughty Boy

'Who else waan challenge di country boy?!!' Snarls the man in the Benfica kit, smashing his way through the door and leering aggressively at those inside. A terrified Harbour View man leaps into the arms of an equally horrified Boys' Town player, while the Portmore representative simply turns and runs, desperate to get away from the fearsome intruder blasting into their territory.

Published for the first time after round one is a monthly Premier League magazine presented in the *Observer*, a brand new initiative launched by the PLCA with the aim of getting the competition to reach a wider audience. The paper's resident cartoonist was called on to contribute and picked up on Benfica's astonishing run of results in recent weeks as the story of the first round, depicting the vanquished big boys, all victims of the upstarts from St. Ann's, running scared and leaping for cover.

The next side to challenge the country boy is in fact Tivoli, looking every bit the team to beat this season after hammering Waterhouse 5-1 in the End of Round Final at the National Stadium and seemingly scoring goals for fun. All logic suggests that the resurgent newcomers should be firmly put back in their place, but where had logic been while they were recording back-to-back wins over Harbour View and Boys' Town? Sport's magic comes from its stubborn refusal to always walk hand in hand with cold-headed reason.

Conveniently proving that point as we sit in the common room at the Compound are English champions Chelsea, currently in the process of disintegrating against Sunderland live on television. As Nedum Onuoha skips through the home defence to slide the ball past Petr Cech and make it 1-0 to the visitors, the players in the room can barely contain their joy at the misery of Richard Edwards, an ardent Blue, who retains some dignity by graciously conceding that it is a deserved lead. Unfortunately the rest of the game is to go unseen as we have to pack up and move out for the resumption of our own Premier League campaign, and the opening weekend of Round Two has us travelling to May Pen for a rematch with the Humble Lion of Clarendon.

They have struggled so far this season but they replaced coach Christopher Bender with Lenny Hyde Snr. in mid-October and picked up two wins and two draws from their four games since. Tivoli went there a few days ago, to finally play a game that various rainstorms had seen postponed twice since its scheduled date back in September, and could only manage a draw, while we had only beaten them on the League's opening day with that fortuitous John-Ross free kick. Annoyingly, they don't seem to lose anymore.

Humble Lion was started in the 1970s as a Rastafarian-only club and as such the small bleachers of the Effortville Community Centre are painted in the faith's signature gold, red and green colours. Be it a 'religion' *per se* or an ideology or a way of life, the Rastafari movement is an offshoot of Christianity and focuses on a single deity called Jah who takes the form of the Christian Holy Trinity. It is their belief that Emperor Haile Selassie I of Ethiopia, whose pre-regnal title was Ras Tafari, represented the Second Coming of Christ and was therefore a physical manifestation of Jah on earth. Tradition has it that Selassie—known as His Imperial Majesty, or HIM, to Rastas—was part of the Solomanic Dynasty and a direct descendent of the House of David, the bloodline from which Christ sprang in his first incarnation (the semantics of immaculate conception aside), adding weight to the idea of his being Jah in human form.

Clearly not one for humility, Selassie visited Jamaica in 1966, arriving by jet at Norman Manley International to be greeted by a sea of 100,000 drum-beating, ganja-smoking worshippers on the tarmac. National leaders hoped he might dispel the beliefs but were amazed when he completed his trip without at any point taking the chance to tell the masses that he was not the Messiah (nor did his angry mother, for that matter), instead choosing to present Rastafari elders with gold medals embossed with the Ethiopian seal and passing down dictums about liberating the people of Jamaica. It was during this visit that Bob Marley's wife Rita was converted to the faith after claiming to witness the appearance of stigmata on his body as he waved to crowds at the airport.

Despite stereotypical images of Jamaica that are widely held in the western world (derisively known as 'Babylon' to believers), Rastafari has a following that pales in comparison to that of the Christian Church. The census of 2001 stated that less than one per cent of the population followed the faith, although the fact that many Rastas drift between the lines of formal, organised society may distort this figure, with other estimates suggesting it could be as many as five per cent. Either way, it is still very much a minority faith even in its homeland, and this is likely why Humble Lion is no longer an exclusive club.

Unlike the Charlotte Eagles who had visited us earlier in the season, the pressures of competing at the top have stripped religious requirements away from the Lions, but the club does still retain connections to its roots, with many fans swinging large flags proudly bearing the Rasta colours. As well as the bleachers on one touchline, there is also a large concrete clubhouse painted in green, gold and red. Beyond this the whole ground is separated from the outside world by low concrete walls. One enterprising local singer has taken these walls as his canvas to graffiti the address of his MySpace page with impressively thorough regularity.

While the players change, I sit in the away dugout with Jermaine Hue, who had originally hoped to be playing again today, where he explains some sort of complication is causing the healing to take longer than expected. He has been doing some light training without the ball but the physio now says it will be another two difficult weeks before his still-swollen ankle would be up to withstanding the rigours of a match.

As the players who are fit jog out to warm up, a car comes through the gate to the Centre and slowly rolls up the drive around the edge of the pitch and towards the car park. Straddling the open driver-side window, a man holds a large Rasta flag and yells what must be exactly the same insult he yells at every single visiting team to come to Effortvile, 'Bumbaclaat Harbour View!' And yet this lack of novelty does nothing to diminish his passion, delivering the line with such fury that it seems his hatred might just overwhelm him. More than used to hearing such sentiments at away grounds, Hue has other things on his mind as he watches the car slowly wind its way round the pitch. 'How 'im drive?' he muses contemplatively, head cocked to the side as he ponders the logistics of using the pedals while sitting with one foot either side of an open window. The heads of the one or two others loitering around the bench follow the car through a full 180 degrees to watch it pull up behind us in the hope that we might find an answer, but with no one else visibly driving it simply remains one of life's mysteries, a neat snapshot of the admirable lengths of ingenuity a football fan will go to in order to swear at the opposition.

With the players now out warming up, DV wanders over to the bench complaining about the standard of the topsy-turvy pitch and the over-long grass. I ask if the League has a minimum standard to which the clubs have to adhere and the question is laughed away. 'They care more about the stands than the pitch,' Hue tells me. 'The clubs coming into the league have to be able to hold a minimum number of spectators. How much is it coach?' he asks, turning to DV. 'Two thousand', the manager replies without looking away from his players going through a keep-ball drill in front of us. 'Yeah, they all have to be able to fit in two thousand spectators.' I point out that there is no way places like Boys' Town's Collie Smith Drive or even the stands here at Effortville could take that many people and again both men laugh. 'Some clubs are allowed,' they say almost in unison, sharing a cynical tone. Their suggestion is clear and I venture that perhaps Harbour View might not be one of the clubs that would be given such leeway. This time DV does turn around, 'If one lightbulb doesn't work at Harbour View they'll come for us,' he explains. 'And yet other places can have lights like these.' With that he points to the large, wonky poles dotted around the field with a few meek bulbs hanging haphazardly from them.

I gaze upwards, considering the surroundings until the sickening slapping sound of a ball being belted into Oneil Fisher's crotch, forcing him to bend over double to recover his bearings, brings me back to the conversation.

It is not the League itself that makes and breaks these guidelines, I am told, it is the Federation. So does all this stem from the Ricardo Gardener story or is there more to it? 'No, it all just comes from that.' Every club in the world has its psychoses and paranoias that they are unfairly treated, but Harbour View's seem to be more keenly felt. 'There's a lot of politics,' sighs a resigned sounding Hue in conclusion.

The match itself is not a classic. With just over half an hour gone Denzil Watson curls a shot off the inside of our post and in before Christopher Harvey taps in a rebound ten minutes later after Andre Fagan's headed shot from a corner is parried. Half time is enlivened by one of those absurd 'only in Jamaica' moments of comedy which delays the start of the second period. At many grounds the changing rooms are locked during play for security reasons (later in the season the referee's room at Tivoli would be broken into with investigators suspecting the intruder was after a gun belonging to the official, an off-duty policeman) and Effortville is no exception. As the players come out after the break everything appears to be just as it should be, but as the half is about to kick off Carvel's phone rings. On the other end of the line is Jahmali Spence, and he has somehow managed to get himself locked inside the away changing room after everyone else had left. Shouts go down the line and someone is despatched to free our imprisoned striker, and a minute or so later the match resumes with eleven players now lining up at each end. There is little else to speak of and the game ends in a disappointing 1-1 draw. Not a terrible result in isolation but it is now one win in four and the league is slipping away from us.

It could have been far worse though. The wheels came spectacularly off the Benfica country boys' drive to upset the establishment and after some very public off-field problems they went down 5-0 at the Edward Seaga Complex. Between Rounds the club which had been flying so high descended into chaos as club members attempted a *coup d'état* against chairman Iyrone Rose, feeling aggrieved at the way he had recently dismissed two players, and set up their own interim board to assume control. Rose treated this with absolute disdain and asserted that he was very much still the man in charge of the club's administration, but it all meant the team went into Round Two not knowing up from down. Following their hammering at Tivoli the conflict went to arbitration where the JFF adjudicated they would only recognise Rose as the chairman at the club, causing him to sneer: 'I don't know where they got the idea from that they could take over a private club. We are not only the management at Benfica, we are the owners. I don't know where they got that idea from.' He went on to assure fans that 'everything is back to normal'. Only it wasn't. I am sure there is more to the story than anyone on the outside will ever know, as well as there being crippling financial troubles, but what is clear is that the club never really recovered.

Once things start to go wrong on the administrative side of a club the playing side almost always follows, and what better demonstration of that than the day's other big losers. Chelsea's game with Sunderland ended in an astonishing 3-0 home defeat and it comes just days after the bizarre and ugly sacking of assistant manager Ray Wilkins by their madcap owner Roman Abramovich. Over the next few months they join Benfica in a seemingly unstoppable freefall as both sides begin losing games left, right and centre, sliding dramatically down their respective leagues as they go. As I watch them go, safe from my vantage points of Arsenal and Harbour View support, I count my blessings for the stability of those two teams. In an age of super-rich owners waltzing in and out of clubs on a whim, one should never underestimate the value of a management structure that is solid and secure.

On arriving at the Compound a week later for our next game the man at the top of that management structure is shaken. 'We lost, Hugo,' is about all Carvel can muster as we greet each other before kick off, clearly still struggling to come to terms with Arsenal's first home defeat to Tottenham in 17 years the previous day. So much for stability. And Carvel is certainly not alone. I had just finished speaking to Deighton Simpson, a policeman who helps with security at the club and another Gooner, who had been glumly outlining a theory of his that whenever Arsenal lose in England or McLaren do badly in the Formula One, Harbour View invariably follow suit. Fortunately the F1 season had finished last week giving Hamilton, Button et al. no opportunity to dump their poor luck down onto us this weekend, but following yesterday's game at the Emirates the portents are still not good.

I take my seat at the press bench without letting Deighton's theory get me down. Today's opponents are bottom dwellers George's who have amassed a grand total of eight points from the twelve games so far this season, running up a goal difference of minus twelve in the process.

'Clyde your squad's getting younger, soon they'll need signed permission slips from their parents to play,' jokes Paul Hibbert, a former player and manager of the team and a die-hard Harbour View fan, a jest which Carvel refutes by responding wryly, 'Well I usually play at left back.' It is indeed a very young squad and Harbour View had been singled out for praise for bringing through young players, the downside to that though is the frustrating levels of inconsistency we had to deal with in Round One.

Goals from Romario Campbell and Andre Fagan prove wrong Deighton's theory today. The two-nil win should have been more comprehensive though, and afterwards DV sums up what everyone else is thinking as he tells a journalist, 'It is the goal that continues to plague us and it is our greatest difficulty'. While we really should have done so by more, we had at least won.

For me though it is time for a temporary farewell to Harbour View and it had been a solid enough way to part. Now my attention is going international, and tomorrow morning I will be shipping out of Jamaica to join the Reggae Boyz as they set out to defend their Caribbean Cup.

Sunday 31st October Sunday 14th November Sunday 21st November

Arnett Gardens 0 0 St. George's	Tivoli Gardens 5 0 Benfica	Reno 0 0 Arnett Gardens
Benfica 3 2 Reno	St. George's 1 0 Boys' Town	Boys' Town 2 1 Humble Lion
Boys' Town 1 0 Sporting	**Humble Lions 1 1 HVFC**	Village United 1 1 Portmore
Humble Lions 1 2 Waterhouse	Portmore 2 1 Reno	**HVFC 2 0 St. George's**
Tivoli Gardens 2 2 Portmore	Waterhouse 0 1 Sporting	Sporting 1 2 Tivoli Gardens
Village United 2 0 HVFC	Arnett Gardens 1 0 Village United	Benfica 0 0 Waterhouse

National Premier League

	P	GD	Pts.
1. Tivoli Gardens	13	17	29
2. Waterhouse	13	9	26
3. Boys' Town	13	1	23
4. Portmore United	13	5	21
5. HVFC	**13**	**4**	**20**
6. Benfica	13	-7	18
7. Sporting Central	13	2	16
8. Reno	13	1	15
9. Arnett Gardens	13	-5	15
10. Village United	13	-8	13
11. Humble Lion	13	-5	12
12. St. George's	13	-14	8

*Coach DV Hayles faces the media after the 1-1 draw
with Humble Lion at Effortville.*

CHAPTER FIFTEEN

The European Caribbean

My experience of the Reggae Boyz has so far been pretty underwhelming. Two home friendlies, neither of which did much to raise the heart rate, are the sum total of all that the national team has shown me, and they had offered precious little more on the occasions on which they had played abroad. But those fixtures were in preparation for the two weeks which now loom ahead; the Caribbean Cup has arrived, and Theodore Whitmore has to show that the defending champions can fashion a winning team from the merry-go-round of experiments that has been spinning for the past few months.

Since the second of October, 23 teams have been playing over two qualifying rounds, each vying for one of eight spots in the final tournament. As the winners in 2008, Jamaica spent the time sitting back and watching it all happen knowing that they had a free passage to the last eight, a luxury also afforded to the tournament's hosts. And it is the identity of those hosts that gives these particular finals of the Caribbean Cup some fairly unusual surroundings, for, bizarrely, they are to be held within the polished, efficient confines of the European Union. It might be separated from Paris by a few thousand miles of sea, but the island of Martinique is in fact as much a part of France as Brittany or Alsace and its inhabitants spend Euros, travel under French passports and stand to *La Marseillaise*. And now they are to host the biggest event in Caribbean football.

The competition itself began in 1989 and ever since it has been so roundly dominated by Trinidad and Jamaica that only two of the tournament's 15 editions have been won by anybody else: Martinique themselves in 1993 and Haiti in 2007. And it hasn't always been smooth sailing. In 1990 play was suspended when the Muslim organisation

Jamaat al Muslimeen attempted a *coup d'état* in the host nation of Trinidad, holding the Prime Minister and other MPs hostage at gun point for six straight days and tipping the streets of Port of Spain into chaos and anarchy. After sitting through that delay, the tournament was then abandoned completely when Tropical Storm Andrew forced a number of games to be cancelled. A little more stability wouldn't go amiss two decades later in Martinique.

But while Martinique is in the political boundaries of the EU it is unfortunately not in the geographical boundaries of Europe, and as such getting to the island becomes a long, tiring and expensive process. At home it is possible to buy a plane ticket for less than you would spend on a cheap pub meal and find yourself on the other side of the continent a couple of hours later. Not so in the Caribbean where a cross-regional flight costs more than a return to Heathrow and involves several stops of varying lengths along the way.

A day short of three months after I had arrived here, I am again surrounded by the white and glass curves of Kingston's Norman Manley International Airport and waiting to board Caribbean Airways flight BW417 to Trinidad. Businessmen queue at the gate and adopt a lads-on-tour attitude as they are unclipped from the leash of home for a couple of weeks. As the finale to some joke or other one strolls with bravado from the middle of the queue to volunteer his carry-on bag to be searched by a stern-looking female official while his two friends watch, turning to each other and giggling at his daring. A man I don't recognise in a Harbour View shirt meanders thoughtfully up and down the outside, like someone trying to decide where to place the sofa in his new flat, before eventually settling on a spot and ducking into the line.

Like a bus travelling through town, the flight stops here and there to pick people up and drop them off throughout its journey, setting down in St. Maarten and offloading me in Barbados before undertaking its final leg to Port of Spain. After already spending a day travelling I step off the jet into the warm Bajan evening with twelve hours to kill until the small regional airline Liat will be taking me to my final destination early the next morning, and so I eagerly go in search of my accommodation for the night: the departures terminal. There is no checking in and going through to the departure lounge with my flight still so far away, so having to concoct a contribution to the next month's PLCA magazine I buy a pizza and settle in to do some work as an international airport slowly shuts down around me.

By midnight my eyes are starting to droop and my company is little more than the occasional drifting passenger and a few night workers yelling instructions or snippets of gossip to each other across the hollow space, their shouts seeming to bounce around before evaporating into the empty night. This part of the airport sits beneath a canopy roof and has no exterior wall which allowed a cooling breeze to drift through the thick tropical air. Abandoning work, I settle myself onto a concrete bench, scruffily attempting to produce a makeshift pillow from a folded up hoodie, and try vainly to get a couple of hours sleep before life returns again with sunrise.

At some point in the small hours a dreadlocked French Canadian named Benoît arrives nearby. He is on his way to Dominica where he plans to undertake a grand tax dodging scheme that involves going to Guadeloupe, buying a small twin-hulled boat and sailing it back across the open ocean so he can start a snorkelling business on the cheap. Having as little success as me in sleeping away the dead time, he gives up and instead tells me his bizarre, international life story. As he shows me his bags full of electronic guitar-gadgetry, which had apparently thrown the security men at Miami airport into some sort of neurotic tailspin, I suddenly feel very aware of how conventional and 'nine-to-five' I am by comparison. Following football's travelling show brings you into contact with all sorts.

Eventually the sun begins to rise, the ornamental fountains spring back into life and footsteps once again shuffle over the hard floors. After a decidedly uncomfortable night I am relieved to finally be able to trudge up the steps and onto the small propeller plane bound for Martinique. This being the Caribbean though, we have to make one more stop in St. Lucia on the way. The plane lands and taxies to its resting stop where it unloads a large proportion of its passengers before filling the vacated seats with fresh travellers. And looking out of the window at these newcomers, I find myself watching a group of young men striding across the tarmac wearing exactly the same black and white travelling kit as Harbour View. At the front, I feel sure, is Romario Campbell and my sleep deprived brain is suddenly scrambling for reasons as to why on earth he would be in St. Lucia getting onto an aeroplane. It takes a few more of them before I realise the badges on their chest are not those of Harbour View at all, and that actually joining us for the short flight to Fort-De-France is in fact a very confident Trinidad & Tobago squad. They had left Port of Spain earlier that morning to transfer here and now dotted themselves around the spare seats, shouting jokes between one another cloaked indecipherably in their own island's particular twisted form of English.

It is hard to be sure of the etiquette of asking an international footballer who he is. Does he expect everyone to know? Will you come across as both rude and boorish? Or do they rarely get recognised anyway, especially by foreigners? Bound by this confusion, I choose to remain in ignorance over the precise identity of the player who has dropped into the seat next to mine and instead I ask whether or not he feels they will win the tournament. 'Yes', he sneers, as though amazed at my stupidity for even thinking any alternative outcome a possibility, and clearly appalled at my ignorance he turns away to talk to the coach across the aisle instead.

His confidence is understandable: since the competition's inception, eight of the fifteen Cups have been won by this lot and they have only failed to reach the final on three occasions. And on top of that they go into this year's tournament as comfortably the highest ranked team in the region. Despite Jamaica being defending champions. Trinidad are undoubtedly favourites.

As the plane taxies round the runway the stewardess announces that it will be just a fifteen minute journey until we land in Martinique. 'Fifteen minutes?' the player beside me exclaims. 'Fifteen minutes?' He looks to the coach for confirmation before turning to me, apparently prepared to forgive my earlier insolence in return for me clarifying whether or not we really were going to bother with such a short trip, as though it would make much more sense to just swim there instead. 'Fifteen minutes? One-five?' Well, that's what she said.

He is shaken out of his bewilderment by a sharp acceleration for take-off at which he flings his hands down to his sides and clings to the arm-rests. He gives the impression of not being stunningly comfortable with flying, and when he begins muttering nervously to himself mid-flight at the slightest hint of turbulence I decide to distract him by pressing further about his side's chances, in particular whether or not there is any other team he feels could possibly stand a chance? 'Well . . . Jamaica,' he says magnanimously, succumbing to the widely-held belief that this tournament is little more than just another contest between those two old rivals. 'And Cuba too I guess.'

That was an interesting addition. To me the Cubans are an entirely unknown quantity. Indeed, it is a country whose sporting activities are so dominated by baseball that one never really considers it a footballing entity at all. They have been Caribbean Cup runners up three times without ever winning it and go into the tournament sitting just behind Cyprus, and a remarkable 57 places behind those African giants Gabon, in FIFA's world rankings. But they must be doing something right because here they are being singled out by their rivals as one of the teams to beat. And in a convenient twist, the tournament's opening game will shed some light on exactly who is capable of what: a few days later it's going to be Trinidad and Cuba getting the thing underway.

It says a lot about the history of this region that in just 24 hours I had been in three different countries whose reigning monarch is the Queen of England and also technically touched down in the Netherlands before finally arriving in France. That there is not a single country in the Americas that officially speaks its 'own' language powerfully demonstrates the ruthless way the Europeans casually divvied up the New World between themselves, and when you spend time here it is easy to understand why the early settlers liked what they saw.

Like everywhere else in the Caribbean, Martinique is a very nice place to be. In terms of landscape it has many similarities with Jamaica; a hilly, mountainous centre covered in thick, green vegetation sweeping down to beaches tipped with white sand and turquoise seas. The only major physical difference is that at just 436 square miles it is only around a tenth of the size. But where it really veers away is the point at which nature's influence stops and man's takes over. Understandably given its status, Martinique is considerably more wealthy than Jamaica and effectively allows visitors to enjoy all the creature comforts of 'the Western world' while basking on palm fringed beaches under the Caribbean sun. Anyone familiar with the land on the other side of the Channel will recognise the Carrefour and Auchan hypermarkets scattered around the landscape and the typically European brands within them. The architecture of its small towns is uniquely French with whitewashed buildings and small church steeples rising above lazy town squares. It is, for a European wandering the Caribbean, a home a long way from home. I stayed near a small town called Les Trois-Îlets, the road into which faces you with the picturesque town ahead while flanking you with the greenery of steeply rising hills on your left and on your right a drop down into a broad, blue bay. In this glinting enclave the three islets from whom the town gets its name lift their tree-covered heads out of the sparkling Caribbean Sea.

But, beautiful as the island is, you might by now be wondering just how it comes to be that what is actually a region of France can even have its own international football team in the first place? Well the short answer is it doesn't, not really. FIFA statutes stipulate that to gain membership into the organisation, a 'country' must be 'an independent state recognised by the international community'—raising the awkward question of how FIFA has 208 members when the UN agrees that only 193 such states exist, but that is another matter—and these are criteria that Martinique clearly fails to meet. So, like the tournament's other French overseas department Guadeloupe, Martinique is not a member of the global governing body and therefore cannot enter a team into any of its competitions, including the World Cup. CONCACAF and the CFU however, are much more accommodating and gladly welcome these drifting outcasts into their houses on the condition that no player who has represented France in the last five years dons the local shirt in any of their competitions. So, accepted as a country by the CFU but not the UN, Martinique floats happily around the twilight zone that sits between the real world and the football world, and for ten days the rest of the Caribbean would be coming to keep them company.

So I have got myself here. I also have somewhere to stay. I have come prepared. But that's not all that needs sorting, and the checklist is looking discouragingly unchecked so close to the start of the tournament. Press accreditation? No. Transport? Nope. Rudimentary knowledge of what is happening and when? Well, there is a vague article on *Wikipedia* that kind of gives a fixture list, albeit one where the kick off times are wrong. It seems there is work to be done.

A couple of weeks before I got here, the JFF had put me in contact with Maurice Victoire at the CFU. This is the man to know, I was told, and upon e-mailing him he had provided me with his phone number and told me to ring him as soon as I got to the island, so this is what I now seek to do. My isolated hotel exists in a signal black hole outside the omniscient reach of Digicel so I walk down a hill to the nearest village where I can just about muster up a few bars to make the call. Invalid number. I try a few more times but to no avail, so I return to my hotel and e-mail him again. The next day he replies repeating the same number and giving me another one to try as well, just in case. Again neither work, and I have to wonder whether the communication shouldn't be slightly more competent at a tournament sponsored by the region's biggest mobile phone network. Eventually though, standing in an unlikely reception hot spot on a muddy jungle track near my hotel and having tried countless combinations of international dialling codes with various 0s and +s at the beginning, I finally connect to Monsieur Victoire.

'No, I don't have it,' he abruptly informs me. Well why am I speaking to you? Having shot me down he then goes hurriedly on to dismiss me with the sort of disdainful arrogance that can only truly be pulled off by a man with a thick French accent. 'I explained all this to you before. You need to speak to the person at Digicel on the 100 106 number because they sort it out.' Well actually Maurice you didn't explain that to me at all, and besides, that number doesn't work. He insists the number is right and, unable to get this contemptible Englishman off the phone quickly enough, he leaves me to it.

So my initial problem is not even close to being solved, and after a few more failed attempts I e-mail him one more time to explain that as it is now the day before the tournament kicks off it would be nice to get this all sorted, hoping he could clarify the exact number I need to ring and who will be on the other end of the line when I do so. He replies the next morning, the day the tournament begins, with a single sentence: 'Your accreditation was picked up by a colleague at the hotel already.'

Now then, this is something of a twist. Considering that firstly I have no colleagues and secondly I am not staying at the same hotel as the rest of the press it seems to raise more questions than it answers. I sense, though, that I have exhausted all lines of enquiry with Maurice, so thank him for his help and look at other avenues.

The only 'colleague' I can think of is Ian Burnett, Sports Editor of the *Observer* who I worked with on the PLCA magazine and had contacted a day or two earlier to see if he could shed any light on the situation. I e-mail him again and get no reply. It is now a matter of hours until the competition kicks off, I am getting nowhere and have no more cards to play other than to simply hope Ian can get back to me with a solution. Trying to organise your life in the Caribbean can be a frustrating business, but to expect Teutonic levels of efficiency and succumb to tearing your hair out at anything less is a path to insanity and little else. With nothing more at my disposal I therefore adopt the 'It'll-get-sorted' attitude typical of the locals, shut down my computer and disappear off to the beach. When in Rome.

Onto the next item on that checklist, then. Unexpectedly large flight and hotel bills have seen to it that my budget is stretching to breaking point and is rapidly becoming one problem I can't just ignore. But at least I have been assured by various websites that the country's efficient French public transport system would ship me around easily and, most importantly, cheaply. What the websites did not tell me though is that this wonderful system shuts down at six thirty in the evening. And that is the service to and from the capital, Fort-De-France; if I want to catch a bus to Rivière-Pilote, the other host town which sits among the hills on the south coast, I would have to be home a full two hours earlier than that. With two games each evening, held one after the other at the same venue, it means that if I want to get to them on public transport I might, if I really squeezed my time, be able to catch the opening quarter of an hour of the first game each night in the capital. As for the Rivière-Pilote fixtures, well with a little luck I could possibly catch a fleeting glimpse of the warm up before I have to make my way home again. There is yet another unavoidable financial bullet to be bitten, and with gritted teeth I find the cheapest car I can and hire it for the duration of the Cup: the pride of the Romanian automotive industry and that *Top Gear* favourite, a small silver Dacia Sandero.

It is into this that I climb, unaccredited and largely uninformed about the entire competition, to drive the forty five minutes or so into Fort-De-France where Trinidad, Cuba, Guyana and Martinique are waiting at the Stade Pierre-Aliker. Finally, after all the messing about, it is time for some football.

Or at least it will be, when I get there. Cruising unknown roads and with sat-nav nothing more than a hopeful pipe dream, I miss the unmarked exit to the stadium on the outskirts and follow the traffic along the motorway into the city. Before long I am in a multi-story car park in the centre of town waving a battered old tourist map at a very patient attendant trying to explain to me, in a compromise between my rusty French and his rusty English, how I should get myself to the ground. By the time I drive back out, find it, park, buy myself a ticket and settle onto the bleachers I am late and the opening game has already kicked off. Not that you would really know it looking around the ground.

Weekend philosophers have long mused over the question of whether a falling tree makes a sound when there is nobody around to hear it. Along similar lines, an international football match seems to become almost meaningless when there is no one there to see it. The players are representatives of their countries, the achievements they are chasing become achievements of their people, but if none of those people are around to share it the game becomes little more than a bunch of blokes having a kickabout in a deserted bowl and it must be sorely tempting to let the hollowness of it all overwhelm you and just pack up and go home. Of course, there are a few spectators scattered around the 16,000 capacity stands tonight, but it is so quiet that the main noise is coming from the chirruping of swooping birds above and the constant throb of crickets from outside the walls. The only human sounds are snatches of conversation that drift up the stairwells from the mouths of stewards below and out into the stadium bowl.

Like Independence Park, the pitch at the Pierre-Aliker is also surrounded by a running track. There are two large covered grandstands along either touchline with the ubiquitous concrete bleachers occupying the corners. Neither end contains seating but one does hold a disused scoreboard, so decrepit that panels are falling out of it, that is adorned by the sort of white-on-black Omega chronograph clock that graced so many stadia of the 1980s, a feature that stopped working at twenty past five on some long forgotten afternoon. On the pitch a Cuban curls in a free kick that bounces through a crowded area and hops untouched over the bar, eliciting the first signs of life from the meagre audience.

I lean back against the concrete behind me to enjoy the gentle breeze cooling the stadium. So far it is that sort of evening. Cuba are looking a much more organised and coherent side than the relatively hit-and-hope Trinidad lot and it isn't long before something comes of their superiority. A tricky run by the winger leads to him beating two defenders on the byline and pulling the ball back to his captain Jamie Colomé waiting on the edge of the area to strike it with the outside of his left boot, sending it crashing off the post and in. Minutes later their left back airily strings together some stepovers and skips round the Trinidad defender before lifting a cross into the box, looking about as taxed as a man playing against the under 16s on the training pitch. All too easy.

A large black moth bobs and weaves loosely through the air before setting itself down on the white metal barrier at the bottom of the bleachers. In the far grandstand one man bangs a set of clappers together, forlornly trying to raise some sort of atmosphere.

At least I'm not missing a huge amount. With the Premier League carrying on back home Harbour View squandered an opportunity to catch up on a defeated Tivoli with a lame 0-0 draw against Arnett at the Anthony Spaulding Complex. Excitement, it seems, is hard to come by anywhere at the moment.

Half time comes and goes and the ground is gradually filling up as the locals arrive in anticipation of the hosts' opener to follow. Trinidad are slightly improved but it is still Castro's boys making the best of things, putting together one particularly impressive move that ends with a goal being disallowed for offside. The swelling crowd is finally giving the occasion some feeling, and suddenly this is fuel-injected by a large band striking up in the middle of the far grandstand. The sound of drums engulf the stadium, their powerful bass tumbling through the percussive rhythm like boulders crashing down a mountain and out of nowhere a party has landed which seems to push the football to the side and take over whole occasion. The uniform red of the performers suggests that either they are supplied by the sponsors or Trinidad's Soca Warriors are accompanied by the most professional and orchestrated supporters' band in the world. I can't be sure, but either way they certainly knock a trumpeted rendition of *The Great Escape* into a cocked hat.

With a new tension in the air the Cuban left back abandons stepovers and chooses to demonstrate the darker side to his game instead, flinging himself two-footed into a challenge so brutal that both players involved are left writhing on the turf and needing to be stretchered off. It is a car crash of a tackle and as the inundated medics scoop up the casualties and carry them away the twenty remaining players contest one of the most deserved free-kicks you will ever see, one which turns out to be a fairly sorry anti-climax that loops harmlessly out for a goal kick.

Trinidad are now pushing hard for the equaliser, all too aware of the damage a single defeat can do in a group round of just three games, and they are a much improved outfit on the one that had played the first half. But as is so often the way in situations like this, the counter-attacking Cubans break away, hitting them in the spaces they have left open to score another and effectively seal the match. I find it hard not to be slightly amused. The final whistle is not far behind their second goal and it brings to an end a game that did little to reinforce the already questionable reputation of FIFA's ranking system. More significantly though, it also proved that the prediction of the Trinidad player on the plane was a lot more accurate than he would have liked. There is a third guest at this party, and if Trinidad and Jamaica were previously looking at the first nine days as nothing more than a procession to the Final they are in for a shock.

Following that the game between the hosts and Grenada produces a drab 1-1 draw that leaves both sides struggling in the group table. As the final whistle blows on a fairly anti-climactic opening night I unsuccessfully make to beat the rush from the noticeably busier stadium by nipping down the stairs and dashing back to the Dacia. I fail, and twenty five minutes later I am still stuck in the choking gridlock that stifles the car park.

It is at this point, competing fiercely with cars coming from at least two different directions for any space that opens up ahead, that I perform a brief summation of the Caribbean Cup so far in my head. One day into the tournament and I have already blown my budget; I have failed to get hold of my accreditation; I have got myself lost; I have little idea of where I am supposed to go and at what times I am supposed to go there and, to round it all off, at some point during that evening someone on the bleachers had helped themselves to my camera.

Bienvenue Hugo, *au Martinique.* You're off to a flyer.

Wednesday 24ᵗʰ November

Portmore United	3 0	Benfica
Tivoli Gardens	0 2	Boys' Town
Arnett Gardens	**0 0**	**HVFC**
Humble Lion	1 1	Reno
St George's	0 1	Sporting Central
Waterhouse	2 2	Village United

National Premier League

	P	GD	Pts
1. Tivoli Gardens	14	15	29
2. Waterhouse	14	9	27
3. Boys' Town	14	3	26
4. Portmore United	14	8	24
5. HVFC	**14**	**4**	**21**
6. Sporting Central	14	3	19
7. Benfica	14	-10	18
8. Reno	14	1	16
9. Arnett Gardens	14	-5	16
10. Village United	14	-8	14
11. Humble Lion	14	-5	13
12. St. George's	14	-15	8

CHAPTER SIXTEEN

Showdown In Sainte-Luce

It is a miserable day that greets the arrival of the defending champions to the tournament. From morning the tiny island is blanketed by a slate grey sky that tips rain down upon it, while winds sweep down from the mountains and whip fiercely through the palm trees.

During a brief and rare respite from this tumult I arrive at the ground in Rivière-Pilote, fishing into my wallet and once again entering as an unaccredited, paying customer. It is a much smaller ground than the Pierre Aliker with a capacity of just 3,000 people, all of whom are seated in one large grandstand along the touchline opposite the entrance. A wide path carries you there below a tall metal fence which separates you from the running track wrapping itself around yet another pitch.

I arrive still hopelessly uninformed and as I wander along the path the evening's first game between Guadeloupe and Guyana is already half an hour in. With a bit of luck though, that would soon change. Walking up the broad steps into the stand I know that somewhere in this structure sit the Jamaican press contingent and with them, if Maurice Victoire was right, my accreditation. I am within touching distance of finally putting that whole mess behind me.

I amble around the stand searching inside and out for any sign of the press box. Having no luck I approach a man wearing a 'Rivière-Pilote 2010' t-shirt and hope for the best. He wants no proof of identity of any kind, he simply asks if I am with the media myself and upon a positive answer proceeds to guide me to a dimly lit stairwell. At the top of this I find myself entering into a bright, cosy hall where the great, the good and the journalists are all rubbing shoulders, helping themselves to complementary drinks and canapés as they do so. Now all I have to do is find a familiar face.

As I glance around, trying to get my bearings, I turn to see that the very person I am looking for had just followed me up the stairs, Ian Burnett. 'Ah!' he exclaims as he sees me, 'I was just, *just,* downstairs getting your pass. I only saw your e-mails when we got here and set up.' He holds out his hand to reveal a red laminated press pass. Finally, I've got that damned card. He takes me to the small press box, a room of a few metres squared that is positioned above the half way line at the back of the stand, to introduce me around. With him in the Jamaican delegation are Audley Boyd of the *Gleaner,* brother of former national player Walter, and Nicholas Evans, a sports reporter for the radio station *Irie FM.* Some Irish Digicel representatives named Kieran and Gillian dash in and out, barking orders to various dogsbodies and frantically ensuring the tournament runs smoothly.

As I enter nobody seems remotely concerned with the football and instead all are in the midst of trying to solve a technical breakdown involving failing extension leads that leaves the array of laptops along the desk unpowered. Digicel Kieran, burdened with having to update the company's website, is the only one affording even a token glance out to the pitch. Below us a Guyanese forward is hauled down by the last Guadeloupe defender as he bursts into the box. It looked a certain red card but the defender is offered a lifeline by the ref who has tweaked a calf muscle as the play had unfurled. Ingeniously, the defender sees his chance to curry some favour, running to the stricken official and massaging his injury, and in doing so absurdly managing to avoid any further punishment.

'He scored one from much further out in Grenada,' Kieran recalls through a thick Irish twang as Guadeloupe's Jean Luc Lamboude lines up the free-kick. 'Really smashed it in. He's got one hell of a thump on him.' This time the thump goes glaringly off target and Kieran's attention again returns to the computer dramas. 'If you're going to plug it in then really *plug* it in, don't do it half-arsed.' he urges as Ian tries to ram the plug into the socket. Brawn eventually wins out over brain and with one last solid shove crisis is averted and the laptops at the far end of the desk are once again running on full power. Relief sweeps the press box.

With the clock ticking down on the opening fixture of Group I, Guadeloupe hit home a corner to double the advantage they had earned earlier in the half only to have it ruled out for offside. Considering Guyana had been defending the set-piece with a man on the line it seemed an unlikely decision and understandably the players bawl their protests to the ref. One runs to the man strolling nonchalantly away from the post, just an exaggerated whistle away from being the caricature of innocence, and points him out furiously to the official. This causes the suddenly offended defender to break character and shove him firmly in the chest. The referee is entirely disinterested, waving away their horseplay and ordering the game to continue. Three minutes later Guyana break through the Guadeloupe defence and equalise with less than five minutes to go. Final score 1-1. Life's a bitch, especially when it's played out on a football pitch.

So now almost everyone has made an appearance in the tournament, and the last teams to enter the fray are the Reggae Boyz and Antigua & Barbuda. Halfway through the warm ups Richard Edwards, Harbour View's sole representative in the squad, had been dragged away from the subs and sent off on his own routine to 'catch up' with the starters, suggesting a last minute change of plan in the Jamaica camp. Sure enough, with a couple of minutes to go until kick off Digicel Gillian arrives breathlessly into the press box to announce the news. 'That's not the right team,' she pants in reference to the team sheets we had been handed a few minutes earlier. 'There's been a change.' She hands round new sheets showing Edwards' name now ticked as a starter and Omar Cummings crossed out, removed as a precaution after tweaking a quad muscle during the warm up.

In the early minutes a cutting through ball from Keammar Daley releases Dane Richards just inside their half when the linesman raises his flag, calling him offside when he had looked at least a metre on. Cries of disgust go up from our end of the desk, occupied by the three Jamaicans and myself, while a lone Antiguan at the far end mockingly lets out an exaggerated sigh, as though personally offended by just how far beyond the last defender Richards had strayed. A good-humoured argument is ended by Digicel Kieran, caught in the middle and hamming up his role as mediator with arms outstretched towards either party: 'Come on lads, we'll have no fighting in the press box.'

But it isn't long until Richards is set free without the handbrake of the flag being pulled. He chases the ball into the area to cut it back from the by-line where players are queueing up in gaping acres of space around the six yard box to finish it off. It is Luton Shelton who reaches it first and he slots it neatly underneath the keeper. Jamaica's defence of their trophy is up and running.

A one goal lead is not enough to satisfy the hunger of the onlookers and as a few more chances come and go the cynicism of the journalists grows. 'We need to put them out of their misery early,' announces Audley while swigging from a bottle of complimentary beer, 'we want three or four.' In the Antigua goal Keita Decastro is doing his best to help them get there, regularly managing to slice the ball behind himself when dealing with back passes rather than despatching them far upfield, while the defenders in front of him are doing equally little to demonstrate any kind of inclination to mark, tackle or really disrupt the Jamaican attacks in any way whatsoever. As a result it is soon two-nil, with Daley picking the ball up from deep and playing through Shelton who is charging in from the left wing. The pass is exactly where it needs to be as the forward collects it, carries it past the last defender in the box and smashes it over the keeper's head for his, and Jamaica's, second.

And just a few minutes later Audley has the three he wanted. Richards makes a run past the last defender and the perfect through ball sets him free, sweeping across the grass in a beautiful arc that cuts the centre-back completely out of the play and arrives effortlessly into the striker's stride. High on confidence, he carries it forward just a few paces and slips it past the out-rushing keeper from the edge of the area. Game, set and match Jamaica.

With the action frantic the camaraderie of the press box is in full swing as people try to piece together the details of what had happened.

'Who made the pass?'

'I don't know, I was writing something down.'

'Did anyone see who passed it?'

'I think it was Daley.'

'What was the pass like for Richards' goal? Was it a long ball over the top? We'll say it was a long ball over the top.' Digicel Kieran, needing immediate answers for the website, is leaning towards Audley and whispering his suggestion like a naughty schoolboy corroborating a cover story with the rest of his gang. He is grateful to be corrected. Between us we seem to have caught enough glimpses of the move to be able to piece together an accurate picture, and by the half time whistle everyone is satisfied they can recount the goal to the masses in a way that closely resembles reality. With live TV across the entire Caribbean, any incidents of misreporting would be very publicly picked up on.

Early in the second half Antigua are gifted one back but continuously keeping them busy at their own end is Richards and, just as he had been in the friendly against Trinidad a month or so earlier, he is electric. With an hour gone he picks up the ball just inside their half he sets off on his own little Maradona moment, powering through the yards and jinking this way and that between a gauntlet of four or five defenders. One man gone, and another, and another. Just a matter of seconds after receiving the pass he arrives at the edge the six yard box where he squeezes on the trigger and fires.

But fires over.

Quite how he had missed the target when it was easier to hit nobody is sure, but it seems almost to wrong football itself that such a run should go unrewarded. Those wonderful few seconds will now just pass through our short term memories and disappear forever when by rights they should have been embalmed in the splendour of a truly great goal. All the same, such form is undeniable encouragement for the games to come.

The Antiguans go on to produce a few more chances but Jamaica have put down the shutters and see out the game comfortably. The minutes simply tick by to a very satisfying opening scoreline of 3-1. The second half had not been good and the team seemed to have allowed themselves a little complacency but nonetheless, it is a markedly better start than certain others had made.

Yes, he had said to me. And with such confidence too. Yes of course they were going to win it. Maybe one or two others could challenge but really the only foreseeable outcome would be Jack Warner handing the trophy to his own team and them all riding the merry charabanc home to Port of Spain together while everyone else, dizzied and dazed in defeat, miserably watched them into the sunset.

But reality is rarely so forgiving as fantasy and after just two games Trinidad & Tobago are already packing their bags, for following their humbling defeat to Cuba they went down again to Grenada and find themselves in the humiliating position of being the first side dumped out of the tournament. In Group H's other match the Cubans beat Martinique to raise an interesting conundrum for the final game: with fixtures every other day and qualification now assured it would make sense for them to rotate the squad and take the opportunity to rest key players ahead of the semi-final, but Grenada only need a point to progress at the expense of the hosts and allowing them an easy ride would not be a great PR stunt to pull in front of the locals.

But that is their problem to worry about. In the Jamaica camp there are far more troubling issues boiling over that threaten to have us going home early too.

When I arrive at the Stade Rivière-Pilote the Antigua—Guyana game is already well underway and the bored-looking Jamaican journalists, having had to get there early on the communal bus from the hotel, are lounging in their seats browsing the internet news sites. All the talk across the sports pages is of a *Panorama* investigation showing evidence of a number of FIFA executives taking bribes which the BBC had controversially aired in the UK earlier tonight, just a couple of days before England hope to be awarded the 2018 World Cup. The programme had upset the bigwigs in Zurich and it would, many were saying, throw our bid completely out of favour with the Executive Committee and cost us any chance of staging the tournament. The England 2018 bid team labelled it 'an embarrassment to the BBC' and dutifully proceeded to mop Sepp's brow in an effort to assuage any ill effects while, as expected, FIFA are treating the programme with shameless contempt and dismissed its findings entirely.

With a few members of the International Olympic Committee also coming under scrutiny, the IOC immediately requested that the BBC hand over all their evidence so they could conduct a proper investigation. One would imagine that an exemplary organisation which prides itself on being run to the most exacting ethical standards such as FIFA would do the same, grateful that the hard work of the journalists involved had revealed the bad apples in the barrel and allowed the organisation to take steps to remove them. But they did nothing. They simply feigned great offence, shut up shop and refused to even consider the implications of the BBC's findings. And these are the men entrusted with running world football?

As always when the football world is plunged into scandal, the Caribbean is healthily represented by Warner who had tried to sell 2010 World Cup tickets allocated to the CFU to a Norwegian black market company at a fat personal profit to himself. It would have been interesting to see the CFU President in Rivière-Pilote, however the build up to the big vote unfortunately necessitates his presence in Europe. But though he might have been away himself I do, when making a dash to the bar, pass his good friend Captain Burrell, and on any other day he would surely have had something to say on the matter himself. Today though, his thoughts are occupied by his own problems much closer to home.

The game itself is not a particularly entertaining one. A 2-0 win for the Reggae Boyz means it is two games, two wins, five scored and one conceded. We are top of the group and into the semi finals with a game to spare. And the cherry on the top is qualification to the CONCACAF Gold Cup in the summer, with the semi-finalists here being awarded the Caribbean's four places in North American football's biannual showpiece. But the real story of the match is none of these things. The real story had been twenty four hours earlier, and the Guadeloupe game very nearly didn't go ahead at all.

During the last summer's World Cup the planet looked on aghast as the France team had refused to train following an in-camp dispute. Echoes of that now rang through Martinique as the Reggae Boyz reportedly cancelled a training session the previous night over a pay dispute, ordering away the bus that had arrived to take them from the team hotel in the small town of Sainte-Luce to their training pitch, and threatening to pack up and return to Kingston if the issue could not be resolved that evening. 'Whatever we are doing we have to do it tonight,' Raymond Anderson, head of the Jamaican delegation dramatically told the media during the showdown. 'If we are going home then that has to be decided tonight, if there is a resolution then it must be tonight.'

The contested money was the *per diem*—a standard daily 'wage' to compensate for time away from home—that the team is owed by the JFF for the tournament, which they claimed to be US$100 for the squad, plus the percentage of any prize money to be shared around by the men who win it, a figure they set at 80%. But this is not a simple matter of crass greed and mercenary feelings, it is a group of young men who have reached the end of their tether and simply want what they are owed.

For the past twelve international fixtures the players have foregone their payments from the cash-strapped JFF and now they just want to be paid for doing their jobs. But footballers are easy targets for public reprehension and this is a delicate matter, so instead of picking up hearsay I wanted to get to the heart of the problem first hand by speaking to those involved.

And so, sitting beneath a whirring ceiling fan in the wood panelled poolside bar at the players' hotel the morning after the successful Guadeloupe game, two days after the 'strike', I sit with team captain and leader of the revolt Shavar Thomas while he explains his side of the story to me.

'At the Gold Cup a few years ago there was a situation where the captain at the time, Ricardo Gardner, talked about the payment package for the team for the whole Gold Cup and that didn't go down well, again, between the players and the Federation. But it was resolved and everybody moved forward and we took part in the Gold Cup, but I think it affected the whole team camaraderie and performance.'

'A year after the Gold Cup we signed a contract with the Federation, each player. And it states that whenever we play a team, depending on their ranking in the FIFA rankings, we get a certain amount. Let's say we play a team ranked in the top ten—Argentina. We probably—the figures are not correct, I'm just estimating—we probably earn three grand US [per player] and then it goes as to the ranking, but I don't remember the actual terms. That was the contract we signed, it was a one year contract so it expired last August and we haven't signed anything since with the Federation.'

And it was after that expiration date that the relationship between team and Federation began to strain. 'The Federation came to us as players and they say they are financially strapped, they don't have any money,' Thomas continued. 'And we as players extend ourselves and we make the sacrifice, and we did so with a willing heart, trust me.

But it's not easy to work and not get paid, and not just one or two times, but twelve times.'

When footballers do things like this it is very easy to treat them with contempt and nothing more, dismissing their actions as greedy when they should be concentrating on the tournament instead. But if a mechanic serviced twelve cars without pay and then finally turned to his boss and said he won't do any more unless, from now on, he gets his due wage, would the public consider it unreasonable? For these players football is their passion but it is also their job, it is how they earn their living and provide for their families, they just want to be fairly paid for doing it. More than that though, they want the JFF to prove that they aren't all take and no give, and to show some commitment to their players.

But as the news broke the internet provided its usual battleground for observers to throw in their two pennies worth. 'These players are all about money and not the love of the game', one comment bemoans. 'They should ALL be banned for three years,' slams another, while someone else declares that: 'These mercenaries were willing to humiliate their President [Burrell] and embarrass their country irretrievably.' As someone who has spent time within the camp rather than just reading the newspaper reports I can definitively inform 'kris' and the others posting furiously online that this is the last thing the players wanted to do.

'I personally said to the General Secretary that we as players have extended ourselves and made the sacrifice,' Thomas goes on, 'I think that the JFF should, this one time, go to the extent. I know they don't have the money, but can you show us that you're willing to make that sacrifice? And that's all it is. It is not money. We're not asking for winning bonuses, we're not asking for match fees, appearance fees, we're not asking for none of that.' They didn't even ask for the money owed them for past games, it was just about this tournament now. 'And I read in the paper that we *"demanded . . ."* We didn't demand anything, it's what we deserve. But a lot of people will read into it the wrong way. But the ones who have been in and out of the camp, they know. Players before us, they know.'

'I can't bash the fans because if they were in our position and they'd know what is happening, what we deserve, then it would be a different situation. They would say something different. So, not understanding the situation, not being in our position, they are allowed to say, "They should concentrate on the football." So, I won't bash them and say they can't say that but . . . it's just how it is.'

'I was hoping that this wouldn't happen again. That players wouldn't have to be negotiating with the Federation days before the tournament, and there would be a fixed thing in place saying this is what happens, this is what happens so everybody knows what they're getting into, what they're signing up for. I don't want to be a business man when I'm a footballer, that's not my profession. My profession is to play football and I don't want to be a politician going back and forth with people.'

That is the other worry in situations like this one, that the distraction can affect the performance of the team, which is, after all, what they are asking to be paid for in the first place. Thomas admitted himself that Jamaica's showing at the previous Gold Cup suffered because of that particular feud, and the French players' strike at the last World Cup, with which this saga was drawing unfortunate comparisons, came in the middle of what was arguably the most inert and downright woeful tournament showing of any major team in recent memory. I put those thoughts to Thomas.

'I don't know the real situation with the French but I'm pretty sure those guys weren't playing for the money because all of them are millionaires, so if they are arguing about $1,200 . . . ! I think it's more principle. And if you compare to France, those guys completely checked out because they have an arduous schedule through the year before the World Cup. I'm not saying they should have done that, I think they should have continued playing because once you go across the line it's not the Federation anymore, it's the guy next to you, it's the guys sitting on the bench that you're playing for. It's the people of your country that you're playing for. And not the French Federation or the Jamaica Football Federation, it's the players next to you. And we maintained that focus. Regardless of what's been happening we know that we still have a job at hand that we have to do.'

The 'strike' was led by four senior players—Thomas himself, Rudolph Austin, Luton Shelton and Jermaine Taylor—three of whom earn their livings in wealthier leagues overseas, leading them to tell the mass media that their actions were motivated by principle rather than finance because the **per diems** in question were 'pocket change' to them. But there are a number of players in the squad not receiving fat foreign pay-cheques and so I go in search of one of them, Harbour View captain Richard Edwards, to see if he had anything to add, and I am fairly surprised to hear a note of uncertainty in his opening words.

'Teams are symbols and if the leader is saying one thing it matters that I support it because I don't want to be this person that disrupts the team. At the end of the day, team bonding is much stronger than just thinking about yourself so I support the majority.'

So does that mean he was not too certain about the action taken? 'It could have happened a different way, in a different manner,' he tells me, 'I guess we were pushed to the limit where we ended up having to go the route that we have gone. And I think it's the best possible way in which we could have got the results because for the past year I think we have made a lot of sacrifices for our country and we are just asking them to do us one favour . . . we haven't asked for match fees, bonuses; we haven't taken that step. We just want our *per diems.*'

His conviction in the righteousness of the strike seems to be growing as our conversation goes on. 'We're not here for the money, we're here for the opportunity that can happen for us by representing our country. The situation is all based on the fact we have a worldwide financial meltdown, and most of us that play at home we are playing for little or nothing, but at the same time I know that the clubs are making a gallant effort to make things better. I just want the Federation to go ahead and take the same stance as them. It's not even what we are owed, it's what we were guaranteed because it was what they told us that's what we would normally get.'

There seems to have been an element of naivety on the players' part that is surfacing at times in this story: falling back on contracts that expired 16 months ago, talking of verbal assurances which have no solid backing. But this does not detract from the principle that they should have been paid for their work and weren't. It is one of those situations where the natural reaction is to cast blame at one party or the other, and as such the internet message boards have also been abuzz with people backing the players and criticising the JFF, saying things like: 'The Federation has treated the Jamaican team like dirt for a long while.' But the truth is that, in just the same way the players shouldn't be lambasted for just wanting to be paid for their work, neither should the JFF be strung up because it tried to seek an alternative payment scheme when it simply does not have the money to offer the full amount. One columnist in the *Star* sensibly commented that the deal is the players go out and play while the JFF raises the money to pay them, but he didn't allow scope for the fact that in the midst of a global recession corporate Jamaica just isn't putting the money into sport, putting the JFF squarely between a large rock and a very hard place.

The negotiations carried on late into the night, leaving the public back home on edge as the next day's newspaper reports went to press with the situation still unresolved and offering no indication as to whether the Guadeloupe game would go ahead or not. In the end an agreement was reached when Captain Burrell personally paid the extra money, a total of $14,000 US, from his own funds and delivered an emotional speech to the media in which he said: 'If we were to strike and not play this would create tremendous embarrassment on the country. Not Burrell, on poor Jamaica, and as such I would die before I allow this to happen . . . I will not subject Jamaica to ridicule.' His heroism is something we will come back to later.

It was undoubtedly a messy and unpleasant affair and one that everyone would rather not have happened, but it did. And really both sides were right and both sides were wrong, but instead of trying to cast either party as the guilty one everybody should instead be concentrating their efforts on avoiding any repeats. Thankfully steps are taken on the squad's return home a couple of weeks later and with a bit of luck and some careful thought they will put an end to such ugliness for good. One certainly hopes so at least, because Jamaica really is better than that.

For the immediate future the most important thing is that everything was sorted and that the team was not thrown off-course by the way the 'strike' played out, as the 2-0 victory the following night demonstrated. With the whole saga put to bed, for the time being at least, the last word will go to Edwards. Had the Federation not paid, I ask him, would the players really have followed through on their threat and just gone home?

'What we came to agree on is that if they don't give us our full *per diem* and they want to give us 50 percent, we won't take it, we prefer to play for free. And the prize money that they said we would get 50 percent, we wouldn't take it at all. We just play to win. Because each and every player leaves Jamaica to represent their country, to represent themselves and to make their family feel proud. And we nuh leave Jamaica to come here and fail, we want to win.'

Caribbean Cup Finals, Group Stage

Group H

Trinidad & Tobago 0 2 Cuba
Martinique 1 1 Grenada
Grenada 1 0 Trinidad & Tobago
Martinique 0 1 Cuba
Cuba 0 0 Grenada
Martinique 0 1 Trinidad & Tobago

Group I

Guyana 1 1 Guadeloupe
Jamaica 3 1 Antigua & Barbuda
Antigua & Barbuda 1 0 Guyana
Guadeloupe 0 2 Jamaica
Guadeloupe 1 0 Antigua & Barbuda
Guyana 0 4 Jamaica

Group H

	P	GD	Pts.
1. Cuba	3	3	7
2. Grenada	3	1	5
3. Trinidad & Tobago	3	-2	3
4. Martinique	3	-2	1

Group I

	P	GD	Pts.
1. Jamaica	**3**	**8**	**9**
2. Guadeloupe	3	-1	4
3. Antigua & Barbuda	3	-2	3
4. Guyana	3	-5	1

Sunday 28th November

Boys' Town	0 2	Arnett Gardens
Sporting Central	1 1	Humble Lion
HVFC	**1 0**	**Portmore United**
Benfica	2 1	St. George's
Village United	1 1	Tivoli Gardens
Reno	1 1	Waterhouse

National Premier League

	P	GD	Pts.
1. Tivoli Gardens	15	17	30
2. Waterhouse	15	8	28
3. Boys' Town	15	1	26
4. Portmore United	15	7	24
5. HVFC	**15**	**5**	**24**
6. Benfica	15	-9	21
7. Sporting Central	15	3	20
8. Arnett Gardens	15	-3	19
9. Reno	15	1	17
10. Village United	15	-8	15
11. Humble Lion	15	-5	13
12. St. George's	15	-16	8

CHAPTER SEVENTEEN

Win Or Bust

When a football team starts kicking up a fuss over money and making the sort of demands that the public will decry as mercenary it puts itself in a very difficult position. After their actions during the group stage, the Reggae Boyz now have to justify their behaviour and win back the support and affections of the fans back home. In effect, losing now has gone from not desirable to not an option. They have to make good on their new position as favourites to win the tournament or face months of the public raking over every last detail of their 'strike' and undoubtedly concluding that none of them are fit to wear the shirt.

They were looking good so far but tournament football can be a strange beast to grapple with and it is uncanny how often the freescoring side which set alight the group stage crumbles when the pressure of the latter rounds stifles and kills their open style. They will have to adapt to a whole new set of challenges in order to retain their title, and should they fail to do so there is a lynch mob back in Kingston already tying the nooses.

I arrive at the Pierre Aliker just as the first semi final is starting, and ninety minutes later Guadeloupe have satisfied the locals by writing their name on the bill for Sunday's final at the expense of the Cubans. On paper it is clear that Jamaica should be joining them. 'If you lot can't beat Grenada I'm going to personally go into that changing room and kick all of their arses,' Digicel Kieran informs Ian, Audley and Nick when they arrive, but if all life's twists were played out on paper then Cuba and Trinidad would both still be in the running too. That they aren't should be warning enough to Jamaica about the dangers of complacency.

But it takes just seven minutes for the Boyz to strike their first blow. A loose pass strays towards the corner flag and Ryan Johnson chases it down, dragging the defender with him as he does so. Richards spots the space which has opened up and darts into it to receive a perfect pass, taking one steadying touch before sliding the ball low inside the near post. What's all this nonsense about the knockout stages getting tougher? This is easier than the last game! Now we can just sit back, relax and enjoy the flow of goals.

But within minutes Granada have hit back, and at half time it remains 1-1. The second half is dominated by Jamaica with only the occasional break giving cause for concern, but no goal. They are just putting together one such counter when, about forty yards from goal, Edwards flies in hard and from behind, leaving the man on the ball lying in a heap on the floor. He knows his error and immediately gets up and scampers away when the foul is given, but the ref is whistling and calling him back. Having been booked earlier in the tournament, he is just one yellow card away from missing the final. It was a rash challenge and Edwards turns and holds out his arms, pleading with the official not to show him that critical card for it. Suddenly the mists of time swirl and I see Gazza shrouded by a balmy Turin night two decades earlier, using his white shirt to wipe away those infamous tears. Gary Lineker now floats into view, gesturing to the England bench to keep an eye on the young star after his semi-final booking ruled him out of the World Cup Final. Back in September, Edwards had spoken to me of how anxious he was to get a chance to play in the Caribbean Cup, never having had the opportunity to play in such a tournament before, and now I am looking down from the stands as this referee marches across, seemingly set to end it. But there is no card, just a quiet word. The Harbour View captain has his reprieve. From a distance I breathe a sigh of relief on his behalf.

And just like that famous semi final with Germany, normal time cannot produce a winning goal. Six minutes into extra time, the breakthrough finally comes. Rudolph Austin gets the ball by the corner flag, turns inside and hits a deep cross over the heads of the defenders which lands smoothly at the feet of Troy Smith. After taking one touch he hits it low across the goal and into the far corner. It is a goal that takes Reggae Boyz to where they so acutely need to be, a goal that sees them into the Caribbean Cup Final this coming Sunday. One step closer to their salvation.

So what is it like for an international football team on the day of a tournament final? What do the players feel? What is the routine? What is the atmosphere like among the group and around their hotel?

Quiet, would be the short answer. I have come to Sainte-Luce to see what the mood is and how they are spending their morning ahead of the evening's grand occasion and found very little sign of life anywhere. After doing a light workout in the pool almost the entire squad had returned to their rooms to relax and the only player to be seen now is Dane Richards, sitting in the shade outside the bar and looking at Facebook on his laptop. This is the man whose talents had really shone throughout the tournament, and whose goals had carried Jamaica to the final that is now a matter of hours away. I take the opportunity of the quiet period to speak to him about the night ahead, and to try to get to know the man behind the skills.

'Everybody's really confident,' he tells me after we have moved and placed ourselves near a fountain outside. 'Not over confident but confident that we can go out there and do it. We can be confident all we want but if we don't go out there and play well we're not going to win the championship so we've just got to be confident off the pitch and on the pitch and hopefully we can get the job done.' His assessment of the night ahead is pure football platitudes. 'We've just to go out there and play our best and hopefully it's good enough to win the championship,' he adds.

Richards is a player about whose own personal development I have been curious, for he has built his career the **other** way. Put simply, Jamaican footballers have two routes to the bigger leagues; the first is that being chased by all those at Harbour View and everyone else back in the Premier League, and that is to impress domestically, reach the national squad and hope that a foreign coach spots you and offers you a trial and then a contract. The second is the way players like Richards, Omar Cummings and Shavar Thomas made it, namely through the American collegiate system and without ever setting foot on a Jamaica Premier League pitch.

Richards' own route began in his home town of Montego Bay, where he starred in his high school team at Cornwall College and helped them to the DaCosta Cup and then the Olivier Shield, the top prize in schoolboy football. He was also drawn into the youth ranks of Seba United, a Premier League side at the time, but left for America before playing for the first team. He earned a place at San Jacinto College in Houston after a couple of older friends had been there and tipped off the coach to his talents, then he won a scholarship to attend Clemson University in South Carolina. In 2007, having scored freely throughout his college days, he was picked by the New York Red Bulls in the second round of the MLS SuperDraft, instantly making a name for himself in the first team and ending his first season with a nomination for the rookie of the year award.

He has since firmly established himself in the New York side and ended the recently concluded campaign (the MLS season runs from March to November) with five goals in the last seven matches that carried the Red Bulls to the Eastern Conference title. It is obvious that he stands apart from most of his countrymen and with all the talk about facilities that had been going on in Jamaica in recent months, I am curious as to how he feels his development as a footballer has been aided by his education in the States.

'Going to America definitely helped me,' he says. 'I started at junior college and I went to Div. 1 football and then I went pro, and each year I developed as a player. You can get quality weight rooms to make you stronger, quality pitches to play on that make passing better, and the style of play is different so it definitely helps. America really helps you develop.'

One of the big advantages the American sporting system has over the way we do things in England is that, being largely university and college based as it is, a high level of formal education is a necessity alongside training. Unlike the English horror stories, there are no children there who don't quite make the cut and are then dumped with little or nothing to fall back on. Simply put, if you want to be a sportsman you have to have the school grades too. Richards explains: 'You've got to balance it so you can move on. If you don't get the grades you can't move on, so I had to balance my school work and soccer as well.'

Some might consider this a barrier but in truth the most promising sportsmen are given a certain amount of leniency in meeting those requirements, and the education such a system provides means those who don't make it have an alternative life opened up for them. The other real benefit though is that the children of countries like Jamaica will look at the star striker of their national football team and see that he reached his position by 'staying in school'. While Jamaica's school attendance rates are actually fairly good for a country of its level of development, they are still by no means perfect and someone like Richards can only be a positive role model in demonstrating what can come of not just attending school, but by working hard and getting good grades while there.

'Definitely kids sometimes say I'm a role model and I take that as a compliment,' he says, before explaining what has motivated him in his own progress: 'I'm just the bearer of my life and my family life so I just keep doing it because I have to do it so that my family can be better off.'

These days he counts as team mates Rafael Marquez—of Barcelona and Mexico fame—and, until recently, former Aston Villa and Colombia striker Juan Pablo Angel. But the real star name in his team is Thierry Henry, whose impressive history with Arsenal, Barcelona and France includes winning the World Cup, the European Championship, the English Premier League, The FA Cup, La Liga, the Copa del Ray, the Champions League, the European Super Cup and the World Club Cup among other titles, as well as multiple Player of the Year and European Golden Shoe awards. Richards has been fairly passive throughout our conversation to this point, but at the mention of Henry his entire face suddenly lights up with enthusiasm.

'It's unbelievable! Growing up watching him and seeing the great things that he has done, and actually now he's my team mate beside me in the locker room,' he pauses and gently shakes his head. 'Unbelievable feeling. But when you get out on the pitch you can't be thinking about that, you've got to be focussed on your game. If you're not focussed on your game then you won't be his team mate anymore because they will find another player. But he's a quality player and I try and learn from him each day so I'm feeling my game can get a lot better through him. He's won everything in soccer so I'm definitely learning a lot from him.'

So how does he feel Dane Richard fits in alongside these stars? 'Rafa, Henry, Juan Pablo; those guys are quality players who have played in Europe and all over. Now playing with them I'm like, "This is unbelievable." But I've just got to stay focussed and continue playing with them or even move to Europe because they have been there and done that already and just to get a taste of it,' again he trails off for a moment as he pictures great opportunities. 'I would love to get a taste of it.'

Physically Richards is not a large player, only around five foot seven in height and of fairly slender build. Some might consider this an obstacle to success in the more physical European leagues but he dismisses this by evidencing the evolution of the game and the sort of modern players who have been on top of the world in recent years: 'I used to think that it could be a problem, but now I see a lot of players not gifted with height and they're doing well also. Messi is not gifted with height, Iniesta is not gifted with height but they are quality players. I've just got to go out there and do my stuff.'

They are the same names Richard Edwards, known as 'Shortman', once mentioned to me as examples of players who prove that height need no longer be an issue in the modern game. You wonder if those mould-breaking stars of Barcelona realise the inspiration they give to their fellow professionals around the world.

And yet for all this talk of Europe and America, one comment he makes is particularly telling: 'If the money was good in Jamaica I'd prefer to be at home, trust me.' Again, this is the sort of thing footballers often let slip just before being called a 'mercenary' by the public, but we are not talking about the difference between earning £55,000 a week here and £60,000 a week there, we are talking the difference between struggling to survive in a league that is not even fully professional yet and earning a very comfortable living elsewhere. Although a salary cap on squads means the MLS cannot offer wages like Europe does, it can still compensate a player in a way the Jamaica Premier League could never even dream of—I overheard it said by one player that a certain member of that Jamaican team was the lowest paid player in the league on a healthy US$80,000 a year—and Richards had explicitly mentioned earlier that providing the best for his family is one of his chief motivators. So they are not the words of a 'mercenary', they are just yet more evidence of what Jamaican domestic football is missing out on because of its lack of financial power.

We have spoken of his career but there is an international cup final just hours ahead and thoughts can only stay away from the more immediate business for so long. They go into tonight's game as defending champions. I wonder if, in the mind of a player, that might provide extra motivation. 'That's two years ago. I won't forget because that's why we're defending champions but I just want to go out there and focus on tonight then afterwards we can say, "We are back-to-back champions". But right now we just focus on tonight.'

Just focus on tonight. On such a note I leave him to do exactly that and, with all the other players still in their rooms, I go back to my own hotel. In just a few short hours we will be meeting again at the Pierre Aliker, and the Caribbean Cup Final will be decided.

'You fucking eejit!' Up in the media centre Digicel Kieran is not impressed. With Jack Warner appearing at the final, the downstairs bar area has been cordoned off and us insignificant press men, who have followed the entire tournament, are no longer allowed in unless we can present a special pink wrist band. Kieran, as the organiser-in-chief, had attained one of these and passed it on to me so I could get the drinks in on the strict condition that I didn't, under any circumstances, actually put it on. What he failed to anticipate though, was that the bouncers on the door flatly refused to let me in unless it was secured, irreversibly, around my wrist. When I return, therefore, with the full order of beers and soft drinks but the bracelet permanently fastened to me I am not welcomed warmly.

'Right lads,' he says turning to the Jamaicans along our press desk, the one where the English speakers in the media are concentrated. 'All drinks for the press are now on him because he's got the bracelet wrapped around his fucking wrist, like,' he hesitates momentarily, waiting for the appropriate simile to come to him. 'Like a fucking carrier pigeon.'

The third and fourth place play-off between Cuba and Grenada is playing out down on the pitch while he and Digicel Karl, added to the team during the final group game, skit back and forth to ensure that the website is continually updated, the VIPs are happy and that the whole occasion goes smoothly. It always struck me as odd that the organising of the tournament is left to representatives of the sponsors rather than the CFU, but perhaps that's the sort of control they want for their money. There aren't even many Digicel people here, and none of them look the wrong side of 35, but to the credit of those individuals they are doing a very good job indeed.

The glow from the setting sun drapes itself across the far stand like an orange blanket and nobody is really paying any attention whatsoever to the match going on. The ground is still practically empty and since Cuba took the lead in the twelfth minute the only tension has been coming from the worried mutterings of Digicels Karl and Kieran, living in fear that an equaliser would bring extra time and throw the entire evening's schedule off course. 'I know they're going to score, I can feel it,' Karl complains while Kieran, as usual, is somewhat more colourful with his selection of language: 'Just you watch, we'll get to fucking stoppage time and they'll get a fucking equaliser. I'm telling you.'

Having not created a single chance all match, Grenada do indeed wait until fucking stoppage time before Kithson Bain puts the ball across the face of goal to where substitute Lancaster Joseph is running in to finish from just two yards. The Digicels hold their breath as the move unfolds, then let out huge sighs of relief as Joseph somehow contrives to put the ball over, while the rest of us simply gasp in disbelief. Rushing along the media platform to where the French commentators have television monitors set up on their desks, I get confirmation from the replay that suspicions of offside were unfounded, it had simply been an impossible miss.

So the organisers' wish is granted. The game finishes 1-0 to Cuba and as Karl goes with Captain Burrell to the running track where the prize cheques are presented to the teams, Kieran sets about undertaking the kind of hidden preparations one doesn't even normally consider when watching events like this. The trophy must be tracked to ensure it is moved from the television studio tent to the mouth of the tunnel where the players will pass it when coming out for the final, and the whims of Jack Warner's wife must be met, and her desire for a complimentary Digicel t-shirt satisfied.

As this is all going on the floodlights fail at one end of the pitch, giving them yet more to worry about. A troupe of local dancers twirl their skirts and flip their hats in an effort to entertain the audience during the dead time, while mechanics scramble to get power restored in time for the kick off. About an hour after the last game ended things are finally ready. The lights are on, the trophy is in place, Mrs Warner has a t-shirt and the team talks are being rounded off in the changing rooms.

I venture down to the running track and position myself in a small group of photographers that has clustered at the opening of the tunnel. Inside the players slowly gather before organising themselves into their formal lines. At the head of the Jamaican troupe, clad in their second strip of emerald green, Shavar Thomas looks both focussed and relaxed, staring dead ahead one second then turning to me with a smile and a confident thumbs-up the next. Next to him the dreadlocked Guadeloupe captain Stephane Auvray appears similarly prepared, while behind them players stretch and jump on the spot, getting their bodies ready for the exertion ahead.

The stadium has now filled to near-enough its maximum 16,000 capacity and when the FIFA anthem strikes up the referee and linesmen lead the procession out onto the pitch, passing either side of the small table onto which the trophy has successfully completed its odyssey. As superstition dictates, no one touches it. They line up for the national anthems and I make my way back up to the press area while former France international goalkeeper Bernard Lama, raised in French Guiana, goes through the process of toe-punting a ball down the pitch in what they called a 'ceremonial kick off'.

The early pressure all comes from Guadeloupe. They waste a chance, and then another. Then Richards makes some progress and wins a corner for Jamaica, but it is headed clear. It is no more than respite for the Jamaicans, with Guadeloupe coming through the midfield too easily and creating frequent openings. At the back Thomas is having to put in his best performance of the tournament to deal with their constant surges. But then the Boyz start to get into the occasion. Austin hits a freekick that skims the roof of the net. Richards has a close range shot deflected wide.

Then, just past half an hour in, Jamaica take the lead. Austin breaks down the wing and crosses deep to Shelton who in turn heads it back towards Cummings in a central position no more than six yards out. With his back to goal the ball comes across his body, he follows it on the turn and with one hit he hooks it high above the keeper and into the net.

But it takes just four minutes for Guadeloupe to equalise. Larry Hanany picks a gap in the Jamaican defence with a bouncing through ball to where Ludovic Gotin is running onto it in space. It sits up perfectly into his stride and he smashes it first time into the net. The crowd filling the stadium erupt. They are all backing their French compatriots and now Jamaica are under pressure. A minute later Dwayne Miller, in goal for Richard McCallum, is forced into another save, and then another. We need half time, we need to settle the game down again.

When the break comes there was very little conversation among the Jamaicans on the desk, they just stare intently at their work in a way they had never felt the need to do when the team was winning. The tension continues to rise in the second half. With an hour gone Adrian Reid misjudges a high ball, getting drawn out of position and allowing Clavier to steal in behind him. A short pass then finds Cedric Collet who places a curled attempt from twenty yards that dips just wide of the far post.

Collet then turns playmaker, breaking down the right and squaring across the box to his captain who sends a shot just over the bar. We respond with a series of attacks but none of them produce anything more threatening than a corner before Guadeloupe bounce back to attack again. A mis-hit Clavier cross swings dangerously through the area as everyone on the press desk holds their breath, praying no one is running onto it. The second half is flying by and the crowd are getting more and more animated, fiercely planting themselves behind their team.

As the game draws into its closing period Jamaica start to take control for the first time. Shelton heads a long ball from Troy Smith back towards Austin on the edge of the area. As it bounces in front of him he shapes to strike but fails to get over the ball and sends it flying over the bar.

We need to get Richards into the game, but it's not something we are able to do until the 80 minute. But at that point Austin finds him, sliding a perfect ball through the defence into his run. Richards sprints forward, closing in on the ball with goal now open in front of him. He meets the ball's path but it's not clean. His touch never lets him down, and yet he fumbles, it spills away from him, suddenly he is way out of position. He tries to salvage something and pulls it back to Cummings but the shot goes wide of the post.

Guadeloupe hit back. Gendrey hits a flat cross towards Gotin who has pulled off the last defender and finds himself clear in the area to receive it, but the cross is just too high, skimming his head and going wide. As another cross then goes in at the other end a lady in the crowd screams, the intensity becoming all too much for her. It is headed clear.

There are just two minutes to go when Richards breaks down the right but he is dispossessed too easily by Gendrey. The Frenchman comes forward, turns inside slightly and drills a shot from thirty yards. It's powerful, it's accurate, Miller is dancing his feet helplessly across his goal line to try and get to it but he can't. The crowd rise to their feet as the ball simmers goalwards. The net shakes as it whooshes millimetres over the crossbar. Reprieve for Jamaica, and with it relief.

Once more it goes to extra time. Suddenly the band strike up again having played sporadically throughout the tournament, booming their rhythms through the night as the players defy fatigue and push onwards. Clavier hits a free kick into the wall from just outside the area. It squirts away, rolling teasingly across a bustling group of players and wide. Vernon then plays in Richards who is tackled, the clearance bouncing just in front of Austin. It sits perfectly for him, again he shapes and this time he gets over it perfectly, connecting powerfully. It is moving fast and towards the bottom corner, only for the keeper to somehow stretch down low to turn it away.

Half time comes and the tension among the three Jamaicans of the press is palpable. They have long since given up on the desk and have for some time been occupying the seats in front instead. Now they are rising, marching around, trying to ease their nerves. But the second half is different. The game has slowed as though everyone is happier to settle the matter with a shootout than risk making the mistake that would cost them the tournament. And so the play becomes more cautious, tiredness also finally making an imprint on the game. Occasional chances still come but the finishing is tired and lackadaisical. Everybody seems to know what is coming and acceptance of this fate settles upon the entire occasion well before the end. With one last free kick lobbed hopefully but unsuccessfully into the box the game is up. The ref can offer no more chances; his whistle finally brings play to an end and the players slink away for a brief rest.

Penalties. Everyone seems to hate them, especially the English. 'The cruellest way to decide a game,' say some. 'A lottery,' say others. Of course, our own national dislike is fuelled more by the fact that we're so useless at them that they invariably end any tournament we enter than anything else, our consistency of failure perhaps suggesting that they are not such a lottery after all. But we only really seem to hate them when we are involved and, as always seems to be the way, losing. As a neutral there is nothing more dramatic to watch. On this occasion, though, I do not feel like a neutral and tonight the break before the start of the shootout seems to drag on for hours.

It is football reduced to its rawest form. One striker, one goalkeeper, one kick. And always, without exception, one winner and one loser. Economists have often studied the humble penalty kick as possibly the finest real-world example of what they call 'game theory', the squaring-off of one foe against another where A's choice of strategy counters B's and vice versa until one of them comes out victorious. Does the taker go left or right, up or down? The same options, of course, are open to the keeper: where does he dive? The best penalty takers and savers have ways of manipulating the odds in their favour, but for the average participant it is simply a case of choosing the right area and hoping your opponent's choice of strategy allows for the success of your own. Perhaps, therefore, it is just a lottery after all.

Still the players sat, discussing who was taking what. In the second minute of the 1974 World Cup final the penalty was made a little more complicated by Johan Neeskens, one of the great Dutch masters of 'total football', who scored one against the Germans by whacking it straight down the middle. With that seemingly obvious tactic introduced to the world, perceptions began to change and the middle then became a third choice of line for the kicker: the Neeskens variant, as it has been coined. This option is a difficult one to choose though because going central seems a fairly passive move in comparison to the more proactive options of right and left; the keeper starts in the centre so to actually aim a shot there and have it saved would make the taker look very foolish indeed. But keepers too have the burden of needing to give off the illusion of doing something—to dive and go the wrong way is far more preferable than to miss by just standing still and hoping the ball comes right at you—so they too are less likely to lump their fortunes on 'middle'. Interestingly, a study by Ofer H. Azar and Michael Bar-Eli of 286 kicks from professional leagues around the world found that keepers chose to dive to one of the sides a massive 93.7% of the time, and yet, assuming he cannot see which way the ball is going at the moment he makes his decision, the best way for the keeper to maximise his chances of saving would actually be to stand his ground, slap bang in the centre. Of course if they took this on board and always chose the middle the strategy of kickers would change in response, necessitating another re-think.

The chances are that very little of this is going through Rudolph Austin's mind when finally he steps forward to take the first penalty. Most likely some of it is though, a simple right, middle or left; up or down. What will I do? What will he do? The permutations for both kicker and keeper are endless and ever-changing. Austin goes for bottom right; the keeper doesn't. One—nil Jamaica. Larry Clavier swaggers forward for Guadeloupe, giving off an air of ultimate confidence, or at least trying to. 'He's going to miss,' declares Kieran. 'He's too interested in his fucking walk-up.' He and Dwayne Miller in goal both choose the same way, but he chooses up and Miller chooses down. Kieran and the keeper were both wrong, one—all. Next Luton Shelton, like Neeskens did, chooses middle and wins. Two—one. Then two—all. Three—two. Three—three. Kicker and keeper choosing different directions, or choosing the same direction but at different heights. Four—three. Four—four. Shawn Francis comes forward for Jamaica. This time it is the keeper who chooses the middle, Francis goes for the bottom corner. Five—four. It is Jean-Luc Lamboude who marches towards the box last for Guadeloupe. 'He's got one hell of a thump on him.' Their star of the tournament, striding purposefully toward Miller's goal. Score and it's sudden death, miss and the game is up. Right, left or middle. Up or down. Where will I go? Where will he go? Lamboude confidently runs into his kick, his choice made, and fires.

Friday 3rd December

Semi-finals

Cuba **1 2** Guadeloupe
Jamaica **2 1** **Grenada**
aet

Sunday 5th December

3rd/4th Place Play-Off

Cuba 1 0 Grenada

Sunday 5th December

Sporting Central	3	0	Arnett Gardens
Village United	1	2	Benfica
Reno	0	0	Boys' Town
Waterhouse	**1**	**0**	**HVFC**
Tivoli Gardens	1	0	Humble Lion
Portmore United	1	0	St. George's

National Premier League

	P	GD	Pts.
1. Tivoli Gardens	16	16	33
2. Waterhouse	16	10	31
3. Portmore United	16	8	27
4. Boys' Town	16	1	27
5. HVFC	**16**	**4**	**24**
6. Benfica	16	-8	24
7. Sporting Central	16	6	23
8. Arnett Gardens	16	-6	19
9. Reno	16	1	18
10. Village United	16	-9	15
11. Humble Lion	16	-6	13
12. St. George's	16	-17	8

CHAPTER EIGHTEEN

'So Afraid Of Jack'

The morning after the night before. As quickly as football had descended on this small corner of France it then packs up and moves out again once the party is over. With the confetti still blowing around the deserted steps of the Pierre Aliker, the Caribbean Cup tourists are jetting out of Fort-De-France's airport and back to wherever it is that their normal lives tick by.

It is an early start in the Liat check-in queue and in front of me the Grenadan team are laughing and joking between themselves, a number of sharp London accents from British-born players conspicuous among the Caribbean burrs. Looking slightly lost at the side stand Jack Warner with his wife and press secretary, bereft of Sepp Blatter's coat-tails to hold onto and drag them into private jets and helicopters, waiting for their seats to be arranged by one of the various FIFA lackeys dotted about in their official blazers. As the bright, fresh Martinique sunlight pours in through the large windows I watch them all go about their business, the storybook men of television screens and newspaper cuttings occupying a very human scene.

Grenada's local liaison warns one of the coaches that it might be difficult to get seats for all of them on the small plane before disappearing to the front of the line where he successfully answers duty's final call by securing the lot, and then goes up the line to bid an emotional goodbye to each individual. The media men, some of whom still haven't even got round to removing their passes from around their necks from last night, bid one another goodbye, breaking ties that have been forged over the last couple of weeks inside the tightly enclosed bubble of tournament football.

As the procession moves to security everyone is held up by a problem with one of the Grenadans. The passport control official has been trying to explain to defender David Cyrus, in French, that the name on his boarding pass had been incorrectly spelled and that as a result he is not going anywhere, while the bemused, uncomprehending player simply stares blankly back at him. 'It's always the fucking English one isn't it!' one of the London accents yells forward ironically as the squad's one French speaking player, holding the giant novelty-sized prize cheque they had been awarded the night before tightly in his hand, edges through from the back to assist. The team soon get bored of making jokes about Cyrus and, while the problem is being smoothed over, they instead turn their attentions to another English-born player who had arrived in the country and apparently told at least two of the squad that he plays for Arsenal's reserves, a subject that keeps them occupied for just about the entire journey.

On passing through, Warner and his group take themselves away from the main body of passengers and occupy a couple of small benches in an empty part of the departure lounge, hiding from the possibility of anyone asking about his latest scandal which still lingers freshly in the air. The players lounge on the benches nearer the gate, playing with their phones or continuing their joke-filled chatter. When it comes to boarding they happily stand back to allow the Warner clan to cut into the front of the queue and laugh sycophantically as he makes some jovial remark. Such a move may not have been so well received at Heathrow, but he is a more popular man on home turf.

By the time I board with the rest of the mere mortals, Uncle Jack has long since bagged himself the front seat of the tiny plane and settled in with a Lee Child thriller to while away the flight. The players, meanwhile, are still getting their kicks from the claims of the 'Arsenal Reserve'. 'I can just see him and Theo driving to training together!' one cries as the others all screech with laughter. They continue to paint imaginary scenes of their team mate duelling with Walcott et al. on the practice pitches of London Colney as the plane cranks its propellers into action. We trundle along the runway then sweep upwards. Behind us the tiny island of Martinique shrinks into the distance.

Rewind less than twelve hours and Jean Luc Lamboude is running in to take his penalty. He reaches the ball, instantly making his choice about where he is putting it and striking it hard. Miller also silently makes his own strategic choice, diving to his left, but this time he needn't have bothered. Lamboude's shot flies wide of the post. As the striker's head drops the lined up Jamaican team break rank and sprint towards their keeper. They had done it the hard way but they had retained their title.

Up at the top of the stand Ian, Audley and Nick jump around and hug each other while the players descend on Miller in a mass of jubilant shouts and flying bodies. They shake hands with their defeated opponents then run off to the bench, picking up Whitmore and tossing him up into the air above their heads before emptying the contents of the water cooler over him. Others simply spray their drinks over the whole scene, soaking players, coaches and management alike.

Guadeloupe glumly parade up the stadium steps to collect their silver medals from Warner, having to observe the torturous formalities of watching the winners celebrate before they can slip into their changing rooms and out of sight. By now the line of green-clad Jamaicans is forming at the bottom of the steps with players looking to individuals in the crowd and raising their arms in victory. One by one they come up and have the shiny gold medals placed around their necks, grouping together at the side of the crowded VIP platform. Last up is the captain. Shavar Thomas is handed the trophy by Warner and, with one triumphal thrust, punches it into the sky. His team mates jump around him as confetti guns explode into the air, and with this final humiliation done the Guadeloupe players slink away.

The celebration party is directed back down onto the field where the squad pose for endless photos with their prize. With a flash of my media pass at the gate I am out to join them, high-fiving an ecstatic Thomas on the running track and taking a picture as he tosses his medal into his mouth in that classic pose. The players are taking it in turns to enjoy the trophy, holding it and kissing the ever-smiling Digicel girls while the delighted photographers snap away. To the side Dane Richards stands with Ryan Johnson, both watching on and looking oddly glum as though somehow it is not their victory to celebrate. Johnson, despite playing a big role in the tournament, missed the final and whether Richards is just sympathising with his friend or not

I don't know. After congratulating them I move on to the Harbour View man.

Richard Edwards is buzzing. This had been his dream and now it is happening. He high-fives and hugs me as I wander over to him. I ask how he feels. With eyes wide he just blows his cheeks out and shakes his head in disbelief. He picked up an injury in the semi final that so nearly kept him out of this, he says, but now here he is. Before we separate he runs off to wrest the trophy from his team mates so I can take a couple of photos of him holding it, copies of which I would later give him when we are back at Harbour View. With one final handshake I leave him to return to the celebrations and walk back away from the pitch for the formal media duties of the post-match press conference.

Beside me, ensconced again in the insides of the grandstand, Audley grumbles as question after question is asked and answered in French. When finally the chance comes to speak English it is, of course, just full of the usual politically correct banalities about how it had been a 'tough game' against a 'good team' and when Whitmore utters the words, 'The boys really had to dig deep tonight,' it feels like we could be listening to any one of those old school British managers running through their favourite post-battle clichés.

With very little to report from the press conference we go in search of other stories. I briefly let my guard down, accosting Digicel Kieran to pose for a photo with the trophy then stopping to chat with Ian, during which time Audley has broken from the pack, slipping into the VVIP area reserved only for Jack and friends and privately cornering Captain Burrell. Sensing we are missing some vital material, Ian, Nicholas and I quickly dash through the cordon and stuff our Dictaphones under the Captain's nose.

'I think that there is a lot more to come from Coach Whitmore,' he is saying. 'He is a confident coach, he is a disciplined coach. When you exhibit those qualities you can only go from strength to strength. So again, congratulations to Coach Whitmore, his coaching staff and all who worked together in achieving this victory for Jamaica.' Maybe not such groundbreaking stuff then. What about the players' strike?

'I have decided not to speak of that now,' is his sensible response. 'I think this is a time to enjoy the victory, right now is a time for celebrations. It is a time for Jamaicans at home and in the diaspora around the world to celebrate this very important victory. And it shows that our football is certainly on track. We are going into the Gold Cup next and we hope to build on this resounding victory in an attempt to qualify for the World Cup in Brazil.'

It might have been a bit disappointing from our point of view but he is right, this evening is not the time to be speaking in negative ways about the players or their actions. But this view is apparently not universally shared. From the sofas next to where we stand, Warner's voice, lisping and soft, pipes up. Unlike Burrell, he has decided that he wants to tell us exactly what he thinks of the strike. And so there we are, just Ian, Audley, Nicholas and I being ranted at by one of the most powerful men in world football, champagne glass in hand, while the President of the JFF looks on and cringes. Within days his words to the four of us will spread around the entire Caribbean, and in doing so they will cause a minor storm.

'I have felt in many ways the pain of Captain Burrell because what he had to go through to reach this stage was tough. To be held to ransom and, in my humble view, be blackmailed by a team is unacceptable. And I want to say to you that the pain he has felt, I feel for him, for the Caribbean. Because it is a precedent that will be set in the Caribbean unless we begin to stop it at this point in time. In fact I have told him that even the rules shall be amended to facilitate countries bringing in teams at the last minute that face this situation.'

'National pride must take precedent over money. National pride must take precedent over mercenary feelings. And in that context, therefore, I am pained. But at the end of the day the Captain stood up, as a big man, and he has saved the day and today Jamaica and the Caribbean is happy.'

At this point he deviates to take a veiled side swipe at poor Guadeloupe for not being what he calls 'a **bona fide** country' before getting back to his main thrust.

'But you guys in the media make the point that at the end of the day national pride must be the be-all and end-all. And that is why, in many ways, I am pained for my Captain. And I want to say again, to him, congratulations, I am very happy for him and Jamaica. But equally I am pained, I am pained for the suffering and the pain he went through to reach this final.'

So just where do you start with all this? Firstly, the hypocrisy of Warner being saddened by people putting money over football strikes you like a freight train. Only the most heartless of mercenaries could actually want to be *paid* for doing his job! Sentiments coming, of course, from a man who ruthlessly exploits the game's dirtiest recesses in order to line his own pockets. Where was Warner's 'national pride' when he was trying to avoid paying his 2006 World Cup squad for their historic achievement, you might ask? And when he was trying to syphon the TTFF's share of the gate receipts against Scotland into his own account?

But the story gets worse, and his crimes get more severe than mere hypocrisy. On being asked by Ian about his own side's performances he had said, 'We played badly and we paid the price for playing badly.' It's true, they did play badly, but only to Warner would this be seen as an excuse not to pay them.

Lasana Liburd is a journalist from Trinidad. It was he who first uncovered Warner's 2006 World Cup ticket scandal before the world's media picked up on it and he has dedicated his career to exposing the lies in his country's sporting set up. A few months after the Caribbean Cup final, in February, he meets with a small group of anonymous Trinidad players and coaching staff in the car park of their national stadium and they talk to him about Jack Warner.

'Why is it we always have to fight for what is rightfully ours?' questions one, in a sentiment startlingly reminiscent of what was said to me by the Reggae Boyz. 'Everybody is so afraid of Jack and it is overbearing.'

For the Finals of the Caribbean Cup they were informed that their match fees would be TT$9,363 (a little over £900) per player per win, TT$6,242 (£600) per draw and TT$3,120 (£300) per loss. 'One or two players grumbled,' one says. 'But we felt that if we argued we might end up with nothing so we decided to go with that.' But while it might seem dictatorial they did not have any say in what they earned, what is really scandalous is that in the end they received just TT$500 for the solitary win over Martinique and not a single cent for their two defeats.

'They complained about the players' performances,' the same player goes on. 'But what you sow is what you reap. Not that we go out to play badly, but there is a god above . . .'

'The TTFF never live up to their end of the bargain,' complains another. 'We just want to be paid what they said was entitled to us, even if was just one dollar. How can Jack say after the event that he isn't paying any money for losses, or is giving us less for certain matches? If they want to make the 2014 World Cup a priority they have to change the relationship with the players.'

Basically, the TTFF had told the players what they would be paid, forgoing any sort of negotiating process in doing so, and then backed out of even paying them that. That was not the start of it either; the team had barely been paid all year and there was an outstanding bill of TT$437,255 (£42,460) owed to them, not to mention the technical staff who had not been paid since the previous September. The simple reason being that when their World Cup qualifying campaign ended unsuccessfully with a draw against Mexico that October, Warner sacked the entire backroom staff and refused to pay them for their final month's work, before later re-hiring them and still not paying them.

What is bizarre is that it is not even the TTFF who have to pay, but the Sport Company of Trinidad and Tobago, a subsidiary of the Ministry of Sport, and unlike the Jamaican situation the money was there and ready, just waiting for somebody from the TTFF to sign off on the payments. But nobody came. As Liburd writes, 'False promises, fear, victimisation and emasculation are all tools of Warner's trade and, after 38 years in the business, he wields them skilfully.'

One member of the unpaid technical staff outlines the stand-off: 'The last salary anyone got was September 2009 [17 months previously]. There were always meetings when we were told that we are going to be paid at the end of the week or next month or when we return from a trip or after the Budget. Then we were told by the Sport Company that Richard Groden [general secretary of the TTFF] just had to come in and sign our accounting sheet and we would be paid. That was back on December 3 , but today is February 3 . It is so peculiar. No one could imagine it would go so far.'

But the trouble is that so little can be done about it. 'Who do we go to when things like this happen? That is a good question,' wonders a member of the technical staff. They had complained to the Ministry of Sport but Warner is a senior member of the ruling Government and has even acted as Prime Minister. He is also President of both the

CFU and CONCACAF, and Vice President of FIFA. Football and politics have, astonishingly, allowed so much power to be concentrated in the hands of one such corrupt individual that it leaves those under him with nowhere to go. 'The governing body is who we are supposed to turn to when there is a problem,' says one player. 'But what do you do when they are the ones who are victimising you?'

So this is the order in which the man running football in the Caribbean and in North America keeps his own house, and the actions of the man with whom Jamaica's Captain Burrell is such close friends. The Trinidad players chose not to take the same action as the Reggae Boyz, though, when perhaps they should have done. 'We always try to solve things in an amicable way but it proves futile,' one player says of their battles with the TTFF. 'They are not people of their word and they are not to be trusted.'

Liburd spoke to one of the anonymous Soca Warriors about the Jamaicans' strike and although the quotes were never published, he was kind enough to pass them on to me for this book. 'I admire Jamaica because the night I heard they were going to strike I said, "They really have belly to strike in a major tournament like this." I admire the way they stood up as a team. That is what we don't have in the Trinidad team. From 24 players, when things get tough it goes down to ten.'

'My mother always told me it is better to get victimised fighting for our rights than to get victimised for doing nothing. In Martinique we discussed refusing to play until we got paid but when the time came the guys said they wanted their caps so they could get the chance to play abroad and so on. I told them we would struggle to get our money when we got home.'

'When I spoke to the young players on the Jamaica team they said, "If the senior players striking then we a strike too because them want betterment for we."'

That is the special unity of which Richard Edwards spoke to me, and the special unity which saw the Reggae Boyz get their wages and then get their trophy.

My return flight again takes me to Barbados, where a three night stay means I miss Harbour View's one-nil win over Reno. When I do get back to Kingston, though, things have still not settled down. While I was still away, the KSA Business House Football Association honoured Carvel with an award for outstanding administrative service to football in Jamaica—a richly deserved award after a 43 year career—and he took the opportunity to publicly criticise Warner's words against the Jamaica team and announce that the PLCA would be sending a letter to both the CFU and the JFF about the matter. This is one of the things I like most about Harbour View and its people, it is not a club where anyone is afraid to speak their mind, they do not blindly tow the party line like others seem to and they will always say what they feel is right, regardless of who they upset. Perhaps their persecution complex gives them a feeling that they have nothing to lose by upsetting the authorities anyway, but all the same they do not shirk away from criticising those who should be criticised and I find that one of the more endearing features of the club's management.

Pouring water on the flames though are the national players themselves. On landing back at Norman Manly International it is revealed that they had written a letter to the Federation stating that they 'unreservedly apologise to the JFF, the people of Jamaica, our families and all the Reggae Boyz fans.'

'We have concluded,' the letter went on, 'that our actions, even though not intended, caused undue embarrassment to the country.' My initial reaction is one of surprise, not least because it was written by Thomas himself, and I wonder what had happened to convert his stonewall belief in their cause into this apology. What is less surprising was that one of the seven other players to sign the letter was Edwards, although even he had sounded thoroughly convinced by the validity of their stance once his initial uncertainty was out the way.

But by the time I have finished reading the newspaper reports it has already become clear that the letter was little more than a superficial move. Having spoken to him in Martinique, I would bet my last pound that Shavar is not even remotely sorry—at least not to the JFF—but by publicly saying he is, the fans are presented with the image of a united front between players and Federation and everybody can move on from the whole episode. They had won the cup and they have apologised, and now nobody can possibly have any gripes with the national team. It is all smiles again.

Over the next week or so, during which time Harbour View succumb to defeats against Village and Boys' Town so miserable they barely warrant mention, contracts are drawn up by the JFF to stave off the possibility of future repeats. Instead of the one year contracts that had expired sixteen months ago, these will last for four years and will have to be signed by any player wanting to be eligible to represent the national team. On top of this, the board of directors agree that any player who takes similar action again in future would face a two year ban from international football. The players may have won the Battle of Saint-Luce, but the JFF are ruthlessly winning the war.

Burrell laid the guilt onto the players, telling them that they are responsible for earning income for the Federation and should therefore wield their roles more carefully in order to afford the current youth players the same opportunities they had enjoyed. It was a neat piece of spin in the JFF's thorough propaganda campaign, and was an interpretation that differed wildly from the genuine intentions of the senior members of the team who were largely motivated by precisely that same thing, ensuring better circumstances for the younger players.

People can only make up their own minds about whether the team was right or wrong to strike, but the fact is it forced the JFF into long-overdue action. And they might now be firmly harnessed in by the authoritative response of the Federation, but at least Jamaica's players will get paid from now on. Which is more than can be said about anyone playing for Warner.

Richard Edwards holds the Caribbean Cup trophy on the pitch after winning the final at the Stade Pierre-Aliker.

Sunday 5th December

Guadeloupe **1 1** **Jamaica**
aet
4 5
pens

Wednesday 8th December

Humble Lion 0 1 Portmore United
HVFC **1 0** **Reno**
Benfica 1 2 Sporting Central
St. George's 0 1 Tivoli Gardens
Boys' Town 0 1 Village United
Arnett Gardens 3 1 Waterhouse

Sunday 12th December

St. George's 1 0 Arnett Gardens
Reno 4 1 Benfica
Sporting Central 1 1 Boys' Town
Waterhouse 1 0 Humble Lion
Portmore United 2 0 Tivoli Gardens
HVFC **0 1** **Village United**

Wednesday 15th December

Arnett Gardens 1 0 Benfica
Boys' Town **2 1** **HVFC**
Village United 0 1 Reno
Portmore United 1 0 Sporting Central
Humble Lion 2 0 St. George's
Tivoli Gardens 1 1 Waterhouse

National Premier League

	P	GD	Pts.
1. Tivoli Gardens	19	15	37
2. Portmore United	19	12	36
3. Waterhouse	19	9	35
4. Boys' Town	19	1	31
5. Sporting Central	19	6	27
6. HVFC	**19**	**3**	**27**
7. Arnett Gardens	19	-4	25
8. Reno	19	4	24
9. Benfica	19	-13	24
10. Village United	19	-8	21
11. Humble Lion	19	-6	16
12. St. George's	19	-19	11

CHAPTER NINETEEN

Superstar Friends

When you talk to Jamaicans about the history of football in their country there is always one name that will come up. Alan 'Skill' Cole is a dreadlocked Rastafarian who is widely considered to be the greatest player the country has ever produced, appearing for the national team as a 15 year old schoolboy back in the 1960s and going on to an illustrious playing career that took him to the fabled North American Soccer League as well as a stint in Brazil, home at the time to arguably the finest national side in the history of the game. When he returned to Jamaica he was a superstar player and became the only professional in the country before going on to coach both at home and in Africa, spending four years working in Ethiopia. His, clearly, is not the average life, but there is yet more to 'Skill' that makes him even more remarkable. The week before I meet him he had signed a contract with a Hollywood studio for a film written by the Oscar-winners behind *Rain Man*, a movie that deals with those years in his life where he was not just a footballer but also the best friend, manager and confidante of Jamaica's greatest icon, Bob Marley.

Today he has little involvement in football. The way it is run in his country has plumbed such depths that he barely even affords it any attention. 'It makes me sick to watch,' he tells me. 'When it comes on TV I get away, I go outside and read. It's so sad.' He is highly opinionated and remains hugely passionate, desperately wanting Jamaica to reach, as he sees it, the highs of back when he was playing himself. He paints himself as the outspoken rebel and speaks glowingly about his own talents as not just a player and coach but as a friend and even a social reformer too, making it seem a little ill-fitting when he pointedly spells out the importance of not succumbing to lofty 'cockiness'. In the hour and a half I spend with him it becomes clear that is he a fairly complex character and very probably not an easy man to work with, but he comfortably reveals a wry sense of humour and expresses a deep admiration for his old friend. Humility and exaggerated self-promotion make an odd concoction within Cole's fluid personality. He is also what you might call stereotypically Jamaican in his laid back approach to life, and when I ask if he has any plans for the future, he responds with: 'I don't like to talk about plans. Tomorrow morning something will happen and if the vibe is right you just go along with it, and everything will work out.' As our interview unfolds it becomes clear that such thinking has been a guiding principle throughout his life.

I have arranged lunch with him at New Kingston's Ashanti Restaurant, a place whose vegetarian cuisine makes it popular amongst the capital's more well-to-do Rastafarians. He arrives on his bike a little later than planned, wearing a workout vest and with a small towel across his shoulders, illustrating his continuing dedication to health and fitness. Now into his 60s, his locks and beard have greyed, the only real outward sign of his age. He joins me at an outside table, and talking over the churning traffic noises of the city centre he tells me about his remarkable life. 'I was a little boy when I moved up central near to Sabina Park, near St George's College.' Sabina Park is Jamaica's Test cricket venue, in the rougher downtown region. 'And all those areas over there are football areas, you have many clubs there so I was fortunate at that time to have been in that area. We are products of our environments and I was close to all these ball fields. My father used to take me to the ball fields with a football and I'd be kicking with both feet: right, left, right, left. From there my father was my only coach as a youngster.'

'So I lived in this area and watched these early players before me, the good players. I used to watch them and I adapted good things from them. And then I took Jamaican football to another level. So I'm a product of all those people that came before me: I saw them, I took a little piece of them and I took it to another level. Fortunately for me, as I said, I was around the park and football was my everything. I ate football and I became a master of it. I was able to talk to it, to communicate with it. I took it to that level.'

It wasn't until his teenage years that a recognised coach came his way and it was an Englishman, instilling in him the virtues of fitness and stamina to couple with the more Jamaican attributes of skill and dribbling. It was this man Cole credits with making him into enough of a complete player to break into the national team at such an extraordinarily young age. The same coach also tried to persuade him to move to England and worked on lining up a move to Aston Villa, but one thing stopped the move ever happening: 'It's too cold,' he says dismissively. 'I love playing soccer but I don't love money, I don't love money to the extent where I'm going to go to the cold and play for it. I'm not a materialist. Maybe now. It's very lucrative now, maybe it would have tempted me. Once you play in England you don't have to work again. But in my time it wasn't all that lucrative and I wasn't prepared to go and play in the winter.'

Instead he signed for the Atlanta Chiefs in the nascent NASL, the infamous but ultimately doomed American league that would employ Pele, Best, Beckenbauer and Cruijff during its heyday of the late 70s and early 80s, but before that time the names were slightly more parochial. 'They got most of the top players in the Caribbean,' Cole reflects. 'That was a vast exodus. They signed me when I was 15, my father signed me to them when I was 15 and they gave me a retainer so I didn't leave until I was 17. I was the youngest player to ever play in the NASL. And I won the championship when I was 17, I don't think it has ever been done again.' It is hard to tell where understandable pride stops and a less endearing need to drive home the impressiveness of his achievements begins, all the more so because of a certain hardness in his character that wards one away from sympathy. What is clear though is that America held no further glory for him. Following that season he went home and stayed there, because he just didn't fancy seeing out the second year of his deal. 'I didn't go back,' he says. 'They called me and . . . 'he shrugs his shoulders indicating his disinterest in a return. 'I just wanted to stay home.' Nothing suggests any remorse about breaking his contract; indeed, his steeliness returns as though his employers had displayed unacceptable temerity in expecting him to go back there. This is another trait that unsettles me about Cole, he is very quick to condemn others' faults but seems unable to see wrong in his own actions, even when they are patently out of order.

So he signed for Mona and then went on to Boys' Town from where he got the big move of his career, signing for Nautica in the Brazilian second division. It was, he says, 'a new world', but one that he seems to have enjoyed thoroughly. 'I played against all these top guys: Rivelino, Tostao, Pele, Jairzinho, you name them. Clodoaldo, Edu, all of these guys. Football in Brazil was fantastic in those days, it was the top league at that time in the world. It was really tough, it was really tough. Only three other foreign players played in Brazil at that time: Gival from Argentina—he was the top player in Argentina at that time—de la Rocha from Uruguay—a very famous name—and the goalkeeper at Santos was in the Argentinean national team, and myself. So we were the only three nations from outside of Brazil that time. It was secluded in those days. I was the first ever person from CONCACAF to play in Brazil.'

You might expect a young man to be intimidated in such circumstances, but Alan was not like most young men. 'In my days when I played I had so much confidence, I wasn't afraid of playing against nobody. There was no complex, it wasn't like some people who might go there with a complex. I'm going to beat you. My team qualified for the championship in 1958-59. There were only two teams that were champions for that area, even now they're the champions again; Santa Cruz and Esporte. And I went there and I said, "It's got to change." And things changed, I helped to change it. And we qualified for the national championships. All the big teams that qualified played in the national championship and we played right around, it was the biggest thing in Brazil. They make a lot of money, big money. So that was very exciting. That was *the* thing: you go to Brazil, you want to play in the national championship. It's like going to the Superbowl. You play all around the circuit.'

But ultimately it was another adventure that ended ingloriously when a new director took over the club and demanded that he cut his sacred dreadlocks. 'We're talking about 1973, the world wasn't civilised then,' he says plainly about the disagreement, still deeply offended by the religious affront and unwilling to elaborate further. The lack of empathy for his beliefs and Cole's stubborn nature meant he was unprepared to make any attempt to repair the damage with his club. 'I was happy to come home. I just got fed up and leave. They wanted me there, they didn't want to release me and have me transferred because Marinho [Nautica's other big name] had just been transferred to Botafogo. We were the two stars in the team so if I go the team is dead, they wouldn't want that. But they were messing around so I got my tax clearance and . . . 'he claps his hands loudly. 'Fuck it,' is his succinct summation of the events, before adding something altogether more poignant and somehow more fitting: 'These things I don't question, I just got to go. This is my life.'

On returning to Jamaica he joined Santos and dominated the national league, but at the same time saw his international career curtailed by the JFF's archaic rules against professionalism. 'I would have been the most capped player in the history of this country,' he asserts, his voice containing none of the self pity displayed by the man I had met in the park during my first week. 'But because I became professional so early I couldn't play many of these games. I just used to watch.'

After his playing days he moved onto coaching local teams, with a large degree of success, and this served as a prelude to his next great saga. His explanation of his move to Ethiopia is perhaps Cole in a nutshell, the encapsulation of Jamaican football's greatest legend and his easy approach to life. He arrived in the Rastafari holyland on a pilgrimage and took something of a shine to the place. 'I went for six weeks but ended up staying for four years,' he says casually, before shrugging and adding: 'It just happened.' Vast cultural differences made him pine for his beloved home country, and he doesn't dwell for long on his time in Africa. 'I was coaching in the province for a year then I came to Adis Ababa and I made my name in Adis Ababa. It was revolution, you know. It was a time of communists and you had to be very careful.'

The nation he returned home to was not at the same sporting level as it had been when he left it behind, and he rues the state of Jamaican football in the modern age, criticising players, coaches and particularly administrators. 'The JFF are just clowns,' is his forthright opinion. And the way to improve things? 'Get rid of them. Get rid of all of them.' Given statements like these it is little wonder he and the Federation have not managed to work together in recent years, a barrier he assures me is not put in place by him. 'I don't have a problem with nobody, they have a problem with me, my personality.' But despite his insistence that he bears no grudges he seems hurt by the way he has been treated: 'I'm here before all of them. I used to pay the bills, my presence used to pay the bills and to keep the stadium going in the 60s and 70s. When I played the JFF made money, when

I don't play the games went down. But these guys come into the system and it's like my personality is too rich for them.

'It's too much of the politics of football. That is the problem, the politics of football. These guys, I don't know if they love the game, they probably love their pockets more. It's more about putting money in their pocket. Football is going nowhere because they have the wrong personnel, they have the wrong people doing the wrong jobs. I don't think they understand football and they make it look so difficult. Now they have the monopoly on football and it's going nowhere, because you have a lot of people in football that are causing a lot of problems—people that are no good—and that is why football is going nowhere. Everybody knows, everybody knows who they are but nobody wants to come out and talk. I can't talk. They must leave football.' I don't suppose there will a job offer from Captain Burrell in the post any time soon.

But Cole the football man is only half his story, and it is not the half that caused Hollywood to come knocking. What they were interested in was the Cole that used to drift into Trenchtown as a youth and got to know one Robert Nesta Marley while there, along with the friends who would eventually become The Wailers. As their music grew, Cole became increasingly involved. He had chosen to play for Mona between his stints with Atlanta and Boys' Town simply because the team manager was also involved in music and would school them in the business. When Cole and Marley registered Tuff Gong records nobody else knew, not even the other members of the band and when they toured the world he would organise training to keep them physically fit. 'They were fun,' he says of the tours. 'Sometimes wild, really. In the music business there are a lot of crazy people. Like everything you have good and bad, it would depend on the cities that you go to.' He enthusiastically cites Amsterdam as his favourite destination, followed less keenly by London, Berlin and New York. It was the latter city where the beginning of the end came as Marley's cancer took control and his body gave way one day while they were out running. 'He collapsed in my arms in Central Park,' Cole recalls sadly. 'That was it, destiny.' Marley died in Germany just a matter of months later.

I am curious about the personal nature of his relationship with one of popular culture's great global icons, and inquire as to what

Marley had been like to know. 'Very quiet. Secluded. He was very shy. People don't realise that but he was shy. I managed to bring him out and he became more sociable. He was somebody who refrained from people; very quiet, very secluded. He would talk to some people and they would be afraid of him because his face was screwed all the time. But it wasn't actually that, it was just his view, just his perception of life, and it came out in his features. Inside he was cool, it was a different person. But people got carried away with his personality, they were afraid of him because he didn't talk.'

Football allowed a release for the young singer though, and despite not being a natural talent he improved under the guidance of his friend. 'When I first started teaching him he was very wild,' Cole tells me. 'I got him to master control: refined, rhythm, coordination. He learnt well, and he loved it with a passion. Oh my God! That man loved soccer! Right next to music—unbelievable! He learned. You have to play every day if you want to learn to be a footballer. After I had him for a while he became very tough; control, passing, very athletic. He loved it!'

As it became more evident that Marley was going on to big things the people working with him undertook a long process to make him more personable and media friendly. 'Bob's life was just Trenchtown in those days. From Nine Mile to Trenchtown. Jamaica was open but he was pressed down to one area so I had to bring him out, meet people. He was afraid, he couldn't talk to people. So we had to bring him out. He was the same man but he had to integrate, be around people, socialise; it becomes a part of your environment. So I had to break him out until he becomes more social, speaking more to people, speaking to people who had a different level of understanding. People who had gone to university and come home—my friends—would come over to the yard in the night time and he would listen and become a part of it.

'It was the early days. The man couldn't speak to people, he couldn't approach, he was afraid. He didn't talk much. And at that time people didn't earn much but he learned, and his writing went to another level. You can define Marley's music, his writing, if you study it as a period of his environment and you can understand. And you can see it. It becomes more hopeful, broader, because of the environment.

'When people came back from overseas with Masters, Bachelors, professors—that was the type of environment he was exposed to now, and he listened. He listened. Bob could tell me everything a guy said. The next day he could tell me what Tom, Harry, Dick said; all of that, he was fantastic. And he took from them and he wrote songs. He depicted all good things. I remember we went to England in '79 and I said, "How do you write all these songs?" And he said, "The people around me". It's environment. Bob listened to everybody, he was quiet. Fantastic human. Fantastic. He was fantastic.' The notion of people being products of their environment is one that Cole feels strongly about, citing environment as what shaped both his and Marley's careers. To a large extent the idea is evident too in Jamaican society as a whole.

When I ask what life around Jamaica's pair of superstar friends was like in the 1970s he modestly describes it as, 'just nice and great'. As Marley became a worldwide star the money began to flow in and they could afford to move from Trenchtown to a large house uptown on Hope Road, conveniently just around the corner from where I myself live in Kingston. In Cole's ever-modest eyes the move instigated a social reform. 'When we started living up at Hope Road, me and Bob, everything changed because they didn't have Rastamen in that area in those days. We'd play football on the lawn every evening and people used to walk off the street to see the Rastaman playing football. We changed it, we broke the barrier between the middle class. We were specifically responsible for breaking that barrier and integrating the Rastafarian with the middle class in the seventies.'

The house is now the widely-visited Bob Marley Museum, and while there the guides tell visitors with mischievous glee that the neighbours would often complain about the parties and activities going on in the young rebel's house. I ask Cole, was this really was the case? 'No, we didn't keep parties up there. But at that time, as I said, Rastafarians were something new and there was still discrimination. But we were too powerful at that time, they couldn't trouble us. We were moving; we were rising and they were declining. In the early days Rastafarians were looked down on, and we brought that change in the system, Bob and myself, we brought that change to the system. It was part of the plan, part of the divine plan.'

Alan 'Skill' Cole in his own modest words. Great player, great coach, great manager and, last but not least, earthly medium for Jah's social reformation. I leave the restaurant with the vague feeling that he may have done as Jamaicans tend to do and slightly embellished the roles he played within his own stories, but in truth he may even have played them down for all I knew. Whatever the dry reality though, there is little doubt that he was the country's original football superstar, and that he remains today one of its truly great characters.

CHAPTER TWENTY

'He Made Them What They Are'

'He told me he was going to shoot me,' Richard Edwards nonchalantly explains to me, recalling his run-in with the opposition player whose hands had been around his throat a few minutes before. From the away changing room shouts of 'Far Right you're dead,' had been emanating violently in the direction of Rafeik Thomas, and even now that it lies empty and silent a tension still lingers. The visiting players and fans, who had only just finished scuffling in the tunnel area, have been mostly shipped out and the riled humours of the Harbour View contingent are returning to normal. Just another Sunday night at the Compound in many ways, but one with an added twist.

Harbour View and Tivoli Gardens have never enjoyed an easy relationship. The two biggest sides in any country will inevitably develop a spiky rivalry but added to that here is the concept that Harbour View is traditionally a PNP community, although not necessarily strongly enough to really unsettle everyone. And besides, unlike some of the others in the league, the football club itself is distanced from local politics. The main reason for any hostilities between the two, so I am told by people in yellow and blue at least, is that Tivoli hate being beaten, and that is a fate they tend to suffer more against Harbour View than against most other clubs. Whatever the roots of the friction, tonight has been just the latest chapter in a long history.

The evening was tense from the start. They had come here leading the table with the most goals scored and the second fewest conceded but having begun to look fallible in recent weeks, picking up just a single point from their last two games. Harbour View, though, had one fewer than even that. It was potentially a season-defining game. Drifting ten points from the top, if we lost this we could kiss goodbye to the title once and for all. Win it though, and we would be in a position where we could top the league by bettering Tivoli's result in just three of the 18 games left. So let's now rewind a few hours.

The teams have finished warming up and are preparing to come back out to the pitch. A healthy number of away fans have followed their team across town and they are creating a decent noise away to our left. One man presses himself up against the fence to our 'VIP' section, snarling swear words at those inside. The team sheets are produced and offer another small brick in the wall of this rivalry between Jamaica's big two: Rafeik Thomas starts.

Rafeik lives in Denham Town, he was brought up by Tivoli and then he switched to Harbour View because the club provided an atmosphere in which he felt more comfortable. He is by no means the only player to have made the switch but for whatever reason the people of Tivoli have never forgiven him for it, and players and fans alike single him out for 'special treatment' every time the two sides meet. When asked about it he shrugs it off, giving the dignified impression that he finds it all a little silly.

But tonight it certainly seems to give him a little extra motivation as he flies at them from the start, tearing down the wings, holding off powerful challenges, making chances, bouncing up from heavy kicks. He seems to be making himself the centre of all our attacks. As we moved out of defence he picks the ball up with his back to goal 30 yards out and deflects a couple of tackles before dragging the ball back and shooting, sending it just wide of Edsel Scott's goal.

With less than twenty minutes gone Lemar Nelson collects the ball inside their half and launches into a determined run, attacking the Tivoli right back who needs help from the centre half to deal with him. Between them they slow Nelson up as he gets into the box and usher him out wide, but he spins on the ball and hits it back to the edge of the area where Wolfe flicks it up and launches himself into a spectacular flying volley. He hammers the ball towards the goal, on the path to which it is blocked by the raised arm of the defender. Penalty!

After the game Tivoli boss Glendon Bailey is thoroughly unhappy about it. 'Almost every game we play now the referees call a penalty against us for handball and I feel they should just let the game play', he tells the press, clearly mortified by the unfairness that Tivoli aren't allowed five goalkeepers. Perhaps more useful words would have been somewhere along the lines of, 'Just keep your bloody hands down, lads.' But what do I know?

It is Harvey squaring off against the explosive Scott, the ups, downs, lefts and rights running through their minds. Or even middle. They both choose opposite sides and as Harvey strokes it along the floor into the net the keeper goes the other way. 1-0 Harbour View, and we fully deserve it.

We don't let off, tearing into them straight away from the kick off. Thomas is buzzing, riding challenges, winning chances, even making hefty tackles himself and all while playing with a controlled intelligence that suggests he is thoroughly enjoying himself.

But for a moment his coolness vanishes. Tivoli captain Kasai Hinds throws himself dangerously at Rafeik, flooring him and giving away a free kick. Having been battered all match, Thomas finally loses his cool, leaping up and shoving Hinds away. It is the spark that causes the match to ignite. The two teams erupt as players fly in on the scuffle from all over the pitch. In the melee it becomes hard to tell which arms are trying to keep the peace and which are on the attack and the ref charges around with his whistle, desperately trying to regain control of the occasion. It is only a minor flare-up but it sets the tone for the rest of the match and hints at what is to come later.

In his bid to cool things the down, the referee is becoming over-zealous and awards Tivoli a free kick just inside our half for absolutely nothing whatsoever. 'Who dis ref?' asks Ian Burnett, who has appeared behind me on the media desk. ''Im clearly another idiot.' Ian had only just published an article in the PLCA magazine criticising the country's officials and this one is doing little to prove him wrong. The free kick is hit high and fairly aimlessly into our box and Dicoy is the first to make contact, heading it out but not far enough to make it safe. His weak clearance drops nicely for Roland Dean who watches it carefully and shapes himself perfectly to meet it first time. He hits a spectacular volley that flies hard into the top corner of the net.

As the Tivoli players run away celebrating the Harbour View heads drop and players stand around the pitch with hands on hips. But it doesn't last long. From the kick off we pour back into their half and win a corner, taken by Hue, which bounces into the box and slaps almost comically into the forehead of Tivoli's Victor Thompson. Whether he was trying to guide it into the hands of his keeper or he was just taken by surprise only he will know, but it pops up off his head and straight into his own goal. They had been level for less than a minute and had now handed the lead back to us.

Tivoli don't like to lose. The game becomes violent again not long after. After comfortably defending a free kick outside our box we spring out on the break with Nelson charging out down the left. Thomas makes a run outside him but instead the youngster cuts inside, coming towards the half way line where others are sprinting out of defence to join him. He is being shepherded across the field by Kemar Flemmings who is doing a good job of slowing the move down until suddenly, and for no reason at all, he raises a hand and belts Nelson in the face. It happened in the centre circle but it was a loud enough slap to be audible in the stands and the Harbour View player drops to the floor holding his nose. The referee does the only thing he can and shows Flemmings the red card while the dazed Nelson has to take a good few minutes of attention from the medics before he has recovered his awareness enough to return to the game.

Half time comes to rescue the visitors a couple of minutes later and Bailey looks miserable. His side are failing for the third successive game and their discipline is falling apart rapidly. He seems to have done something right with the break though when, early in the second half, Boyd, having started brightly but faded as the game became more tempestuous, attacks a wide open gap down the right wing, carrying the ball into the box, cutting inside John-Ross and shooting from close range. Robert Williams manages to make up the ground and throws himself in front of the shot, sending it ricocheting off his shin. For a split second it looks like a carbon copy of the goal they had beaten us with at the Edward Seaga Complex, but the ball balloons high and over the bar and our advantage is preserved.

Devon Hodges then attacks down the left and is fouled by Edwards to win a free kick. Raymond Williamson takes it, planting it straight into the wall before winning the second ball and putting in a much improved cross. It sails into the box and is headed on to an unmarked Boyd who thankfully gives us a momentary reprieve by shooting tamely wide. Just sixty seconds later John-Ross miscontrols and is robbed by Damien Gerdon who puts it out wide before receiving the return ball, taking one touch forward and firing over. They are starting to reverse the pressure onto us, to win this we are going to need another goal at least.

It seems fitting that Thomas should be involved in the scoring of it. He drifts out wide on the right and receives a pass from Harvey. After fighting off a couple of defenders he lays the ball back and Harvey strokes it into the path of John-Ross who takes two touches and curls a shot towards the far corner. Scott manages to get a hand to the shot but it isn't enough and the Harbour View players run deliriously to the fans to celebrate. ***Three-one***!

Tivoli don't like to lose. A high ball into our box is headed out and as Edwards brings the dropping clearance under control Williamson runs in with a ferocious tackle, connecting hard with our captain's shins and earning a yellow card. Edwards goes off for a brief checking over by the physios but soon returns to the field. It is not the last time those two will clash.

Inevitably, and with no small thanks to the ref, things are not going to be easy. Minutes after Thomas is given a yellow card that nobody in the press box could explain, Tivoli break down the right. The winger turns on the ball and runs straight into Kimorlee Brissett, bouncing off and falling to the floor to inexplicably win a free kick near the corner flag. It is sent in too close to the goal, in a very comfortable place for Barrett to claim. Only he doesn't. He takes the catch in front of his face and then drops it, landing it at the feet of an amazed Hodges who pokes it in from three yards. It was the simplest of catches and the most embarrassing of errors for the keeper who has been nothing short of impressive all season, barely putting a foot wrong. As the Tivoli players grab the ball out of the net and run back to the centre circle, Barrett holds his hands on his hips and looks completely gobsmacked at his own laxness. Three—two.

As it approaches the end another cross comes in and is headed away to the edge of the area. Wolfe is underneath it and he raises a foot to control its descent, unaware that Christopher Jackson is charging in from behind to head it back goalwards. Studs clashed with forehead and the ref blows his whistle and gives Wolfe his second yellow card. The last few minutes would be ten against ten.

From the free kick the referee again displays his inability to track the game properly. It is hit straight into the wall and presents itself neatly for a second attempt as Tivoli attackers dash into our area.

The next cross again hits a defender, bouncing off and going behind where the ref whistles and awards a corner. Harbour View are furious; what they and everyone else in the ground have seen is the linesman flagging for offside and it is only the blundering ref who seems to have missed it. 'The ref's a dunce,' mutters a dispirited Ian behind me, while down on the bench DV vociferously informs the official that he is 'a disgrace'.

With our defence creaking under pressure we start to fight back. Thomas has a couple of chances while Steele—who 'always scores against Tivoli', according to Clyde—is coming close too. But there is no more time for goals. The ref finally blows his whistle. Three-two Harbour View.

But Tivoli don't like to lose. As the players approach the gate Williamson is shouting at Edwards who in turn is responding by yelling with a wild fury I have never seen before. With eyes wide, shouting turns to shoving as they pass through the gate and outside the changing rooms, just below the press desk, players from both sides run to take up the fight for their respective men, with a hand being placed at the throat of our violently bellowing captain. Players and onlookers alike try to calm Edwards and get him away from the scene, bundling him up the steps to the side which leads to the seating where Mally and others try to defuse him. As Ian and I look down the incident passes and everything settles, but not for long.

Moments later a Harbour View official runs to the pitchside gate to beckon a security officer. Ian and I both whip to the other side of our platform and peer down to see Carvel, of all people, pushing a Tivoli follower and yelling with almost the same animalistic fury as Edwards, demanding that the man be removed from the ground. Quite what had been said or done is unclear but this now sparks round three and players and followers begin shoving and screaming at anyone in sight. Again, security manage to quash the uprising fairly quickly but a tension remains as I make my way downstairs to the tunnel area. Their keeper Edsel Scott, who had spent the game berating his own players with such venom that he had been booked for it, bangs his boots against a wall while shouting with a deranged fury, seemingly at no one in particular. The shouts 'Far Right you're dead' sweep from the visiting dressing room and members of the away support continue to break into sporadic demonstrations of anger.

With the Tivoli representatives finally gone I am speaking to Edwards outside the changing room and he is all too familiar with the scenario. I ask him what had sparked his own personal fight and he explains that as the last-minute free kick was taken Williamson had punched him in the stomach and then made his threat to shoot him as they walked from the pitch. The casual picture he paints of his own response doesn't quite match with what I had seen but I suspect it is little more than bravado on his part.

In the car afterwards Carvel is visibly upset and points out that, 'we went to Tivoli earlier in the season and lost one-nil and we just turned round and went home. Nobody said any more about it.' When the shoe is on the other foot things don't go so smoothly it seems. As we approach my building he gets a phone call from Vin Blaine who explains that Tivoli thought Thomas had slapped Hinds at the beginning of the small fight early in the match. As everyone else in the ground had seen though, it had actually been a push to the chest and no more. It certainly is no excuse for the way the community had gone on to represent itself afterwards.

But what had been really remarkable about the spat is where it happened. The Tivoli fans in our area of the ground were not a rag-tag bunch of 'badmen' from the most desperate streets of West Kingston, they were the upper echelons of the club's support, the supposed VIPs, and they had still conducted themselves in such an aggressive, lawless manner. And where had Edward Seaga been while it was happening? Only he knows, but he certainly was not trying to mediate.

The people and the way they carry themselves are the result of Seaga's policies and spring from his 'model', as he called it. The environment of modern-day Tivoli and those who come from it are not quirks of geographical chance but products of circumstance and, as much as he would like to blame external PNP forces for things going wrong, and no doubt with some justification, the person ultimately responsible for those circumstances is him. A few days later, travelling in Bowa's car back from Benfica's Drax Hall, the ruck is once again the topic of conversation. Seaga must have been embarrassed by the behaviour of his community's residents, opines under 21 coach Harold Thomas. To that Bowa gives a reply as damning as it is concise: 'He made them what they are.'

Sunday 19ᵗʰ December

Waterhouse	0 1	Boys' Town
Benfica	0 1	Humble Lion
Arnett Gardens	2 1	Portmore United
St. George's	2 0	Reno
HVFC	**3 2**	**Tivoli Gardens**
Sporting Central	4 3	Village United

National Premier League

	P	GD	Pts.
1. Tivoli Gardens	20	14	37
2. Portmore United	20	11	36
3. Waterhouse	20	8	35
4. Boys' Town	20	2	34
5. Sporting Central	20	7	30
6. HVFC	**20**	**4**	**30**
7. Arnett Gardens	20	-3	28
8. Reno	20	2	24
9. Benfica	20	-14	24
10. Village United	20	-9	21
11. Humble Lion	20	-5	19
12. St. George's	20	-17	14

CHAPTER TWENTY ONE

Here To Stay

'Oh yeah, I know Swindon well,' the man says to me as I hone in on the area of England from which I hail under his persistent questioning. 'I used to deal heroin there.' We have travelled to the north coast where Harbour View will be looking to exact revenge on Benfica for the shock 1-0 at the Compound earlier in the season and I have been drawn into a bizarre conversation with a ganja-rolling onlooker purely by dint of my clothing: wearing a navy blue England cricket shirt as I walked past the side by side portakabins which formed the changing rooms at Drax Hall, I had evidently appeared a kindred spirit to this man and he called me over to share his story. He had lived all over England for 14 years and as such his accent was an odd blend of London and Jamaican. After Class As he moves the conversation on to something altogether more sinister, telling me with a great deal of pride about his 'cousins' who are currently serving life in prison for the murders of Letisha Shakespeare and Charlene Ellis in Birmingham in early 2003, the 'New Year shootings' as they came to be known in the British press. He seemed to have been expecting to receive a wave of sheer admiration for his proximity to such dangerous men and he becomes terribly deflated as I explain that, off the top of my head, I couldn't actually remember those particular killings. 'Are you sure? It was the biggest news story in Britain all year,' he pleads, keen to revel in the vicarious recognition that my recollection of the crimes would bring him.

The way he speaks sums up so much of the difficulty facing the Jamaican authorities in their struggle to reduce crime: gang life, and all the killing and drug dealing that goes with it, has become a mark of credibility among so many of the youth. When these behaviours are the last resort of the desperate then at least you know that by providing jobs and other socio-economic necessities the problems should go away, but when many of the people involved actually *want* to be badmen, how on earth do you fight it then?

I make my excuses and return to the Harbour View camp in time for kick-off, placing myself on the small metal stand by the side of the pitch next to DV who is serving a touchline ban for some past indiscretion. Benfica are a club struggling to stay afloat financially and Drax Hall really is a park football venue. In the absence of a sound system to play the FIFA and national anthems one man parks his car by the touchline and, with all four doors open and the volume on his stereo right up, the anthems bleat from his speakers while the visiting players stand dutifully for the formalities wearing an array of bemused looks. I am already losing count of the number of times this season on which I have had to remind myself that this is the national *Premier* League.

The start of the game is equally surreal. After four minutes a cross zips into their box and is met with the weakest of clearing headers which sends it directly to the feet of Marcelino Blackburn just a few yards from goal. Hardly able to believe his luck, Blackburn controls it then smashes it over the keeper's head and in. And three minutes later a Harvey cross is met by Thomas who, under no pressure whatsoever, can just stand and guide it past the keeper. Seven minutes have gone past and we are two-nil up, and the odd thing is the home defence don't even seem to be there. There is no urgency in their play whatsoever, to the extent where I have to ask myself if those goals had actually been real or just imagined, because a team in that situation at home couldn't possibly look that lackadaisical.

And even more strange than that is just how badly we are playing for our lead. Passes go astray all over the pitch and I have never seen us so loose in possession. We scored those two early goals in spite of ourselves rather than because of dominant play. As Thomas puts in John-Ross only for him to slide a shot wide of the goal it is clear that if we play well we can score as many as we like. But we don't play well, and soon they shake themselves out of their stupor and begin to take firm control of the midfield. The pitch is abysmal and the ball is popping up over feet and round legs. We do manage to muster a corner which is met by a dismal clearance straight to Thomas who is allowed two attempts at goal that are both blocked, but little more. If someone had just turned up in Jamaica and this was their first experience of the Premier League they would be shaking their head in disbelief. Both sides are horribly underselling themselves.

With half time approaching one of the Benfica subs can no longer contain himself and nips through the gate at the side of the pitch and round behind our stand to piss up against the wall. As his back is turned his teammates sweep into our box and create their best chance of the game, missing what turns out to be an absolute sitter. The rest of the half is lost in a mess of stray passes and poor control until the whistle brings to it a grateful close.

For DV at half time there is no need to undertake Mourinho-esque feats of espionage in trolleys full of dirty laundry. To get illegal instructions to his team today he simply goes down to the front and leans over the fence as they sit around the dugout sipping their energy drinks. He is one of those managers who seem to experience every pass and every kick even more than his players and spends half the game screaming at the top of his voice, much to the amusement of many opposing fans. Minutes into the second period Michard Barrett throws the ball down the centre of the pitch, as opposed to utilising the space on the flanks, and DV is furious. 'Button! BUTTON!' He jumps up to express his annoyance with greater force. 'DON'T TROW DOWN DI MIGGLE!' Realising the futility of trying to shout over such distances he turns instead to Bowa, deputising for him on the bench. 'BOWA! TELL 'IM NOT TO TROW DOWN DI MIGGLE!' Bowa has seen it all before though: 'Calm down and drink your beer,' he says turning round wearily as a frustrated DV plops back into his seat and gulps again from the bottle of Red Stripe in his hand. It is a small quirk of Jamaican speech that double letters at the apex of words are often replaced by hard 'G' or 'ck' sounds, meaning 'middle' becomes 'miggle' and words like 'bottle' become 'bokkle'. They are twists that we in Britain normally associate with early childhood and they sound amusingly out of place when screamed furiously in the testosterone-heavy atmosphere of professional sport.

As the second half draws on it is becoming clear that Benfica are not getting back into the game and with Kemar Petrekin introduced from the bench we are suddenly looking dangerous again, and indeed it is he who wraps up the game for us. As Benfica pour forward desperately they leave amateur amounts of space at the back and a through ball sets Petrekin clear, rounding the one remaining defender then knocking it along the ground past the advancing keeper.

In stoppage time we complete the humiliation, cutting out a Benfica attack and flying forward in numbers. The home team have all but given up, the midfielders not even bothering to chase back and watching from a distance as Petrekin takes it round their keeper and makes it four-nil with his second. It has been the worst I have seen us play and the fact that we produced such an impressive scoreline speaks volumes for just how woeful Benfica's defending has been. And amazingly, this is the first time since the opening fixtures against Humble Lion and St. George's back in August and early September that we have managed to win consecutive league matches. This streak (for want of a better word) now sets us up to go into the ten day 'winter break' with an outside chance of making the End of Round Final and, more importantly, we have another three points as we push for our title.

The mood is buoyant and easy going as we journey home. Speeding in Bowa's car down the dual carriageway carrying traffic back into Kingston, DV, an occasional driver who seems to be thoroughly enjoying himself tonight, comes level with us with a huge smile and bellows out of his open window, 'Tivoli draw!'. Sure enough, they had been held one-all at home in the latest episode in their rivalry with Arnett, meaning that the gap between us and the leaders is now down to five points, the exact number we have gained on them over just the last two games.

Going through Downtown we stop at traffic lights and DV, who had fallen behind, pulls up beside us again. 'I just can't shake you can I,' Bowa shouts, leaning across to the open passenger side window as DV looks back at him challengingly. It's clear where this is going. The lights ping to green and both cars speed away, yo-yoing past and behind each other as we fire along the straight roads of the grid system. Approaching the end the traffic light above the roundabout flicks from green to amber, causing both drivers to accelerate hard only to see it turning red just before we reach it. Bowa brakes while DV shoots on through and disappears out of sight down the road, leaving the humbled younger coach to look on ruefully and endure the comments of his passengers who make him fully aware of just how smug his boss will be when we arrive back at the Compound in a few more minutes. Another red light further up the road end any hopes Bowa may have of staving off humiliation and we pull into the car park to see DV already out of his car and greeting us with a celebratory jig, the biggest grin yet spread across his joyful face.

This winter is a good time at Harbour View Football Club. With the last two fixtures of the year we have put ourselves squarely back in the title race, and with a bit of luck January will see the start of a triumphant run-in for the reigning Champions.

Christmas is generally considered the point in the football season at which things start to fall into place. Whoever spends Christmas Day at the foot of the table, they say, is almost certain to go down in May, while you will also have a good idea of who will be fighting it out for the title as the winter months turn to spring. But St. George's, sitting glumly on the bottom, have been turning around their form spectacularly in the last few weeks, while we're still looking at half the league as potential Champions and need to get all the way down to Arnett in seventh before it really starts to seem a bridge too far. It has been the strangest of seasons so far, when is this league going to start telling us something concrete?

But for a couple of days at least football is to take a back seat as attentions in this party-crazed and highly religious land turn to festivities. As with the rest of the world, a Jamaican Christmas is a very family focussed event and it says much for local hospitality that I get invited into two of those families for the day. It is about as far removed from what I am used to as possible, but I spend Christmas morning at the home of one of Carvel's sons with four generations of the Stewart family—including Carvel's nephew Christopher Harvey—eating a traditional Jamaican breakfast of seafood, cooked banana, fried dumpling and the national fruit ackee while sitting under the shade of a gazebo as a warm breeze gently blew through the trees. As the day moves on I am transferred to Clyde's house for a Christmas dinner of assorted meats and array of traditional side dishes. Sitting in a t-shirt enjoying 28 degree sunshine means it doesn't feel much like Christmas, but it is a lovely day nonetheless.

As one celebration moves into another and the New Year fireworks flash through the sky above Kingston, the nation reflects on the conclusion of what the *Observer* calls a 'most difficult' year, one that has seen the country suffer with the rest of the world through the economic depression while also being scarred by the Dudus uprising and the Nicole flooding. It has certainly not been a year as tough as it was for the island's beset neighbours in Haiti but it was still one that had most Jamaicans looking forward rather than back as the nation's leaders speak of pulling together to ensure the future be better than the past. Going into the New Year, Governor General Sir Patrick Allen warns, 'We know we will experience crises but we also believe we can overcome them with the strength and vigour of our minds. The beauty and greatness of our people must not be marred by the ugly spectre of crime.'

Leader of the Opposition Portia Simpson-Miller also calls for unity as she urges, 'Let us all step forth bravely as one people and be that agent of change for a better future and a better Jamaica.' But while it all makes for pretty rhetoric, the public are less than impressed, putting forth a strong voice demanding that the leaders take their own advice before expecting everyone else to put their differences aside. The persistent failures of the nation's leadership to deal with crime both on the streets and in Parliament itself has resulted in a broken trust that the public seem to be struggling to overcome, and clearly the easy words of the politicians are not going to be swallowed down like the spoonful of sugar their speakers had hoped for.

A timely demonstration of the fractures between the public and the authorities comes in the first days of January when police kill Horace 'Pugu' Ramsey, leader of the New World Order gang in Central Kingston, itself a splinter of the infamous One Order gang of Spanish Town in St. Catherine. While police report a shoot out that resulted in his death, local residents say no such thing happened and that he was killed in cold blood as his wife and children looked on. Such discrepancies between the two sides are common—the Tivoli uprising was full of them—and clearly do not paint a picture of residents and security forces working together to combat crime. But what is really telling about the depth of Jamaica's problems are the warnings one woman gives afterwards. 'Police better stand guard cos a now shot a go buss. Pugu used to protect we and now them kill him.' In other words, the police have to come in and fill the security vacuum left by the killing of the 'don' because otherwise the residents are exposed and helpless at the hands of outside gangs. It is not the authorities who bring law and order to the lives of these citizens but the criminal big men, and that is a very dangerous state of affairs.

All this makes the 'apology' of the Reggae Boyz a couple of weeks ago all the more important. So often sport is an escape route; while it can and does have profound effects on a society it also exists on a more superficial level and provides something to turn to when the life and death realities of the everyday become too much—our politics may be rotten to the core but at least we have our football team to be proud of and for 90 minutes we can watch them fight for our glory. Whether anyone feels they were right or wrong to 'strike', this is about national opinion and if they had failed to win in Fort-De-France and not penned their apology afterwards then the average Jamaican would simply be looking at one more rotten apple in the barrel of the public sphere, an effect that would also have trickled down to the Premier League—where Harbour View open the year with a cheerless 0-0 draw at home to Sporting—and damaged the image of the sport as a whole. As it is they can still look to the football pitch and feel some pride while forgetting the antics of Parliament.

On the flip side of the 'distraction' coin are the deeper roots that sport has in society, where a national football team, not to mention a world beating track & field team, can be precisely the sort of unifying factor for which the politicians are crying out. In tough times sport can appear at its most extraneous, but often this is precisely when its importance is greatest.

There is some good news leading into the New Year. In their end of year summary, the police report a seven per cent drop in serious crime—including murder, shootings, rape, robbery and larceny—for the first time this century. There is relief at a total of 1,428 murders committed compared to 1,682 the year before. Of course this is still terrifyingly high for a country with a population of under 2.9 million—especially when put into the context of just 615 homicides having been committed in the whole of England and Wales during the same period—but all the same it is an extra 254 lives still being lived. Police commissioner Glenmore Hinds puts the reduction down to new initiatives that have been implemented and large-scale security operations that have been carried out around the island, most notably the Tivoli Gardens assault.

There is a deep and tangled web of problems, far beyond the scope of this book, which stimulate crime in Jamaican society but the fact is it is not the only country in the world dealing with poverty and mass unemployment and yet the people of Bolivia, Haiti and Cameroon don't slaughter each other on such a devastating scale. There must be, therefore, something that stands Jamaica out. And there is. Whenever the issue of crime is raised there is one call that is always made by members of the public but rejected as unfeasible by most experts, namely for the politicians to break up and dissolve their own strongholds. Common sense seems to cry out to tear down the garrisons.

There is one expert who, far from dismissing it, has been actively championing the idea. Back in October Paul Buchanan, the former boss of an initiative which aimed to provide poor and working class people with state-owned land, had given an address in which he outlined a plan to pull apart Tivoli and Arnett and turn them into non-residential districts of retail and innovation, 'Jamaica's "Silicone Valley" of the future' as he termed it. 'The ultimate garrisons must be dismantled,' he had said. 'Built to accommodate the exploding population of Back-O-Wall and Kingston 12, Tivoli and Arnett Gardens soon became zones of political war, exclusion and entrenchment. But at the same time both have developed a welcome notoriety in sports'. By removing the people from these areas and placing them elsewhere, the traditional divides would be broken and the partisan clusters would become mixed, not just removing *en bloc* political tribalism from the capital but also alienating the gangs from one another and interrupting the flow of revenge and rivalry conflicts in their day to day lives.

'Let the programmers, sportsmen, artists, musicians, tradesmen and brilliant scholars be the face of the new Tivoli, Arnett Gardens, Spanish Town and other such garrison communities,' Buchanan continued. And it is those words that bring us once again to the importance of football, something that goes way beyond match reports and league tables and into the very fabric of a nation. While the rest of his list is made up of side-projects and future hopes, it is the sportsmen who exist now, in four garrison-based Premier League football teams, as lights shining out from these communities. Pass the flag to football, he is effectively saying. Let it be the standard bearer as we march into a bold new tomorrow, let sport be the vehicle carrying us towards peace and harmony.

But the obvious flaw in disbanding communities residentially and hoping their football clubs will continue to act as some sort of conduit for local pride is that there are no longer any local people in which that pride can manifest. Jamaica's 'football culture' domestically is fragile enough as it is, if you relocate someone from Arnett to Denham Town and place them next door to a family from Tivoli, for how long will they continue to make the journey up the Collie Smith Drive to watch games at the Anthony Spaulding Complex in a locale that has been turned into a glorified retail park? Football teams are extensions of the people they represent and they live off the continued loyalty of those supporters, what will become of Tivoli Gardens FC if the only community it stands for is a few corporate office buildings? Buchanan identifies sport as the bearer on whose back Kingston can be carried out of its garrison age, but in doing so would it actually be cutting off its own lifeblood and causing its own demise? And that's not to mention all the other obvious difficulties in ripping down and displacing entire residential communities. 'You can't tell people where to live,' as Edward Seaga would later say to me. That tangled web just seems to get ever more messy the more you try to unravel it. The garrisons, it seems, are here to stay.

Wednesday 22nd December

Benfica	**0 4**	**HVFC**
Humble Lions	3 0	Village United
Portmore United	0 0	Boys' Town
Reno	1 1	Sporting Central
Tivoli Gardens	1 1	Arnett Gardens
St. George's	1 0	Waterhouse

Sunday 2nd January

Humble Lion	1 0	Arnett Gardens
Boys' Town	1 1	Benfica
Waterhouse	1 1	Portmore United
HVFC	**0 0**	**Sporting Central**
Village United	0 1	St. George's
Reno	1 0	Tivoli Gardens

National Premier League

	P	GD	Pts.
1. Tivoli Gardens	22	13	38
2. Portmore United	22	11	38
3. Waterhouse	22	7	36
4. Boys' Town	22	2	36
5. HVFC	**22**	**8**	**34**
6. Sporting Central	22	7	32
7. Arnett Gardens	22	-4	29
8. Reno	22	3	28
9. Humble Lion	22	-1	25
10. Benfica	22	-18	25
11. Village United	22	-13	21
12. St. George's	22	-15	20

CHAPTER TWENTY TWO

Juiced

The second Round had ended with the Premier League world being torn apart at its seams as the big guns collapsed and the little men rose up from nowhere. All sense of reason seems to have disappeared in the last few weeks—Tivoli have not won in five games, losing three of those, while Portmore and Waterhouse have a grand total of three wins between them from their last five each. St. George's and Humble Lion, however, having spent most of the season casting themselves further and further adrift behind everyone else, are the form teams of the league with 12 points each from the last 15 on offer. With the form guide showing Ws, Ds and Ls in all the wrong places, the Rastas of Clarendon have even managed to claw themselves out of the relegation zone and put four points between themselves and the drop—new coach Lenny Hyde Snr. has clearly been doing something right.

As per the first two rounds, it is to be those Humble Lions that will provide our opening opponents for round three. This is the last of the full-sized rounds before the League splits into two groups of six for the home straight and it is one that we really have to dominate. After training on Friday DV had sat his players down and told them: 'This is the fatigue round, the round that sorts Champions from also-rans. The team that copes best with the fatigue and mental strain wins. Last season it was us, that's why we were Champions.'

I have always liked DV. He is a manager who was described by Carvel as 'the most technically sound coach in the league' last May and he lives for football—he once described how he will always tell a woman never to ask whether he loves her more than football because there will only ever be one answer, and it will not be one she likes. As a teenager at Kingston College he kept wicket for the school cricket team that included West Indies legend Michael Holding, whose bowling DV unshowily describes as 'very fast'. The pair used to spend a lot of time together and that increased further when Holding found a girlfriend in Harbour View and used DV's family as his cover story for regular sojourns to the community. He was also a decent sprinter, growing up close to four-time Olympic medallist Donald Quarrie, and sacrificed his place at the national championships for a keen friend to whom the event meant much more. 'That was his thing, it wasn't mine,' he says. 'Mine was football.' And today it still is. One of his great strengths beyond sound tactics is as a speaker and his ability to produce stirring team talks at key moments, always promoting the belief that Harbour View have a little something extra as a team that nobody else does.

Friday was another of those occasions, rousing the spirits of his squad as they went into this most crucial of periods. After the Sporting match people had proffered various theories about exactly what was required from round three in order to set us up to retain the title. Eight wins minimum said some, getting through unbeaten was another suggestion. One thing that is certain was that we have to perform better than anyone else and we cannot rely on our rivals slipping up like they have over the last month or two. This is the time for Harbour View to stand up tall and stride through the herd, regardless of who or what should stand in their way. Because that is what champions do.

With Humble Lion arriving after four straight wins—two more than we have managed to string together at any point this season—we need an authoritative performance. There are a number of debutantes in the squad and on Friday DV emphasised the need for them to work hard and take their opportunities to cement a place in the team. He announced their inclusion while reading out the squad for the upcoming game as the senior players all clapped encouragingly, congratulating the newcomers on making the step up and welcoming them to the fold. It was one of these names in particular that caused a stir; having read out the list as a very formal procession of full names, DV rounded it off with his wild card: '. . . and of course, the great, Juice.'

Juice, or Elton Thompson to use his real name, is a young player whose profligacy in front of goal has reached comical levels in the under 21s, a striker whose finishing is almost a running joke around the club. But he is young—a truly great finisher at 18 is rare enough to be a £40 million player at 26—and he is a good footballer nonetheless, solid on the ball, a tireless runner and, most importantly, he has that Michael Owen-like ability to get himself those chances in the first place. He is a player who looks like he will score a lot of goals when he is older and has tightened his shooting, and who even now will cause a lot of problems for opposing teams by constantly buzzing around the attacking third and continuously popping up in all the places defenders do not want him to be, something it is now hoped would draw fouls from a physical and slightly clumsy Humble Lion back line should he get the chance to play. And he doesn't always miss—on the day it was announced he would be joining the Premier League team for the first time he celebrated by scoring the winner for the under 21s, a nicely taken goal he slipped low past the keeper. I may be largely alone, but I have a good feeling about his step up.

When we arrive at the Compound on match day, we find out he isn't just in the squad, he's starting. Jamahli Spence has been struggling with a foot injury all week and is only fit enough for a place on the bench and our lack of strikers means Juice is thrown into the fray alongside Rafeik Thomas, as the locals watch on in amazement.

And after just a few minutes their incredulity grows when Christopher Harvey attacks down the right and belts a swerving cross over the box to the far post. A yellow and blue shirt sprints in to meet it, connecting powerfully with his head and hammering it past a helpless keeper from close range. Mixing fate and fairy tale, there is only one person it could possibly have been: eight minutes into his début, Juice has scored the opener.

Rarely have I ever seen a goal celebrated in such a way. Like Toto Schillaci at *Italia 90* he sprints away looking so overjoyed that he's not quite sure what to do with himself and within seconds his delirious team mates wrestle him to the ground and jump on him until he is buried beneath the entire Harbour View side. But he is not to be halted there and once the pyramid has dissolved he is up and running again, this time heading to the bench where every player, coach and staff member has risen to clap the young striker. Making his way down the line he high-fives each one before finally reaching DV, the manager who had given him his chance, wrapping his arms around the coach and burying his head in his chest with a grateful hug. Behind him everyone else has by now lined up ready to re-start the game and the taken aback coach briefly returns the hug before shaking him off and sending him back onto the pitch, where there are still another 82 minutes of football to play. But what a start.

In the stand Paul Hibbert, having gained no end of pleasure from Juice's misses all season, is still stunned when the game gets going again. Turning round with a look of astonishment he simply mouths the word 'Juice', as though wondering whether or not it had really happened, before standing and bellowing: 'DV, you're the best coach in the world!' A few minutes later and he is now on the phone. 'I'm staying quiet now,' he says, sharing his amazement with some anonymous friend on the other end of the line. 'I'm not saying another word for the rest of the year.'

In the second half, after Blackburn has made it 2-0 with a penalty, the début star is taken off for Ranique Muir and he leaves the field to a standing ovation that he probably wouldn't have even dared dream of this morning when he looked forward to the game ahead. But what marks him out as significant here, beyond his slightly Cinderella-hued story, is what he represents. Jamaican clubs live in a continuous struggle to survive. They must bring up a young player, build him up to a level worthy of the bigger leagues and sell him on for a small fee before turning back to the pool for another youngster with whom the endless circular process can be repeated. But that, as it is, is just a faceless theory written factually on paper. Juice, with Fagan and Bryan both having gone to Vietnam, is that cycle made real. He is the next person to be pushed up the ladder, the next potential pay cheque to help Harbour View's survival. Or so goes the plan, at least. But he is a reminder that football's minnows do not trade in names on a team sheet but in real people, real boys with their own dreams and hopes and loves and desires and flaws. Behind all football's dollars are real lives, and Juice's life, for the foreseeable future, is now dedicated to getting that move abroad, and raising Harbour View some vital cash. But, more immediately, he will discover in the next few days that this sporting life is not all about the ups.

The game ends at two-nil. Elsewhere Tivoli, Portmore and Boys' Town have also won and order has been restored to the previously choppy waters. The latest column of the form guide now shows Ws for the top four, Ls for four of the bottom five and Ds for everyone in the middle. Everything is back in its rightful place. How relieving it is for the establishment to see such symmetry again.

The structure of Jamaican cup competitions works somewhat differently to our own. There is an island-wide cup competition, the PFAJ Champions Cup, which begins in March, but the smallest teams from Westmoreland cannot really afford to be carting their whole squad to Kingston for a game and Jamaican football as a whole is not capable of sustaining a national cup competition of the depth and scale of our own FA Cup, and yet it seems unfair to rob the little teams of their chance to compete. So the problem is solved by giving each of the four regions its own tournament earlier in the season from which the top teams qualify for the Champions Cup.

The provincial regions finished weeks ago to allow administrators time to organise who would be appearing in the national tournament. Kingston and St. Andrew, however, is so strong that all eight teams entering qualify for the 'grown up' Cup automatically and so, by the time the glory of Humble Lion and the other regional winners has almost been forgotten, the KSAFA clubs are only just starting out on their own road to the Champions Cup.

The long name for our local competition is the KSAFA Jackie Bell Knockout. Winthorpe 'Jackie' Bell and a colleague of his, Dennis Ziadie, were killed in a car accident during the 1986 World Cup in Mexico and they are still fondly remembered today. Both had been international footballers and before they went to Mexico Bell had been named national team coach while Ziadie was given an important role in youth development. In October, on National Heroes Day, I had played in a charity match held annually in their memory while KSAFA also had come up with a way to ensure they were never forgotten, naming their cup competition after Bell.

The tale of their accident may be ringing a bell. When watching the Masters' training game in Heroes Park on my first evening with Harbour View back in August, the Kolo Toure lookalike had bemoaned the fact that the deaths of two JFF officials had destroyed his chances of playing for the national team. They were, of course, Bell and Ziadie. And it is convenient that the Toure lookalike's story becomes relevant again here because he represents the other, less glorified, avenue that lies ahead for a boy like Juice. The avenue that leads to afternoons in the park laying bare the lingering disappointments of the past to unknown listeners. To him the fact that two people had lost their lives seemed almost insignificant in the shadow of his personal woe, so great was his tragedy, but to the rest of Jamaica he is a forgotten man.

Juice would again be starting in the first leg of our quarter final, for which Harbour View have been drawn against Tivoli. A huge clash, you might think. How excited people must have been to see those two drawn against one another early on. Well actually, it happens with such unlikely regularity that both clubs became convinced it is rigged, and so for the last three years Clyde has made the effort to be present at every draw to personally ensure that everything was above board. Indeed it is, and still the draws continue to throw the two clubs together.

Tivoli may have ended their winless run a few days ago but tonight they look ragged and woefully short of creativity. In the first half Juice is booked for throwing the ball away in anger after having a foul given against him, but with an hour or so gone he experiences a moment he will never forget, whatever the rest of his career has in store for him.

Making yet another enthusiastic run, a ball is played through for him to chase. As it bounces into the area the keeper comes to meet it, getting to the ball slightly before the striker. In his naïve excitement, Juice still challenges for it and he catches the keeper's hand with his boots. It is the sort of thing a young player who is desperate to impress will do when a more experienced player might have known better, and a foul is rightfully given. But the keeper is not one for making allowances and, after a quick roll of pain to ensure everyone knows just how grievously he's been assaulted, he leaps up and headbutts the striker. Immediately the ref is over and produces his red card, and then he approaches Juice. Reaching into his pocket he brings out a yellow, followed by another waving of the red. Every ounce of elation on Sunday is now matched by despair. He covers his face with his hands and walks from the field in tears, a young boy overcome by his emotions and unable to hide them from the crowd surrounding him. The Tivoli fans scream bilious abuse his way as he departed and Hibbert, so often his chief critic in the past, now becomes his chief guardian and vents his own fury back at them.

Our games with Tivoli never go smoothly and their unpleasant fans grow more and more uproarious as the match progresses, but for all their side's impotence Harbour View cannot break them down and the game ends goalless. It was a game we really should have won by three or four, but it simply didn't happen. The second leg will give us 'all to play for', as they say, and the elder heads around the ground merely nod in acceptance of a disappointing result and move on. The youngest head, though, had been imprinted with a scolding lesson in life's harsh realities. It's not all fate and fairytales. Being a young professional footballer grasping for that next rung on the ladder is a tough position to get used to, as the man who was denied his big chance by Jackie Bell's death can attest, and Juice is just starting to find out why.

Sunday 16th January

Benfica	2 3	Tivoli Gardens
Boys' Town	2 0	St. George's
HVFC	**2 0**	**Humble Lions**
Reno	1 2	Portmore United
Sporting Central	0 0	Waterhouse
Village United	0 0	Arnett Gardens

National Premier League

	P	GD	Pts.
1. Tivoli Gardens	23	14	41
2. Portmore United	23	12	41
3. Boys' Town	23	4	39
4. HVFC	**23**	**6**	**37**
5. Waterhouse	23	7	37
6. Sporting Central	23	7	33
7. Arnett Gardens	23	-4	30
8. Reno	23	2	28
9. Humble Lions	23	-3	25
10. Benfica	23	-19	25
11. Village United	23	-13	22
12. St. George's	23	-17	20

CHAPTER TWENTY THREE

Guns, Pitches & Bling

Saturday's papers make grim reading. On what was dubbed 'Fatal Friday', five people were killed when an attempted bus robbery went wrong in New Kingston. The bus system had for a long time laboured under the stigma of safety deficiencies—just last week the *Observer* had run an online poll questioning whether people considered public transport too dangerous to use—and this was a prime example as to why. Halfway through the bus' route the three robbers had produced guns and ordered it down a quiet side street where they proceeded to claim the possessions of the passengers. It was to their considerable misfortune that one of those passengers happened to be illegally armed himself and a shootout ensued, a scenario which then escalated when the police arrived soon afterwards. The result was two dead gunmen and three dead passengers.

But it did not end there. The same article goes on to look further into an incident from the day before, the Thursday, in which five people were shot dead in Portmore—where Harbour View are about to go. They had been playing dominoes in the Portsmouth area of the town when ten gun men jumped out of two vehicles and opened fire. Police called the two incidents 'barbaric' and said that they represent a clear message from the criminal community that they are prepared to push the security forces to the very limits of their will and determination to maintain law and order, as though humbled by the end-of-year crime figures and wanting to prove the positivity of the new year to be nothing more than over-optimistic folly. There are also reports of a well known entertainer's adopted son being shot dead outside the gate of his home, an incident which, like the bus robbery, had occurred uptown in New Kingston. The hopeful atmosphere of the past few weeks is once again being spiked by fear.

Having seen off one of the League's form teams on round three's opening weekend Harbour View now have to visit the other one. The impressive road to St. George's takes us back through the winding mountains and steamy rainforest. The wet season finished a couple of months ago and the river, whose torrent had bubbled and spat when we first travelled to Buff Bay in September, is little more than a stream ebbing between the large, round rocks sitting across the expanse of its dry exposed bed. This is not a seasonal day though and rain falls from the grey sky onto the roads and rising peaks, among which columns of jungle mist rise as though billowing from chimneys hidden by the dense trees.

For Portland itself this weather is not an anomaly. Indeed, it has been on the receiving end of more than its fair share of rain recently and this shows in the pitch when we arrive at Lynch Park. It had once been a cricket pitch and has large amounts of clay in it which is now wet and very slippery. But that is not the only problem, and the ground is also so uneven in places that it is almost dangerous. 'Bumpy, bumpy,' DV observes as he walks down the centre before kick off, his accent making the words almost onomatopoeic as it bounces the syllables around. Bowa is more concise, walking past me near the centre circle and moaning: 'This isn't a pitch, it's a pasture.' In one penalty area it is almost like marshland and the whole thing seems to have gone weeks without seeing a mower, tufts of grass in some places reaching a good seven or eight inches long.

In conditions like this you rarely get a great game of football and today proves no exception. While men around me brazenly ignore the 'NO GANJA' sign, despite a policeman standing among them, the players on the pitch battle out a scoreless draw. At the end Richard Edwards comes off with no complaints at the result. 'At least it's a point so we'll have to take it,' he says, seeming to recognise, as the rest of us did, that George's had actually played better football than the champions. He goes on to say that the pitch had worked against them before going off to change. And that's that, more points dropped, and on a day where Tivoli, Boys' Town and Waterhouse have all won.

'Bumbaclaaaat,' exhales Daveion Woodhouse in the stands at the Compound. It is another cloudy day and the Under 13s, the side formerly captained by Martin Davis before he skipped off to Valencia, are playing against a team from Spanish Town, and they have just conceded an almost laughably error-strewn goal to go two nil behind. The first goal was fairly poor, causing Michard Barrett to bury his head in his hands as he watched the terrified looking keeper come out to meet a striker in a one on one situation with all the conviction of a timid man trying to shoo an angry bear, but this next one had been simply farcical. The original shot had hit the post and, with countless legs Riverdancing through the scramble in the way they so often do with children playing football, a follow-up had been cleared off the line and then the other post was struck before the ball was finally placed in the net at the fourth time of asking.

A number of the first team squad have come out to watch and they struggled to hide their amusement at aspects of the spectacle being played out in front of them. What is impressive though is the support they offered the youngsters as well, they even knew all the names of the little players and their personal strengths and weaknesses. What a lift it must be for a child to get such attention from the professionals of the Premier League champions. But now they are being called away. The buses are ready and the men must leave the boys to it. Portmore are waiting for them across town.

Yesterday large areas of Portmore were under curfew. For 24 hours from 6pm on Friday to the same time on Saturday evening, residents of the Westchester and Portsmouth communities had to remain indoors unless given written authorisation from the security forces moving into the area. 'The soldiers have to find out what is what. The violence flares up here all the time,' said the Corporal running the mission. 'The operation is nowhere as big as Tivoli but within a couple of days this will all be sorted out. We are here to get the guns, drugs, ammunition and criminal elements.' There was no Coke-figure involved and there was no mass uprising, but the absence of global news cameras does not make it any less significant to the people who have to look out of their living room window at soldiers pushing through their streets.

As promised it has all been 'sorted out' today. An eagle circles overhead as we scour the pitch at Ferdie Neita Park, taking in its own view of the field. What it looks down on is even worse than the pasture had been at George's, with hard bumps and long grass. Most amazingly of all, there are large areas on which thick shrubbery is growing. I walk past DV outside the penalty area and he demonstrates how easy it would be for players to catch their feet in it and trip. 'That's the Jamaica Premier League,' he laughs as he wanders off to inspect the other flank. Pitch quality is a real issue here, especially considering there is a culture of playing more with their feet than their heads, but like everything else it all comes back to that one thing. The crucial element is, as always, money.

The English and Spanish leagues have no such concerns. They enjoy massive resources and these come primarily from television, sport's great provider. The total amount the Premier League raised from selling its TV rights in the UK and abroad for the 2010-2013 period was £3.182 billion; that's over a billion pounds a year for the 20 clubs to play with just from one income stream alone. In Spain clubs are allowed to negotiate their own TV contracts and from them Real Madrid and Barcelona bring in around £106 million each per season. Any amount the Jamaica Premier League gets from TV will, of course, pale in comparison to that. But exactly how much is it, you might ask. What relative pittance do the media companies here give to the League for its product? The answer is nothing. In fact, the League actually *pays* CVM to broadcast its games.

In short, it is in the league's interest to get the games shown on television in order to make its sponsorship rights more valuable. Showing the games is less in CVM's interest because as far as they are concerned there was very little market for local football on TV (viewing figures are not measured in Jamaica) and so the PLCA, unlike *La Liga* and the Premier League, negotiates from a position of weakness. Earlier in the season a major sponsor had stepped in, spinning an absorbing rhetoric about high production values and a more attractive end product, but this particular backer didn't enjoy a good past relationship with CVM and refused to work with them. So the league did what it had to do and severed its ties with the network, only for the new sponsor to suddenly get cold feet and pull out.

This happened at around the time Harbour View travelled to Humble Lion at the beginning of round two, and since then the league has been aired on a temporary new home at Hype TV, a cable channel aimed primarily at the 'MTV generation' where they had to pay their own production costs. But now they are starting to build bridges with CVM again and have been allowed to come back to the larger network on new terms: the PLCA are to continue to produce their own shows at their own cost, and they must also pay the network for the airtime, a double whammy of expenses.

But it's not all bad. They are pleased to have editorial control over what the public sees, and the sabbatical to Hype has opened the league up to a whole new audience that didn't previously watch the local league. Within the PLCA they are privately confident this will make the rights more valuable and so, while they have to endure this season paying out two different costs for television, that might actually turn into a profit when renegotiation time comes around in summer. Television money is the basis for all football's wealth, in Jamaica they are just daring to dream that some of it might finally be coming their way.

It is a gloomy evening and from the church near the corner songs of praise drift over the pitch as the home side make threatening early moves. We are six points behind Tivoli and three behind Portmore themselves who sit second. Depending on Boys' Town's result away at Arnett, a win could take us second and potentially to within one result of the top. Before long, with Kimorlee Brissett stranded upfield, a long ball gets tossed into the left hand side of our area, a difficult one for Barrett to judge but, unlike the poor 13 year old keeper this afternoon, he times his movement perfectly and spreads himself well to push the ball away from the striker's feet. But they collide heavily. He staggers to his feet and limps to the loose ball to send it out for a throw before collapsing to the floor again to receive treatment. It's always worrying to see a keeper shakily get to his feet after a collision: what if his vision is blurred, you wonder? What if his reactions are dulled? He is the one player on the pitch with absolutely no room for error, can he still do his job properly?

It doesn't take long before the balletic star of our previous game here, Steven Morrissey, is back to his old tricks. A high ball loops up on the edge of our area; he raises his foot and plants it firmly into Richard Edwards' chest. Instantly he screams and falls to the floor while holding his leg in the air, as through trying to fully exhibit the damage done to it by our captain's ribs. About two seconds later he realises the game has continued and that no one is paying him any attention whatsoever and springs to his feet, the latest in a string of miracle recoveries so extensive he is becoming a walking scrapbook of Jesus' greatest hits. They are clearly singing the right songs over in that church.

With the game stretching, Portmore are making opportunities down our left as Brissett is too often finding himself stranded high up the pitch from his attacking explorations. For now though he is being let off by an inordinate number of misplaced passes from those trying to exploit the gaps. After Thomas hits a shot just wide, his strike partner, Juice, is clattered into by an over-zealous defender. It has been happening frequently and they are being allowed to get away with it. 'One, two, three, four,' DV shouts towards the ref, counting off the unpunished fouls on his fingers. The official is clearly cowed by the abuse and a few minutes later an innocuous challenge is harshly rewarded with the home side's first booking.

Sport and schadenfraude go together like tea and biscuits. Indeed, others' misery is often one of our greatest joys as fans, and while it is not nice to see a player injured it can sometimes be hard not to smile when it brings with it the most richly delicious of ironies. Making a dash into some space in the centre of the pitch, Steven Morrissey pulls up and begins to limp. There is nobody within metres of him and even by his standards trying to buy a foul there was taking the piss, this is for real. Like the hypochondriac coming to terms with the news that this time he actually *is* ill, this is one occasion on which there is no screaming and no drama as he plops down to the floor, he just sits down before looking forlornly to the bench for help. Perhaps his substitution is more a precaution than anything else—he is due in America for a trial the following morning—but he is immediately replaced, and I find it difficult not to feel slightly smug as he limps from the pitch.

During the half time break news comes through over the phones that Tivoli have drawn at home with Village. Not just that but everyone in the league, with the exception of Waterhouse, have also drawn. This isn't just a chance to get one over on one of our title rivals now, it is a chance to get one over on *all* of them. But both sides have this inspiration and the second half begins evenly. With about an hour gone a high ball bounces deep into their half and Juice is first to it.

A split second later a defender arrives and throws his boot into the space the ball had been, now occupied by our striker's knee. Juice tumbles to the floor and the ref blows for a free kick. There will be a card for this and everyone waits anxiously to see what colour it will be. Will they be playing the last half an hour with ten men?

The current FIFA Laws of the Game state that a player should be sent off for 'serious foul play'. They don't elaborate exactly what this rather vague adjective means, but if going hard and studs-up into an opposing player's knee isn't a 'serious' foul then what is? Yet Portmore is the club that people in Jamaica tend to acknowledge as getting privileged treatment. They have a number of officials high up in the JFF and will quietly do as they are told rather than ever rocking the boat in the way that other clubs might. Perhaps this is the reason that the referee waves away the defender without so much as a talking-to as the Harbour View bench erupts in fury, or perhaps he is just another refereeing 'dunce', as Ian Burnett might say. Either way it is a decision so ludicrous that even a local stretcher bearer in a Portmore United shirt laughs out loud, looking over at DV and declaring, 'That's a red card,' while our coach can only bring himself to respond with exasperated sigh.

It gets worse when they break down our right. Christopher Harvey gets a tackle in and sends it out off the attacking player for a goal kick. Except the ref gives a corner. The stretcher man bursts out in laughter again, gaining endless delight from the absurdity of the decisions going his team's way, yet sympathising all the same with the fuming Harbour View bench next to him. The corner is dealt with, but the game is getting more and more desperate. This is a massive opportunity for both sides in the title race and the minutes are running out.

With the game lurching from end to end they press through our right. There are five minutes to go when the ball comes to Portmore's rising talent Tremaine Stewart. He is about thirty yards from goal, looks up and sees his chance with Barrett a few yards off his line. He unleashes a howitzer shot, hard and flat and swerving through the air, the apex of the shot rising only just above the bar before it dips. And the dip is crucial, for it brings with it the realisation that this strike is heading for the top corner. Barrett shifts his feet but the swing is carrying the ball too far away from him. He leaps vainly and throws one hand up towards it but can't reach as it sails past him.

Ping! It strikes the top of the bar and goes over. Somehow it hadn't quite dipped enough. The groans of agony from the home crowd are met by sighs of relief from the few in Harbour View colours.

Both sides give everything as the last minutes pass. Then, in the final seconds of injury time, we are awarded a free kick around 35 yards from goal. Jermaine Hue stands behind it, eyeing his targets carefully he sends a high ball into the area. Ranique Muir gets to it ahead of anyone else and directs a pass across the box to Thomas who has found impossible amounts of space on the far side of the area. He controls it—there is no time left at all—and with what must be the last kick of the entire game he shoots low across the goal. It seems to take forever but there is no doubt about it: it's going in! I am already out of my chair celebrating; heart pounding and adrenaline surging, my mouth opening to release a scream of triumph.

But it doesn't go in. As if in slow motion, time's whims prolonging and drawing out the anguish, it rolls along the floor and just outside the post.

I fall back into my seat. How had that gone wide? How are we not celebrating the latest of late winners? Harbour View players collapse to their knees in disbelief. That had been it, that had been us taking the initiative in this chaotic title race. But it wasn't.

On this same January night the league in Spain was effectively sewn up. Real Madrid lost 1-0 away at Osasuna while Barcelona avenged their early-season defeat to Hercules with a 3-0 win, putting them seven points clear at the top. That is not an unassailable lead with four months to go you might think, but this is no ordinary league. The £106 million each a year I mentioned earlier means that Barça and Real are competing on a different plain to everyone else. *La Liga*, this year more than any other, is a two-team league. And Barcelona's record in that league now reads: played 21, won 19, drawn 1, lost 1. They have just won their 15 consecutive match, there is no way they would drop enough points in the remaining 17 games to let Real back in and now everyone, even the ever-biased Madridista media houses, is conceding the title before they have even woken to the first chilly dawn of February. Could you design a more boring, lifeless competition? And yet it is watched fanatically by millions of fans all over the globe, fans from whom all that limitless TV and merchandising money richly flows.

That night I lie in bed replaying Rafeik's shot over and over in my head, as though the outcome might eventually change if I go through it enough times. And if that is going through my mind, I wonder, what on earth must be going through his? No doubt the 'What If' thoughts of how he could have done things differently will haunt him for days. That is the life of a sportsman.

Of the five teams in the title hunt, two had drawn while we had been millimetres from inflicting a loss on one of the others and picking up three enormous points ourselves, points which would have put us four off the top and left us with all the momentum. But it wasn't to be and we remain in fifth place, separated still by six points from Tivoli. But who cares, right? No foreign broadcasters are paying billions of pounds to show these games because who wants to see them? Christ, just to get it shown at home the league has to *pay* the TV stations, who on earth is bothered by this bling-free competition?

Well you can keep your *La Liga* parades. While the world looks the other way, Jamaica is producing one of the most frustrating, agonising, exciting title races you could imagine. So they might not have Messi or Ronaldo, they might not have the Camp Nou or the Bernabéu, they might not have the glitz or the glamour and yes, they might have bushes growing on their bumpy, pasture-like pitches, but I for one would take this mad, crazy Jamaican Premier League over a one-team procession any day.

Hugo Saye

Sunday 23rd January   Wednesday 26th January   Sunday 30th January

Arnett Gardens 1 1 Reno	Benfica 0 1 Portmore	Arnett Gardens 1 1 Boys' Town
Humble Lion 0 1 Boys' Town	Boys' Town 0 1 Tivoli Gardens	Humble Lions 0 0 Sporting
Portmore 0 2 Village United	**HVFC 1 0 Arnett Gardens**	**Portmore 0 0 HVFC**
St. George's 0 0 HVFC	Reno 2 0 Humble Lions	St. George's 1 1 Benfica
Tivoli Gardens 1 0 Sporting	Sporting 1 1 St. George's	Tivoli Gardens 0 0 Village
Waterhouse 4 0 Benfica	Village United 3 2 Waterhouse	Waterhouse 2 1 Reno

National Premier League

	P	GD	Pts.
1. Tivoli Gardens	26	16	48
2. Portmore United	26	11	45
3. Waterhouse	26	11	43
4. Boys' Town	26	4	43
5. HVFC	**26**	**11**	**42**
6. Sporting Central	26	6	35
7. Reno	26	3	32
8. Arnett Gardens	26	-5	32
9. Village United	26	-10	29
10. Humble Lions	26	-6	26
11. Benfica	26	-24	26
12. St. George's	26	-17	23

CHAPTER TWENTY FOUR

Two Sides Of The Ghetto

I worry that so far I have portrayed Tivoli Gardens as the pantomime villain of the piece. All I have said may paint it as a dark and sinister place, at the centre of which, were this Hollywood, would lie their foreboding stadium, shrouded by a permanent black storm cloud, the kind which strikes the goalposts with regular cracks of lightning. Home to a demonic team of rabid red-eyed monsters waiting to be slain by the gallant, noble warriors of Harbour View. But real life of course does not have its pantomime villains and this is no more realistic a description than the rustic paradise I firmly said it was not in chapter nine. I feel I should rectify the situation, for the truth, as always, lies somewhere in the middle.

And so it is under a sky of the brightest cobalt blue that Harbour View arrive at the Edward Seaga Complex for the Jackie Bell Cup quarter final, today being the second leg after our 0-0 draw and Juice's red card at the Compound. The only imperfections are the smallest white clouds and these tufts do nothing to stop the glorious sunlight pouring down onto players who are now darting about a pitch that is a lush, glowing green. The atmosphere around the ground is light and relaxed, like that which flits airily around a warm day early in the English summer. West Kingston's not so bad after all, why would you want to be anywhere else?

'Fuck yuh mother, referee!'

Oh yes, the people. They don't make it easy to be generous to them. Wherever you go in any football league there is abuse and swearing, but the people of Tivoli just seem to be more bitter than anybody else, the chip on their shoulder always seems that much larger than anybody else's. They simmer with resentment and anger, constantly spilling hate into the world.

'Batty bwoy linesman!'

About 15 minutes of the match have gone and Navion Boyd has just been chopped down in the area by Fabian Campbell, leaving the Tivoli striker rolling on the floor and banging his fist on the turf in pain but the referee has given nothing more than a goal kick. It is an odd decision: the ref is clearly stating that it wasn't a foul, but by giving a goal kick as opposed to a corner he is also saying that Campbell's challenge didn't actually get the ball. That only leaves the option that Boyd dived, in which case why wasn't he booked? I couldn't tell you; from where I was sitting it looked what they call a 'stonewall' penalty. But, as they always say, these things tend to even themselves out.

'Harbour View a batty man side!'

The people leaning over the fence between the stand and the pitch are clearly as bemused as me by the decision, although they do choose slightly different ways to express it. It's not long until they find a new target for their scolding.

'Lick out di Junglist blood claat legs!'

A midfielder is now tussling with Marcelino Blackburn on the far side of the pitch. In Jamaica to 'lick' is to 'hit' and this particular fan wants our midfielder stopped by his legs being swiped out from underneath him. A Junglist is someone from Arnett Gardens area which, when in Tivoli, qualifies Blackburn for verbal persecution as a resident of Trenchtown. Garrison rivalries might be tamed but they are still alive and well, despite what people may like to claim.

Like I said, the law of the cliché stipulates that dodgy decisions will even themselves out. After about half an hour a ball is played into their area and Andre Steele scampers after it, bringing it under control only to have a defender smash into his legs. The tackle was absolutely nowhere near the ball and the Harbour View bench all jump to their feet screaming for a penalty. Goal kick. The fans respond with an explosion of bile so furious and constant that it is almost impossible to make out any words. They are swearing at us on the bench, they are swearing at our players, they are swearing at the officials—although quite what the ref and linesman have done to anger them by turning down an obvious penalty for the opposition is unclear. Jermaine Hue, a sub to give his ankle a rest, was the loudest advocate for a penalty and now he prowls the technical area like an angry tiger, receiving a hail of personal insults from just a few feet away.

And then, after nearly 135 minutes of the tie, goals start to come. With the coaching staff on either side readying themselves for half time, Campbell slides a pass along the ground to Ranique Muir who controls and lays it off to Steele on the edge of the area. Steele plays it straight back into the path of Muir who has continued his run, he in turn hits it hard first-time with his left foot.

'Goooooooooooooooooool!' Hue is back on his feet, turning to the silenced fans with his arms raised in celebration and a cheeky grin spread across his face. He's been around long enough to know exactly what's coming.

'Fuck yuh mother, Jermaine Hue!'

'Batty bwoy, Jermaine Hue!'

The torrent is as instantaneous as someone flicking a switch but this time it burns brightly and quickly dies out, a cathartic purging of tension after going a goal behind as much as anything else. What seems odd about so much of the swearing from Tivoli fans is that a lot of it comes from women. 'That's the ghetto way, the women are like that,' Clyde explains to me the next morning. 'In front of all the big men there's always a woman.' Sometimes literally. Just a week or two ago the police finally ended months of searching in their quest to find Jamaica's most wanted criminal, the fearsome Christopher 'Dog Paw' Linton. He was wanted for numerous murders and shootings in the August Town area of Kingston—home to our second keeper Devon Haughton—and had been found cowering in the house of two women. According to an *Observer* journalist whom he had contacted moments before his arrest, his voice was 'trembling' with fear. As one online commenter said: 'These big bad gun men are all cowards. They create mayhem and when they are caught they are like babies. The amount of lives they have destroyed means nothing to them but they are so concerned about theirs.' The ghetto way. A tearful gangsta sheltering behind two ladies. A nation of contradictions.

With an hour gone a cross is headed clear of the home defence and lands for Fabian Campbell to volley speculatively from thirty yards. It is blocked but Andre Steele—who always scores against Tivoli—is first to the second ball, curling it with his right foot from outside the area and pinging it off the post into the net. The celebrations this time are even bigger; two up, with away goals meaning they now have to score three to win it.

It should be all over when Steele plays through Muir but the chance is smothered by the keeper. From that point, though, it is all Tivoli. Thomas is withdrawn to keep him out of the way of the fierce tackles and the structure of the side seems to disintegrate. In the 69 minute a long ball is headed away from our box by Dicoy only to be hit first time straight back and into our top corner. Not long afterwards, a foul by Andre McFarlane gives them a free kick twenty yards out. As it is taken Barrett shifts his weight early in the wrong direction and is incapable of getting back across. It flies into the corner to make it two-all on the night.

The fans in the Edward Seaga Complex go crazy, they seem to think 2-2 is enough for them. It's not and away goals mean we are the ones still going through at the moment, but the momentum is all against us. Bowa shouts to the team to fight, Vin tells them to keep calm. As if these players didn't have enough to deal with, they also had to decode the conflicting messages of their coaches. But whether through fighting or staying calm, we hold out. The final whistle blows and puts us into the semi final where we will square off with Boys' Town in just a couple of days time. Another meeting with west Kingston, another clash with the ghetto football fans.

It is interesting to wonder why the residents of Tivoli are what they are. Of course, we are not all 'just people', united by one pan-species behavioural code—people here do not act in the same way as someone from a gentrified village in the Oxfordshire countryside might, for example. We are, as Alan 'Skill' Cole was at pains to express, products of our environment. We will probably never know for sure what about the Tivoli environment shaped its residents, if it really was Edward Seaga who made them what they are or whether their attitudes stem from the stresses brought to bear on them by external political forces. Certainly there seems to be something of the embattled, us-against-the-rest siege defier about them, fighting the world because the world fights them, and this can draw some sympathy with their situation. But there seems to be no desire to break through that stigma, with people instead appearing happy to spit at the outside while labouring under a victim mentality and for that fingers must point towards community leaders, and Seaga. The semi-final would be illustrative of this because Boys' Town is also a traditionally JLP area, and a much smaller one than Tivoli, and yet its people offer a different experience entirely.

The semi-finals are to be held at Harbour View. The announcement had been made just a couple of days before the event after club director Ludlow Bernard had come to an agreement with KSAFA, and so on Sunday Waterhouse, Arnett and Boys' Town all pitch up at the Compound. The former two play out a dreary game that sees Arnett into the final prior to some between-game entertainment from sponsors Claro. Mr G, since performing his hit *Swaggarific* at half time during the international against Costa Rica in August, has been taken over by this mobile phone network and his masterpiece has been re-processed, re-packaged and re-branded as *Clarorific*, a phrase that became the main focus of all their subsequent advertising, and tonight he is due to perform in the show. A month or two ago Claro had ambled even further into their Clarorific yonder by introducing a ten year old 'mini-me' to their advertising stable, dressing him up in the sort of expensive-looking clothes every rap video features—with the obligatory sunglasses permanently on his face to boot—and now this little scamp is also singing live in front of the biggest crowd at the Compound all season.

When he finishes his repertoire the host approaches with a microphone and some questions about his life:

'What do you do during the day?' the host asks.

'I go to school every single day and I listen carefully to my teachers so I can grow up clever and well educated,' is the answer.

'And what happens when you get home from school?'

'I do all my homework, and then I sit down with my dad and we do some extra sums.' This wonderfully contrived back-and-forth is ended fairly abruptly by the appearance of Mr G himself, who seems to have spent so long whirling about the corporate merry-go-round that he is no longer sure whether he is supposed to be *Swaggarific,* *Clarorific* or any other *rific* and so spends the next couple of minutes switching shapelessly between them before performing a Beenie Man track from the same 'riddim'. Actually writing a new song, it seems, is entirely implausible.

My parents have come over for the week and have been looking forward to their first experience of Harbour View. What they get as the game begins, though, is as unimpressive and shambolic as it gets. After just five minutes a Boys' Town free kick is hit into the area where Montrose Phinn heads out weakly. It falls to Jermaine Hardware who takes an almighty swing only to completely scuff his strike. This scuff sends the ball looping comically over Barrett's head and into the goal as the desperate keeper scrambles frantically back. So it is one-nil to them, and not a start to awe the visitors.

In fact my father is becoming increasingly unimpressed by what is a very limp performance by both sides. 'Is it always just long ball like this?' he asks as yet another punt goes aimlessly upfield from the back. Some free kicks bring a couple of half-chances our way but nothing came of them.

By half time we are level. With five minutes to go Christopher Harvey, the only player to have done anything positive in my father's eyes, plays a long ball past an isolated defender into the path of Thomas. The striker's run ensured the centre-back is dragged wide with him and out of position, allowing Wolfe to find space on the edge of the six yard box. Thomas picks him out and the shot is slipped under the keeper's dive. One all.

But the start of the second half is not played to a much higher standard than the first had been. 'Which is the player that you rate?' my father asks, and I point out Hue in the centre. 'Well I think he looks very average.' His contrary attitude is not without some grounding as Hue is certainly having one of his quieter days, but he still shows his ability in flashes and is impressing others. In fact, so perfect is one through ball that the announcer—provided by Claro and nothing to do with Harbour View—feels compelled to share his feelings about it with the entire stadium and picks up his microphone. 'Another peach of a pass by Jermaine Hue,' he declares over the speakers. 'We need to see more of that in the national team!'

'You're speaking to the deaf!' cry the home fans, tired of constantly seeing their star player overlooked by the Reggae Boyz selectors. But where the national team misses out, Harbour View does not. There are 88 minutes gone and everyone is readying themselves for extra time when Hue sees Andre Steele's run down the right and plays the ball neatly into his path. Steele takes a couple of touches and then belts it right into the top corner. Two-one in the dying seconds. It is glorious, it is Hollywood, it is exactly what my parents came to see.

And yet the Boys' Town contingent maintain their dignity throughout, even while the Harbour View fans hurl mocking shouts their way. They are not like the people of Tivoli. They are no angels—who is?—but they do not conduct themselves with the apparent hatred that Tivoli seem to. Did the same external PNP forces not apply themselves to Boys' Town? Not as ruthlessly as to Tivoli, that must be acknowledged, but the contrast in actions and behaviour does 'Garden' no favours.

So with dignity, Boys' Town crash out. But more importantly, Harbour View march on, and are in the cup final.

Wednesday 2nd February

Tivoli Gardens   2 2   HVFC

Agg. 2 2
HVFC through on away goals

Sunday 6th February

HVFC   2 1   Boys' Town

CHAPTER TWENTY FIVE

The Present And The Future

It is another hot, sunny Wednesday afternoon in Kingston. Wearing shorts and a distinctive bright pink t-shirt, Richard Edwards sits on a fixed seat facing a wall of football boots in one of three air conditioned branches of Western Sports located at the Twin Gates shopping plaza in the Halfway Tree area of town. Behind him a small crowd of staff and customers are looking eagerly up at a television hanging from the wall that is showing live coverage of a friendly between Portugal and Argentina in Geneva. Cristiano Ronaldo v Lionel Messi is the clear undertone to the game and that battle has all the European papers, and the fixated group in the shop, enthralled far more than which team actually comes out victorious. Edwards, though, is barely paying it any attention. He has other things on his mind.

At 4 am tomorrow morning he will be leaving his home in Portmore to fly to Texas where he has a 17 day trial with the MLS side Houston Dynamo. The trial itself, it had been explained to me by officials at Harbour View, is little more than a formality; they are keen and just want to have a closer look before finalising any deal. 'I really want to help this club, and in order to do that financially I'll have to gain a contract overseas,' Edwards himself had told me back in September. Now it seems he is about to do just that.

The position of this one player seems to sum up everything important, both sporting and economic, about the dynamic of top level football in all developing countries throughout the world: fall in love with the game, nurture the exceptional talent, reach the top in your own nation then perform the final duty for the club and country that raised you by securing a lucrative move elsewhere. If Juice is the face of the young player at the bottom, Richard Edwards is now the face of the lucky ones. He has outgrown this particular pond.

I had rung his mobile earlier and now join him as he waits for a pair of boots to arrive. He needs a spare pair for the trial just in case his first pair break so has come out to this sport shop to find a pair. Like everyone else he does not have a sponsorship deal and so has to buy his own at the club's expense—as a senior player he is afforded the luxury of having no price limit—but has to twiddle his thumbs while a van goes out to fetch some in the right size. This is an international footballer and captain of the Premier League champions—the equivalent of John Terry sitting quietly in JJB waiting for a courier van. But he is smiling and uncomplaining, excitedly anticipating what the future is about to bring.

'This is my opportunity that, as a player, you look forward to. I'm really happy and optimistic about being overseas and being able to earn a transfer. That's my focus right now, I'm pretty much confident. From before, my main friends at Harbour View, they've all gone abroad—[Dwayne] Miller, Kavin [Bryan] and [Lovel] Palmer. So I'm the only one left.' Palmer in fact is already at Houston, having transferred from Harbour View the previous January, and has been in regular contact with Edwards about what is coming up.

'We speak like every day. Even just now we were talking, look at my phone,' he holds out his Blackberry to show a text conversation between the pair. They have even made plans to live together. 'I don't know much about Houston but I think Lovel has a friend, someone who has been there since last year, and he's staying at this friend's house on one front door. He's waiting on me to come and do my stuff and hopefully they sign me so that we can get a two bedroom apartment ourselves.'

I can't help but wonder if Lovel played any part in getting him the trial in the first place, but this, he feels, had no direct cause. 'Put it like this: I don't know if it's because of his performance last season that the coach came to the Caribbean Cup. So I knew that the coach and Ryan Johnson were sitting beside each other and after the semi final Ryan Johnson came to me and said the coach liked what he saw. So that was good news! All I have to do is go into the final and do what I did before. But I got an injury in the semi final so I couldn't be my normal self.' It seems he had still done enough though.

Not every aspect of moving on is favourable and his girlfriend and children, for now, would have to remain back in Kingston. 'As far as I know about joining the MLS—I spoke to Lovel—and you have to be in the league for a year first, one season, before they start processing Green Cards for your family. But I don't mind. I'm going to be disappointed about not being able to have my family with me but at the same time I guess they'll have to understand. She's okay, but not really okay,' he adds about his girlfriend. She is still happy for him though, 'Because it's my time. I want it all these years.'

Of course it will not just be family he is leaving but also the football club he has been a part of for six years. 'Yes I'm going to be sad but it's another opportunity for another player to step up to the plate and show his true worth. If I'm here I'm obviously going to be in someone's way preventing them from showing their true potential, but if I leave that means one more person can establish themselves in the club.' He then speculates at who the next will be, expressing both confidence and concern at the effect on the team. 'Fabian Campbell I think. Preferably him because he's kind of a player like me. But,' he pauses and sighs, 'he doesn't link up the play in the midfield like I do. He's 22, and that comes with experience, playing a lot of games. He has stepped up to the plate on many occasions before and with him playing regularly now I don't think it will be different. But I think that is a problem when players are young: Harbour View players they have a tendency, when they become established and people start telling them that, "Yeah, you performed well," and stuff like that, they get complacent. Once that happens, performance drops. And they don't know how to pick themselves back up. So that's my only concern where he's concerned. But he's a level headed person, it's going to be good for him.'

In Martinique Dane Richards had firmly insisted to me that if the opportunities were the same at home, he would rather be playing his football in Jamaica. I wonder if this is the case for Edwards too. 'I wouldn't say I would stay because a player wants to go outside their country and meet people over there on a football platform. Because I have proved myself here for many years now and I think it's time for me to move somewhere else.'

'I think as much as it might be rough, it'll be fun. Because like I said I'm meeting new people, going into a different environment;

you're basically starting out a whole new life. As much as how it will be challenging I think it will be fun, and I'm up to it. Actually, I'm happy.'

He won't be the only Jamaican on trial at Houston: Jermaine Taylor is there as well as three others, among them Portmore's Steven Morrissey who had travelled the day after going off injured against Harbour View. 'Probably he was just showing a front, not wanting to risk his health before he's going off. He's that type of player. He, Navion Boyd, they are both that type of player. If I touch them: drop. They just want you to get sent off.' Richard Edwards: if he has something to say he will say it. I suggest that while Morrissey had distinguished himself I haven't noticed it so much in Boyd's play. 'Probably because he was injured and you don't see him that often but he is that type of player. Once it gets rough, physical—and his team is that type of team, very physical—once the game gets that way, the least touch: drop. They seem to love it in Jamaica but as much as how a lot of people like him as a player—even I like him as a player—I don't like the whole diving thing and wanting to get cards. I don't like it.'

And in that he is largely alone in his country, where in all walks of life deception is so often king. 'They seem to like it! If there is a skill player, once you mash up the player, even if you mash up a player and get the ball and the skill player dives or creates something, they go for the skill player. Jamaicans go for skill. You have been around many games now. For example at Harbour View, if the team's not scoring the stadium is silent. If a player gets the ball and shifts another the stadium erupts. They only go like that for the skill, the shift, and goals. Otherwise silent.'

It is interesting that he should bring up the atmosphere in the stadiums as, coming from England, the silence has been the thing I have found most striking about the audiences at national games. 'You know I really want to have an experience playing in England. I get a lot of energy from the supporters. I don't know about any other players but that's me. You get that sort of lift.'

'I've played in one of the World Cup stadiums at Bloemfontein. I've played in that stadium before and it was full to capacity. I remember being on that pitch with the noise and everything. I might be right beside you and I can't hear you. You have to be looking, every chance you get, you have to be looking.' He jumps up, adopts a ready stance and shifts his head around rapidly. 'The vuvuzela was more distracting than anything else I've experienced because your team mate could be there and he could be the right pass to make but because of the noise you don't even recognise him.'

The talk of stadia brought to mind another point Dane Richards had made to me in Martinique, namely that one of the biggest perks to playing in the US is the impressive facilities. Is this something that Edwards, too, is particularly enticed by? 'I wouldn't say facilities because being around the national team you get to see a lot of different facilities. You don't try to compare to Jamaica—those countries have better resources than Jamaica. But the challenge of playing amongst quality players, that's going to be a bit of fun for me. I know I can match them.'

This idea comes to the heart of, from my experience, Edwards as a person: he simply loves football. It is not the money that draws him to the MLS or the glamorous surroundings but the fundamental longing to play the game he lives for somewhere new and against some of the most decorated names in the modern game. The MLS, for all our scoffing of it in Europe, currently hosts Thierry Henry, Rafael Marquez, David Beckham . . .'. . . Landon Donovan. You can call the names,' he says taking over the list with enthusiasm. 'As a matter of fact in my career so far I've played against some great players. I remember playing for Harbour View in a game against DC United and they had this player named Marcelo Gallardo who played in the Argentina team in the '98 World Cup, and I closed him out.' The last bit is said with a distinct tone of pride. 'The name doesn't challenge me at all because I'm this type of player. Look at these guys,' he gestures to the group crowded round the game on the shop's TV. 'They watch Cristiano Ronaldo and Messi and they get excited about their shifts and things like that. I'm not that type of person; I *study* players' movements and what their top move is. Messi's top move is he'll shape up like he's going to his right, but he's going to his left. No matter what he's going to his left. So I tend to study someone because if you want to be a top class player you have to imagine facing players like that. And I watch Beckham and Thierry Henry and I try to study them and hopefully when, *if*, the time comes I'll close them out.'

While on that subject I choose to satisfy my curiosity about encountering the greats. The Reggae Boyz had gone to Argentina for a friendly a year or so ago but Messi himself had not played. I have always wondered whether such occurrences are disappointing to a player, or a relief. 'I wasn't disappointed because it's a perfect opportunity at the time to beat them and be a part of history. I mean you don't just get up on any day and beat Argentina, it doesn't matter which eleven they put out, it just doesn't happen. Because sometimes psychologically before you go on the pitch you're already beaten. I didn't mind him not playing but we played against a pretty good Argentina team.' And they so nearly had made history as the first Jamaican side to win against them. 'We led until the 85th minute, they scored in the 86th and the 89th. But you know, it's a good experience.'

This brings me to his place within the national team and whether moving to the bigger leagues might solidify it ahead of the Gold Cup. 'Not really because even now while playing for the national team I have conceded the fact that two people are ahead of me in the position I play, I concede that. But I'm not going to make their job be easy, I'm not that sort of person. I'm a hard worker and I'll forever be a hard worker.

'Speaking about the national coach, he was here not too long ago with me,' he indicates to the seat I am sitting in. 'We were talking for a bit. He didn't know about the trial so I told him. He said it's a long time he's been telling me that I shouldn't be here playing football because right now I'm way above the level of the league in Jamaica. So all I have to do is just go and be myself, go and do what I do best which is work hard as ever. He is the type of person like this—just like not knowing you before and knowing you now,' he nods toward me. 'You can sit down with him and have any sort of conversation. And it's good because he was a player before. He used to play in England for Hull'

At this point his boots finally arrive and he inspects them with a distinctly unimpressed look on his face. He's not happy with the studs and doesn't even seem sure if they are proper boots or astro shoes. 'I'll have to take them because we've waited so long, but . . . 'he peters out, as though he can't even be bothered to waste further words on them, before going to pay on the Harbour View credit card he had been given.

As he walks out he swings a shopping bag by his side filled with Jamaican biscuits that he has bought to take over to Houston for Lovel, and explains the origin of a slight limp he walks with. Six years ago, he says, while playing for his old club Waterhouse *against* Harbour View, he had broken his foot in a tackle. He noted with satisfaction that he had also scored in that game and played for a further six matches before actually going to see a doctor about the pain. 'And guess who it was that broke it?' he asks, grinning. 'Lovel!'

We walk through the bustling streets of Halfway Tree, packed with shoppers hurrying about and cars blasting their horns. The tree of the area's name, which these days no longer stands but is instead marked by a clock tower, was used as a quiet resting stop for merchants on their way to market in the days before it was engulfed by the expanding city. Now it is one of the busiest and most chaotic parts of town. As we stroll along untroubled by the passing crowds I become curious as to whether he ever gets recognised in public, given that players here do not have the same high profiles as the top English players. 'Yeah sometimes,' he explains. 'But I don't like it because when they come up to me when I'm with my girlfriend they just want to talk about football and she just has to stand there and wait. So I try not to stop when they talk to me.' As he finishes speaking a stranger approaches and asks about the upcoming cup final, as though he had been listening to us and wanted to prove the point.

As we walk on Edwards asks a few questions about life in Britain and then we talk more about things over here. Approaching the taxi rank a small group of men sit in a recess on the busy pavement throwing down cash as they gamble on dice. 'Jamaica!' Edwards chuckles as we pass, and I get the sense that for all his excitement about leaving he will miss this place too. But the next chapter is beginning for him, and for Harbour View. We say our goodbyes as I get into a car. In just a few hours he will be flying out of Kingston and, hopefully, into the MLS.

A few short days later the team have to take their first steps without the captain. As we had expected it is Fabian Campbell who takes over his role against Waterhouse and he seems to thoroughly enjoy the opportunity. 'Not too far, stay back!' he yells to Phinn as the defender drifts forward, displaying the vocal and organisational abilities that make his captain so important. It is his head that rises above every other to clear every corner and he organises the team well. He seems confident, if a little raw.

With a few minutes to go until half time, by which point Harvey has headed us into a one-nil lead, I feel my phone vibrate in my pocket. Fittingly, on the screen is a text from Edwards telling me of the impressive result he had helped Houston achieve in a friendly last night. In my hand are the excited words of the top man moving on while on the pitch in front of me is the young player growing into the void, hopefully to make a name worthy of a transfer fee a few years further on. You might say the old and the new, but given the nature of football business here perhaps the present and the future might be more appropriate.

I congratulate Edwards on the result and keep him updated with the score at the Compound during the second half. But there are no more goals to tell him of and by the time the final whistle goes we have not only boosted our own charge but dented Waterhouse's with a one-nil win. And that is not the end of the good news: Portmore had lost to George's by the same score, as had Tivoli away at Humble Lion. Of the group of five that has pulled away at the top we were the only ones to have won and now move into second, with the entire pack separated by just five points. Spain could only dream of a battle like this one, the final few months of the season are shaping up to be sensational.

'I'm really happy for the team and the coach,' Edwards says when I fill him in on the news. And they are really happy for him too. This is his chance to move on up, and no one would begrudge him that.

Sunday 13th February

Arnett Gardens	2 0	Sporting Central
Benfica	0 0	Village United
Boys' Town	0 0	Reno
HVFC	**1 0**	**Waterhouse**
Humble Lion	1 0	Tivoli Gardens
St. George's	1 0	Portmore United

National Premier League

	P	GD	Pts
1. Tivoli Gardens	27	15	48
2. HVFC	27	12	45
3. Portmore United	27	10	45
4. Boys' Town	27	4	44
5. Waterhouse	27	10	43
6. Sporting Central	27	4	35
7. Arnett Gardens	27	-3	35
8. Reno	27	3	33
9. Village United	27	-10	30
10. Humble Lion	27	-5	29
11. Benfica	27	-24	27
12. St. George's	27	-16	26

CHAPTER TWENTY SIX

The Fan's Life

Supporting a football team is a strange thing. I have never met the Arsenal players. I have never had a conversation with Arsène Wenger or Robin van Persie. I can't even claim that the club represents my home town or my roots, having been born in the middle of nowhere and turning to the team because my older brothers ensured I knew about The Arsenal before I even really knew about football. To think logically, there is no reason why the success of Arsenal should mean anything to me, they are just a group of men playing a game that is essentially immaterial to the trials of real life.

Harbour View at least have a personal connection to me. They have welcomed me into the heart of the club. The coaches, the players, the management; I know them all and spend time with them all. Their success, therefore, has more of a direct impact onto my life than that of imported millionaires. But even then it is still only football, it is still just a game.

So why is it then, that on the 16th of February I am sitting at the side of the pitch at the Edward Seaga Complex watching Arnett Gardens rain down shots on the Harbour View goal as those lads I know contest a cup final, and barely even notice? Why is my mind occupied almost entirely by a match 4,500 miles away that I watched earlier over a grainy, jerky internet stream involving a load of people I have never had, and never will have, any sort of personal connection with? And why do I even really care about either game?

Earlier today, Arsenal came from behind to beat the great Barcelona 2-1 in the Champions League. Barça would later overcome the defeat in the second leg and go on to win the cup for the third time in six years but this night isn't about that and I am left with one of those games that stays with you for years, in the same way that I can still see Thierry Henry gliding through the Real Madrid defence to score the winner at the Bernabéu, or Sylvain Wiltord, clad in that garish gold strip, sweeping in the rebound from Freddie Ljungberg's shot to win the League at Old Trafford. I didn't know any of them either. So why do I care?

The Buju Banton retrial began this week and, as it had been the first time round, it is all over the papers. 'Banton's attorney David Oscar Markus said they were in the middle of a battle which they intended to win,' writes the reporter in the *Observer*. I flick to the back pages and see DV warning that Arnett 'will come with all guns blazing to win' that evening. Turning again to the front of the paper and Buju tells the press: 'I am fighting'. 'We will make sure that we fight until the end,' Barcelona manager Pep Guardiola declared before the Arsenal game.

All these quotes could come from the same story, such are the similarities between language and sentiments. But on the one side you have guns, drugs and prison—the fiercest things 'real life' can offer—and on the other side you have football, that shallow little game. But what these illustrate is that football is not 'only a game', the lines between it and 'real life' are so blurred that they have become one entity meshed together. A subject is only as important as people make it and football stirs in us something so strong that it has become as important as anything else in our day to day lives. Arnett coach Paul 'Tegat' Davis told the press: 'Yesterday I was reminded by an old lady that they long for something to jump for, so this would be for the supporters and people of Arnett Gardens.' Even in one of the most dangerous areas of one of the most dangerous cities on the planet, where annual murders in the community can be counted in the tens or hundreds, the people are craving sporting success. And that is because football matters.

'Arsenal! Arsenal!' Shouts one of the locals, seeing the shirt I still have on, as our car edges through the crowd outside the gates of the Edward Seaga Complex, venue for the Jackie Bell Knockout Final. A few others look round and also start shouting and cheering. One man in a tatty Barcelona shirt scurries away to the stand. These people most likely have never been to either London or Barcelona and most probably never will, but they had all seen the game earlier on and they all cared.

'Ball them Arnett, ball them!' A lady has pushed through the thin crowd leaning against the fence and shrieks with such volume right behind Clyde's head that he jumps and moves away. 'Ball them Arnett!' Her voice is hoarse and gravelly, her hair closely cropped and her eyes have a shallow, vacant property which removes all depth from her smile. Below this hollow face she has a malnourished-looking body that is skinny and boyish. All the same, she appears to be full of life and is thoroughly enjoying herself as she bellows and claps before suddenly switching allegiances. 'Ball them Harbour View, ball them!' Clearly team loyalty is not quite so ingrained in everyone.

Arnett are edging the early exchanges but as yet things are scoreless. To me though, the match is going on before my eyes but it isn't really sinking in. It feels odd to be here so soon after watching the other game earlier. Normally after a result like that you spend the rest of the evening celebrating it and the next few days savouring it, you are not thrown into a cup final less than an hour and a half after the final whistle.

Arguments brew behind us. 'Harbour View are the biggest team in Jamaica,' trumpets someone. 'Who else has won the Caribbean Cup three times?' Another denies it. Mixing Harbour View, Arnett and Tivoli was always going to lead to some disagreements. 'Harbour View are the biggest team in the Caribbean,' returns the first man, upping the ante considerably in the face of his opponent's rebuttal. 'Blood claat Harbour View!' shouts someone else, weighing in without reason but with commitment in spades. Jamaicans simply love to shout and argue but very rarely is there any real crowd trouble, something that seems inconsistent with the violent nature of society at large.

As another chance goes wide midway through the second half the announcer, who has been busily plugging phones all game long, is overcome by the excitement of this goal-free encounter and trills: 'What a Clarorific game!' I know the battle with Digicel is fierce and you want your slogan to be heard as much as possible, but if this is the definition of 'Clarorific' it does you no favours whatsoever. It has been scrappy, disappointing. But in the 73 minute Arnett's Dennis McKinley gets the ball on the edge of the box, shifts past the defender and hits low across goal, beating a stretching Barrett as it slides into the bottom corner. The fans cry out behind me, a scattered mix of 'Goal!' and 'Bumbaclaat!' depending on their affections.

My head is returning to the here and now. 1-0 down with quarter of an hour to go the nerves are now tingling, the heart beating faster. It could be two a few minutes later when Barrett, making one of the only misjudgements of his entire season, rushes out to meet Adrian Reid in a one on one but gets it wrong, finding himself stranded on the edge of the area as the ball is squared across the face of his goal. Under pressure from our converging defenders their striker hits powerfully but inaccurately and it flies wide. 'Bumbaclaaaat!' howl five hundred exasperated Arnett fans in the stand behind me, beautifully in unison.

With just seconds left in injury time we sense our last chance and lump a free kick into their box. In the middle of the scramble Dicoy raises his head and pokes the ball forward. The keeper is coming out to collect but Steele, scorer of the decider in each of the last two rounds, is racing him to it from the other direction. It is the man in the yellow and blue who gets to it first, pushing it with his head past the keeper's grasping hands. It's not powerful. It drops, bounces, defenders chase it, but they can't get to it.

Goal! The bench are on their feet, the yellow section of the crowd is jumping, the players chase a rocket-fuelled Steele as he runs past the opposing fans with his hand to his ear. In the 92 minute!

Once again I am watching the preparations for extra time. This season is determined not to make things easy for me. The players take an unusually long break. One Arnett follower who has been particularly vocal all match long is reacting to our late equaliser by outlining a theory that Carvel has paid off the ref to get decisions going his way. 'That's what Jamaican football is,' he says. 'Bare bloodclot corruption.'

But the night before we had been watching the under 21s in their end of round final against Sporting. 'Find another way to supplement your income, because you're ruining football.' Deighton—the supporter whose theory it is that Harbour View's results always follow Arsenal's—had shouted to the fourth official. So last night the officials had been bribed against us and tonight they have been bribed for us? As I have said before, every team has its paranoias, and if you were to listen to everything said in the stands the referees are taking bribes both for and against everyone. The more likely scenario of course is just that they get things wrong, plain and simple, but as fans we love to feel that the world is against us, that we are fighting against the odds. We want to feel that our victories have come from our own team's skill rather than outside help and we want to feel the exact opposite of our failures. This victim psychology makes winning all the sweeter while giving us a readymade excuse for failing—it wasn't our fault, the authorities conspired against us. Of course this is not unique to football. The model 'was thrown out of gear in the 1970s,' Seaga had said of his Tivoli Gardens project on TVJ. 'That is not the fault of the model, it is the fault of pressures that were brought to bear on the model from external forces.'

The plotted-against football fan only notices wrong decisions when they go against his team and conveniently ignores those that go his way, or else has another way of explaining them. What is this particular supporter's response whenever a dodgy decision clearly goes in Arnett's favour? 'You need to give them more money Carvel Stewart! Whatever you paid the referee isn't enough!' This convenient get-out clause allows him to seamlessly fit contradictory evidence into his oppressed worldview.

This carries on as play finally gets going again. 'Batty bwoy referee. Suck yuh mother!' the fan shouts at will towards the supposedly corrupt official. And it is coming from both sides: 'Referee, what is this?' implores DV as a clear foul on Brissett goes unpunished. 'Refereeeeee!' screams Barrett from all the way back in his goal as Juice is tripped and nothing is given. 'Jamaica's full of corruption. Especially Harbour View a corrupted side,' someone is saying behind me. What a jumble of victims and villains it all is.

Meanwhile the announcers are still fervently pushing their wares over the loudspeakers. 'You'll be so disappointed if you leave here without buying a Claro phone,' we are told. 'They're worth 14,000 and we're giving them away for 2,500—you can sell them on and still make money!' Well there's nothing like an official endorsement to keep the black market thriving healthily. 'Yes, thank you for your wise words, Mr Rogers,' interjects his embarrassed sounding colleague.

Extra time is flowing by without really doing anything. A few shots come at either end but neither keeper is particularly troubled. Half an hour is gone, the ref raises his whistle to his lips and blows. Just like in Martinique, the final will be decided with a penalty shoot out.

The first ones are both put in. Next up is Kevin 'Pele' Wilson, Arnett's senior player and the scorer of the winning goal against us early in the season. He hits it low and hard but Barrett guesses well, diving down to his right. The shot is too close to the middle, Barrett gets behind it and pushes it back with a strong hand. Saved! Harvey then comes forward and makes it 2-1. The goals keep coming on both sides, Dicoy then Nelson tipping us back ahead every time they level. At 4-4 it is Steele who strides forward from the centre circle, places the ball on the spot and steps back to his run up for the crucial kick. This to win. He runs forward, thumps his foot at the ball and sends it to his left. The keeper is nowhere near it.

The bench, huddled together during the shoot out, breaks up and sprints onto the pitch. High fives, hugs, congratulations—everybody is embracing everybody. Gene, Twinny, Teet, Barry, Mally; all people who make their contributions to making Harbour View happen. These are the 'fans' in Jamaica to whom winning *really* means everything because their investment in their club is literal as well as spiritual. They physically give their lives to their club and these are the moments when it all pays off. While the players are dancing on the pitch and posing for photos with the trophy the fans in the stands had long since gone home, but not those who work with the club.

It is the first trophy of a potential three this season and with this in mind the celebrations are heartfelt but short lived. There is a game on Sunday, and a League to win. We haven't even left the pitch before thoughts are turning to the next training session, the next game, the next step. Within about half an hour we are in Clyde's car doing the usual round of town dropping players back at their homes. Dicoy in Mountain View, Devon Haughton in August Town. It has been quite a day and the players have earned tomorrow off, but after that it is back to business.

Some people scoff at sport. To them it is something that only the unwashed, uncivilised and uneducated masses care to trouble themselves with and by even admitting an interest in it they are rendering themselves unable to be a true 'intellectual'. They do not allow their thoughts to rot on matters so banal and as such they turn their minds to other pursuits far more deserving of their valuable time.

I've always felt sorry for these people. They will never have a day like this. Whether they occupy their time with art, literature, music, opera, theatre, cinema or sex there is nothing on earth that will ever give them that feeling shared by so many when Andrei Arshavin scored to put Arsenal ahead of Barcelona. None of those things could ever possibly provide that sudden moment of unbridled collective euphoria, a second of such raw emotion that they fall into pandemonium, jumping, screaming at the top of their lungs and embracing complete strangers. They will never be so overcome with joy that they lose all control and all they can do is raise their faces to the sky and roar with passion. They will never sprint across a pitch to celebrate with a player who has just won a cup final on a penalty shoot out nor will they ever know the buzz that lingers for days after results like these. Perhaps they wouldn't want to be seen acting in such a primitive manner anyway, but that doesn't make their stance any less joyless.

No matter how much satisfaction they might gain from a symphony or a play, I will never be convinced that those lives are not to some extent hollowed by a void that can never be adequately filled by sport's surrogates. Their pursuits are all well and good but they are all deviations from the real world and no more. Beethoven composed his work hundreds of years ago and it is what it is and always will be, it will never change and it will never impact lives to any great extent. The same can never be said of sport, it *is* the real world. It is the most unpredictable, the most thrilling and the most real of dramas, but because of some fatuous notion of intellectual pride such people will never know that. And for that they will always be worse off, while the fan's life is a rich one indeed.

*Above: The Harbour View bench watch on
nervously during the penalty shootout in the Jackie
Bell KSAFA Knockout final at the Edward Seaga
Complex. L-R: Carvel, DV, Barry, Teet, Hue, Twinny.
Below: The players celebrate with the trophy.*

CHAPTER TWENTY SEVEN

The Growth Of
A Caribbean Giant

In the early 70s Jamaican football went through a controversial and fundamental transformation. Up to that point the game at senior level had been dominated by the footballing arm of cricket clubs or other organisations such as the YMCA or the military, but this was felt in some quarters to be an unsustainable model. The flaws in it were deep: for one thing it meant football was not taken seriously and its organisation was haphazard as it played a very secondary role to cricket. It was also a system that saw the best talent haemorrhaging out of the game when many young players came out of school having starred in the Manning Cup only to turn away from it because they had no desire to join a cricket club in order to continue. And even more damaging was the lack of relevance it had to the wider public and the apathy it was treated with as a result. As DV puts it: 'Arnett Gardens, Tivoli Gardens, they are not going to go and watch a cricket club playing a football match—it don't mean anything to them.'

In the late 60s the old domination of the cricket clubs was beginning to give way to a new breed: community based teams. The cricketers were losing control of KSAFA and in 1973 a new administration took control of the organisation which completely reformed the struggling game in the Corporate Area, guided by the foresight of president Neville Glanville and his enthusiastic team. They had a clear vision of where the future of football lay and, writing in the prospectus *KSAFA Plans New Football Deal,* vice president Russell Bell, brother of Jackie, laid down the outlines: 'With the clear understanding that it is illogical to encourage or promote activities which in reality act against the development of the game; and with the forceful vision that it is essential that we afford youth a progressively organised programme, we are forced to promote football on a community basis.'

With this they formed the Major League, a senior level competition throughout Kingston & St. Andrew, and invited all communities to form a structured team and enter if they felt they were up to it. Like all radical reform, it was not a popular idea at first. 'You're bringing in a lower division, you're bringing in everybody, you're lowering the standard of what it was and breaking down social classes and barriers. It will just be war and disorganised and so there was a lot fuss. But it worked. It worked.' Clyde says of the change. DV describes a higher level of hysteria amongst the establishment: '"This a rude bwoy ting and yuh gwaan have violence cos now Tivoli Gardens can play and now Waterhouse can play,"' is how he describes their feelings at the time. 'All these communities which were very violent—worse than now in those days—and had no control would now be playing football in the highest league in Jamaica.'

When the Major League first began the media turned against it, attempting to sabotage the rebellious new structure before it could take off by refusing to report on it and exaggerating the violence the game encouraged in order to pressure the government into banning it. But despite having no newspaper reports or television updates the crowds were coming in their droves to support their local teams and it only took six or seven weeks of the new season before the press cracked and returned to football. There were clashes, there was violence, there were knives, bottles and stones regularly present among both supporters and players, but what all this demonstrated was passion. And the public loved it.

Many of the old teams dropped out, giving up on football entirely, while some of the bigger and less cricket-orientated clubs were able to adapt and ride the transition. But these relatively faceless teams, the likes of Santos and Cavaliers, had to deal with losing a number of players as their stars returned to represent the communities they grew up in now that the opportunity presented itself at senior level. Harbour View was one such community and reshuffled their pack, bringing back players like Shawny Hayles and Owen Stewart to mix with a strong but young core formed of the '72 Minor League winning team. In the first year the decision was taken that the team would enter into the division below the Major League in order to allow the new structure to fuse properly, and then in 1974, the year they were officially formed, Harbour View entered the top league for the first time.

Money was the club's initial problem, and the solution was one that made the club. All the youngsters involved with the team spent their weekends going around Harbour View collecting bottles which could be turned in for recycling in return for a small amount of cash. 'We'd take maybe our road and the next two roads beside it and then we go gate to gate, door to door . . . . That's how we funded the team,' Clyde tells me. 'We packed them and then the cars came and collected them from off the pavement and they carried it to the back of Carvel's house. We sorted them and then we carried them down to the liquor store and we traded them in.' The true genius of this plan though was not simply the funds it amassed, it also raised awareness of the team and garnered invaluable support. Clyde recalls: 'It galvanised and it bonded everybody, and it made the community aware that this is what we're doing. And so the community bought into it and everybody came together. The whole site of Harbour View were really into it.'

They were so successful in this that they were able to equip themselves in new kit, taking their inspiration from the great Brazil with golden shirts and blue shorts, and arriving on the scene with an immediate impact. But they were also playing well, and in the first year they won the eastern zone and made it to the final stage at the national stadium where they appeared in their most daring gear yet. Vin Blaine had taken a trip to England and came back with a set of blue, long sleeved Chelsea tracksuits for the team to run out in. 'We came out in spanking new outfits and everybody was proud,' says Clyde. 'We were slick man, and proud of it.' To this day Harbour View walk out onto the pitch in blue tracksuit tops—although they no longer come from Stamford Bridge—and they remain the only side in the country to do so. This earned them their ongoing reputation as the side where all the money is and drew jealousy from other teams. 'Sweatsuits were a rare commodity in Jamaica, so in those days when a person buy a sweatsuit you have to have money,' DV told me. 'They were so stunned.' That first year they defied the negative expectations of outsiders by winning their first game in the final round 7-1 and going on to finish third overall in front of a packed crowd at the national stadium. And they did it all while playing a new and attractive style of football that earned them the media nickname 'Cinderallas of the East'.

They weren't the only ways in which Harbour View were taking the initiative: their facilities were also streaking ahead of their rivals. DV describes playing conditions in the early years of the competition: 'In those days people would sometimes encroach on the field when them watching the game and if the ball went near everybody would come and look, so they had a man with a stick that run down the line and shout "Line, line, line!" And once the ball come over that side him run with the stick and shout "Step back, step back, step back!" so the referee or the linesman could get a likkle chance to see. So when we came in the competition we planted some posts, bought some nylon rope at the top and bottom so nobody could walk out, we had a barrier. But we put in blue and gold rope and we lined the field with it. The field was all dirt but we rake up so it looked nice for matchday, paint it. It was just stone and dirt, nothing else, not a blade of grass. And it would have glass bottles on it so we have to make sure on matchdays we try and get as much of it as we can. Referees, when they used to go to the games they had to find a tree to go and change; we provided a changing room in a house so they could go there and use the bathroom. So those are the little things we did different.'

The people at KSAFA saw this and took inspiration, implementing new rules that every team had to rope off their fields so as to allow the games to be played properly. This expenditure being imposed drew further ire from rival clubs, but that did nothing to dampen the spirits. Harbour View had money, they had kit, they had girls aplenty coming to their games and they were performing on the pitch. Everything was about perfect. This came to a peak in 1976 when the team won the Major League for the first time, while the younger generation also won the Minor League. The win sparked wild celebrations, with the shopping centre near the harbour front being cordoned off for a big party at which a number of well known artists were invited to perform in honour of the first trophy Harbour View won in open-age football.

But there was another step to be taken. Jackie Bell, in charge of Santos, had been one of the most fervent opponents to his brother's plans in forming the Major League and took the step of approaching cigarette manufacturers Craven A for sponsorship of a new island-wide competition instead. He boycotted the Major League and his Santos side, the team of Alan 'Skill' Cole among other stars, dominated the new National League by winning each of the first five seasons. But the downside to it all was that people had no real interest in it, and fan support was far greater for the community based Major League back in the capital. After a few years Jackie accepted defeat and submitted to the Major League, allowing his brother to take over the National League format. Instead of continuing to run them against one another, Russell fused the two competitions so that the top sides from each region would gain entry into the island-wide competition and turned it into the country's top attraction. It was the birth of club football's modern format in Jamaica and the country has gone from strength to strength ever since.

So Harbour View entered the National League the year after their Major League success, finishing second, and throughout that era the current crop of Premier League clubs began to emerge at the head of Jamaican football. The 'garrison' clubs to the west of town—Tivoli, Arnett, Waterhouse and Boys' Town—all made big strides forward during the 70s and 80s with the politicians in the areas seeing them as potential vote winners and victory as a way to boost the morale of the community. Boys' Town were particularly talented and over the next ten to fifteen years they had a series of what Clyde describes as 'epic battles' with Harbour View as both competed for dominance of the Corporate Area.

It was also during this period that the club management were first made aware of the potential value of their players as an income stream. In 1979 they played an international contest with AIK Phoenix of Trinidad and during the away leg a 16 year old in the Minor League team named Keith Cunningham impressed their hosts enough to become the first ever Harbour View player invited for an overseas trial. While that particular trial was unsuccessful it was at least an eye opener and in the 80s a match in Guadeloupe resulted in the transfer of Altimont 'Freddy' Butler to the local side L'Etoile. But Clyde laughs off the suggestion that, even as late as 1987, Harbour View might have managed to get a transfer fee out of the deal:

'Get What! We didn't know about that! It was a good opportunity for any player in Jamaica. It was great for him, and for us. So when we got the opportunity we just helped him to go, "That's great! Go!"' It was the club's first steps into the modern business though and they proceeded to tour the Caribbean as frequently as possible, taking up all invitations from clubs in countries like Cayman or Trinidad to stay with them and play a few matches. They also undertook further initiatives to ensure that the talent was continuously produced and Carvel proposed a summer 'mini-league', a summer contest whereby the senior people within the club each coached a group of young children into teams to compete against each other. It worked well and today Clyde speaks with pride that his side—named 'Arantes' after Pele—produced a future national captain in the form of Linval McKenzie.

But in the early 90s things started to deteriorate as the people who had built the club, and had moved over the years from players to coaches and administrators, were drawn away by everyday work commitments—Clyde in advertising, Carvel an engineering entrepreneur, DV a fireman with the Airport Authority. The people taking up the more prominent roles became complacent and disorganised and so the conscious decision was made that everybody had to return to the club and focus on nailing down a permanent place in the National League. They branched out from the community for the first time and began bringing in players and staff from further afield, some of whom worked out and some of whom did not. As a club made by people who had all known each other since childhood, it became difficult to express any negativity to outsiders in the way that they could to each other without causing undue personal offence, but on the whole the broader horizons reaped rewards and in 1995 they won the Major League again, earning a spot back in the National League that they have not relinquished since.

In the summer of that same year was an ambitious attempt by an organisation calling themselves Caribbean Major League Football to establish a regional competition of franchise teams from the islands. To a large extent these were effectively national teams, with each country generally being given one franchise. Jamaica had one side based in Montego Bay called the Cornwall County Lions but Harbour View slightly cheekily requested that they might be given one too, and their daring paid off when the league agreed. The CMLF itself went bankrupt before it could really take off but it was through their brief involvement that Harbour View were given the funding to build the current stadium on a relative shoestring through Carvel's construction company. It was the sort of facility no other club in the country, if not the entire Caribbean, could enjoy at that time.

Once again, after a comparatively unsuccessful period through the late 80s and early 90s, Harbour View were putting themselves at the vanguard of Jamaican football development. They sent more players than any other club to the 1998 World Cup with the national team and from there we enter the modern age, with the Ricardo Gardner transfer squabble and the ugly saga that has followed it.

Titles continued to come and in the years between then and last week's Jackie Bell Knockout win they have won the Premier League three times and the CFU Club Championship twice, making them the most successful side in Jamaica. And this year they are trying to add to their proud history by chasing the one feat that has so far evaded them, something that has only been achieved once by anyone in the last twenty years: retaining the Premier League title. In achieving that, a 2-1 defeat against Reno means they will go into their game with Village, the turning point of the entire season, six points off the top.

Sunday 20th February

Portmore United	0 0	Humble Lions
Reno	**2 1**	**HVFC**
Sporting Central	1 1	Benfica
Tivoli Gardens	2 1	St. George's
Village United	0 1	Boys' Town
Waterhouse	1 1	Arnett Gardens

National Premier League

	P	GD	Pts.
1. Tivoli Gardens	28	16	51
2. Boys' Town	28	5	47
3. Portmore United	28	10	46
4. HVFC	**28**	**11**	**45**
5. Waterhouse	28	10	44
6. Reno	28	4	36
7. Sporting Central	28	4	36
8. Arnett Gardens	28	-3	36
9. Humble Lions	28	-5	30
10. Village United	28	-11	30
11. Benfica	28	-24	28
12. St. George's	28	-17	26

CHAPTER TWENTY EIGHT

Crime And Punishment

Guilty!

The Buju verdict has finally arrived and the nation has gone into mourning as twelve Florida jurors agreed that the charges against him of 'conspiracy to possess with intent to distribute five or more kilogrammes of cocaine', 'possession of a firearm in furtherance of a drug-trafficking offence' and 'using the wires to facilitate a drug-trafficking offence' were to be upheld. He was innocent of one further drug charge but that was of little consolation; his bail had been revoked and when the sentencing comes his lawyers expect him to get 15 years to life.

The reaction around Jamaica was one of horror. Supporters were in tears and conspiracies abounded: 'This is another attempt by the USA to keep countries like Jamaica down,' one man fumed on the *Observer* website, another declared that Buju had been 'caught in the white man's trap' as revenge for his most infamous anti-gay song *Boom Bye Bye*. They were determinedly blaming everyone but the criminal. Many were staying away from such theories but were sympathising instead. 'You still my number one artiste and we will always love you no matter what the situation,' said someone. Others blended both reactions: 'OK Buju, we know you're not as innocent as you want us to believe but you are not as guilty as they have made you to be.'

What these all amount to is a picture of one of the most infuriating things about the Jamaican psyche. All too often there is evidence of a victim mentality that fuses itself with a refusal to accept responsibility and hold criminals—criminals they like, anyway—publicly accountable for their lawbreaking. Jamaicans cry foul and want freedom for their man. The least heard reaction to the verdict—by a long, long way—was that Buju got his just desserts. And this is not something that only the young felt, or the poor, it is shared throughout all sectors of society. Even newspaper editorials voice the hope that his sentence would be as light as possible. The people desperately want him free to roam the streets again and cannot accept that he would be going to prison. And they wonder why they have a society that breeds so much crime?

Musicians setting up drug deals, politicians giving guns to gangsters, football administrators breaking every law in the book in order to line their own pockets; they are all the same. And yet the people of Jamaica are immediately prepared to turn a blind eye to crime so long as the criminal serves some purpose for them. The most absurd of all comments was by a man called Island Patriot and he summed up Jamaica's problem perfectly: 'Unfortunately when it comes to justice American-style it's hard to get off charges when not only oral testimony but also video and audio recordings of you committing the crime is available.' And this, apparently, is a bad thing when the man in the dock is someone the public happen to be fond of.

Twelve fair, objective men and women looked at the evidence presented to them and decided that Buju Banton's actions violated federal laws and, while wrong verdicts do happen, the chances are they were right to do so. He was not set up by vengeful homosexuals and, with all due respect, the American state has better things to do than launch a national conspiracy aimed at 'keeping Jamaica down'. The overwhelmingly likely reality is that he is a criminal and therefore the best place for him is jail. That Jamaicans so passionately refuse to agree says much about the wrongs and hypocrisies of their society.

The road connecting Ocho Rios and Montego Bay is about as pristine and faultless as you could imagine. It is where the tourists travel, it is blemish free, neatly lined with immaculate golf courses and well tended resort hotels. The day after Buju was sent to prison I am travelling along it in the back of Carvel's car en route to Montego Bay for another meeting with Village. It is the second league game running where the combination of a long journey and the Jackie Bell winnings means the team is staying away in a hotel overnight, and this time I will be joining them.

With a trip like this there are logistics to address. What rooms do we have? Who is sharing with whom? The team bus left town late so is still a couple of hours away, and as we sit waiting in the car park of our hotel Carvel rings Bowa who has supposedly drawn up a room list. Only, the list has been lost. Or left behind. Either way it isn't where it should be. Snatches of conversation tell half stories as the squad list is read out and written down so Carvel can engineer the solution at our end.

'Where's Dicoy? Why's Dicoy not on the list? . . . He was injured in training this morning? Oh . . . No, Vin's gone back to town tonight . . . Are you sharing with DV? . . . The two keepers together . . . Fame and Beckett . . . Jerry and Cliffy . . . Ohh, you forgot about Andrea didn't you?'

A group booking had been made for thirty people and with twenty players plus staff that limit is being stretched with additions such as myself and Andrea, Carvel's girlfriend. But, after at least an hour in the car manoeuvring the names, everything finally seems to fall into place just as the first bus arrives from Kingston and a handful of players spills out.

The hotel itself is not the luxury you might associate with professional football, or indeed with this particular stretch of coastline. The grubby, dull paintwork in my room is peppered with holes from where old appliances had once been screwed to the wall, the shower is just a pipe over a bath and, most creepily of all, the sheets have blood stains on them. But at least it's a cheap bed for the night. The layout is of two double-storey buildings facing each other which house all the rooms and lead down to an artificial beach by the sea. Here an assortment of piers overhang the shallow water—all of which is hidden by the dark night—and a kitchen area, around which the players soon descend in anticipation of their evening meal. A counter with a screen over it separates the outside from the kitchen and behind it club cook Ebba busily applies the finishing touches to a large pot of beef stew.

As the food is handed out Carvel and Andrea arrive. 'Is there enough for Hugo?' the chairman asks. 'He needs a lot, he's a growing lad.' It has been a number of years since I have been referred to as 'a growing lad' but I am at least a hungry lad and gladly receive a polystyrene plate of stew with, of course, rice and peas. Players wander up to collect their plates and shuffle off to sit on the chairs on the deck. It is at about this point that Bowa and DV finally arrive with a triumphal look about them, the last guests to the party having left town even later than the rest of the team.

I stand at the far end of the counter eating and on the other side Jermaine Hue lolls lazily in a high chair, watching people come and go without taking anything for himself. 'I already ate on the way over here,' he explains. I ask him what they normally do on trips like these and whether they have to adhere to a strict bed time. 'We don't go to bed early but we usually go to our rooms early, just because there's nothing to do.'

He isn't wrong. As people finish their meals some sit around talking but one by one they drift off back to their rooms and by the time I retire to mine there are only a handful of people left. It is about nine-thirty.

There is no strict itinerary in place for match day. At about ten o'clock I venture down towards the kitchen area and look upon the beach and sea in daylight for the first time. It is not the tidiest of settings with a few tatty boats bobbing on the water and the jetty structures have a distinctly ramshackle nature about them. The clear, turquoise shallows flow over white sand and stretch way out to a distant reef, their expanse punctuated by islands of thick green mangrove bushes which rise out of the pristine water.

Some of the earlier rising players loiter by the kitchen waiting to be served their breakfast. Barrett and Hodges stand near the counter while Harvey, known as Jammel within the team, has placed a high chair by the service hatch and is complaining heavily to Ebba about the wait he so endlessly has to endure.

'Good morning sir, yuh good?' Twinny greets me as I approach, before fetching some freshly made hot chocolate from the stove and handing it to me in a polystyrene cup. Brissett comes down carrying his laptop with a persistent dancehall beat ticking out of its tinny speakers while Harvey continues to poke fun at the large cook, delivering one particularly cheeky remark and suddenly springing out of his chair to retreat to a safer distance as the chef lunges forward on the attack.

'Hugo!' Ebba then calls out from behind the screen, before poking his head out of the hatch and looking at me. 'Jammel a cunt.'

Harvey immediately responds. 'You know what a cunt is?' he asks me, as though it was another incomprehensible patois word. After I assure him that I am indeed familiar with the word's meaning he makes his move. 'Well he's got both.' Ebba ignores the accusation and seeks some praise instead. 'Hugo, how was the beef last night?' I let him know it had been great but Harvey, now returning to his seat, again sees his chance to sting. 'You can be honest with him Hugo, tell him it was the worst fucking beef you ever had.'

They continue to spar with each other while the others look on and laugh. Finally Harvey pushes the boundaries too far and Ebba grabs a cup and fills it with water. Harvey sees what is coming and leaps up to run for cover, ducking behind me just as Ebba leans out of the hatch and dispatches the water directly into my face. For Barrett and Hodges, who have been watching the entire episode, it couldn't have ended any better and both collapse with laughter. There is a distinctly relaxed mood ahead of the afternoon's game.

I am still wiping the water away when DV and Bowa arrive and the food is finally dished out. 'He wanted more ackee but you gave me more than him even though I didn't want any,' complains DV as Beckett walks off with helpings evidently not in proportion with what he had requested, 'It's a waste.' I come next and Bowa leans out of the service hatch to declare, 'We have American breakfast, English breakfast, Continental breakfast or Jamaican breakfast. What would you like?' I needn't answer as my plate is already being loaded up with the only option really available, the typically local fare of callaloo, dumplings, boiled bananas and ackee and saltfish. Such a combination can require a fairly strong stomach early in the morning.

I sit on the top deck with a number of the team who all come and go as they finish their food. Spence arrives and seems in a buoyant mood. 'How long's it been since they heard on the radio: "Jahmali Spence turns, shoots and scores"? Months!' he laments, his cause not having been helped by injury in recent weeks. 'I'm going to make a comeback though,' he insists. John-Ross sits opposite him and agrees with the sentiment, adding that he too is after a goal today. His own injury meant he hasn't played in months so just getting him back in the team was a bonus, that alone is seemingly not enough to satiate the appetite of a professional footballer though.

After breakfast most players return to their rooms. Bowa retreats instead to the most distant deck, along a narrow thirty foot boardwalk, where he places himself in a shaded hammock and sings along to songs that are playing out of his mobile phone. Fabian Campbell and Devon Haughton sit by the pool with Robert Williams, but apart from that there is very little sign of life. Relaxation is clearly the main aim of the morning.

As the hour to leave approaches they return, coming to the kitchen to pick up a light snack before all gathering round a long table on the main deck where DV addresses his team. His pep talk drifts over the sand to where I sit on a beach chair. 'We have to defend the flanks,' he impresses upon them. 'Jerry, use the space ahead of you. And forwards, you've got to make runs to receive the ball and then keep possession.' The sun is roasting today and kick off is mid afternoon—given the choice between having to sprint and fight for possession and sitting in a stand watching them the sane choice is clear. But that is what they are paid to do, what they train to do and what they gear every aspect of their entire lives to doing. For the player, chasing that ball is his life regardless of how hot the sun might be.

'We cyaan let them take nine points off us,' DV is saying—'cyaan', pronounced like 'yarn' with a strong K at the beginning, being the Jamaican word for 'can't'—reminding his team of the two defeats Village have already inflicted on us this season. '**Nine points!** It's too much. We are a big team, no likkle team, or any team, can take nine points off us in a season. It doesn't happen; in England, France, Spain, Germany, Jamaica, it doesn't happen.' A deep silence settles on the group as he looks around his players, then he rounds off by stressing the importance of not just being the better team technically but also mentally. 'Attitude wins games. *Will* is more important than skill.' Again the group sit in a contemplative silence before everyone is sent away to gather their things with a few final words.

Falmouth is a small town. A grand cruise ship pier had finally opened a couple of weeks ago after long delays in construction and today its largest incumbent yet is docked there. It looms over the entire town, a gleaming white monument to the gulf between 'us' and 'them', the 'haves' and 'have-nots' with Royal Caribbean's anchor logo perched regally on the top. Blurring the lines of that gulf with increased trade is of course the purpose of the pier being there but as we sit on the bench waiting for the players to change, the ship dominating the landscape behind one of the goals, debate rages as to just how successful it is in bringing foreign money to Falmouth. Corey, another regular member of the Harbour View troupe, blasts that all the visitors just get off the boat and get on a bus to Montego Bay so what is the point, while the JFF's Match Commissioner—'Trelawny born and bred'—defends it with the reasonless passion of the man on the defensive. He seems to think that the situation will be improved in the future when the local businesses catch up. Those amenities, Corey returns, should have all been built at the same time as the pier, not after it. It is Jamaican inefficiency, he derides, and before long the phrase 'policy-making' is used.

If it isn't clear by now, pretty much everything in Jamaica comes back to 'policy-making' and the politicians. 'It's policy-making,' DV had been telling me just a couple of minutes earlier as we walked around the pitch. The grass wasn't looking bad but in the past it had been a different story. 'Last year it was all over the place,' he said. 'When the ref arrived he had to re-mark the pitch.' So why are they allowed to get away with it? Because a Vice President at the JFF is heavily involved with the club and he had to keep them sweet so he could continue to count on the local votes when crucial elections came round. 'They play in red,' he had continued, still on the theme of their previous encounter here. 'Red's their colour. But last year they decided they wanted to play in yellow which meant we had to change our kits. But I said, "No, my team plays in yellow, you play in red." And they insisted that they were the home team so they get to choose. So they went to the referee and he agreed with them, and then they went to the Vice President, who was here, and he sided with them. But I said, "No, red is your registered colour so you play in red. My team plays in yellow." This was all going on before the game and in the end we had to ring the Federation back in town and get them to sort it out,' And so what was the verdict? 'I was right,' he said with a satisfied smile.

After that he turned back to the subject of the ground. 'There's so much potential here, all that space. You could put stands along there with a car park behind,' he pointed to the field behind the benches that was occupied only by some young schoolchildren enjoying some sort of sports day. 'And stands behind the goal, and there's room for a practice pitch.' So is it just money holding them back? 'No, that's not the problem. It's policy-making. Or if Village wanted to they could even use the stadium built for the Cricket World Cup but they don't.' This white elephant is mentioned a lot when Jamaican facilities are debated. The Greenfield Stadium in Trelawny was built specifically for some warm up matches and the opening ceremony of the 2007 Cricket World Cup and has sat virtually unused ever since. With this in mind it is worth thinking back to August when Captain Burrell was so determined to build four venues to host a FIFA tournament of some description. Village, though, chose not to use the Greenfield Stadium: 'They'd have to ask the Government and sort it with them, and Village don't want to pay for the upkeep; they'd rather live for free.'

And so they do, at the Elliston Wakeland Centre where one touchline has a couple of small, metal framed bleachers and another, even smaller, concrete stand in front of the clubhouse behind the goal. It is on this which I sit with the ten or so people from Harbour View to watch a game that is largely won, in accordance with his wishes at breakfast, by the returning Jahmali Spence. Their only sniff comes after quarter of an hour when Barrett collects a corner and is clattered in mid-air by a striker who sends both keeper and ball crashing over the line. The 'goal' is rightfully disallowed and soon after we take control.

Brissett plays a ball from the back down the left wing to Blackburn who clips a first time ball over the top of the defence into the path of Spence. The striker, who has been derided as 'the fat man' for the entire game by one man in the stand, races forward and beats the keeper to it, just touching it past his advance and towards the goal. Not to take chances, new signing Lennox Creary hares after it and boots it solidly into the empty net from no more than two yards, claiming the goal for himself while Spence takes the real credit. 'See fat man deh!' bays the man next to me towards the abusive Village fan a few metres away. 'See fat man deh!' Spence is large and wide—his size often making him the butt of jokes within the club—but there is certainly no fat on him, and right now he is celebrating giving his side the lead while his agitator in the stand sits staring silently forward.

At half time the home fans are unhappy. 'The coach a fucking idiot,' moans one about Village's Brazilian manager. 'He cyaan even hold and distribute the ball.' The comments foreshadow ugly scenes at the final whistle. In the second half the home team push hard, firing a shot over from 40 yards and then just missing the target with a spectacular bicycle kick from a corner. Their fans are up, roaring their team on and Harbour View are beginning to look flustered. As they walk away from a corner Fabian Campbell, growing into his new role within the squad, is conspicuous in shouting encouragement to the players around him while waving his arms in a downward motion, impressing on his team mates the need to calm things down and regain control.

With about ten minutes to go they do just that. As Village send another hopeful ball into our box Barrett dashes out and scoops it up, immediately rolling it out to the right where Harvey is waiting. Bringing it forward he finds Steele in the centre who takes one touch then curls a neat low ball back out onto the flank into the run of the advancing Muir. The move has swept us to within ten yards of the byline when Muir squares the ball to Spence who controls and hits low past the isolated keeper. There was no turn preceding it, but those listening to the commentary back home are once again hearing those brilliant words, 'Jamahli Spence shoots and scores!'

At full time some home fans run on and form a tight knot around the Village coach as he walks to the changing rooms, barking furious insults in his face which he does his dignified best to ignore. His coaching staff come to break up the melee and it turns into a minor scuffle as the Brazilian finally loses his cool and begins to snap back. It is one of those scenes that, walking past towards the Harbour View bench, it is hard not smirk at. Our camp laugh, looking on with smiles of amused surprise at the conflict they had brought upon the home club. It is easy to be smug after an important victory and there is distinct optimism about the coming weeks. 'The way I see it, we have nine games to win it,' Carvel surmises as we are gathering up to leave.

Tomorrow morning, however, our fun is to end. In fact, from this point our entire league season will start to disintegrate. We are unaware of it as we drive away from Falmouth, but like Buju, Harbour View have fallen foul of the law. And like Buju, our punishment will be severe.

Wednesday 23rd February

Arnett Gardens	0 1	St. George's
Boys' Town	0 0	Sporting Central
Humble Lion	2 0	Waterhouse
Tivoli Gardens	1 1	Portmore United

Thursday 24th February

Benfica	0 1	Reno
Village United	**0 2**	**HVFC**

National Premier League

	P	GD	Pts
1. Tivoli Gardens	29	16	52
2. HVFC	**29**	**13**	**48**
3. Boys' Town	29	5	48
4. Portmore United	29	10	47
5. Waterhouse	29	8	44
6. Reno	29	5	39
7. Sporting Central	29	4	37
8. Arnett Gardens	29	-4	36
9. Humble Lion	29	-3	33
10. Village United	29	-13	30
11. St. George's	29	-16	29
12. Benfica	29	-25	28

CHAPTER TWENTY NINE

The Silence After The Cheers

Lou Gehrig's Disease, they call it. Or amyotrophic lateral sclerosis in the words of a doctor. Whatever words you want to attach to it, it is a terrible degenerative illness, one for which there is no cure, and a couple of years ago it hit a Harbour View legend. Barrington Gaynor was known throughout his playing days as 'Cobra', such was his striking presence on the pitch and he had lived for the game, captaining both Harbour View and the national team, before coaching at Bull Bay F.C. and Waterhouse. During the latter stages of his career, his charitable Barrington Gaynor Foundation donated large sums of money to local schools and children to demonstrate his passionate belief in education and helping the community.

But by the time he was doing that work his movement was starting to lose its fluency. It soon became clear that something was wrong with this fitness-obsessed athlete and after travelling the world for a diagnosis it was a Jamaican doctor who finally told him that he was in the early stages of ALS in 2008. The condition, the same Stephen Hawking suffers from and known in the North American public consciousness after a New York Yankees' baseball player who became the first high profile sufferer in the 1930s, attacks the central nervous system and destroys the motor neurones. When voluntary movement becomes impossible the muscles throughout the body, unable to function, weaken and atrophy. Its symptoms cannot be reversed, only slowed, and its causes are still unknown but it does seem to be something former athletes are particularly prone to, a chilling indicator of the effects that a life of the most intense and strenuous fitness can have on the body.

A couple of years after the disease began ravaging his nervous system, Gaynor now sits in a wheelchair, his muscles almost entirely wasted and shrivelled, and he communicates by using his eyes to indicate towards letters on a piece of Perspex held up by his carers. Sometimes his face breaks out into a smile which carries a powerful reminder that underneath the small and frail exterior there dwells a man whose mental capabilities are still fully functioning and intact. In the car after the Jackie Bell Cup semi final Clyde's wife Judith, who works for Air Jamaica, had recalled a story about how she and some colleagues had helped him off a plane in the earlier stages of his illness and afterwards she had sat in one of the seats and cried at the sight of the once-proud athlete so crippled by disease, something she admits she still struggles with now. 'He used to be like Shortman, that sort of build,' she had said sorrowfully, referring to the solid and muscular physique of Richard Edwards, so different to what he has become.

Gaynor had been at the aforementioned Cup match and now the coming league meeting between Harbour View and Boys' Town is to be a testimonial. The club has been granted special dispensation from both the JFF and PLCA to break the $300 ceiling and charge $500 for entry to the game, with the extra going to a fund to help the family with medical expenses. Through the Sports Development Foundation the Government has given $200,000 (around £1,500) and Waterhouse donated $25,000, while the JFF will also later contribute $100,000.

Unfortunately the game itself can't live up to its billing. Before half-time, when some presentations are made, the only thing to happen of note is the appearance of Edwards in the starting XI. He had arrived back in Jamaica an hour and a half before kick off having played 70 minutes for Houston last night but was keen to get himself back into the yellow and blue to help his team again while waiting for the transfer to be completed.

During the break Gaynor is taken out to the centre circle with his family to be presented with some ceremonial cheques and small tokens by Carvel, Captain Burrell's old facilities adversary David Mais of the SDF and a representative of Bull Bay F.C. It is on seeing his youthful wife and five year old daughter that it becomes striking just how young the fragile man in the wheelchair really is, and how devastating the effects of his illness. In his early forties, the life has been sucked out of his body, leaving a healthy and active mind behind.

But there is another Harbour View hero returning to the Compound tonight, albeit one of a slightly (but not much) younger generation. Shortly after half time DV withdraws Spence, who is limping after taking a kick, and replaces him with Fabian Taylor. Taylor joined the club as a teenager and spent eight seasons in the first team, a run punctuated by a season on loan at the New York MetroStars (now the Red Bulls) before leaving to be one of many Jamaican players plying their trade in Scandinavia, joining Notodden FK in southern Norway who, despite having a stadium half the size, could pay a more comfortable wage than Harbour View. His two years there had been ruined by a broken ankle and a serious knee injury and he had considered retirement in October but now marriage brings him home and Harbour View have brought him back into the fold. In an added twist to his story, just two days before the Jackie Bell Cup final Taylor's brother was cycling in Portmore and was shot in the foot after getting caught in the crossfire of the seemingly continuous battles raging in the small town. It was a turbulent wave that brought him back to the Compound, but here he is nonetheless.

Unfortunately he has very little chance to show what Harbour View have been missing. Hopes are high that he might regain his fitness and become the final piece of the jigsaw in a season that has seen us dominate games but be frustratingly wasteful in front of goal. But while the odd flash is there he looks understandably rusty, and most of the play happens at the other end. Boys' Town supporters groan as they watch their team waste three chances from inside the six yard box over the course of the second half and when the referee ends what has been a truly drab top of the table clash it is we who are the more grateful for the point.

In the changing room after the game Spence shrugs off the idea that his injury might be serious in the dismissive, 'It's nothing' way that all men adopt when asked about their pains. As he does so Rafeik Thomas comes in, telling me that his own long-ish term injury will be healed in time for him to be back in action for the next match—that one being away at the home of his old friends Tivoli. As the players sit around chatting I go over to Edwards, who had limped off himself with a very forgivable case of cramp, and as he sits there in nothing more than a pair of pants he tells me about his time in America.

He does not know at this point whether he will be definitely signed up or not and has no idea of the coach's plans because 'he's not that kind of person' and keeps his cards very close to his chest. But he had been pleased with his own performances and feels quietly confident that all will go to plan. And even if Houston don't sign him there is a Florida-based side in USL 1, one league below the MLS, that want him for sure. He certainly seems to have fallen in love with the US football scene though and cannot wait to return.

'You should have seen me last night,' he taps me on the knee to emphasise his point and speaks with an enthusiastic gleam in his eye. 'After the game I went out and all the little kids were asking for my autograph! They liked it because I had been winning a lot of headers against players who were six foot plus.' As we speak the children of Harbour View have found their way into the changing room and are chasing each other round in one of those games that is bound by rules invisible to an outsider, and Edwards seems thrilled to have spent time in a position where players are treated with such professional reverence.

Houston is certainly an attractive destination for him because it offers that connection to home with Lovel Palmer. When the room has emptied a bit he tells me quietly, and in strict confidence, that Clyde had said the New York Red Bulls have also expressed a strong interest should Houston turn him down. This would of course be another exciting destination, bringing him into the same team as New York's superstars and his national team mate Dane Richards. It is a circumstance he looks more than happy to contemplate, but for now his thoughts are in Texas and rightly so; a couple of days later Houston send through an offer to Clyde.

So it has been a day of mixed feelings. Emotional for those seeing a former hero, 'a true son of Harbour View' as Clyde had called him on KLAS radio a few days before, in a wheelchair. Exciting for Edwards who has only been back in the country for a few hours, and frustrating for those hoping to see a big win over title rivals on an evening when Tivoli had beaten Waterhouse 2-1 at Drewsland.

But this is not the full story of the title race. I have not yet given the complete picture of the league table. What I have not explained yet is that in the days before and after this fixture a scandal unfolds that rips the heart out of the league season, and effectively kills it stone dead.

A few weeks previously I had written this in the wake of our draw at Portmore in relation to the Spanish *La Liga*: 'I for one would take this mad, crazy Jamaica Premier League over a one-team procession any day.' How hollow that all became within just two days of this Boys' Town game. It had all begun the morning following our win against Village. A solid win, we thought, and we had made the four hour drive home that night feeling very satisfied with the events of the day. But someone at the PLCA noticed that something had been awry with our team selection. Blackburn had picked up a yellow card against Reno and, that being his third of the season, it earned him a one game suspension. The problem was that in amongst all the hassles of organising the trip to Trelawny and booking the hotel this fact had somehow slipped through the cracks and he had been included in the team, even playing the pass to Spence for the first goal. There was no arguing the facts, no chance to moan that the authorities have it in for Harbour View; it was irrefutable and the automatic punishment gave the three points to Village by default, bringing DV's pre-match fears to fruition and making them the only team to take nine points from us this season. The more important statistic though was that instead of going into the game against Boys' Town looking to chase down a four point gap on Tivoli we were suddenly seven points back, and the 0-0 draw made that nine.

But even that is not the end of it. The PLCA clearly smelled blood and they went on the offensive, reviewing the entire season so far for other such misdemeanours that might have been missed. Their search comes up with spoils that reverberate throughout the table. On the Tuesday after Boys' Town, the Professional Football Association of Jamaica (PFAJ—another of the myriad organisations running the game here) sends an e-mail around announcing that three other illegitimate players had found their way onto the league's pitches, the most significant from our point of view being Omar Parker of Humble Lion during their match against Tivoli just eleven days before Blackburn's appearance had brought the issue to light. What is so shattering is that this game had turned up a shock 1-0 defeat for the league leaders and that has now been turned, by default, into a 3-0 win for them. Portmore also lost a point for illegally playing Tramaine

Stewart in their 0-0 draw with Humble Lion while Benfica received the boost of a 3-0 over Sporting to aid their relegation battle.

The upshot of this is that Tivoli are now a full twelve points ahead of Harbour View and nine above their nearest pursuer—an honour now held exclusively by Boys' Town—with just eight games of the season to go. Even if we win all eight of those remaining fixtures—a streak the likes of which no one has even come close to producing all season—we would need Tivoli to lose half of their games and still have to hope that the damage on their goal difference is sufficient to put us ahead. It is, for all intents and purposes, game over for Harbour View's title hopes and pretty much those of everyone else too. In the space of five days Tivoli Gardens have gone from being in the thick of a tight championship battle to Champions-in-waiting without really having to do very much at all.

So all my words after the Portmore game are now deadwood. What has been a turbulent, exciting fight for the league has now become exactly the sort of one-horse race I had been deriding in Spain, only with an even greater points vacuum separating the leaders from the chasers. The people running the game have shot themselves in the foot, they took their wonderful contest and ruthlessly snapped its neck to leave it lying limp on the ground. But they didn't have a choice. This is one breaking of the rules to which the authorities couldn't possibly have turned a blind eye and so they did what was necessary. It just so happened that what was necessary was something that benefited nobody, with the obvious exception of Tivoli, and left everything that had been so vibrant feeling shattered and hollow. It was fun while it lasted but, with two months still to play, this season's Premier League now appears like it is just about over. The silence after the cheers feels very cold indeed.

Sunday 27ᵗʰ February

Benfica	2	1	Arnett Gardens
HVFC	**0**	**0**	**Boys' Town**
Reno	0	3	Village United
Sporting Central	1	1	Portmore United
St. George's	0	0	Humble Lion
Waterhouse	1	2	Tivoli Gardens

National Premier League

	P	W	GD	Pts.
1. Tivoli Gardens	30	17	21	58
2. Boys' Town	30	13	5	49
3. Portmore United	30	12	7	47
4. HVFC	**30**	**13**	**8**	**46**
5. Waterhouse	30	12	7	44
6. Reno	30	10	2	39
7. Sporting Central	30	9	1	37
8. Village United	30	9	-5	36
9. Arnett Gardens	30	8	-5	36
10. Humble Lions	30	8	-4	33
11. Benfica	30	9	-21	33
12. St. George's	30	8	-16	30

Barrington 'Cobra' Gaynor (third left) receives presentations from Carvel (third right), David Mais of the SDF (far right) and others. Seated on the floor, one of Harbour View's biggest fans shows his appreciation for the former player.

CHAPTER THIRTY

The Hands Of Mortals

As my taxi rattles shakily towards a junction in Mountain View, on the way to the Compound, I look out of the window and wonder if there is a way for Harbour View to get back into this title race. The twelve point gap is a daunting one, and even if we put together an unprecedented run of form ourselves we will be relying on the teams ahead of us to each suffer a spectacular collapse.

But at this dispiriting point hope strikes me from the heavens and a divine solution presents itself. 'Evening Service and Miracle Healings, Wednesday 9 , 5pm' proclaims a sign that hangs from a lamp post on the corner, giving the address of a local church. There it is, I suddenly think, Miracle Healings! It is amazing how the mortal men of Christianity have the power of their omnipotent God so completely harnessed in their own fleshy hands that they can schedule his miracles and advertise them to the public for an appointed hour, but how useful it will be to find ourselves on the receiving end. That, it seems, is about all that can prevent Harbour View's crown from falling off and landing into the grateful clutch of Edward Seaga and his Tivoli troupe.

'Every day holds the possibility of a miracle,' Elizabeth David once wrote, and today will have to be the day when ours begins. It isn't just any game either, it's Tivoli away. Today we will either surrender the league or give ourselves hope, however slight, that we might find a way back. A loss will leave us 15 points behind and out of it completely, but a win would have us just nine away and from there we might, if everything falls our way for the rest of the season, be able to pull off the impossible. At the very least we can claim a moral victory of sorts: get ourselves to within six points of them by the end of the season and the proof will be there that the better team had *not* won, that this would be a league table where everything did *not* fall where it belonged, and that they had only won their title by dint of points penalties. But even that is hopeful at this stage. Harbour View have a lot of work to do.

On arrival at the Compound it is clear that we aren't the only ones needing a hand from above. The players have gathered round the television showing Ireland's struggle against an India team that is running away to victory in the Cricket World Cup. The heavenly inbox is clearly spilling over on this Sunday afternoon. But we don't hang around long enough to see the Indian victory crush the Irish prayers, we have our own pleas that need answering. We have to go chasing our own audacious dream.

It begins in inauspicious circumstances. Fuzzy's is the only bus we have today and even after filling that and all the cars there are still five players and a number of staff left standing around the baked car park. Carvel is on his way over to pick some up and AnnMarie Massey, a member of the management at the club, would go back for another run after dropping myself, DV, Barry and Corey at the Edward Seaga Complex. 'They eat too much before the game,' surmises Corey in the car as DV complains that the players left behind hadn't even been ready to go because they had been in the toilet. It is at moments like these that it is most easy to understand Edwards' seduction by the professionalism of the MLS.

Edwards himself is in the stand today, not selected by DV despite his deal with Houston still not yet being completed. An injury now would be the cruellest of blows. This time it is Beckett filling that role in midfield with Fame taking his place on the bench, suggesting the management are still not completely sure about which direction to take in the absence of the captain. But the main problem today, as with every day this season it seems, would be not in midfield but up front.

From the fence behind us comes the usual torrent of verbal abuse, perhaps the strongest and most persistent yet and certainly with the least sense of irony.

'Suck yuh mother pussy, referee! Blood clot, referee! Harbour View a batty man side!'

We are making some chances but we aren't finishing them off. A goal mouth scramble sees the ball just miss Spence's outstretched foot, Hue curls in a free kick that produces a decent if over-spectacular save from the keeper. Divine intervention, though, is just around the corner.

When Harvey brings the ball into their half there is about half an hour gone. He sends a long pass into the box which causes mass confusion, everyone seems to be leaving it for everyone else to deal with. Blackburn takes advantage to run across the front of the keeper and jump through the path of the ball with an arm raised. Did he touch it? With minimal deviation, if any, the ball continues on its path and bounces absurdly past Scott in the Tivoli goal and into the net. The Harbour View players wheel away celebrating but immediately something is wrong. The linesman is flagging and the referee blows his whistle—no goal! Instead he reaches to his pocket and shows Blackburn a yellow card for hand ball, evidently feeling he *had* touched it past the keeper.

No Englishman needs to be reminded of Diego Maradona's Hand of God and no Irishman can forget what the tabloids imaginatively dubbed 'Le Hand of God' after Thierry Henry handled in setting up the vital goal that qualified France for the 2010 World Cup at Ireland's expense. Both those goals stood, both were absolutely crucial for their team. Perhaps Marcelino Blackburn is not high-profile enough to command deities into his limbs, and so today the influence of his mortal hand is punished rather than rewarded. If we are going to get our miracle it is looking increasingly likely that we will have to produce it ourselves.

The argument of whether Harbour View are the biggest side in the Caribbean is rearing again behind us. 'Harbour View not even the biggest side in Jamaica, you can't even pick a team properly,' mocks the main antagonist, understandably enjoying the fallout of the illegitimate players scandal. 'Harbour View inna di batty man club,' he then offers, as though this crucial evidence would seal the argument. Carvel then turns round in his chair and rides to the defence of his team: 'You know the batty man club well because you're in it too,' he says in his calm, dead-pan way, delivering a response as effective as it is childish and causing everyone around to laugh at the remark's target. 'Like knows like, fish swim with fish.' The full Harbour View staff is looking round and laughing at the man who has fallen into embarrassed silence, and even those on his own side take pleasure in his humiliation.

A few mumbled bumbaclaats seem to be all he can muster but no Jamaican can be silenced for long. When Scott picks up an injury the home fans take the opportunity to curse the players nearest to them. 'Fuck yuh mother, twenty seven! Number twenty seven a batty bwoy! Suck yuh mother pussy, twenty seven!' the man yells with his fellow supporters towards Harvey, who responds with a small gesture indicating for them to come onto the pitch and discuss their thoughts in a more personal manner. 'Concentrate Jammel, leave it,' shout the Harbour View coaches, not wanting their player to react and become distracted. Fabian Taylor, enjoying his first start since returning to the club, also patrols the near flank and finds himself a target for local attention too. 'Number eleven you need to change your pad, the blood's running down your leg! It's all over your boots!' screams one woman, making a refreshing yet graphic deviation from the usual phrasebook of insults so tiredly overused. It has to be said that the word 'ladylike' is not one that can be applied too liberally to the females of the Kingston ghetto.

The second half sees the game turn ugly. 'Once the game gets that way, the least touch: drop,' Edwards had once said to me about Navion Boyd's antics when things get physical. Today he might not be diving but he certainly loses his temperament as the temperature rises. The signs are there when he tries to shield the ball from Brissett's attentions to win a throw and turns to barge our left back in the chest instead of using his frame legitimately. The ref ignores this, as he does the shove on Beckett, a former high school team mate of the Tivoli forward's, a few seconds later. But nonetheless Boyd only has about a minute left on the pitch.

Again trying to shield the ball, he is tripped by Wolfe and as he falls he turns and lashes out, catching the Harbour View midfielder in the face with his hand and being shown a straight red card when he gets to his feet again. He walks off in the emotional huff of an angry schoolboy while the fans up their already-impressive quota of curses in the referee's direction.

Around ten minutes after that it is ten a side as Blackburn goes in late for a tackle and clatters his opposite number to the floor. The

Harbour View bench howl in rage as he is shown a second yellow card but in truth there is no way the decision can be argued. Hardly an inconspicuous return for the player who has only just emerged from the centre of the suspension controversy. We could have been down to nine a few minutes later when Beckett catches a Tivoli player with a flying elbow but he is lucky to only be given a yellow. The unhappy home fans tell the ref, yet again, exactly what he should do to his mother.

There are about ten minutes to go when Hue, over on the far side of the pitch, is brought off for the return of Romario Campbell to the first team. On seeing his number raised he turns and walks over towards the bench when suddenly a yellow card is being held over his head. The ref, it transpires, had wanted him to leave the pitch on the other side and then booked him for not doing so. No laws of the game had been contravened, not even an unwritten but accepted practice, and yet the ref decided it was a bookable offence all the same. 'Where have you *ever* seen anything like it outside Jamaica?' Hue says to me after the game, and in the car park later on, still in furious disbelief, he adds, 'If you watch *good* football they never leave that side of the pitch. This could only happen in Jamaica.' As he walks from the field he makes his disgust very clear and the home fans are outraged at this show of indiscipline towards the official. 'Respect the referee, Jermaine Hue!' they cry, deeply offended on the poor ref's behalf. 'That's not respect!' And with their sermonising done he leaves the pitch. 'Fuck yuh mother, referee!' they yell, mere seconds later.

But while all this is going on the one thing the second half never really looks like producing is the one thing we really need from it: a goal. The length of stoppage time is announced like a dead-man-walking call and our final minutes slip by without salvation. The whistle blows, this game is over and our game is surely up. The mood on the bench is solemn, Bowa sits staring stonily at the floor as the players crowd over and drop to the ground to sip their Lucozades in silence. The gap remains unchanged but we really have little chance now. You do not catch up twelve points in seven matches, it simply does not happen, and our last flicker of hope is now dancing precariously in the breeze.

Miracles, of course, are little more than a human construct to give depth and meaning to extreme coincidence. The evidence supporting them is much like the evidence supporting every football fan's belief that the referees want their team to lose. Contradictory evidence is ignored or explained away and only the events that support the belief are recalled and recounted. It is what psychologists call a confirmation bias: I prayed for something to happen and it did, therefore God *is* looking after me, despite the times my prayers may have gone unanswered. The blatant foul wasn't given therefore the refs **have** been bought by the other team, the wrong decisions in our favour just show they haven't been paid enough.

But it doesn't matter how much anyone prays for it, taking Barrington 'Cobra' Gaynor to that Mountain View church on the night it hands out its miracles will not have him striding purposefully up and down the wing at the Compound again. And similarly, no matter how we try to incite the heavens in our favour it is now almost certain that Harbour View will not be lifting that league trophy come May. That is the hard and bitter truth of the ungodly world. 'A fact never went into partnership with a miracle,' American lawyer Robert Green Ingersall said once. 'Truth scorns the assistance of wonders.'

Sunday 6th March

Boys' Town	2	1	Waterhouse
Humble Lion	0	2	Benfica
Portmore United	0	1	Arnett Gardens
Reno	1	2	St. George's
Tivoli Gardens	**0**	**0**	**HVFC**
Village United	1	1	Sporting Central

National Premier League

	P	GD	Pts
1. Tivoli Gardens	31	21	59
2. Boys' Town	31	6	52
3. HVFC	**31**	**8**	**47**
4. Portmore United	31	6	47
5. Waterhouse	31	6	44
6. Reno	31	1	39
7. Arnett Gardens	31	-4	39
8. Sporting Central	31	1	38
9. Village United	31	-5	37
10. Benfica	31	-19	36
11. Humble Lions	31	-6	33
12. St. George's	31	-15	33

CHAPTER THIRTY ONE

What Happens In Football

I sit on a chair looking at the impressively decorated walls while the secretary types and answers phone calls at her desk nearby. In the adjacent office, nestled behind closed doors above the library on the UWI campus at Mona, the Right Honourable Edward Seaga is finishing off his lunch. The small waiting room is cluttered with so many reminders of the significance of his life that there simply isn't room to display them all. Various knick-knacks—if you could call them that, for these are not carriage clocks and porcelain dogs—are starting to pile up on the floor. Photos of the former Prime Minister with the rich, famous and powerful lean against the walls, keys to various global cities are proudly displayed in a glass fronted case and letters of friendship from powerful world leaders are framed and hung. None of which is doing anything to calm my nerves. Interviewing sportsmen is a fairly easy affair—they tend to be a similar age to me and are generally pretty easy going—but this is a different proposition entirely.

Seaga has spent a lifetime battling through some of the most ferocious politics on the planet, leading the JLP from 1974 until Bruce Golding finally took over in 2005. But even then he did not slip quietly into retirement to spend his days pottering around the rose garden. At 80 years old he still holds numerous positions in football and life at large and rarely has a moment to spare. That I have managed to pin him down for an interview at all is a rare privilege that only came from months of Clyde working to set it up during their weekly encounters at the PLCA meetings. And, to put it lightly, he has not achieved what he has by suffering fools gladly. So when I am summoned into his office, where he then explains pointedly that he isn't really sure what it is I want, it's fair to say I'm not quite as relaxed as I am for other interviews. I dip my toe in the water by asking about the early development of his Tivoli Gardens project, and he is happy to oblige.

'It was something that I designed as a sociologist and anthropologist to satisfy the needs of all aspects of community development. There was an intense swamp and garbage dump, and people living in little huts in that area which was,' he pauses to find the right word, 'indescribable. It also was a den where criminals used to hide. So in every respect it was something that could not survive because it was a great stain on the community and to that extent we decided to demolish the area and replace it with a modern community.'

A modern community that was only open to his supporters, or so his critics would have us believe. Unsurprisingly, he paints a different picture. 'It's about a thousand units and we told people who were living there that they should make applications if they wanted to come back and live in that community. Very few of them did, for two reasons. One, they had settled elsewhere and two, they were mostly aligned politically to the other side. And in all of the waterfront constituencies you'll find people in areas of great political polarity who don't like to live among each other because they are afraid of hostilities. So you'll find that people cluster where they can.'

Essentially he is saying the concentration of his supporters was a result of the choices made by the people themselves rather than his party, and he is very definitive in absolving himself of blame. To fully address the issue I ask him outright if he had ever approved residents' applications based on their political affiliation. 'No, no, no,' is his unequivocal response. 'People who were in Tivoli Gardens came from within that community and the people in the little ramshackle huts were told they could make applications but as I said they went to another area and settled. They wouldn't necessarily want to live among people who had the opposite political persuasion, so that was the reason why we never got a substantial number of them.'

As he continues he seems to pinpoint this as the origin of Kingston's massive troubles since. 'That's a pattern,' he goes on about this political grouping. 'It's a pattern that goes on. And this has, in the succeeding period, created a number of serious hostilities which have broken out into street fighting. Western Kingston is the only one of a JLP persuasion, all the others that surround it are PNP and so it came under a lot of political pressure. That led to the community having to try and defend itself because you wouldn't get the police trying to help out in circumstances like that. And this went on for years until the definitive election in 1980 which settled the matter of the JLP and the standing of the Western Kingston constituency.'

It is, of course, worth bearing in mind just who these words are coming from. Seaga paints his JLP as a picture of innocence throughout our conversation, always the victim and never the antagonist, a perennial underdog bullied and battered by the hostile PNP. These are clearly the words of a JLP politician.

It was said that during the 1970s Seaga and Michael Manley were not just political rivals but also shared a great mutual loathing of one another personally, and hints of this also appear when he speaks scathingly about Anthony Spaulding who, he says, created Arnett Gardens specifically to copy the JLP's flagship Tivoli project. He lays much of the blame for the violence of those dark decades squarely at Spaulding's feet with the assertion that he was, 'very, very partisan.'

'That set the tone for the area. If he had been like Omar Davies it would never have happened. He certainly was someone who, by his actions and his speech, made it clear that he saw the JLP as enemies and so the posture of antagonists really came about through that militaristic interpretation. And that came out of the fact that the government at the time was moving in a very radical socialist direction and militarism was a part of that ideology in the sense of that's how you keep the people under control. But politically we fought that off in the 70s and got rid of it. But it was a nasty period.'

He is now into his 80s and his age shows in a body that is beginning to look hunched and frail, and a face blemished with liver spots, but his eyes still flash with passion and something approaching menace, while his conviction in speaking shows his resolve is as strong as ever. His words are powerful and emotive, and his accusations are vast. The PNP, he asserts, used the army to fight a war against its own citizens. It seems more like something from the dictatorships of South America than a strictly democratic Commonwealth nation. 'If I'd known that that is what you wanted to talk about I would have given you some material that shows twice when the state forces attacked Tivoli Gardens without any reason. The reasons were created in order to be able to attack it, so they claimed that they were the government there and they wanted to apprehend criminals. And the killings that took place by the security forces, the amount of ammunition fired etc. etc. and not one gun, not one bullet was found. And that was in May 1997, and then the second time was in July 2001 and this time it was worse. This time they stood in a high rise building nearby and snipered people just walking on the street. 27 people were killed and the hospital was full of wounded, and again it was on a created antagonism that they went into the community at 4 o'clock in the morning and they drove up and down the streets firing shots and they claimed they were being fired at. And they called in reinforcements and the reinforcements started to attack.'

'They had a commission of inquiry, which I asked for, but I didn't know they were going to use people who were partisan to them as the commissioners. So naturally the findings were to their suiting. We really needn't bother to attend.' What is most staggering about this is that they cannot be dismissed as just an old politician's partisan memories, the words he speaks are the verifiable truth. The attacks on Tivoli really happened and the director of Amnesty International UK said that the inquiry, 'failed to fulfil its obligations under international law to fully investigate these killings. There can be no justice for the victims and their families until their voices are heard, their deaths adequately explained and those responsible held to account where the law has been violated.' There was little or no representation for the victims and no independent investigators, so evidence came almost entirely from the very security personnel who were on trial. A British human rights barrister called it, 'a travesty of the legal and evidential tests which a public enquiry into killings by state agents is required to perform by international law.' That the PNP needed to skew the enquiry so spectacularly speaks volumes for their culpability, and this wasn't even back in the violent 70s. As recently as 2001, the Jamaican government murdered its own innocent civilians in the streets. And that's not to mention the controversy of the Dudus affair.

I move the conversation on to the Shower Posse and how they came to such prominence within Tivoli. 'Every community has a Shower Posse,' he responds. 'Every one of them. This one just got more publicity because of the lack of assistance it got from the police in dealing with problems, and therefore it got into problems with the opponents more than the other groups. And it was supposed to be these groups that kept Tivoli free of crime and also it kept out intruders, and that was why the people there welcomed their position because they appreciated that they were doing what the police wouldn't do, and that's protecting them from intruders coming in and shooting up the community.'

And its links with the party? 'There is not a link in the sense that the JLP **needed** the Shower Posse, and I don't think the PNP needed the other posses that existed either. Because in all of these communities the margin of victory is very large, you don't really need anybody to do anything to help you. Politically you would be very well established.' It makes sense but still seems to ride over a lot of accepted wisdom, so I put to him the words of the former gangster who had described himself as a 'political enforcer' for the JLP. 'Well they will tell you that they were connected, obviously they have political affiliations, but not on the instruction of the JLP or expectation of the JLP. Or on the PNP side.'

Although it seems he is backtracking slightly, I sense his patience was running short on that line of questioning and so I take the conversation to what I had really come to discuss with him in the first place: football. He describes garrison politics as 'history' and I want to know why. Dr Sives at the University of Liverpool had stated expressly that football was not directly responsible, but this contradicted exactly Captain Burrell's words at the League launch, words that were taken from Seaga himself. I am eager to hear more on where this peace came from between Tivoli and Arnett and the role football played.

'In the mid 90s Dr Omar Davies, who is the member of parliament for Arnett Gardens, built a football stadium and said to me that we should have a match between Tivoli Gardens and Arnett Gardens. Prior to that we weren't able to play in each other's community, we had to go to some neutral ground. So we broke ground on a trial basis and it worked. And it worked very well. And that opened the gate for games to be played in other areas that were politically hostile. The intermingling of people made it even better because people started to become friends and so on.

'And it really created a transformation, a real transformation that nothing else had been able to do. And on that basis we now have the football league, and the other competitions below that, playing in places that some time ago were hostile.'

In fact, so convinced is he of what football has done for Jamaica that he looks at me as if I am mad when I suggest that the tribal nature of fandom might actually make the divisions worse. 'Worse? No. No. While we played outside the community it was possible to play a game, but not really with any level of friendship between the two teams. But when we broke the ice and started to play in each others' communities it became just a normal friendship that will exist between any two sets of people.'

I then ask him how football could be used to soften the rivalries even further, but he insists there was no more scope for change. 'Those rivalries don't exist anymore. They don't exist so there is no need for football to do any further work there. Football is just going along now as a normal sport would.' The game's work, in Seaga's opinion, is done. Having seen the abuse Marcelino Blackburn and other Trenchtown residents still get while playing at Tivoli I am slightly more sceptical, but the evidence is piling up that football has indeed given something to Jamaican society that nothing else could, that it has broken barriers and soothed hostilities where everything else had proved impotent. Proof indeed that sport's value is way beyond that of a simple hobby.

Before I leave I want to ask him one last thing. I am curious to hear his thoughts on the Dudus invasion and how much it had hurt Tivoli. 'Very deeply,' he sounds mournful as he speaks. 'No community has ever been exposed to that, Tivoli is the only one. Because of the hostilities that are ingrained in the state forces through their own political feelings, Tivoli is always the one that is under attack. And in this instance, to attack it with mortar shells and things like that, it has never been done before. And they wiped out, they say, 73, but people there say it is much more than that. But they never really allowed anybody to take a proper count.'

Seventy three dead civilians, at a conservative estimate, because of the JLP-ordered actions taken by what Seaga insists is a heavily PNP-supporting security force. So has the community managed to recover yet? 'It's recovering. And what has been happening with football has been very helpful because it has allowed the process to work and for them to build back their self confidence, because Tivoli was built out of an area that was the most despised area in the country. It was a slum, a dump, it was everything that was bad.

And therefore the people in the entire constituency got that stigma, that they are not worthy of anything and that they are all from a background of evil and that sort of thing. And we have changed that image through the community and through the projects that I did in that area so that people are proud to be in Tivoli and proud to be known to be Tivoli because the programmes were succeeding so well. And it was the kind of place that if you wanted to live there you would find a much improved location than where you were before. And they want to get back to that stage.' And football, that shallow game of over-paid prima donas, is the prime social mover in making that social recovery happen.

On that note, then, we turn back to the Premier League.

Richard Edwards' transfer to Houston is on the rocks. Harbour View received an offer a couple of weeks ago but now contact with the middle man orchestrating the deal has all but dried up, while the Americans had told their press that they are still uncertain about whether or not they even want him. Clyde is very unsure about what is happening, and the mixed messages and lack of answers from the agent are making life very difficult indeed for the club. On the plus side though, it means we have our captain back in the side for Benfica's return to the Compound this weekend.

The other good news is that six other players have been called up to the provisional national training squad. Two of those, John-Ross and Romario Campbell, fire early shots in the first minutes before Wolfe receives a perfect ball from Lamar Hodges in the 14 to put Harbour View one ahead. Edwards makes it two with his first of the season and John-Ross puts us three ahead before an injury time consolation made the final score 3-1. With Tivoli drawing with Arnett the gap between us and them was down to ten points, but with only six games to go it is still looking desperate.

'I still harbour hopes of winning the league,' DV tells me in defiance after the game. 'I have seen stranger things happen in football. There are still six more games to go, and the leader dropped two points which just goes to show that anything can happen. All we have to do is make sure we are in a position so if it does happen we can take the lead.'

While Edwards may have been available tonight, Dicoy Williams was not. He was away on a short trial with Toronto F.C., a new MLS expansion team under the guidance of former Dutch international Aron Winter, and his return flight landed at about the same time our final whistle blew at the Compound. It therefore fell to Clyde, who so often drives Dicoy home after matches, to pick him up.

While his car circles the looped road in front of the arrivals terminal, I jump out to go in search of our international defender. After a lengthy wait, punctuated by shrugs towards Clyde with every wasted lap, his tall frame lumbers out of the sliding doors and he seems to have mixed emotions. 'Did you see my match?' he keenly asks. An e-mail had been sent to everyone involved with the club containing a link to watch his trial game online. I tell him that I had and opine that he seemed to have given a solid performance. He too was pleased with how it gone but that had been the only game of his trial, which probably isn't a positive omen. Added to that, their squad is near its limit of foreign players and he is in the wrong position. 'The manager wants a midfielder and a striker,' he says miserably as he climbs into the back seat of the BMW.

So it is a pleasant surprise when Toronto send through a solid offer and within days Dicoy is packing his bags for a new career in the MLS. 'It is very good news, I'm excited,' he tells me over the phone for an interview feature I was asked to do for the PLCA's magazine. 'I can't wait to be there and see if I can get a spot in the team. It's going to be a tough challenge.'

And as this is happening Edwards' transfer to Houston falls through entirely. By this stage the Red Bulls have also moved on to new targets and despite Clyde trying to push his services on to other clubs none are really looking for overseas players so late in the transfer window. Given his excitement before he left for the trial it must have been a brutal disappointment for him, but he finds solace in his deep religious faith and, as is the way with the modern age, in Facebook. 'Thank you Lord,' he posts on there when the news comes through. 'When God takes something from your grasp he is not punishing you, but merely opening your hands to receive something better.' And if he is downbeat he doesn't let it show, expressing to me his confidence that something else would come along and stressing the need to just keep working hard to make it happen. 'The story, it just didn't sound straight to me either,' he agrees when I say it had all seemed a bit dodgy, but exactly what went wrong and where seemed to get lost in the mess. So it turns out that Dicoy is unexpectedly gone and Edwards is unexpectedly still around. Funny how these things turn out. Funny what happens in football.

Sunday 12th March

Arnett Gardens	2 2	Tivoli Gardens	
Boys' Town	1 0	Portmore United	
HVFC	**3 1**	**Benfica**	
Sporting Central	1 1	Reno	
Village United	2 1	Humble Lion	
Waterhouse	0 1	St. George's	

National Premier League

	P	GD	Pts.
1. Tivoli Gardens	32	21	60
2. Boys' Town	32	7	56
3. HVFC	**32**	**10**	**50**
4. Portmore United	32	5	47
5. Waterhouse	32	5	44
6. Reno	32	1	40
7. Village United	32	-4	40
8. Arnett Gardens	32	-4	40
9. Sporting Central	32	1	39
10. St. George's	32	-14	36
11. Benfica	32	-21	36
12. Humble Lions	32	-7	34

CHAPTER THIRTY TWO

Machiavellian Intent

The league may have been dealt a severe and dampening blow but important things are still happening in football politics. On a regional level, Jack Warner and his mob get themselves re-elected unopposed into their positions at the top of CONCACAF for another four years of raping and pillaging the beautiful game, and in the same week that Sepp Blatter's re-election campaign on a global level receives a heavy boost. Next to this it is a small, barely-noticed event that is striking on a local level, and it holds imposing consequences for Jamaica's own sporting governance.

In Jamaica each of the parishes has its own football association—with the exception of Kingston and St. Andrew, who together form KSAFA—which gives rise to a total of thirteen local organisations. It is on the 21 of March that one of these, the Hanover FA, signs a lucrative new sponsorship deal worth $1.2 million with the *Captain's Bakeries* restaurant chain. Like I said, we are talking about a small event here, but it is the contextual meaning that is important rather than the happening itself. This is a business that is very active in Jamaican football and the agreement means it now has similar deals with nine of the thirteen parish associations across the island. And it is the individuals within in these associations, a total of just over 100 people, who vote in the elections that decide all the major positions within the JFF, which potentially gives the businesses that fund them a certain degree of influence over the outcome should they desire to interfere. So, with this in mind, one might ask the question of who it is that wields this influence? Who is the businessman that owns the far-reaching *Captain's Bakeries*? I fear you may have guessed the answer already.

This seems like a good time to take a closer look at Captain Horace Burrell.

I had left the Pierre Aliker in Martinique with Burrell having grown on me considerably. He was passionate about Jamaican football, he seemed a nice enough bloke and he had just enabled the Reggae Boyz to win the tournament by paying their wages from his own personal pocket. And his reluctance to dwell on the strike that evening, compared with Warner's bizarre, and possibly slightly intoxicated, rant, cast him in a very favourable light. He might be Warner's best friend, I thought back then, but he didn't seem too bad himself. But with the help of Trinidadian journalist Lasana Liburd again, I did some further research that was far less favourable.

A former military man, hence his prefix, Burrell became President of the JFF for the first time in 1994. He quickly made all the right friends and two years after assuming office he cemented his place as Warner's right hand man with a turn of mendaciousness of which the Trinidadian himself would have been proud. There was a vote at a FIFA Congress in Zurich to give CONCACAF a third seat on the Executive Council, a move that would significantly boost Warner's power within the world governing body, and all national football association heads were to be present in order to mark their ballot. But this was not a hugely popular motion and Warner needed all the votes he could get. Unfortunately for him, news broke on the eve of the Congress that Jean-Marie Kyss of Haïti would not be able to make it and without him there was panic in the CONCACAF camp.

Luckily Burrell was on hand, and he wasn't in Zurich alone. He had acquired some company in the form an apparently stunning young woman named Vincy Jalal ('I surround myself with a lot of ladies . . . In my business, of course!' he had joked at the League launch) and everybody fervently agreed when he ingeniously proposed that in these tight circumstances she might pose as the head of Haïtian Football Federation to cast her vote for Warner.

So she took her place in the Haïtian seat and at the role call she exhausted her knowledge of the French language by responding with a heavily-accented, 'Oui'. Then when the time came for business everybody in the hall looked on admiringly as she sashayed forward in her tightly-fitting dress and voted for Uncle Jack, an action captured on video and stored for posterity in the FIFA archives. From that moment the Burrell—Warner friendship was sealed, and it would prove to be a very useful tool indeed a few years later.

In 2003 Burrell encountered the biggest threat yet to his position as the head of Jamaican football in the form of Crenston Boxhill. Prior to the election, the President received what was seen as a veiled endorsement from Blatter, who turned up to break ground on what would become the failed technical centre in Portmore, but as debts piled up many people had become keen for change. It was a tight electoral race and Boxhill showed his intent by turning up on the day with around 50 voting officials in his entourage. The stunt worked and a couple of hours later he ousted Burrell as President of the JFF.

Captain, though, was beaten but by no means broken, and it is the four year stint of the Boxhill administration that demonstrates just how important it is to have the right friends and to play the right games within FIFA. Immediately on his election defeat Burrell announced that the Federation was $30 million in debt, around half of which was owed to him personally in the form of money he had lent to cover costs, and now he wanted it repaid. So what could the new administrators do? Burrell had recently splashed out to build a swanky new headquarters for the organisation in New Kingston and so, in order to pay off their debts, Boxhill decided the only option he now had was to sell it. But Captain's powerful friends swooped and made it very clear that if such a move were to happen Jamaica would be thrown out of FIFA because, as general secretary Urs Linsi wrote to the Federation, 'we will consider this action to be a misuse of FIFA funds.'

It was a development that stunned then-JFF treasurer Carlton Barclay. 'In that letter it didn't quote any regulation we breached, none whatsoever,' he told the *Star* newspaper at the time. 'We wouldn't want to be disqualified so the sale of the building is scrapped but what I am saying is there is no regulation. Obviously if there was a regulation it would have been noted and we would not think about selling the building.' But they would have to get used to such treatment and the Boxhill administration would spend its entire term being squeezed and undermined by FIFA and CONCACAF.

There were two threats made against them that they would lose their FIFA funding and they were fined US$5,000 just for failing to present a copy of the national anthem at the start of the Caribbean Cup. Boxhill was no angel, as evidenced by his failure to pay the English FA £153,431.94 that was owed after a friendly at Old Trafford, but he was doing a solid job. The Reggae Boyz won the 2005 Caribbean Cup, the under 18 boys and under 20 girls won regional tournaments, Harbour View became Caribbean Club champions and the JFF turned an un-audited profit of $7.5 million in 2005. And, to top it off, they were clean: 'There is no corruption, embezzlement or fraud in Jamaican football now,' Boxhill told Liburd. 'I can proudly say that no such charges can be levelled at this present organisation.' Yet despite all this they went into the 2006 AGM having to deal with a vote of no confidence for the second consecutive year as Burrell and his supporters, at home and abroad, continued to make life impossible.

'We are beginning to see Machiavellian intent,' noted the *Observer* in a contemporary editorial. 'It is unfortunate that this administration has not been allowed to settle, with seeming collusion of the FIFA hierarchy . . . The administration ought not to be undermined by international guerrilla tactics.'

The beleaguered Boxhill claimed that such harassment was 'unheard of in Jamaican football,' and he went on to leave little doubt as to where it was coming from: 'One individual is behind all of this,' he said. 'In Jamaica we all know who the individual is.'

That individual, who still held posts at CONCACAF and FIFA, would be successful in his campaign and won back the Presidency in 2007. What is telling is that despite being the incumbent, Boxhill did not even bother to stand in that election such was the hopelessness of the situation. At that point *Captain's Bakeries* was the chief sponsor of seven of the thirteen parish associations while indirectly funding two more via a deal with the Western Confederation, and Boxhill, in acknowledging the futility of running against this power, told the press that Burrell was 'compromising the process'.

Since then, of course, the JFF has not been attacked from the outside. In fact, it's been quite the opposite and they have received generous help from FIFA's best friends. Friends such as Peter Hargitay, a Swiss-Hungarian spin doctor who has risen to prominence with football politics. Earlier in his career Hargitay was behind Union Carbide's successful battle to avoid paying compensation to the impoverished victims of an explosion at one of the company's chemical factories in India that killed 16,000 people and left many thousands more maimed for life, a feat that Andrew Jennings reports Hargitay boasted of proudly on his website. That is just one of many unpleasant chapters in his past and for the last few years he has been a 'Special Advisor' to Blatter at FIFA, helping the President deflect the many media stories of corruption within the ranks. It was Sepp's friend Hargitay who was instrumental in securing the JFF's largest ever sponsorship deal, worth US$1.7 million over two years, with the Italian sportswear company Kappa. It was also he who, having been shamefully hired to help the 2018 World Cup bid, helped broker a deal with the English FA to give the JFF more time to repay its debts. Boxhill would never have dared dream of receiving that sort of help from the outside.

It is worth now casting a fresh look over that moment in Martinique when Burrell dipped into his own pocket and paid around US$14,000 to the Reggae Boyz on behalf of the cash-strapped JFF. Given the light cast on him by his response to the 2003 election defeat, this suddenly seems much less an act of generosity than another axe to hold over the Federation when someone does finally come along who would be willing to run against him.

There is an air of secrecy around the finances of Burrell's Federation that could undoubtedly hide various ills. It is reported that a favourite trick of Warner's is to negotiate the TTFF's sponsorship deals personally so the funds then become intertwined with his own personal accounts, making it almost impossible to see where his money ends and the TTFF's begins. The trail then gets even harder to follow because he might claim a deal to be worth *x* amount today and *y* amount next week, while the sponsors themselves could say it is another, more significant, figure entirely. So what has happened to the difference? A large show will then be made of personally paying the players from his own account and when attempts are made to oust him he simply recalls his debts, which are impossible to substantiate because nobody knows whose dollars are whose.

There are feelings among some members of the Caribbean press that Burrell copied this ploy in Martinique. While there is no presentable evidence to cement the theory, there is an odd shroud around the Federation that makes it unusually opaque, and this speaks volumes. A quick Google search will tell you all you could want to know about the details of the English FA's various sponsorship deals. For the JFF, though, the only similar details to be found are of two deals struck by Boxhill, and when I asked personal contacts highly-placed within two of the Federation's primary sponsors about the length and monetary value of their agreements as well as who negotiated them, I was told that 'corporate confidentiality' prevented such things from being revealed. Odd that our FA didn't feel the need for such measures, despite their deals being substantially more valuable. There are people within all these organisations that hold the dirt on the Captain but they know it is not worth the cost to speak out, sadly including the *Observer* and its reporters. Burrell insulates himself well, and has nurtured Teflon tendencies.

There are generally two schools of thought about him in his home country. The vocal but outnumbered minority feel he is corrupt and self-serving and needs to go. The other vein of feeling, one that manifests itself from fans to national players, is that Burrell is power-mad and has many faults but these can be accepted with little more than an occasional grumble because he has friends in all the right places and puts little Jamaica in touch with the core of the global decision-making in a way that nobody else could. Abroad he has pals who are far more certain about him. Blatter has awarded him with FIFA's Order of Merit, ludicrously placed him on the disciplinary commission and appointed him as an instructor on the 'Com-Unity Programme'. As Jennings icily puts it, 'Burrell tours the world dispensing advice to football officials. For the good of the game.' So there goes the neighbourhood. Horace, Jack and Sepp: cleaning up world football as best they can.

The day following Burrell's deal with the Hanover FA, Harbour View are to travel back to Clarendon to face Sporting Central in the last fixture of Round Three. With the top five having been effectively settled months ago, there are still four teams separated by one point all vying for the final place in the upper half before the league splits into two. Reno are in possession for now but are level on points with Village and Arnett, while our opponents, Sporting, sit one point behind but with a superior goal difference to two of the three teams ahead of them. It is tight.

Through a combination of the geography of those teams occupying the top places and the way the fixture list has already played out, whatever happens this will be the last time we leave the Corporate

Area all season. Round four holds away meetings with Boys' Town, Waterhouse and, should they make it, Arnett while all other opponents would come to us. It is a strange feeling gathering for a cross country trek for the final time. Driving past the cement works in Mally's car, the same road along which I had passed in the airport taxi after landing in Jamaica, it strikes me how my perceptions have changed since that first experience. This is no longer an alien land, Kingston no longer holds any fear for me. I know these roads and I know these people, I feel at home here.

I realised a couple of weeks ago that I am going to miss these journeys, barrelling along the highways and twisting through the mountains in anticipation of the game ahead and returning under darkness to the broad, glowing skyline of the capital. I had come to Jamaica to see what life is like for the top football teams and found trips which are startlingly familiar to those I know from my own adventures in village-level sport back home. The lunchtime meetings, the milling around the car park arranging who would get lifts with whom, heading off in a haphazard convoy to the game and then checking every driver is carrying everyone they brought with them before leaving for home afterwards.

And it is on these trips that I have formed my closest bonds with the club, when you are not just part of the gathered crowd but one of only a few people journeying with the players to the far side of the island. It is those few faces who also make it to Sav or MoBay that are the real core of Harbour View and it is that core that I am now, however waywardly, beginning to feel connected to. And now this is the last journey, after today it will only be home games or quick hops across town.

A few days ago 'Cobra' Gaynor had finally succumbed to his illness and died in a New York hospital. It has been a sad time for the club and before the game Sporting allow for a minute's silence to be held in his honour. With that complete it is time to get back to business. DV had said that he still harboured hopes of winning the league, despite the ten point deficit but a limp two-two draw suggests he had been hopelessly optimistic about the state of his team.

Somehow Village jumped into sixth at the last moment to be the team joining the top half of the table in round four, but it is hard to really care. Harbour View dropped more foolish points having taken the lead twice on an evening when we could have reduced the gap to Tivoli to just eight, and that is the familiarly frustrating feeling pervading all thoughts on the way home. After Benfica, DV had spoken of how he relishes the challenge of maintaining the side's motivation. On tonight's evidence he is fighting a losing battle. Unless they can rediscover their focus, Harbour View are going to disintegrate completely.

Sunday 20th March

Arnett Gardens	0 0	Humble Lion
Benfica	1 1	Boys' Town
Portmore United	0 1	Waterhouse
Sporting Central	**2 2**	**HVFC**
St. George's	0 1	Village United
Tivoli Gardens	1 1	Reno

National Premier League

	P	GD	Pts.
1. Tivoli Gardens	33	21	61
2. Boys' Town	33	7	56
3. HVFC	**33**	**10**	**51**
4. Waterhouse	33	6	47
5. Portmore United	33	4	43
6. Village United	33	-3	43
7. Reno	33	1	41
8. Arnett Gardens	33	-4	41
9. Sporting Central	33	1	40
10. Benfica	33	-21	37
11. St. George's	33	-15	36
12. Humble Lions	33	-7	34

CHAPTER THIRTY THREE

Champs

'The Jamaican sprint factory', many people call it, that phenomenon whereby Jamaica seems to churn out far more than its fair share of world class sprinters. People then often look to explain it by offering lazy and patronising theories about a 'hunger' to get out of poverty, or because poor people have to walk places instead of driving so they are built to run from an early age.

Yes, that'll do. That's a satisfactory explanation, that must be why these Jamaicans keep popping up on the podiums at sprint events; because they have less money than we do. But, of course, that really has very little to do with it at all, because otherwise every poor country would shine and the USA would be nowhere to be seen. And, more importantly, Jamaicans would be motivated to lead the world in the sport that is the real gold mine: football. But the poor countries don't all shine, the USA is always at the top of medals tables and in nearly two decades of FIFA rankings Jamaica has spent a total of just six months among the world's top 30 football teams, one *less* than it has spent drifting though the wasteland outside the top 100.

But back to sprinting, and first we should probably ask just how good they really are. Let's ignore the question of *why* for now and consider instead *what* their achievements on the track are. In thinking about this there is one very obvious starting point, one athlete that it is hard to look beyond, because when you think of Jamaican sprinting you inevitably think of one man.

Every so often a sportsman comes along whose influence spans the globe, transcending common loyalties towards a team, nation or sport to become something much larger than a simple athlete. These are people who have sat atop their chosen field with a greatness so complete that they become a landmark in history, and yet have done so in such a way that they remained entirely human and a person the ordinary man can always still relate to. These men do not just inspire their traditional demographic but people of all backgrounds and races, extending themselves beyond the realms of sport to become global cultural icons. Pelé and Muhammad Ali certainly belong in this category, probably too Johan Cruijff. In the modern age of the instantly accessible cult hero it could be that Tiger Woods and Lance Armstrong have earned the right to be mentioned alongside those names, while only time will reveal if the likes of Roger Federer and Lionel Messi can sit among them too.

And there is another. Usain Bolt's inclusion into that club is not difficult to argue. He turned up at the 2008 Olympics as the man to beat, he left them as the man impossible to beat. As the gold medal winner in the 100m, 200m and 4 x 100m at both the Olympics and then the World Championships—the only person ever to hold those titles simultaneously—he did not just break the world records in those events but smashed them. And then did it again. And now he speaks of running a previously unthinkable 100m time of 9.4 seconds. He is quite literally redefining the boundaries of what is possible in his sport, and he is loved for it. As the world prepares for the London Olympics he was already the star of the Games long, long before the flame was even lit.

So sure Jamaica has Bolt, but a freakish athlete can appear in any country, that doesn't warrant the label of a 'sprint factory'. Yet Bolt is just the start of it. Going into the 2010 Commonwealth Games in Delhi, an event to which the country sent none of its big names, Jamaica held *all* the World, Commonwealth and Olympic gold medals in the 100m, 200m and 4 x 100m events in both the men's *and* women's competitions with just two exceptions; the women's World 200m, in which they could only manage silver, and the women's Olympic 4 x 100m, where they were widely expected to win but were disqualified for overrunning a baton change in the final. Which means that from a total of 18 sprint golds available in the major international championships, 16 were held by Jamaicans. Add to this that three of the seven fastest women and three of the four fastest men to ever run the 100m are Jamaican, and you have a quite phenomenal set of statistics for a nation of under 2.9 million people and with such scant resources. That doesn't happen by accident, nor does is it happen simply by having poverty on your side. Jamaicans are doing something very, very right.

This week, the last week of March, is Champs. Formally called the ISSA/GraceKennedy Boys' and Girls' Athletics Championships, it is a four day meeting of the top school athletes on the island in front of a sold-out national stadium. The day before the competition starts the *Gleaner* sends its online cameras to capture the chaotic scenes at the ticket office, where people have been queuing since 4am (eight hours before it opens) in order to get hold of the last few thousand tickets when they go on sale. With demand far exceeding supply disappointment is rife. One man in particular is flustered because he has five 'baby mommas' and only three tickets to hand out to them. 'Where have all the tickets gone?' he asks the camera pointedly. They have gone to the ravenous masses, meaning that once again this year a total of around 120,000 people over the course of the four days will pack the stadium to watch what is essentially a glorified school sports day, while many more tune in on live TV and live internet streaming around the world. And again that same question arises as before: why?

First let's tackle Champs. It's so huge because, for obvious reasons, track and field is huge in Jamaica. But more than that, school sport is huge too. During the autumn term school football dominates the back pages of the national papers as the major trophies are fought over: in the Corporate Area they play for the Manning Cup while the rest of the country contests the Da Costa Cup before the two winners square off for the Olivier Shield, and these competitions are almost as big as the Premier League. The reason for that returns again to the relative weakness of the 'football culture' here: people were not brought up living for their football clubs in the same way that we in England were and so the strongest attachment the average Jamaican sport fan feels is often to his *alma mater* rather than a professional club.

Which brings us back to Champs. With athletics obviously offering even less attachment from fans to the pro clubs than football does, when the island's top young athletes compete under the banners of their schools the alumni sit in the stands and cheer them on passionately. To win Champs is to lord it over all other schools in the country and the athletes involved train for hours every day and hone their bodies like a professional for months beforehand in preparation. It is the biggest event in Jamaican sport: a few years ago IOC President Jacques Rogge came to see what all the fuss was about and left scarcely able to believe the spectacle he had witnessed. Champs got big because of Jamaicans' fanaticism for school sport and now continues to grow in a self-fulfilling whirlwind of its own hype to become something truly amazing. When Jamaica College, a private school in Kingston, picked up this year's title to put alongside the Manning Cup and Olivier Shield wins they had also managed, it rounded off a spectacular school year that saw JC thoroughly dominate not just the youth landscape but the entire national sporting Zeitgeist.

Some largely attribute Jamaica's success in producing world class athletes to Champs itself, feeling that the enormity of such a competition offers a huge inspiration to excel that children in other countries do not have, as well as preparing them for the rigours of a life in professional athletics from a young age. Undoubtedly there is something in this idea but, again, there is more to Jamaica's performance than just that.

For a start there is a theory that Jamaicans are genetically predisposed to run well because of their ancestral roots. People of West African descent are known to have a denser muscle structure that is better suited to explosive movement than that of other ethnicities, as well as having lower levels of subcutaneous fat, longer limbs and narrower hips. When the population was being uprooted from Africa to the New World it was the strongest of these men that were selected as slaves and then the strongest of those that managed to survive the journey across the Middle Passage and the fierce life that followed. This theoretically filled the Caribbean with only the best of the best and had a eugenics effect that has turned the modern West Indies into a melting pot of the finest athletic DNA. A study found that 75% of Jamaican Olympians carry a strong form of the alpha actinin 3 gene, a component relating to explosive fast-twitch muscle fibres.

But even now we have not answered the question. The problem with all the explanations outlined so far—poverty, the importance of school sports, breeding—is that they seem rather to suggest that Jamaica has arrived at its outstanding position as if by accident, and this is to do the country a huge disservice. In truth they take these factors and then draw out every last bit of potential by pouring them into what is arguably the best and most thorough track and field development system in the world.

It begins at an early age, with facilities existing for children aged just three to five years at basic school. In the primary schools, many of which have their own qualified coaches, inter-house competitions then allow the best runners to go into district and then parish teams and vie for selection to compete at the national championships. As their profiles rise, these young children will be watched by scouts from the secondary schools where better facilities, training and nutrition means things start to get more serious.

Here is where arguably the single most important factor in Jamaica's success lies. Almost all secondary schools have their own graduate from the G.C. Foster College, an institution that churns out highly-skilled and deeply qualified coaches by the truck load. The quality and quantity of coaches is not an accident of poverty, and the nation's rich picking at international meets can be attributed largely to them. This also helps to explain the discrepancy between their dominance in track and field and relatively minor global role in other sports. One theory is that Jamaicans are free-spirited people who like to take the glory themselves rather than form part of a team, but that is not the only reason. When I had spoken to Major Brown I asked him why a country with such obvious athletic ability might trail so far behind the rest of the world in football, he had told me about the importance of coaching and the role of G.C. Foster College:

'People go there for three years or four years and track is one of the major components. There is a little football but not much. When those coaches leave they know track and field. In fact part of the reason why we do so well is that almost every school—primary school, basic school—everybody has a qualified track coach. The JAAA [Jamaica Amateur Athletic Association] organises ongoing training for upgrading our coaches on a regular basis. What does the JFF have? A four month course? I personally have spoken to Captain Burrell, because he's my friend, and said, "It is not going to work." I recommended to them that I like the Dutch system, especially with youth. I reckon we get two guys on their way out of coaching in Europe to come down here and spend some time at G.C. Foster training our coaches.'

'Most of our coaches like the game, they love it. One of the things I suggested was to try and get an apprentice system with some of these big clubs: Manchester United for instance. Send a man over for two years and they can understand and learn what coaching is all about, and we will get the kind of coaches where when a coach tells a player to do something he respects it. Most of them don't, especially the ones who go away and come back, and when they see the difference between the coaching they get at Bolton and the coaching they get out here . . .'he trailed off, allowing his point to simply illustrate itself.

'Once the player believes that the coach can give him something he listens. Look at Bolt: whatever the coach tells Bolt to do, he does! Because he believes the coach! To me you have to deal with the coach. The coach is the bottom line and you start at kindergarten and work your way up. Because as you said we are naturally athletic, we have the skills, but we put it together as a team and we just can't get there.'

So while football proves a struggle Jamaica adorns its schools with track and field coaches unlike anywhere else in the world and it reaps the rewards. But what is most remarkable about these coaches is that much of their work is unpaid, their motivation coming from a love of the sport and a fierce desire to uphold the island's proud history. And as well as simply being school coaches, they often personally sponsor their most needy children, paying for kit or nutrition from their own pockets and even housing them. A friend of mine that I met at Harbour View, a man named Clive 'Busy' Campbell, took in and provided for Usain Bolt when he first moved from Trelawny to Kingston and he now manages Jermaine Gonzalez, a rising star of 400m running.

At adult level the training continues. At the University of Technology (UTech) in Kingston, both the High Performance Training Centre and the MVP Athletics Club are housed and between those three organisations senior Jamaican athletics has been freed from a past reliance on foreign coaching at the adult level and flourished to reach its strongest ever state. At all levels Jamaica makes the most of measly economic resources to produce the world's best track and field performers. Not by accident, not by luck, and certainly not because of poverty, but through intelligence, efficiency and passion.

The league is now entering into its fourth and final round. There are just five games remaining but with top teams only playing top teams and bottom teams only playing bottom teams, points will be dropped and gained all over the place and the two mini-tables could end up looking markedly different to how they now stand. The relegation battle is, to be honest, far more exciting than the mutated title race, with the bottom six separated by six points and the bottom three by just two. At our end of the table things are more straightforward. We sit third, five points behind Boys' Town, with Tivoli perched on top a further five ahead of them.

An international break over the last couple of weeks had been elongated when a fire in the fuel depot of Miami airport held up the Reggae Boyz on their journey to a friendly in El Salvador, a game in which two goals from Dane Richards and one from Omar Cummings gave them a narrow 3-2 win as preparations for the Gold Cup continued. The delay meant another reshuffle of the Premier League schedule, and so it is three days after we were originally due to that we arrive at the Collie Smith Drive for our round opener with Boys' Town.

With Tivoli away at Village, the significance of our game is this: get the same result as Tivoli or better and we can carry on dreaming of a miracle for another week at least, but lose when they win and it is mathematically all over for us, the title would be gone.

It is a steaming hot day. I was last here on Teach's grand tour of West Kingston back in September—our previous away game against Boys' Town had been played at Arnett's Anthony Spaulding Complex—and on that occasion the pitch had been half flooded. Today it is dry, brown and dusty. They have a well on the site but, as had happened at Harbour View earlier in the season, their pump had broken and the pitch is now desperately short of water.

This is today's choice for the TV game on CVM so instead of going with the team I get a lift with Clyde, and when we arrive Bowa is already setting out cones for the warm up drills. The players, as usual, meander out of the changing rooms in ones and twos towards the bench where they put their match shirts and shin pads down and drift off to warm up. 'I read your article,' Christopher Harvey says as he greets me. 'It was excellent.' Thank you very much.

This was an article I had done for the PLCA's monthly magazine in which I accused the PLCA themselves of, 'robbing the loyal followers of the Jamaica Premier League of one of the most memorable climaxes in its history' with regards to the points scandal. Given its subject matter I'm not particularly surprised that it is garnering favourable reviews from the others at Harbour View but it raised, I felt, a valid point all the same. 'I liked your article, I agree with what you say.' DV tells me when he comes across a minute or so later. I had argued not that we should have been let off—we had broken the rules, plain and simple—but that the authorities could have found a different punishment, such as a fine for the club or an extended ban for the player, and kept the integrity and joy of the competition still alive.

DV sits on the bench next to me and we talk about the madness of potentially seeing a side miss out on the league or, in Humble Lions' case, get relegated as a result of punishments for what is a relatively minor offence. He then questions something that has also crossed my mind since the offence occurred, asking what exactly the match commissioner is there for if it isn't to spot oversights like this? Surely these men, sent by the JFF to oversee each fixture and ensure that every game runs legitimately, should come with a list of players who should be suspended and then cross reference that with the team sheets? It does not require much to do. The organisers are aware of who shouldn't be playing, as evidenced by them catching us out just the morning after the Village game, so why don't they come prepared with that knowledge beforehand? Harbour View had made the mistake and been in the wrong, but the authorities' own laxness offers no help to the struggling clubs. It is, as they say here, a joke business.

But despite it all we still have our hopes, however slim they might be. I sit on the wooden bench running through wishful scenarios in my head. If we win and Tivoli lose there's just seven points in it, then if that happens again next week it's down to four with three games to play, one of which is against them at home. Some football fans are the most committed of pessimists, I am one of those at the other end of the spectrum who is constantly fashioning unlikely but heroic triumphs in my head even in the bleakest of circumstances, and then convincing myself that they are actually the most probable outcome.

Yes, I conclude, we *can* still win this league. My book will be about the greatest come-back in the history of league football!

'That sun is red hot,' DV sighs at the far end of the bench, taking off his baseball cap and holding it out in front of him in a bid to shield more of his face from the scorching heat. The players have by now finished their drills and are spending the last couple of minutes before kick off sheltering in a small patch of shade cast by a large Digicel billboard behind the goal. When the time comes for them to line up along the touchline for the ceremonial march onto the pitch a local man prowls in the field on the other side of the fence behind our bench shouting impassioned obscenities at the players a few feet in front of him and, particularly, at DV. Largely nonplussed by the abuse they get everywhere they go, the players and coaches just watch him blankly before breaking into small laughs as his rant continues. 'Mad man dis,' surmises Jermaine Hue, captain today with Edwards suspended, with a slightly bemused look on his face.

His piece said, the man wanders away down the touchline leaving the Harbour View players to their business. For them it is win or die, there are no more lives.

The overall flow of the early exchanges goes against us and Boys' Town squander one or two unforgivable chances to take the lead. Where they are failing though, people elsewhere are making things happen. Corey stands on the other side of the fence behind us watching the TV coverage on his phone which gives him privileged access to the latest scores from the rest of the league, and he has news: Tivoli have fallen behind against Village.

And things then get even better. It's not long after this that we break the run of play to take the lead ourselves with a move of the most savage beauty. Having had to absorb most of the game's attacking intent we suddenly spring out with a long ball from left back towards Hue in the centre circle. Running forward, he leaps balletically into the air with his right boot outstretched to catch the ball's flight. In one deft touch it is under his spell and before he has even landed again he has already used the other foot to send it forward to Fabian Taylor in acres of space on the right. 'Baaaall,' gasp admiring home fans behind us, and without breaking stride Taylor collects the pass and charges menacingly at the left back. Dancing his feet around the ball he shifts inside onto his left then hammers it with brutal power from

25 yards. It flies hard, rising just high enough to evade the keeper's desperate leap before dipping again, clipping the underside of the bar and bouncing down across the line. Goal! Stunning, astonishing goal! I jump to my feet. Beside me Carvel barely even flinches. 'That's Fabian Taylor,' he says dryly. 'That's what Fabian Taylor can do.' And how we've missed that this season. Seven point gap here we come, league on!

As the half draws on the news from Trelawny goes downhill. 'Tree-one,' some are saying. 'No, two-one.' Either way it seems Tivoli have reversed the deficit and now lead. At half time a young boy walks past us and confirms, 'Garden a lead tree-one.' Not to worry, at least we're winning too, and that keeps us alive.

But when the second half starts we aren't playing well. Our midfield is too attack minded, not doing enough with it in possession to keep the pressure off our defence and then doing too little to help them out when it was coming back at them. Trying to break the cycle, John-Ross plays a lofted ball to Taylor just inside the area then continues his run. Taylor lets it bounce then lobs it high over the keeper with his instep but the shot falls wide. John-Ross remonstrates with the striker for not passing back, as does Wolfe who had a made a run from the other side, but while they do so Boys' Town are flying forward into our half, slicing past Brissett at left back and squaring into a crowded area. It is Xavian Virgo who runs onto it to tap in from just a few yards out and the home fans jump from their seats in celebration. One-all, and the momentum is now all with them.

Behind me Edwards is despondent at the shambolic state of a midfield bereft of his organising presence: 'We had two midfielders out of position,' he laments. 'Zidane and John-Ross were just arguing with Koji.' Carvel responds in his usual calm manner. 'It's the whole match, Richard. It's just pure attacking they do, no defending.' Nicholas Beckett had played the holding role in the cup game with Tivoli and produced his best performance of the season, but he can't yet command his team mates in the way the captain does and today he is being overwhelmed. And with his alternative, Fabian Campbell, offering more energy and volume but a still-raw sense of positioning it is comforting, from a playing point of view at least, that Edwards' transfer did indeed fall through. The young team doesn't seem ready for life without him just yet.

And things get worse. I have to admit that when they score the winning goal I have absolutely no inclination to write notes and so I can't say afterwards exactly how it happens, only that it does. I know it's scrappy, another tap in from a few yards out, but that is not really the point. The point is it puts us two-one down. With Tivoli three-one up. And try as we might there is no way back for us, we don't even really create any more chances. Full time comes and with it the absolute confirmation that there are no gods guiding Harbour View to recovery this season. We are now thirteen points behind with only twelve available from the remaining fixtures, it really is all over.

Even now my over-optimistic imagination conjures ideas that Tivoli might commit a sin as grievous as ours and be docked points too before the season was out, but it is clutching at the wispiest of straws and the maths now confirms our fate. The time has come to accept finally that there is to be no miracle, no triumphal recovery, just four more games in which to watch Boys' Town and Tivoli scrap to pick our fallen crown from off the dusty floor.

And we can complain all we like about the methods of the PLCA following the illegitimate players débâcle, but the truth is that even without the six point swing it afforded Tivoli we would still be seven points behind them. They have been the better and more efficient team, they have led the table throughout the entire season and their goal difference is now 23 when no one else has even climbed into double figures. It tastes bitter after Clyde's remarks on the eve of the season, but their strikers have been scoring freely while we have struggled for goals all season, and that quite possibly cost us the title. Different clubs have different ideas and pursue different agendas; sometimes it is Harbour View's that work best, this year it appears to have been Tivoli's. Boys' Town are still in it themselves, but even they have five points to make up in the last four games.

As fans leave at full time a brawl breaks out at the bottom of the bleachers on the far side of the pitch. 'It's a gang war . . .'sighs one local behind us, a tinge of irony evident in his voice, while children run across to watch the melee. After briefly looking over to see the cause of the commotion, where wild punches are now being liberally thrown, thoughts return elsewhere. No one in the Harbour View camp is particularly interested in the ruckus. Most of the players solemnly collect their drinks from the cool boxes and go straight off to the changing rooms, as though they had grudgingly accepted the inevitability of this moment long ago. After a few minutes only Spence and Beckett remain on the bench, the former staring down and tugging moodily at his socks while the latter just sits with his head in his hands, his dejected gaze fixed on the floor. I walk past with a pat on the shoulder and a futile attempt at a consolatory word or two but it doesn't register, it is a different Beckett to the man who had greeted me determinedly less than two hours ago.

As I go through the fence to the field behind, Bowa begins complaining loudly about the attitude of one of the younger members of the side. ''Im on the field and im show no fuckin' emotion,' he yells animatedly to Beckett. 'See how you're pissed now? Well 'im the same whether good, bad, whatever. 'Im nuh upset about nothing.'

This is the life of the professional athlete. Your every move scrutinised, your every action needing to hit the perfect middle ground. He lost his cool, he didn't show enough passion; he didn't push forward enough, he over-committed; he panicked in possession, he was too casual on the ball. Then of course there are the personal disappointments which, unless you are Usain Bolt, will far outnumber the trophies. For every time these Harbour View lads win the league they will have three or four seasons like this one. It is the same ratio of hurt for fans too of course, but at least they can find solace in their everyday lives; for these guys this *is* their everyday life. And this is the life all those boys and girls at Champs dream of, the life every kid in the Premier League's youth teams dreams of. The life of the athlete is generally one of disappointment, and today is that life encapsulated.

Sunday 3rd April

Boys' Town	**2 1**	**HVFC**
Village United	1 3	Tivoli Gardens
Waterhouse	1 0	Portmore United
Benfica	1 2	St. George's
Humble Lion	1 0	Reno
Sporting Central	4 0	Arnett Gardens

National Premier League

	P	GD	Pts.
1. Tivoli Gardens	34	23	64
2. Boys' Town	34	8	59
3. HVFC	**34**	**9**	**51**
4. Waterhouse	34	7	50
5. Portmore United	34	3	47
6. Village United	34	-5	43
7. Sporting Central	34	5	43
8. Reno	34	0	41
9. Arnett Gardens	34	-8	41
10. St. George's	34	-14	39
11. Humble Lion	34	-6	37
12. Benfica	34	-22	37

CHAPTER THIRTY FOUR

We Definitely Need Help

So the league is gone. Harbour View are champions in name only and will cease to be even that in a couple of weeks time. Next up is our final away game of the season. The remaining three fixtures after today will all be at home, and so it is for the last time that I step out of a taxi into the car park at the Compound below the afternoon sun and go into the common room upstairs. I am later than usual and with the players already in their meeting it is the likes of Teet, Corey and Bowa who are sitting in front of the TV watching Humble Lion and Arnett cancel each other out as Clyde adds his expertise to the commentary.

Only a few minutes after my arrival we are preparing to leave. Richard Edwards had married his long-term girlfriend just yesterday, a fairly spontaneous move, and he beams broadly when I congratulate him on it as he comes out of the team meeting. The honeymoon, though, is on ice until the end of the season.

As the team convoy enters Downtown the bus is pulled over for a random police check and Fuzzy is made to get out and present his licence to the officer. It happens all over Jamaica, sometimes as genuine attempts to reduce minor crime and other times as disguised efforts to search out a wanted criminal, neither of which are presented by the Harbour View minibus. With that interruption out of the way we are rolling again and within fifteen minutes we are approaching Waterhouse. It is here that Nicholas Beckett lives, and nearby Olympic Gardens is where Edwards grew up; this is not enemy territory but home to a number of our squad.

Turning down the narrow lane towards the Drewsland stadium a mural on a wall on the corner celebrates a local gang and mourns the loss of a young man, employing the phrase seen on many of Kingston's walls: 'Gone too soon'. Back in February police had moved to quell the violence here after tensions were rising and a drive-by shooting hit four men. An arrest was made soon afterwards but the incident was linked to an escalating feud between the area's gangs and police activity increased in order to maintain the relatively low murder rate from the start of the year. Just a few minutes before passing this mural, Corey, with whom I am travelling, revved his engine hard and aggressively overtook one patrolling police car on a residential street without reproach. The authorities here have relatively little interest in traffic offences.

Considering I have been multiple times to many grounds—and five times to Tivoli—it seems odd that my last trip anywhere is my first to Drewsland. The rear of the main stand sits on the edge of a broad, deep flood gully—of the sort shown atmospherically in movies of downtown LA—and is said to hold around 5,000 people. It is, as always, made largely of concrete bleachers painted in the club's blue and yellow colours, with a central structure of iron that holds the VIP seats and media platforms. The rest of the ground is surrounded by billboards backing onto a concrete wall, with the dugouts on the far touchline facing the solitary stand.

'We're in danger of not even finishing third,' Carvel says to me as we walk across a truly dreadful pitch, sounding concerned at his team's slide this season. He is right. A recent upturn in form means Waterhouse are now just one point behind us and another loss today would send us even further down the table than we already are. Of course, neither side have anything tangible to play for any more but pride is a powerful motivator and Harbour View are undoubtedly a club suffering from what has happened to them in the last months of the season.

With over an hour still to go until kick off I sit in the dugout waiting for the players to come out and warm up. It is an empty feeling as a supporter going into the game knowing that there is nothing left to compete for this season, just four games to make up the numbers and fulfil our obligations. For most of Jamaica's football followers, thoughts are by now beginning to turn to the upcoming Gold Cup in America, for which the management are targeting an ambitious top four finish.

With such thoughts in my mind too I had, just this morning, sat in the lobby of the Alhambra Inn, just across the road from the national stadium, where I spoke at length to Tappa Whitmore. A warm if possibly slightly shy man, he talked openly about his role as national coach and his days playing in the heart of the Reggae Boyz midfield during their finest hour.

The Alhambra is a strange place. Eccentric you might even call it. Tappa is running late from a kickabout up at Mona so I wait on a sofa in the lobby. Being in the tropics though, this lobby has no walls and the scented air from the lush gardens spills in. All around are old radios and jukeboxes, with metal advertising signs from the 1940s and 50s attached to various walls forming an unusual décor that somehow seems to work. As I watch a number of well-heeled businessmen taking cups of coffee into a conference room opposite me, Tappa strides through the reception area, full of apologies for his timekeeping. 'Sorry to keep you waiting,' he says, still sweating from the morning's exertions. 'I'm just going to take a quick shower and then I'll be with you.'

His job did not come easily. He was assistant coach and filled in once or twice between managers before eventually being given the position full time. 'Life is a challenge,' he says of the in-and-out nature of his role. 'You have to prepare, but I knew one day I'd be offered the job because I always wanted to be the best.' He was also a player of some quality, playing in England and currently holding the honour of being the only person ever to score a winning goal for Jamaica at the World Cup, not to mention being the first person to win the Caribbean Cup as a player and a coach. He is, therefore, a man who is more familiar than most with the ins and outs of life among football's professionals in Jamaica. When he returns from his shower he settles onto the sofa next to mine and I ask for his thoughts on what makes football important to a society like Jamaica's.

'Football is very important—sport in general—because, for me, football has changed my life and it has changed a lot of young players. If you look around at the amount of players who have been out there playing in Europe, the MLS, all over, you have a lot of players. So football has changed a lot of lives in Jamaica so I just hope the younger players coming up can see and emulate that strength and follow.'

It is different to the more politically-minded responses of others to that question, but it gives the fresh perspective of the player rather than the social commentator and offers a new line of thought, that football changes lives more directly by allowing those with the talent to escape poverty. Unfortunately, as Major Brown had also lamented, this importance doesn't seem to be recognised by society at large.

'I don't think Jamaica really treats the game how it should be treated. Our people only support the game *sometimes.* Like leading up to the World Cup and you see the Jamaica team might make it to the World Cup, that's when we get the support. But *now* is the time we need it. Take for instance in Europe when a team is going out, that's when the support comes. You see people crying, you don't get that sort of thing here. We have a game in the national stadium now and we have to be begging people to come out and support. You know it's not like that in Central America, it's not like that in Europe. Only when things are happening people want to come out and support the team, but it's *now* the team needs the support. Now.'

While people love the game, and I reiterate that it is by far the most popular sport in the country, they are less prepared to act on that love in the form of solid support than fans in other places. What follows from a lack of public support is a lack of commercial support, and financial restraints make player development that much harder. 'It is very difficult. Very, very difficult. We'd like to run a programme so to speak, where we can have a pool of players in a camp so we have a base—leave out our players who play abroad—and we have a base and we work. Now and again we can select two players from abroad to come and join us right where we need them. But we can't do that because we don't have the money, and everything comes down to money. So what I'm saying is if you are helping the programme by coming on board now, believing in the programme, then we can run a long term thing. We definitely need help, we need that.'

'When you go abroad you experience the sort of fields and the sort of facilities they have and you compare them to when you come back here to train. Our last training session, our players came from abroad and they are complaining about the field; every time we finish a training session players have to be icing their feet. Again it's something we need, we need facilities, we need fields to train on. It's so sad to say that the national team doesn't have a field for our own;

we have to keep borrowing from Waterhouse, Tivoli, UWI. If we were getting the sort of help and support we need we could be looking at our own training centre.' That, of course, is what Sepp Blatter had come to break ground on back in September, but it is not yet solving all the problems. 'The UWI one is taking its time.' Tappa continues. 'Take for instance now: our under 17 team is in preparation for the World Cup, we have the Gold Cup, our under 20 just finished. So it's a busy schedule, but we don't have the grounds. The under 17s are now in camp, so what? The seniors can't come in camp now. We have two important tournaments coming up—we have the Gold Cup and we have the under 17 World Cup—but two teams can't be in camp at the same time. Fields are a problem, and financially it's a problem because two teams can't stay at the house so the senior team probably needs a hotel. Everything takes money, everything takes money.'

I wonder, as someone who played in England himself, how important he thinks it is for a Jamaican player to get that experience overseas. 'When these players go abroad it helps when they can come back and lend that sort of attitude, the professionalism, to our local players here. Take for instance, if you're late for a team bus or if you're late for a training session you know the penalty. No one wants to lose money. I used to play in Hull City and you have to be *there*. Here the bus leaves at ten o'clock and we try to be on the bus at one to ten, playing abroad you are late. You're late. You need to be fifteen minutes, half an hour before, sitting on the bus so on time the bus can leave. Fifteen to ten everyone is sitting there. We have to wait on the last minute, that's the difference.' Richard Edwards had spoken to me once of how much can be learned from just sharing a changing room with players who go overseas. Football, like everything else in the world, has a knowledge network and it is vital for the smaller countries to keep in touch with it in order to not be left even further behind the more powerful nations.

But inflated stature can bring inflated egos, and I am curious as to whether players ever return home being difficult to handle. 'Sometimes those are the ones who are late for camp because they came and they "didn't know" or some sort of excuse. It's just simple little things. They knew, but it's just their excuse for an evening off training or something like that. They knew; we sent the information to them before they even left so they knew.' So they come back to the less restricted conditions of Jamaica and think they can get away with things? 'Exactly, so you have to say, "Listen, you can't do it there and you can't do it here."'

. 'But I've never had real problems with any player because it's simple; if you fall out of line, there are repercussions. I always choose to pick on the foreign players, the overseas players so those are the players I fine most of all. So when a local player can see it with the Ricardo Gardners, the Ricardo Fullers it's easier to deal with them, because they know. Right in that room there,' he points to the conference room that is currently filled with coffee-drinking businessmen, 'I fined Ricardo Fuller, I fined Damian Stewart big. **Big.** Hit them hard in the pocket. When I do fine a player now it's because they're travelling and they don't wear the right pants or something, or probably late, something simple. Nothing detrimental.'

He then speaks, from his own experiences with countryman Ian Goodison in the late 1990s, of how tough it can be for a Jamaican player adapting to life abroad. 'When I first moved to England it was with Hull City, in division three at that time, and they played from back to front and I was in the middle, and I love to get on the ball. But I think the coach helped me and Goodison a lot because every time they wanted me to get on the ball. Warren Joyce, the coach at that time, he helped me a lot then Brian Little came in and he's the one who likes to play football, so it was easy to adapt.'

'We used to go to Birmingham and buy our Jamaican food and then we could cook. That is the most important thing: once you have the right food nothing else is a problem. Life is like that, and what happened is that we were prepared. We were living a life where we were away most of the time from family, from home so we were aligned together and it's something you get accustomed to. So it was much easier.'

In 1998 came the peak of Jamaica's footballing history. It was the year they finally made their mark as a global presence by appearing at the World Cup. The people still remember it fondly, while whispering their discontent that they have not even come close since, and Tappa was the player who delivered their finest moment. Having lost 3-1 to Croatia and then 5-0 to Argentina in the first two group games, Whitmore scored twice to give them a 2-1 win over Japan. It was not enough to save them from elimination, but it salvaged some respectability at least.

'For every player—not just in Jamaica—there are a lot of players all over the world whose greatest wish is to play in the World Cup. And there are a lot of good players out there who have played in the World Cup and haven't scored a goal so I would say that's the most stand out moment of my career.' I press him about those famous goals.

'To be honest it was pre-meditated. The night before the game, myself, Ian Goodison and Ricardo Gardner—we are very close to each other—we were sitting there and we were talking and we said that we can recall that in the first World Cup qualifying game against Suriname, in Suriname, I started it. We beat Suriname one-zero and I scored that goal so they were saying, "OK, you started it so I guess you have to finish it." So it was our last game in the World Cup and they were saying, "You need to score. You need to have a good game." Because the saying was that every time Theodore Whitmore had a good game for Jamaica, the Jamaica team wins. So my mind was set: "I have to go out there and I *have* to perform." The rest is history.'

By this stage he is laughing fondly at the memory. Gary Linker once described scoring a goal for England as better than sex. How would Tappa describe the feelings he experienced as those goals went in? 'It's unexplainable. As I said before, every four years you sit and you get your TV tuned in to watch the World Cup, and we were actually there, we were out there scoring. And I just imagine what the people of Jamaica are thinking now!' Again he's laughing and smiling broadly. 'It was a great feeling. A great, great feeling.'

I had seen footage of the day they qualified for the tournament: a packed out national stadium, flags being waved everywhere, countless faces unable to contain their joy. I ask him for his own memories of that day. 'I recall I was substituted in the game because I was *really* tired but you could see me with that flag, running all over the field! It was a wonderful feeling, a wonderful feeling. And the atmosphere was lovely. You had the likes of Jimmy Cliff and all these big artists playing. It was one of only two times in my life I ever saw Jimmy Cliff perform and it was at the national stadium and we'd qualified for the World Cup. It was lovely.'

Once in France for the tournament, though, things did not run smoothly. In a story that is wearingly familiar for those involved, financial disagreements with the JFF unsettled the team, and Tappa lays part of the blame for their poor performances in the first two matches on that disruption. 'That damaged the team for the first game against Croatia and we never recovered from that. And then there was the Argentina game. And then we had a meeting and we were a bit more free for the last game against Japan, and that was the game we performed. But the only problems with the Jamaica national team are always financial, and the Federation now has put things into place so the players sign a contract to say what is there for them, what tournament, what practice games and all of that. We keep making that mistake and it's costing us, so the Federation has now put things in place. I don't think we'll ever hear of that sort of problem again.'

As for the experience as a whole, were the players disappointed to go out after the Argentina game or just pleased to have been there at all? 'Disappointed. I don't know which word we could have used. But after the Argentina game we sit and we discuss it because it was the last game, we are out but we can't leave the competition embarrassed, humiliated. But the last game we went out there and we made amends. Fighting for pride. And this is what we need back in this present national team.

'We need players who gonna **represent** the country. We can't just have the skill and the talent, we need people who are gonna go out there willing to fight, willing to die. We need warriors to go out there and fight because that's the difference with the '98 team. We had leaders, the likes of Peter Cargill, Warren Barrett, Durrant Brown. They are players who go out there willing to die for the team. Ian Goodison, Shorty Malcolm. These are players who play with their heart, they always want to win.

'I think it's our culture. People are afraid to talk to people. For example if we are close I will be afraid to say something to you that might hurt you, that might hurt our friendship. But at the end of the day we need three points, we have to qualify for the World Cup, we have to qualify for the Gold Cup. Now, players are afraid and they tend to relax.' This all seems odd. Not just to hear the national coach being so stinging about the players in his own team, but also because one of the most noticeable things I have seen about Jamaicans was that they passionately speak their mind.

'Yeah we speak our mind but out on the field I say something and you take it a different way. And you take it to your community and say, "Bwoy, you know Tappa say something to me on the field." The easiest thing for us to say now is "Disrespect". Everything is "Disrespect", but at the end of the day you have to realise that, listen to me, we are playing a game, we need three points. We are wanting to win so everybody must be willing to act with pride. Willing to fight. I can remember when one of our strikers got a tackle or was hit or something, our defenders say, "OK, we take care of our opponent's striker." We miss that in the game. If our striker is feeling it up there, your striker is feeling it down here. But that's not the case now.'

I have definitely seen a few players at least who would contradict that, and in fairness he did name a couple in the current squad who do that job, but there does seem a general consensus in the country that, for whatever reason, they no longer have the leaders of old. The likes of Cargill, a former Harbour View player who was killed in a car crash in 2005, are spoken of today in the most glowing terms by people who would love to see another incarnation in the current national team, but no one has quite appeared that can live up to his legend. Our conversation has come full circle and returned to the difficulties he faces in his day job. I therefore leave him to continue with it, and get back to his preparations for the big tournament in the United States this summer. Shaking him by the hand, I get up and bid him farewell. His modesty, perhaps even bashfulness, stands him in stark contrast to Alan Cole, but it can't be doubted that this man's career marks him as another of the true greats of Jamaican football.

'YOU HAVE TO GET TO THE MAN!' Edwards is right in Phinn's face bellowing at him after the defender had backed off a Waterhouse striker and allowed him room to get a shot away. Evidently there are some players left who are still prepared to tell their team mates what's what. Phinn looks slightly taken aback but absorbs his captain's message without shrinking, and at half time they discuss the matter again in a manner that clearly shows no hard feelings are maintained by either party. It has been a poor game with the pitch making it impossible and what seems a general laxness in both sides also affecting the play. In fact, with my stomach rumbling and the calendar showing just three and half weeks before I return home, I spent much of the half with my mind drifting around thoughts of roast beef, pie & chips and bangers & mash instead of paying a huge amount of attention to an unabsorbing game, giving weight to Tappa's words that home food is the greatest loss to the man abroad.

Both sides should have scored in the first half, and in the second one finally does. Fortunately this time it is us, with Fabian Taylor rising to head in Jermaine Hue's cross from six yards. One can only speculate how different this season may have been if this experienced, talented and fruitful partnership had been in place since August. Sadly though we have only enjoyed it for the last few weeks and instead of propelling us towards the title that goal simply solidifies our position in third when it proves to be the only one of the game.

With that there are just three league games to go. Third place is pretty much sealed for us, no more, no less. A similar finish for the national team at the Gold Cup would be very welcome indeed, whether or not Tappa could produce it from the myriad difficulties he has to deal with though, remains to be seen.

Sunday 10th April

Boys' Town	2 1	Village United
Portmore United	0 0	Tivoli Gardens
Waterhouse	**0 1**	**HVFC**
Benfica	0 1	Sporting Central
Humble Lions	0 1	Arnett Gardens
St. George's	2 0	Reno

National Premier League

	P	GD	Pts.
1. Tivoli Gardens	35	23	65
2. Boys' Town	35	9	62
3. HVFC	**35**	**10**	**54**
4. Waterhouse	35	6	50
5. Portmore United	35	3	48
6. Village United	35	-6	43
7. Sporting Central	35	6	46
8. Arnett Gardens	35	-7	44
9. St. George's	35	-12	42
10. Reno	35	-2	41
11. Humble Lions	35	-7	37
12. Benfica	35	-23	37

CHAPTER THIRTY FIVE

The Spider's Legacy

No sooner have I written this league off as dead and dull than it turns into a thriller again. At the beginning of round four it had seemed that the title race was all but over while the yawning hole of relegation could swallow just about any two of the bottom six. The very nature of this final round, though, makes it a nebula whose intensity churns up what once appeared set and spits out fresh possibilities. By throwing the top six and bottom six into their own fight-pits you get five games where the strongest prevail and the weakest are killed off. At the top it takes the very best teams to yield a rich return from five games against only their toughest rivals, while at the bottom it will be the meekest sides who are beaten by the others and cannot avoid the trap. The fourth round is pure football Darwinism.

And so it is this theatre which ensures that by the time everyone has gone bed on Wednesday 13 of April one team is already down with two games to go and the other relegation spot looks pretty much assured too, and that the mixed story of the title is heading for the most dramatic of finales. It is a day which sparks excitement in the league again, and it is a day tinged with a fresh scent of scandal. I've flip-flopped on this issue all season but now my mind is set: the Jamaica Premier League is anything but boring.

After their defeats at the weekend, Humble Lion and Benfica both go into the day deep in the relegation zone, four points from Reno who hover just above. With three games remaining this is a significant deficit and both sides desperately need to win or potentially face relegation this evening. With Benfica being away at Reno there is a big opportunity to close the gap, while Humble Lion are also away, playing their local Clarendon rivals at Brancourt. What sweeter prospect for

Sporting, you would think, than to dump their neighbours out of the Premier League. And this, remember, is a rivalry that one commentator compared to Barcelona-Real Madrid earlier in the season. How they must be relishing the prospect in May Pen!

Which all makes it strange when Sporting, all but safe and with little left to play for, name a squad that includes no more than three or four of their usual first team, and even more strange when Humble Lion are allowed to waltz through their lackadaisical defence and roll in a tame opener inside the first minute. It's the early afternoon kick off live on TV and these things can't be politely ignored, everyone could see there was a dodgy smell around the game. While Reno were recording a 1-0 win over Benfica in the other early match, Humble Lion kept themselves alive with a crucial 2-1 win.

But if Humble Lion are still around to fight another day because their fiercest rivals had just let them take the three points, the obvious question to arise would be, 'why?' While their fans may not like each other much, the two clubs reside very close to each other, sole representatives of the centre of the island in the league and reporting to the same parish association. There are undoubtedly connections forged between the clubs at a management level and who knows what they talk about when they see each other. Nobody can know for sure exactly how or why Sporting looked so weak and lost that game, but everyone seems pretty sure there is some mutual back-scratching going on in Clarendon.

A number of threads have appeared so far in this book which hint that all is not always as it seems in Jamaica: players who dive freely, politicians who help criminals, football officials of questionable integrity and now matches that are strikingly under-contested. And the thing is, the public, much like when they refused to believe Buju's guilt, are often only too keen to look beyond wrongdoing: 'They seem to love it in Jamaica,' Richard Edwards had once said of divers. The likes of Warner and Burrell are widely accepted and can you imagine what would happen to the career of a British MP if they were suspected of giving guns to gangsters? They certainly wouldn't be voted into the positions that they are in Jamaica. So what's it all about? Why does this happen, and why, most pressingly, do the public not really appear to mind?

In West Africa lie the roots of the Jamaican people, and it is from there that the tales of Anancy come. Anancy is a spider, although sometimes he appears in the form of a man, and he frequently uses his trickery and cunning to outwit the bigger, stronger animals around him in order to claim a victory. He is by no means a perfect hero and is known to be greedy, selfish and egotistical, but he has an allure that makes him an integral part of Caribbean folklore, with his stories told by all parents to their children and even from adult to adult.

The tales are thought to originate from the Ashanti people of Ghana, in whose native language the word *anansi* literally means 'spider', and were brought to the Caribbean in the minds of the slaves who were shipped across the Middle Passage from the 1600s onwards. This induced a creolisation of the legends as they were changed to fit the new surroundings and environments of their tellers, and these influences were already starting to shape what would become the Jamaican people. There is one story, one that tells how Anancy came to be the focus of his own tales in the first place, that is particularly illustrative of their function to the early slaves. It is called 'Tiger Stories, Anancy Stories' and it is told a little something like this:

Long ago, it begins, *the countryside was ruled by Tiger, the strongest of all the animals, and his word was law. Anancy was just a small, weak spider whose place was below all the others and he always had to tiptoe around carefully, desperately trying not to upset anyone or fall foul of Tiger's rule. He didn't think this was fair though; he wanted something to call his own and one night, as a storyteller was telling the 'Tiger Stories', Anancy realised these were the prize he so keenly wanted. So he went up to Tiger, in front of all the other animals, and asked if he could have the stories, and if from now on they could be known as the 'Anancy Stories'.*

The animals all laughed. But they were soon silenced in shock when Tiger agreed to the request. 'But,' Tiger said, 'you must do me two favours. I have always wanted my own hive of bees for honey, so you must bring me a large pot filled with live bees.' Again, the animals laughed. Just one or two stings would kill little Anancy, there was no way he could capture all those bees.

'For the second favour,' continued Tiger, 'I have always wanted to speak to Mr Snake but he never comes near me. Bring him to me.' Mr Snake was very large and Anancy would never be able to overpower him; the animals laughed even harder.

But the next morning Anancy got up early and took a large pot to the part of the forest where the bees lived. Upon being asked what he was doing by the Queen Bee, he replied: 'I have a bet with Tiger, he thinks I can't guess how many bees would fit into this pot. I don't know how I could prove him wrong, I fear I'm going to lose the bet.' So the Queen Bee suggested that her workers fly into the pot and Anancy could count them as they went, allowing the spider to win his bet with Tiger. One by one they flew in and he counted as they went, but as the last one entered, rather than let them out again, he quickly shut the lid and carried the pot back to Tiger.

Tiger was amazed to see the spider bring him the bees, and angrily reminded him that he also had to bring Mr Snake. So the next day Anancy took his sword and went to the river where Mr Snake lived. When the snake asked what he was doing he said: 'I have a bet with Tiger. He thinks you are not longer than the tallest bamboo tree, and I don't know how to prove him wrong. You look very long, but I think that tree is taller.'

Offended by this suggestion, Mr Snake insisted Anancy cut the tree down and lie it next to him so he could prove he was longer. He did so and Mr Snake stretched out next to it, but was slightly too short. He needed to stretch more so Anancy tied his tail to the end to give him something to pull against. All the animals around came to watch, 'Stretch, Snake, stretch!' they cried, but he still wasn't long enough. So Anancy tied his middle to the bamboo so he could stretch even more. 'Stretch, Snake, stretch!' shouted the animals of the river, but still he wasn't quite long enough. Then, as he really pushed himself, Anancy tied his head to the bamboo and had him captured. With Mr Snake powerless, he was presented to Tiger. The challenges had been completed successfully, and

> *Tiger had to pay up. From that moment on the stories of the countryside became known as the 'Anancy Stories'.*

But the spider trickster is not just a fairy tale in the same sense that we in Europe tell stories of Hansel and Gretel and the others, he became integral to the development of the African race in the West Indies. This becomes clear when viewing the stories with a few deeper notions in mind. Consider that most of the larger animals were used to represent the white man and suddenly it becomes clear that, rather than simply being enjoyable tales of animal cunning, they are descriptions of the scheming and guile necessary for the survival, and occasional victory, of the black man in a heavily racist world.

By telling these stories of the weak spider outwitting the stronger more powerful animals, the slaves, both telling and listening, were able to live out their fantasies of getting one over on their oppressors. Anancy was symbolic of the potential for transformation and the improvement of the slaves' place in the world, and offered a reminder that they were not feeble and passive but strong, wilful men.

In the above story it is Tiger who represents the white man; he rules the countryside, everyone lives under his law and the history of the land is his history. Slaves telling the tale were able to dream of taking back something to call their own. 'History is written by the victor,' goes the well known phrase, and the fantasy of winning the 'stories' from the white man and having their own history heard was a powerful one. Since emancipation the tales have evolved from inspiration to a symbol of how the freed black men first overcame the fierce racism still inherent in society and then eventually claimed Jamaica for their own.

Of course it is naïve to so generalise an entire population's collective morality and then explain it all with a simple fairy tale, but all Jamaicans will tell you just how important the Anancy stories are to the national psyche. And this appreciation of cunning still exists today. It is imprudent to look at the crafts of Jamaican footballers, administrators and politicians through the prism of British social norms because their history, and as a result their modern society, is so radically different from our own. Morality is often subjective rather than absolute and we are all, as 'Skill' Cole insisted, products of our environment. In Britain we have never been enslaved, we have never been oppressed, we have never been taken from our homes and shipped to strange lands to be treated as cheap commodities simply because of our skin colour. We cannot relate to the past and so we should not tut so readily at the present.

There is still a definite awareness and acceptance that the underhand tricks are 'wrong'—at the end of Anancy stories children will often utter a phrase to the gatekeeper of Heaven to demonstrate their disapproval of his rule breaking—but there is a distinct admiration for them nonetheless, to the extent where many Jamaicans will lack faith in a public figure who doesn't seem to posses this ability to 'play dirty' when needs be. Squeaky clean is under-equipped, and sometimes the rules are there to be bent. The spider's legacy lives on in the Caribbean, and with every dive, every 'compromised' election process and every suspicious football result, the tricks of Anancy are not far away.

So this is the situation by the time we kick off against Village at the Compound. Benfica lost to Reno and Humble Lion beat Sporting in the early games, which means that a point for George's, who are currently playing Arnett in Portland, would send Benfica down. In the top half, Tivoli also played earlier and scraped a 1-0 win over Waterhouse meaning Boys' Town, six points behind as a result and kicking off away at Portmore at the same time as us, know they have to win to keep any realistic hopes of winning the league.

Our game means very little. The defeat for Waterhouse means they have almost no chance of overtaking us for third, while Village's hopes of moving up into fifth are even slimmer. It is, though, a chance to finally take points from them after DV's pre-game speech in Trelawny had been mocked so bitterly by the events that followed it. The tone of that speech had suggested he hadn't expected to play them again this season, and it is quite amazing that we are. At no point since the opening day had they been inside the top six, and as recently as February they had been a full eleven points away from it. But on that crucial day at the end of round three they had somehow sneaked in there and therefore secured freedom from relegation for another season, something they would not have been granted were it not for the points they got from the 'win' against us in Falmouth seven weeks ago. But here they are nonetheless—'they're survivors' someone in the crowd notes at their annual tendency to stay up come what may—and present us with a chance for some semblance of revenge for what feels like a season of wrongs at their hands.

They are obviously out of their depth in the top six and from the early minutes it is clear we will inflict their third loss from three in round four. We should be away and well clear even before Spence scores our first, and Romario Campbell then makes it two before half time. At the break we hear news that George's are beating Arnett by the same scoreline with only around fifteen minutes to go, meaning Benfica are now pinning their survival hopes on a miracle comeback from the Junglists. It isn't to come though, and before we have added any more to our own score, confirmation is announced of Benfica's immediate relegation from their first ever season in the top division.

Today is Fabian Taylor's birthday and, having missed a sitter early on, he makes up for it in the 77 minute. Receiving the ball just outside the box he is faced by two defenders. From a stationary position he twists and turns on the spot to deceive them before opening up his body and curling a shot perfectly into the top left corner from twenty yards. As everyone else erupts Taylor is the calmest person there, doing little more than smiling and raising his hands to acknowledge the crowd, who roar even more loudly when Clyde announces the significance of the day over the PA.

From there the game takes on the jovial, carefree feel of the last day at school before the summer holidays. A misunderstanding between Taylor and Richard Edwards on the near touchline leads to the ball going out of play and they react with light-hearted jokes that are shared with the bench. Edwards himself had wanted to score to celebrate his own birthday just two days later and in injury time he scampers into space down the right to receive a pass, takes it into the box and smashes it under the keeper. Goals for him are rare to come by and it is fair to say his celebration is not so understated as Taylor's, while the bench and the crowd leap up in joy too. The atmosphere of the day means the cheers are more rooted in laughter and fun than passionate screams of victory, but in their way they are equally enjoyable and the final whistle blows soon after. Four-nil is a nice riposte to the results they have inflicted on us in the past, but it can't make up for the effects of the nine points we have lost to them over the course of the season.

At Ferdie Neita Park, Marvin Morgan scored the goal that gave Boys' Town a 2-1 win, while the victories for George's and Reno mean Arnett are now the team staring down at the relegation zone, albeit with a healthy four point cushion from Humble Lion who, by fair means or foul, still have slim hopes of survival. But it is at the top that things are getting exciting. With two matches remaining Tivoli are three points ahead of Boys' Town—the very same three points they were so controversially given when their loss at Humble Lion was reversed—and to make things even juicier the two of them are to face-off against each other in a final day showdown. But before we can talk of that as the potential title-decider they each have one other game to play. Boys' Town will be at Waterhouse in a fixture they will expect to win, and what of Tivoli? They are coming to the Compound, and how Harbour View would love to crash their title bid now.

Wednesday 13th April

Tivoli Gardens	1 0	Waterhouse
Portmore United	1 2	Boys' Town
HVFC	**4 0**	**Village United**
Reno	1 0	Benfica
St. George's	2 0	Arnett Gardens
Sporting Central	1 2	Humble Lions

National Premier League

	P	GD	Pts.
1. Tivoli Gardens	36	24	68
2. Boys' Town	36	10	65
3. HVFC	**36**	**14**	**57**
4. Waterhouse	36	5	50
5. Portmore United	36	2	48
6. Village United	36	-9	43
7. Sporting Central	36	5	46
8. St. George's	36	-10	45
9. Reno	36	-1	44
10. Arnett Gardens	36	-9	44
11. Humble Lion	36	-6	40
R 12. Benfica	36	-24	37

CHAPTER THIRTY SIX

Dropping The Ball

It's only seven in the morning but already the sun is high in the sky and shining warmly over Jamaica. Today is Easter Sunday and even at this hour the sounds of loud singing and drumming sweep out of the churches and through the streets of Montego Bay, the first offerings of praise on this holiest day. Even in Jamaica though, the day is not all about prayer, 'bun and cheese'—Jamaicans' Easter treat—and parties; the Premier League is not to be knocked out of its stride and continues unabashed. There are big games at the bottom of the table with Humble Lion playing St. George's at Effortville needing a win to take their survival hopes into the last day, while at the top there is not so much going on, a dead rubber between Portmore and Village being the only fixture. It is tomorrow night that the title battles resume, with the fixtures between Harbour View and Tivoli, and Boys' Town and Waterhouse postponed for a day because Edward Seaga is away in Cayman. At a time when suspicions are flying around everyone felt it best to make sure every club has 'their people' present if—*if*—something is to happen that smells dodgy.

Like Mr Seaga, I have also left town for the Easter weekend and I have travelled north west to the second city in order to observe a different level of football. For some of the island's most under-privileged children the dramas of the Premier League are the last thing on their minds. For them the only thing that matters is that they are about to pull on the famous strip of the world's biggest football club and go out to play in only the second football match of their young lives.

When one thinks of Real Madrid many images come to mind: the pristine white strip, the imposing Estadio Santiago Bernabéu, the 50s glory years of Di Stéfano and Puskás, the slightly murky ties with the

Spanish Crown, the lavish spending of the *Galactico* eras and more European Cups than any other club can dream of. What you perhaps do not think of are what they call 'Social Integration Academies', establishments that are Real Madrid's contribution to the social power of football that this book has tried to investigate. The Real Madrid Foundation—legally a separate entity to Real Madrid C.F.—has set up a number of them around the world, concentrated largely in Africa and South and Central America, and the expressed aim of them is to, and I quote, 'contribute to the human and social development of children who are at risk of social exclusion by providing them with a series of care services including nutrition, health, psychological aid, education and training through the social sport initiatives associated with the "Real Madrid" brand name.' In other words this great sporting powerhouse has, largely unnoticed by the wider public, set up a network of centres around the world for no reason other than to use football to help disadvantaged children, expressly stating that they have no intention of using them to find future players and that admission into the scheme is decided completely irrespective of gender or ability.

A while ago I had contacted Nicole Caldi of the Real Madrid Foundation for more information about the project and she explained a little further about their goals and methods. 'The aim of the Foundation's social sport academies is to contribute to the social development of underprivileged children and give them opportunities through formal education and professional training. The children involved in our projects make a commitment to stay in school and get help to make that happen,' she told me. 'The Montego Bay school also offers other services such as snacks, medical check-ups and organises activities with families. The ultimate goal of the project is for the children to have more opportunities in future.'

The Foundation itself does not directly finance the school, 'but provides different types of support: training of trainers, sporting equipment, transmitting of Real Madrid's know-how . . . and eventually support securing funds. The school right now is managed by the Spanish-Jamaica Foundation, financed by an association of businessmen and women and the facilities are loaned by the Rose Hall Development.' And she again reiterated that the selection of players is done only by the club and is something the Foundation has nothing to do with.

The project in Montego Bay is run by Aaron Lawrence, a former goalkeeper for the national team and part of the squad that went to France for the World Cup in 1998, and his passion for the work is evident as soon as you see him action. The centre itself though, still lacks the recognition and funding it really needs. 'We're based on the playing fields at the Hilton,' Lawrence told me over the phone a couple of days ago, yet as I turn up at the Hilton none of the staff know anything about it. More than that, they seem pretty anxious to get this stranger, who is evidently not a guest, off the premises as soon as possible and after a fairly wearied back and forth it is soon established that what I am looking for is in fact the playing field next door. So I walk back up the drive, past sprinkler-covered lawns of deep green and down the road where the next gate enters into a dry, brown, dusty field that looks more like the plains of Africa than the beautiful grass on which the Hilton's customers are free to stroll next door.

'Real Madrid Football School for Social Integration' acknowledges a sign on the fence at the front, confirming that this is indeed the right place. The field slopes down from the main road to a public beach at the far end on which large numbers have congregated for what looks like some kind of Easter service. The bulk of the site is taken up by a single pitch, to the far side of which a group of small children are changing and kicking a ball around. Behind the far goal white cranes hop through the sparse grass scanning the dusty surface in the hope of some sort of meal and to the left, just a metal fence away from what looks suspiciously like the Hilton's sewage treatment facilities, is the clubhouse. Not the sleek construction of steel, glass and whatever other materials constitute the architects' trend *du jour* that one might expect from the Real Madrid brand name, this is instead a concrete shed barely big enough to contain their equipment, with a shaded veranda on the front onto which are crammed tables and chairs that are being gradually filled by the swelling group of children.

Lawrence arrives about ten minutes after me, and he is not particularly happy. He calls everyone in for a meeting and urges upon everyone the importance of parental support. 'Raise your hands if you've been here since we opened,' he says to the children as about twelve put their small arms into the air. Yesterday marked exactly a year since the project was founded and in that time over half of the original group have dropped out, due almost entirely to parents not being committed enough to ensure their children turn up regularly. Today there is quite a collection but that is mainly because there is a match to be played, so the centre's Spanish teacher, a lady named Margaret, seizes the chance to get her message across to them as well: 'I beg you, spend just five minutes a day on Spanish class. Just in case they go to Spain.'

The picture being painted is not a positive one and Lawrence again takes up the cause with the parents as the young players run off to warm up. 'We need to know the parents also care,' he pleads. 'A lot of countries would love to have what we have here but we take it for granted.' It seems amazing that a parent could be so nonchalant about their child having a highly privileged place in a Real Madrid soccer school that they don't even bother sending them, but with Lawrence's piece said they begin to fight back and some explanations spill forth. The school operates on Friday, Saturday and Sunday, and it soon becomes clear that at least one of these days should be spent at church instead. Lawrence counters against the parent who insisted her child attend service every Saturday: 'We can't continue like this. The young can't be forced into church when they'd rather be playing football.' It brings to mind Paul Banta's words when the Charlotte Eagles had visited in September, only he had been on the other side of the argument. But in today's clash of these two great Goliaths the trump card is played to secure football's victory. 'You can earn so much money in football, your troubles can be over. That won't happen through church.' The parent is silenced. Madrid, though, have no intention of taking these children to the riches of the Bernabéu yet Lawrence, like Anancy, had managed to win his argument by craftily spinning a lofty tale and selling a pipe dream to those aching to believe. It's only fair though, the church has been notching wins with that tactic for two millennia.

'Look at Stanley,' he continues, picking out one of the parents as a prime example of dedication. 'Stanley has come from Ochi for training every time since day one.' Ochi, the colloquial name for Ocho Rios, is around an hour and half's drive from MoBay and this particular father's commitment is indeed admirable. 'We don't ask you all to be like Stanley. We provide the shoes, kits, snacks; all we ask from the parents is to get your kids here.' At this point he rushes away to pick the starting eleven and by the time he returns he has lost the attention of his audience. He continues to stress the importance of showing more attachment to the cause then running through nutritional advice and outlining future plans, by now though the parents are gazing over towards the pitch where the tiny young players are tearing around enthusiastically after the ball. He ends on an emotional note: 'A lot of people say we are dreaming, but if we don't keep this dream it can never work.' But no one is listening any more.

The score is difficult to follow but it seems Real Madrid are inflicted a heavy defeat after scoring at least two but conceding at least four. But the opposition is an under 15 side that plays in a local league, the Real kids are thirteen at the oldest with many under ten and are playing in only their second game ever. 'They'd hardly even kicked a ball before they came here. I taught them all myself,' Lawrence says to me proudly half way through the game, his earlier bad mood forgotten and replaced by the evident joy of watching his hard work paying off. I have sought to establish the various ways in which sport is vital to a nation like this, and I am now struck by how important it therefore is to have passionate men like him giving children who might otherwise miss out a chance to be included.

But I still can't shake the feeling of astonishment that Lawrence's opening rant was even necessary. What is wrong with those parents, I wonder, that they would be so disinterested in something that provides their children with a unique support network that they could not even dream of under normal circumstances? Are they really that negligent of their children's welfare? A few months ago I had heard Lawrence talking about the project on KLAS. After speaking to him the two presenters, as is their way, spent a few minutes discussing it between themselves. 'We dare not, as a country, drop the ball with a partnership like this,' one stated. It is a fantastic opportunity, there is no doubt, for both the country and the children involved to find positivity through sport. I pray, therefore, that the parents of Montego Bay do not let Jamaica down.

Come evening and the holiday weekend ends in the way that these things inevitably do in Jamaica, with a huge party at a pier front bar where the biggest names in dancehall perform to thousands of excited fans. But before that got going the Premier League sides no longer involved in the title race had all run through their fixtures and the results had been astonishing. Humble Lion beat George's to keep their grasping bid for survival alive into the last week, while Village overturned Portmore just down the road from me at the Elliston Wakeland Centre by an amazing five goals to one. But the most incredible result of all happened at the Anthony Spaulding Complex, where Benfica deigned to turn up with just eleven players plus the head coach and were smashed twelve—nil by Arnett, with Kirk Ramsey shooting to the top of the scoring chart by getting eight of them. They hadn't even bothered to bring matching kit and Arnett had to lend them socks before the game could actually be played. What a contrast to the optimism after the first round, Benfica really are a club broken by the exertions of the Premier League.

On Easter Monday myself and a friend guess our way round the windy mountain roads until we finally end up back in Kingston in time for the evening's two matches. Both are being played at the same time, and both are enormous in the title race. If Boys' Town are to get a worse result at Waterhouse than Tivoli can manage against us it is all over, but if we beat Tivoli and Boys' Town get their expected win then the two will be going into their final day showdown level on points.

Next to me on the Compound press desk, a place that has become my home from home, the radio commentators spend the tight, but fairly drab, opening minutes discussing the factors that could decide the game. 'Navion Boyd has ten goals this season while Harbour View's top scorer, Jermaine Hue, only has five,' offers one to a colleague who is distinctly unimpressed by the statistic. 'I'm not particularly interested in that,' he chides, dismissively. 'It's early but Harbour View look purposeful,' the first one chips in again hopefully, only to have his input batted away once more. 'Harbour View always look purposeful,' returns the second. 'Their results have only been so inconsistent because they are young.'

On the pitch the two aforementioned players are taking centre stage in their differing ways. Boyd is fulfilling our captain's words by tumbling to the ground at every opportunity, while Hue soon finds himself presented with a chance to nab the opener after a foul on Spence. 'Jermaine Hue has a PhD in free kicks,' trumpets a commentator, only for the player to then whack it ingloriously over the bar. Shortly after, as Hue is sending a chipped shot off target following a stray clearance by Scott in the Tivoli goal, news comes in from across town that Boys' Town have taken the lead at Drewsland, and the announcement is greeted with great cheers around the stadium. Before half time they are two up.

In the second half a couple of red cards provide the only excitement as Tivoli hold on grimly for the draw that puts them in charge at the beginning of the final day. The final whistle sounds and our work is done. We have taken two points from them and with no more goals at Drewsland the gap next Sunday will be a single point. The rest of us have done what we can but now it is all down to Boys' Town to finish the job off themselves. There is no one left to help them.

After the game DV, Carvel, Clyde and one or two other members of the management stand around talking, the Benfica shambles of the night before being the main focus as Carvel informs the group that they will be discussed at the PLCA's weekly meeting for bringing the game into disrepute, with a view to possibly banning them from a Premier League return for a couple of seasons. Talk then moves on to the game just finished and DV mentions that someone at the JFF approached him before kick off and suggested he put out a team of younger players instead of his first XI. 'It was just his honest opinion, he didn't mean anything by it,' Clyde presses on me afterwards, seeming keen to wipe away further suggestions of anything untoward, before making clear that this particular individual had a history of bizarre and incompetent thinking.

Disappointment with the way the league leaders had played tonight is evident: 'They didn't even want to win,' someone says of Tivoli, before turning to DV and adding: 'Did they expect you to just give it to them?' The lack of adventure as Tivoli Gardens limp towards the season's finish line is turning the neutral even further against them. 'Boys' Town always play to win,' the coach notes in contrast. 'It's always: Red Brigade . . . Charge!'

And that's exactly what they will have to do next weekend. One last occasion requiring one last charge. Thanks to this evening's results Boys' Town will be going to the Edward Seaga Complex just one point behind Tivoli, and knowing that one final thrust will kill off the wobbling leaders.

Sunday 24th April Monday 25th April

Village United 5 1 Portmore United
Arnett Gardens 12 0 Benfica
Humble Lion 2 0 St. George's
Reno 3 1 Sporting Central

HVFC 0 0 Tivoli Gardens
Waterhouse 0 2 Boys' Town

National Premier League

	P	GD	Pts.
1. Tivoli Gardens	37	24	69
2. Boys' Town	37	12	68
3. HVFC	**37**	**14**	**58**
4. Waterhouse	37	3	50
5. Portmore United	37	-2	48
6. Village United	37	-5	46
7. Reno	37	1	47
8. Arnett Gardens	37	3	47
9. Sporting Central	37	3	46
10. St. George's	37	-12	45
11. Humble Lions	37	-4	43
R 12. Benfica	37	-36	37

Aaron Lawrence (right, standing), goalkeeper for the national team at the 1998 World Cup, runs through some pointers with the children he now coaches at the Real Madrid Football School for Social Integration in Montego Bay.

CHAPTER THIRTY SEVEN

The End Of The Carnival

My last week in Jamaica, and the transformation since my arrival has been remarkable. I got here over eight months ago having never been to the Caribbean, without knowing a single person in Jamaica and with a head full of rumours about what Kingston life is like. Now, though, that city has become my home. For months I have felt comfortable and relaxed here, I know people and I know the place. Since leaving everyone and everything familiar behind I have, in effect, lived a whole other life and it is a life I have come to love, not to mention a life that has taught me the fallacy in the Kingston horror stories.

'The road to the airport is so dangerous that you can't even stop at traffic lights.' An example of the sort of advice that littered the travel websites I had seen before coming here, zesty words dished out by over-panicked American tourists keen to exaggerate the danger and excitement of their experiences. The road to the airport is also the road to Harbour View, and on my countless journeys along it the cars I was in have stopped at every light and every junction, and never once was there even the merest hint of anything remotely disturbing anywhere to be seen. Kingston has its problems, and those problems are undeniably worse than those of most other cities, but on the whole it is just a normal capital city. Even its issues of poverty are less pronounced when walking uptown amongst the plush apartment complexes and bulky 4x4s of Jamaica's well-educated professional classes.

And now I have just a few days left in this new home, of this new life, but what a few days they will be. This weekend is big. It is not only the climax of the Premier League but also the time when Jamaica spills out onto its streets and parties. It is carnival. The Jamaica carnival apes that of Trinidad, with soca music blaring all weekend from the eastern Caribbean's big stars and a madness engulfing the town that eclipses even that of normal Jamaican life.

After a number of 'warm-up' events around the island, Friday night is when the weekend really begins with the 'J'ouvert' (pronounced 'joo-vay') party in New Kingston. There's a couple of them around but the big one is at Mas Camp, essentially a car park for most of the year which becomes the centre of carnival and for j'ouvert it is adorned with thematically decorated bars, booths and stalls around a large, and packed, space that lies below a broad festival stage. From here the deejays scream to the swarming mass of thousands of people in front of them over the high-tempo, energy-filled soca blasting out.

Everyone has been talking about it for days and all the young and beautiful in Kingston seem to be here, thousands of them. Many mill around in the space at the edge and fill up with rum from the bars, but the real party is happening in front of the huge stage. In the bouncing throng drinks are not drunk but thrown through the air over the mad swirl of heads as the teeming mass bounces manically, and the deejay works the crowd like an expert. 'Jump! Jump! Jump!' she cries to the beat. 'Three . . . Two . . . One . . .'screaming now as the hyped crowd prepares to break out to the next level. 'Shove somebody! Shove somebody! Shove somebody!' She is still shouting to the rhythm and chaos breaks out as suddenly everyone is jumping around, pushing and shoving everybody in every direction. Carnage of the most incredible kind.

At about half past one they unleash the main focus of j'ouvert. 'The paint is being put out,' they announce from the stage, and from one corner excitement begins to ripple through the revellers. Moving closer to the war-zone the indicators get denser. Occasional splatters on the floor, people coming back the other way with the effects of battle all over them. And then suddenly we are in the thick of it, large cup-fulls of paint flying overhead and into our faces before finally we reach the buckets ourselves. Cups and upturned hats are swung everywhere, colourful welts of paint being flung out, unfurling through the air then crashing onto their target. Hands swarm all over the place, smearing paint over heads, faces or anywhere else they can as a twisting mob of laughing, screaming strangers cover each other while the music continues to boom. Just minutes after the paint has been put out, most of the thousands of people there are unrecognisable, completely covered from head to toe in grey-ish purple with only eyes peering through the mess.

The party continues. Some people wash their faces in the toilets, others don't care. J'ouvert is the one night out in Jamaica where image becomes completely irrelevant. The great Usain Bolt, always a keen party-goer, is dragged from the crowd and up onto the stage, himself painted all over. Fully taking to the moment, he begins 'wining' sexually with one of the sponsor's girls as the audience screams and cheers. Upon finishing he strikes his signature 'Lightening Bolt' pose. Where else could you find one of the planet's most celebrated sportsmen being so un-removed from the public?

At around three in the morning the party moves out from Mas Camp and gathers in the street outside where they are joined by another nearby j'ouvert and a road march begins. Following speaker-laden trucks the party moves through New Kingston until the sun begins to rise, at which point bed finally calls at the end of carnival's opening night. Not that such a weekend allows for any rest, and various parties on the Saturday precede the truly grand occasion, the Sunday where everything explodes.

The carnival street march. The last day of the Premier League season. The biggest party in Jamaica. The head-to-head title decider. In the space of a few hours on this final Sunday, it is all going to happen.

At about ten in the morning the phone rings. It's Nick, another Englishman who lives up the road in Mona. 'The road march has started already!' It began pretty much outside his flat and he had been woken by the music bellowing from the trucks. With two other friends from Montego Bay who are staying for the weekend, I get out and walk the 150 or so yards to Hope Road where crowds are already gathering under the intense Caribbean summer sun burning down from a bright blue sky. Metal barriers shut out the traffic and police motorbikes are buzzing up and down, ensuring everything goes smoothly, while in the distance can be heard the booming beats of the front trucks. Girls in sparkly underwear with giant feathers on their heads walk past towards the noise, skipping down the road to join the dancing troupe. 'We'll just walk down there and meet it,' they are saying.

Closer and closer the sounds come, then slowly the procession rounds the gentle curve of the road and comes into sight. A large red Digicel truck, gleaming in the sun, leads the way and to the side of it swarm the first dancers, all sparkles, tassels, and elaborate headdresses. Even before the first float draws level the bass is chest-shaking and the soca pounds out of numerous large speakers on each lorry. People lean over the edges with drinks in their hands and the flocks in the streets dance beside it. A Digicel dragon comes second, followed by floats from Appleton and Heineken. By the mid-point all that can be seen in either direction is a river of brightly coloured feathers and lorries as thousands of dancers stream by adorned by greens, blues, yellows and purples. Every now and then the procession halts so more crates of rum could be loaded onto the lorries before they roll on again, driving their way onwards towards Mas Camp. With the last truck crawling past we follow the party down the packed route.

By the time the march turns off down Lady Musgrove Road, the blistering morning sun has been blocked out by dark black clouds sweeping down from the mountains, but still the people continue to dance. Rain feels inevitable, and fittingly on this most theatrical of days it arrives in the most dramatic fashion. Rather than sneaking up and dampening the party, it adds to the electric atmosphere, and when the first loud boom of thunder cracks overhead cheers cry out and horns blare to greet it. The opening drops fall. Giant, tropical balls of rain spilling from the blackened skies onto the crazed streets. Within seconds it is like a monsoon, a mad storm being flung down onto the ecstatic party and drenching everything in sight. 'Are we afraid of a little water, Jamaica?' bellows the female deejay on the last truck and the hoards surrounding it scream in reply. 'Are we going to let a little rain ruin our party?' Again they scream, and already every inch of every item of clothing is soaked through as the incredible deluge intensifies. Only briefly does the procession halt as one or two of the more exposed trucks produce tarpaulins to cover their speakers and then we're going again. In no time at all large puddles engulf the roads and the dancing gets only more frenzied as people bounce through the water. 'Jump in the rain! Jump in the rain! Stamp in the rain!' the deejay yells over the beat as feet spring through the flowing currents that swallow the roads and pavements, sending splashes everywhere. Everything is soon so thoroughly sodden that no one could possibly care about the wetness and all there is to do is party. With water streaming down our faces we all dance. Men in carnival gear scale walls to earn impromptu platforms from which to sway and shake, and for the second time this weekend I find myself wondering where else in the world this could possibly happen outside the Caribbean. This is why I have fallen in love with Jamaica, and this was why I am already feeling pangs of sadness at the impending inevitability of my rapidly approaching departure.

But those thoughts are for another day. Today we must let carnival continue its way down to Mas Camp without us, we have to walk back up to Hope Road for other matters. With barely time to dry ourselves out, football snatches back centre stage.

Today being the climax there is a uniform three thirty kick off time across the league, and there is still plenty to be decided over the course of the final ninety minutes. With this in mind, let us, for one last time, go over what means what and who needs which results. Harbour View, of course, are not part of this story and play Portmore at the Compound for nothing more than pride. At the bottom there is still one relegation spot to be decided where Humble Lion's win over George's last week kept them in with a shout, and it is now almost certainly one of those two sides who will be joining Benfica in the drop. Humble Lion are playing the bottom side at Drax Hall which virtually guarantees them three points, a result that would leave them on 46 and one ahead of George's. Although George's have the better goal difference in total the final places in this league are, oddly, decided by goal difference in the two sides' head-to-heads rather than overall, and this means George's have to win their game at home to Sporting in order to stay ahead of Humble Lion who are four-one to the good in their contests against each other. Simple, no? Once again it seems Sporting are taking up a central role in determining the fate of their local rivals. I had forecast the Humble Lion to survive months ago so for personal satisfaction, if nothing else, I want to see them prevail.

At the top there is no question who I, and apparently pretty much everyone else, will be supporting. Boys' Town have become the neutral's team of choice over these last few weeks and today they have to win the showdown at the Edward Seaga Complex in order to give the fans the result they want. For the record their head-to-head goal difference with their West Kingston rivals is superior but the one point gap means there is no result could possibly bring that factor into play, making Tivoli's desperate draw at the Compound last weekend all the more crucial.

So at half past three the final day springs into life across the island. It takes just three minutes for the first blood to be spilled. Reno take the lead over Arnett in a game that means about as much as ours does, but at least it gets things going. And it's not long until the important goals start going in at Drax Hall where, predictably, Humble Lion take and then stretch a lead over Benfica. This development puts all the pressure on George's who, as yet, are not managing to get anything out of Sporting at Lynch Park.

Not a huge amount is happening at the Compound. From the radio there's a chance at the Edward Seaga Complex . . . goal kick. With two minutes to go until half time Kemar Petrekin, another player whose scoring ability Harbour View have been without for much of the season, finally breaks through to put us ahead, and everyone sits back to await half time updates. But before we even get there the radio brings the big news, that just before the ref's whistle there's a goal in West Kingston. The ball is played in to the striker on the edge of the area, he turns expertly and hits a low shot with his left foot past the desperate keeper and into the corner of the net. It is Navion Boyd. Tivoli are one up and Boys' Town now need two.

The first half had been disappointing and in the second Boys' Town are still failing to produce the sort of play that has seen them win six of their last seven fixtures. The charging Red Brigade is crumbling and nerves seem to have got the better of them on the biggest occasion in many years for the club. Tivoli are not playing well either, but then they haven't played well for months so that comes as no real surprise to anybody. Chances are still coming though, and with the home side looking a little shaky, one for Boys' Town will almost certainly inspire the confidence to get the crucial second.

We also hear of chances for George's in Portland but they're unable to finish any of them off and Sporting seem to be hanging on, knowing they too could potentially be dragged into the relegation equations if they concede. Humble Lion have themselves home and dry with a comfortable lead at Drax Hall so both teams in Buff Bay are becoming desperate. The other three games, our own included, are delivering no more goals, but nobody really cares about them anyway. The stories of interest are all being written elsewhere as full time draws nearer.

'The fat lady is putting on her dress,' says the radio commentator on KLAS as the final minutes run down at the Edward Seaga Complex. Boys' Town keep trying but they've been unable find their previous form and have got very little out of the hosts, making their effort look increasingly futile. 'The fat lady's warming up,' he screeches, continuing the metaphor, as the games move into stoppage time. Nothing for Boys' Town, not even a measly consolation. Come on, charge!

There has barely even been time for another effort in the final seconds of what has been an absorbing, if ultimately disappointing, title race when the final whistle blows. 'Tivoli Gardens are the Premier League champions!' the commentator exalts excitedly before pronouncing them to be thoroughly deserving victors, something that one does have to accept even if it tastes a little sour.

Instantly they go to speak to captain Kasai Hinds who says it is, 'the greatest feeling, for myself, the team and the community. We really had to fight for the community'. And with those words it finally clicks to me that to see Tivoli lifting the trophy is actually the ending I have been looking for all along. I had come to Jamaica to see the role sport plays in the toughest areas in the world and what could be more Hollywood than the people of Tivoli, the most wounded and hurt of all, being lifted from the pain of the Dudus invasion less than a year ago by a proud victory in the Premier League? Suddenly it seems right, it seems fitting. Am I almost even happy for them?

'This is the sweetest,' Hinds carries on when asked how this compares to his past league titles. 'Because of the fight. We had teams chasing us and we had to maintain what we had.' Something about his words strikes at the heart of not just the team's season but the workings of the community as a whole. The resilience, the resistance to outside aggression, the us-against-the-world attitude. They might have to ward off the snarling hounds of the surrounding lands but Tivoli Gardens is still standing, community and football team alike. And congratulations must go to them for it.

While the home fans in Tivoli celebrate, those in Buff Bay mourn as the end arrives at Lynch Park with George's unable to muster the crucial goal. Just like when they played us on the second day, their profligacy cost them and now they are facing next season in the local league having been five points clear with two games to go. Humble Lion had continued to take full advantage of Benfica's spectacular mass implosion and finished off with a 7-0 win that keeps them in the Premier League after looking all but dead just a couple of weeks ago, and they can send hearty thanks to their neighbours for their help in achieving it. Petrekin's was the only goal of our game while the other three drab fixtures raised only one goal between them as Reno clipped Arnett at Frome.

And so this is it. I had come to Jamaica for a whole season and the final final whistle has now blown. Before long the players have all disappeared back to the main building. Bigs is sweeping out the changing rooms and Twinny is putting away the last of the kit as one or two small gaggles of supporters sit in the near-deserted stands. With varying degrees of satisfaction they sit beneath the evening sun and chew over the last eight months, offering analysis of the season now gone. No one is too downcast, and yet a melancholy hangs in the air, the feeling that this is the end of the carnival. As time draws on the last words are said and the last wisecrack cracked, and as they drift out into the dusk the gates to the Compound are padlocked for another summer.

A few nights later the people of the club gather one last time for the end of season dinner. As we drive down the harbour front road to our rendezvous at the Compound a double rainbow appears, rising from the ocean to the right, shaping over the road ahead and disappearing behind the mountain to the left. An expression of delight escapes Clyde and he pulls over to photograph it while I just gaze up at the two graceful arcs mirroring each other's colours in the evening light. The superstitious believe double rainbows to be symbols of transformation and something about that seems appropriate. The budding transformation of one season closing before another begins; the possible transformation of a young squad of players into future winners; the impending transformation of a life that had shifted from

England to Jamaica and is now just hours from being shunted back into its old place again.

The dinner is to be held in Port Royal, a small town at the end of the long spit that forms Kingston's large natural harbour. It was once said to be the richest and wickedest city on earth as the pirates of the Caribbean made it their base until it was devastated in 1692 by an earthquake that left large parts of it underwater. The buccaneer spirit lives on in its residents though, and Clyde talks with enthusiasm about the fierce battles, knives often included, into which football matches against them frequently used to descend back in the 1970s. Fortunately tonight was a much easier going affair.

Our cars and buses pull into a car park outside a busy restaurant on the edge of town called Gloria's and the Harbour View delegation file up some stairs to our own private area. The room we fill is large with windows all around, one bank of which look out over the small town and the other onto the moonlit sea. Everybody is here: first team, under 21s, management, Mally, Barry, Brucky, Ebba and all the rest. I place myself on a table with Hue and Phinn, with Hodges, Ebba and a couple of the under 21 squad also joining us and the atmosphere throughout the place is light and jovial.

'Hugo,' Hodges says to me from the end of the table as polystyrene cups of seafood soup are handed out. 'When you write your book you've got to mention Hodges.' It is as though he is convinced my very limited influence can provide some sort of brush with fame and he seems keen not to miss the opportunity. For many of these players a close encounter with a journalist is as much a novelty as close encounters with Premier League footballers are for me and I promise that his name will indeed be included.

The evening swims by, filled with in-jokes being shouted between tables and childish pranks being pulled. Brucky steals Ebba's drink so Ebba returns the favour later on; Hue spills his and stains his stone coloured trousers with red fruit juice; some sort of gag I don't understand about 'steaming fishies' causes much hilarity between Hue and one of the younger players—a gleeful response to the steamed fish being brought out—before it is shared loudly with an appreciative Clifton Waugh a couple of tables away.

With dinner over Clyde picks up a microphone and sets the ball rolling on the more formal aspect of the evening, beginning with medal presentations. Due to the Tivoli uprising last May the League had never managed to hand out Harbour View's winners' medals until now. It was one of the less obvious by-products of the uprising but finally the medals have been engraved and produced so now, a year late and feeling slightly hollow, they are given to the players tonight. The under 21s go first before the Premier League side rise from their chairs and advance forward to receive theirs. It is when the last player has sat back down that I am surprised with an amazing act of generosity.

'Coach DV Hayles would like to make a special presentation to Hugo Saye,' Clyde says over the microphone, going on to explain that the manager wanted to hand his medal over to me as a leaving gift. I walk forward amidst the applause and insist I couldn't possibly accept something DV had earned, but my protests are short lived. One thing I have learnt about Jamaicans is that they do not make token gestures that one should politely decline, if they offer you something it is considered rude to turn them down. This concept steers me to reluctantly but gratefully accept the inscribed medal. I hopefully see it as confirmation of my feelings that I had gone from a curiosity that many in the club were a bit wary of to an accepted member of the family.

Speeches follow from managers and captain, the general gist of which is that the season has been a disappointing one that has fallen below expectations at one of the Caribbean's biggest clubs. Again I am briefly made the centre of attention as Carvel bids his public goodbye to me. '"Intrepid" would be one word to describe Hugo,' he tells the room, before making his own reference to the attachment I have so evidently formed with the club. 'Hugo came here to write a book about Jamaican football and ended up one of our biggest fans. You should see him when we score a goal, you'd think he'd been here forever!' He chuckles gently at the thought then turns to me and rounds off by saying: 'We hope you come back to see us soon.' I hope that too. I have long abandoned all the distant impartiality of the observing journalist and this country and this club have both drawn me in. It is an amazing world and the idea of leaving it forever is one I do not really want to contemplate. But I must.

The next day my time in Jamaica is over. As Clyde drives me to the airport he muses that perhaps the talk of disappointment last night had been unfair. Someone had approached him that morning and congratulated him on a successful season: one cup and third in the league was a pretty solid outcome in the eyes of this man. 'It just shows the extremely high standards we set for ourselves,' Clyde summarises, sounding noticeably more cheery about the club's lot than he had the night before.

So it turns out the present is not all bad, and on my way home I am given a vision of how the future too is looking bright. We stop to look at a plot of ground right next to the airport that Harbour View are looking to purchase to turn into a couple of training pitches to take the strain off the patchy grass of the Compound, providing they can find sponsorship to finance the deal. It seems obvious that a big club should have somewhere to train, but for them it would be a big leap forward.

And so it might be the end for me but the world I am leaving behind will keep turning and Jamaican football will keep developing at its financially hindered pace, and as always the people of Harbour View will be at the vanguard. Maybe next year they'll win their title back, maybe not. Maybe the star names will be playing in rich American or European leagues by then, or maybe not. Maybe in the coming years Jamaica will solve its problems in both sport and society and finally fulfil its huge potential, or maybe not. My lasting impression of the country is that of a nation perpetually on the cusp of future greatness but never quite being able to turn a bright tomorrow into a prosperous today; perhaps that too might finally change.

But these are all questions to which I will not be around to see the answer. I had fallen in love with this incredible country some time ago but now my family wait at the other end of a nine hour flight to take me back to that familiar life of grey skies and over-priced footballers. Of course I look forward to seeing them again, as well as the friends I've not seen for the best part of a year, but my thoughts can't help but linger for now on what I am walking away from.

Clyde parks up in the unloading bay outside the front of the departures terminal. We pull my bags from the boot of his car and I thank him for everything before we hug goodbye. With mixed emotions I turn to the broad, bustling building behind and walk towards it. The large glass doors slide open in front of me and I step into the air conditioned hall and out of this Jamaican life I have adopted. After eight and half months engulfed in the football of the Caribbean, my last goodbye has now been said. I'm going home.

Sunday 1st May

HVFC	1	0	Portmore United
Tivoli Gardens	1	0	Boys' Town
Waterhouse	0	0	Village United
Benfica	0	7	Humble Lions
Reno	1	0	Arnett Gardens
St. George's	0	0	Sporting Central

National Premier League

			P	GD	Pts.
C	1.	Tivoli Gardens	38	25	72
	2.	Boys' Town	38	11	68
	3.	**HVFC**	**38**	**15**	**61**
	4.	Waterhouse	38	3	51
	5.	Portmore United	38	-3	48
	6.	Village United	38	-5	47
	7.	Reno	38	2	50
	8.	Sporting Central	38	3	47
	9.	Arnett Gardens	38	2	47
	10.	Humble Lions	38	3	46
R	11.	St. George's	38	-12	46
R	12.	Benfica	38	-43	37

EPILOGUE

Back To Reality

I sit in a flat in London trying to tie together the strings that hang loose from the end of this book. It may be summer but outside the sky is grey and a dull rain rattles against the roof. Seeping in through open windows the drone of jet engines from planes flying into Gatwick repeats itself over the incessant sounds of a nearby building site. Next to my laptop is a notepad with scribbled pointers about the various characters and themes from these pages that have thrust themselves into the news since I left Jamaica, each managing to round off their own little stories in their own little ways.

The basics come first. A few days after I left the island, Tivoli beat George's at the national stadium to complete the league and cup Double. Less than a year after the army had waged war upon it, the pained community on the Kingston waterfront had placed itself indisputably above all others and looked proudly over a country it was now king of. Soon after this the Reggae Boys travelled to America for their highly anticipated but ultimately ill-fated Gold Cup campaign. They fell short of their desired top-four finish but they still did themselves proud, winning all three of their group games comfortably (the only Caribbean side to even pick up a point) before an unfortunate twist pitted them against the host nation in the quarter final. A disjointed and unconfident performance resulted in a 2-0 defeat, but they left the tournament with nothing to suggest they cannot claim one of CONCACAF's four places at the next World Cup and entered June impressively ranked at number 38 in the world, ahead of tournament regulars such as Nigeria, South Africa and Colombia.

From January there had been an independent enquiry into the Dudus/Manatt affair that had gripped Jamaica. Being shown live on national TV all day every day it had at times descended into soap-opera farce, especially when PNP attorney K.D. Knight had sparred ingloriously with the Prime Minister, but it ended up answering most of the questions raised when the report was published in June. The JLP, the commission concluded, was the body responsible for the hiring of Manatt, Phelps & Philips to lobby against Dudus' extradition, not the Government, and yet the party 'should not have been involved'. Bruce Golding's personal role was deemed 'inappropriate', hinting strongly that the Prime Minster was far too close and had gone to too much trouble to protect the Tivoli don. However the report concluded that, 'We found no misconduct on the part of the persons we enquired into,' but only 'mistakes and errors of judgement'. Though it did add the mischievous caveat, 'It is regrettable that the memories of some of these witnesses failed them at the enquiry.' The report offered nothing as to the nature of the garrison phenomenon or what the future holds in the fight against crime. A poll in the *Gleaner* even suggested that most Jamaicans desired a return to British rule, but that was unlikely to say the least. While the Tivoli football team sweeps all before it, the evidence piles up to suggest that garrison politics is not yet 'history', as Edward Seaga so insisted to me, and probably would not be for some time.

The really big news happened elsewhere. In the build up to the Gold Cup the little Caribbean Football Union was thrown into the centre of headlines all over the world, creating the biggest scandal ever to hit FIFA and finally putting the nail in Jack Warner's coffin. Five days after I left Jamaica, Mohammed Bin Hammam, Sepp Blatter's opponent in an upcoming FIFA election, flew into Trinidad's Piarco International Airport where he was met by Warner ahead of a meeting of the CFU that had been arranged by the pair. All delegates had their first class travel to the island paid for by Bin Hammam (and booked, naturally, through Warner's family Simpaul travel agency) and sat in a room at the Hyatt Regency Hotel in Port of Spain where they listened to the presidential candidate's vision for the future of FIFA before being invited to meet him individually in a conference room. The officials formed an orderly queue outside the door and when their turn came to enter the room they would be handed a brown envelope containing US$40,000 in cash, to be used, they were told by Warner, in any way they saw fit.

Fortunately, as this book has sought to prove, there is still some positive in football and Fred Lunn, vice president of the Bahamas FA, was not for turning. Instead of pocketing the money he phoned his boss Anton Sealey then queued back up to return the cash, but not before taking a photograph on it on his phone. For Warner it would be one scandal too far and when Sealey phoned Chuck Blazer at CONCACAF, by no means an angel himself, it put in motion the proceedings that would finally end his role in football.

Sepp Blatter, as we know, feigned great offence at the dastardly behaviour of his 'family' members and suspended them both just days before the election. But of course, the fact that his only opponent was suspended was no reason to postpone the election and so Sepp won another four years unopposed. And this having been told beforehand by Warner himself of the plan to offer cash to the CFU associations.

Back in Jamaica it was Captain Burrell who took over as acting president of the CFU but failed, in his capacity as head of the JFF, to speak out about the scandal engulfing his long term ally. It was not until Edward Seaga publicly questioned his silence that Burrell finally said something, acknowledging that it had, 'shamed the reputation of football' before going on to deny that anyone at the JFF had been offered money and telling Seaga, in no uncertain terms, that his PLCA ranks below the JFF and that he should stay quiet about these issues in future, blustering that he, 'seems to have tried, found guilty and passed sentence on an entire region's football associations.' Seaga did not keep quiet though and continued his admirable stand, declaring that Warner had to go before he did any more harm and that a complete change of leadership was required at a regional level. 'He has some chief supporters who are not very much different to him and who are doing the same things,' he added, leaving a deep and unfathomable mystery as to who exactly he might be referring to.

In the end Warner stepped down before he was pushed and gave up all his posts within football. Because of his noble sacrifice, those gallant souls at FIFA dropped their investigations into his conduct and decreed that 'the presumption of innocence is maintained.' A wild presumption indeed, but an easy one to make for such a dedicated long-term supporter of Sepp's good work. Bin Hammam, meanwhile, was banned from football for life.

I had set out the previous August to find the good in football behind all the money and the greed and the people running the game had done their level best throughout the season to make that impossible for me. That doesn't mean that they succeeded though. In Jamaica I found innumerable people who care deeply not about their pay packets but about the sport itself, and who make great personal sacrifices towards its progression, from people like Clyde and Carvel to others such as Lasana Liburd and Major Desmon Brown and many more besides. These people understand the great importance of sport to a society and the very discernible effects it has had on theirs in particular. To paraphrase a well worn cliché, football is the opiate of the masses, and what the masses attach themselves to so strongly cannot possibly be a meaningless void. As I have said before, something is only as important as people make it. And to flog one or two other tired clichés, football is very definitely a social equaliser and a boundary-breaker, it brings people together in places that have been impenetrable to any and everything else. These ideas are parroted endlessly by the game's cheerleaders, generally around the time of a major tournament, but I have seen first hand that the airy platitudes are actually built on solid foundations. To dismiss football is to dismiss one of the world's most powerful social forces.

On top of this, the season made me realise just how lucky the journeymen in our leagues are simply to have been born English, a thought that occurred to me as I shared a minibus with people who had the natural ability to be earning £1,000,000+ a year had they also enjoyed that one great advantage. And these are warm, cheery people, more than happy with the lives they lead and the game they play. They are not 'arseholes'.

So that was enough for me. Even though I had quickly encountered the depressing idea that even here the game is now selling itself as an 'industry' of 'products' and 'brands', the fact that the people involved were so nice and *normal* was pleasing. But there was an extra cherry on top, because by looking in from the outside I rediscovered some pride in the English game too. We might all be able to find countless things about it that we find distasteful but the world loves it. In an age where Britain seems to us to be the shrivelled, indebted heart of a dead empire, we have this one thing for which the entire world looks at us and, crucially, finds joy. Industry, television, DNA, the telephone, antibiotics, the computer, the English language, Shakespeare, Darwin, Dickens . . . we have given the world so much in the past but in the modern era we no longer have a huge amount to offer, and yet almost every person in Jamaica supports an English team ahead of any local team—talking gleefully about the Uniteds, Liverpools and Arsenals—and the same can be said of the majority of the planet. We know its tawdry side only too well but the Premier League is our one great export in the twenty first century, and for that, and the pleasure it brings to so many, we should at least feel a tinge of pride in it.

So have a little faith in football. Yes, there are countless 'arseholes' involved in it, but scratch below the surface and there is still a beautiful game that really does provide huge pleasure and has honourable intentions. In every country on earth there are good people doing good things with what is still a good game. The world needs football, the time to turn our backs on it has not come just yet.